Film and the working class

The feature film in British and American Society

Peter Stead

Senior Lecturer in History, University College of Swansea

D0815574

London and New York

First published 1989 by Routledge
First published in paperback in 1991
by Routledge
11 New Fetter Lane, London EC4P 4EE

Simultaneously published in the USA and Canada
by Routledge
a division of Routledge, Chapman and Hall, Inc.
29 West 35th Streeet, New York, NY 10001

© *1989, 1991 Peter Stead*

Printed in Great Britain by
T.J. Press (Padstow) Ltd., Padstow, Cornwall.

All rights reserved. No part of this book may be
reprinted or reproduced or utilized in any form or
by any electronic, mechanical, or other means, now
known or hereafter invented, including photocopying
and recording, or in any information storage or
retrieval system, without permission in writing from
the publishers.

British Library Cataloguing-in-Publication Data

Stead, Peter
  Film and the working class: the feature film in British
  and American society.
  1. Cinema films. Sociological perspectives
  I. Title
  306.485

  ISBN 0–415–06519–4

Library of Congress Cataloging-in-Publication Data
also available

PN
1995.9
.S6
S74
1991

In memory of my father
John Stead
(1914−72)

Contents

General editor's preface

The pre-eminent popular art form of the first half of the twentieth century has been the cinema. Both in Europe and America from the turn of the century to the 1950s cinema-going has been a regular habit and film-making a major industry. The cinema combined all the other art forms – painting, sculpture, music, the word, the dance – and added a new dimension – an illusion of life. Living, breathing people enacted dramas before the gaze of the audience and not, as in the theatre, bounded by the stage, but with the world as their backdrop. Success at the box office was to be obtained by giving the people something to which they could relate and which therefore reflected themselves. Like the other popular art forms, the cinema has much to tell us about people and their beliefs, their assumptions and their attitudes, their hopes and fears and dreams.

This series of books will examine the connection between films and the societies which produced them. Film as straight historical evidence; film as an unconscious reflection of national preoccupations, film as escapist entertainment; film as a weapon of propaganda – these are the aspects of the question that will concern us. We shall seek to examine and delineate individual film *genres*, the cinematic images of particular nations and the work of key directors who have mirrored national concerns and ideals. For we believe that the rich and multifarious products of the cinema constitute a still largely untapped source of knowledge about the ways in which our world and the people in it have changed since the first flickering images were projected on to the silver screen.

Jeffrey Richards

List of Illustrations

Acknowledgements

I am deeply indebted to the University College of Swansea both for research grants and for a period of sabbatical leave, and to the Leverhulme Trust for a grant which allowed time to be spent in London and the United States. My work was greatly facilitated by the staffs of the British Film Institute, the British Library, the Marx Memorial Library, the Library of Congress, the Wisconsin Center for Film and Theater Research, the Warner Bros. Archive at Princeton, the New York Public Library at the Lincoln Center, and the Bobst Library at New York University. In particular I would like to acknowledge the considerable help I received from Frances Thorpe and Clive Coultass in London, Tony Aldgate at Oxford, Tino Balio, Stephen Vaughn, and my co-researcher John Wiseman at Madison, Dwight Hoover at Muncie, and Robert Sklar and Dan Leab in New York City. Whilst travelling along a parallel track Bert Hogenkamp has provided me with many useful pieces of information. First Glennis Jones and then Glenys Bridges and the staff of Words did wonders with my manuscript. All film stills appear by courtesy of the Stills Division of the National Film Archive.

I first had the notion that I should write about film when reading books by Raymond Durgnat and Jeffrey Richards and I was delighted when the latter asked me to write this book: no editor could have been so encouraging and so well informed. My appreciation of films came naturally but it was conversations with Dai Smith, Ieuan Williams, and Dick Shannon that helped me understand them. My friend Ed Gulick, once of Wellesley College and now of Conway, Mass., has been a constant inspiration. My greatest debts are, as always, to my family but suffice it here to note that it was my parents who first took me to the cinema and that my wife Elizabeth has never ceased asking 'Which day are we going to the pictures?'

1   Showmen and the nature of the movies

Motion pictures were to develop into the great mass entertainment of the twentieth century but they had first been shown in the cities of the late nineteenth century and both as an industry and as a social activity they were never to lose characteristics that had been determined at their birth. What Americans came to call 'the movies' and what in Britain was referred to as 'the pictures' had emerged out of a complex and distinctive metropolitan and urban culture which was very much achieving its quiddity as the nineteenth century came to a close. The nature of the movies was determined at an early stage and to study film history is to be reminded of the extent to which American and British cultural patterns in the modern era were determined within the context of the late nineteenth-century city.

There had always been cities providing a variety of religious, political, and commercial functions but few contemporaries doubted that the industrial city of the nineteenth century was a new phenomenon. What was revolutionary was the rate of growth and the sheer size of the metropolitan and urban populations: cities had become dynamic and populous. Even more revolutionary, though, were the social adjustments that needed to be made to accommodate the new masses. In almost every respect the new city was shaped by the interplay between elites and key leadership groups on the one hand and the masses on the other. To a greater or lesser extent all activity became popular. There was a new pattern of industrial relations, a new range of religious and social agencies, a new democratic politics, and a whole host of leisure-time activities and preoccupations that have been identified by historians as constituting a 'popular culture'. The basic framework of that popular culture was fairly obvious for urban workers not only lived close together in distinctive communities but had also begun to pick up the rudiments of an education and they had both savings and time to spare. They were soon identified as potential customers by tradesmen, bankers, building societies, and insurance companies, then by streetcar and railway companies, by the publishers of newspapers, journals, and cheap novels, and finally by a whole army of showmen whose task it was to inveigle the masses into circuses, fairgrounds, peepshows, roller-skating pavilions, theatres, and sporting fixtures. For many years serious and respectable citizens had worried about the new masses but now at least entrepreneurs and businessmen were able to offer them every service, every distraction, and every entertainment that their wages allowed. It was into this world that the movies, and of course the citizens of the twentieth century, were born.[1]

The movies were something very new and they soon developed a unique and distinctive position within the culture but that position can only be fully understood by reference to that context of nineteenth-century popular culture from which they emerged. The term 'popular culture' is a modern one but it describes what was a readily identifiable reality in the new urban areas of the nineteenth century. One difficulty with the term is that many contemporaries would never have been prepared to apply the word 'culture' to the new preoccupations of the masses. The initial political and social fears of the masses had always been accompanied by a dread of their cultural impact and by a conviction that civilized values and standards could not possibly survive. The emergence of a popular culture confirmed many fears and yet there was some compensation in the fact that things might have been far worse. In general the activities of the masses were though of as mindless but they were at least non-political and in many cases they even encouraged the acceptance of social norms and new routines necessary to urban and industrial life. Furthermore there was in many of these activities at least a hint of some of the better cultural values. Sport for example diverted the energy of the masses into activities that could inculcate both useful and attractive qualities. The content of the new journalism was appalling but at least it indicated that the masses could read and apart from being useful that offered the prospect that readers might move on to better things. Then there was the exciting development of 'live' variety, music-hall in Britain, vaudeville in America. Much of this was not respectable but at least it showed that popular music and humour could be channelled into the conventions of legitimate theatre. The cultural value of all these activities was thought to be negligible but at least some useful qualities were being inculcated and above all their commercial basis bound them in to the mainstream organization and values of middle-class society. Within the culture as a whole these popular activities can be said to have established a limited, unresolved but not entirely unsatisfactory position.[2]

Further objections to the term 'popular culture' have come from left-wing or Socialist historians who also question the cultural value of these activities before going on to ask whether the word 'popular' needs also to be examined.[3] Certainly they conceded that these activities were popular in the sense that millions of people availed themselves of them but their argument had been that only in a very limited way can we talk of these activities as belonging to the masses: rather they represented the expropriation and packaging of what had previously been popular forms by middle-class organizations and in most cases by businessmen and entrepreneurs. What they suggest is that the roots of these activities lay deep in popular or folk culture but that ultimately the new urban manifestation of these activities revealed more about the values of the business classes than they did about the masses themselves. What left-wing historians regret in particular is that the emergence of this new 'popular culture' came at precisely the moment when conditions were favouring the development of a radical working-class political conscious-ness. Just as education, literacy and communications were beginning to prepare the workers for new radical organizations their attention and savings were captured by opportunistic entrepreneurs with a very different set of values. Instead of a new social awareness the masses were given in particular fiction, humour, and music which were apolitical and essentially sentimental in tone. To historians of the left the new popular culture represented a fatal and quite decisive fragmentation of what should have been a working-class consciousness.

Any examination of nineteenth-century popular culture then necessarily involves confronting the basic cultural and political values that have determined British and American society in the modern era. To under-stand the precise position of the movies in this whole process we need first to look more closely at that activity which, at least superficially, seemed to be the direct ancestor of the cinema, that is music-hall or vaudeville. Towards the end of the nineteenth century these forms of 'live' variety seemed to be carrying all before them and they had become almost the symbolic or quintessential entertainment of the new city. Yet their cultural position both for contemporaries and subsequent historians was complex and again is directly relevant to any understanding of the movies. The great difficulty with music-hall and vaudeville, and this is a point of crucial significance to movie historians, is that they have earned or been given a very special place in the popular memory and in social history by those who recall with great fondness those heady pre-1914 days. To understand music-hall and vaudeville one has to fight through layers of myth and romance and one has to undo a whole view of the past that uses nostalgia for pre-1914 as a touchstone. Not surprisingly it is difficult for us to decide both how good and how genuinely popular all live variety was, let alone its precise relationship to the new entertainment of the movies.[4]

Recent writers have suggested that almost everything about the music-halls and vaudeville theatres has been gilded by memory. There must have been some great stars and some ecstatic moments in those cosy halls but there must also have been many second- and third-rate performers, constant recourse to stereotypes, excessive repetition, and buckets of sentimentality. Why is it then that these halls have been recalled with so much pleasure in so much twentieth-century writing? The answer is surely that they occupied a very special place in the lives of many young middle-class men and especially in the lives of those of them who were budding artists, writers, or intellectuals, who in short were Bohemians. To the English writer George Moore the halls were a 'protest against the villa, the circulating library, the club' and, we may add, much else that characterized middle-class life.[5] The halls were hardly respectable and they allowed 'young bucks' to escape for a while to an alternative world that offered not only contact with the masses, humour, and song but also drink, conviviality, and sexual opportunity. The new pattern of variety was an adornment to what Michael Chanan has called 'the night-time city', and the whole beauty of the format was that everything took place not in sordid cellars or popular drinking places but in buildings that had much of the appearance and many of the conventions of legitimate theatre.[6] The Bohemians thought of the halls as catering essentially for the masses but they were delighted that they could take their place beside them as part of what Vachel Lindsay was to call 'a jocular army'.[7] The English writer Max Beerbohm spoke of how the music-halls had 'grown up with reference to nothing but the public's own needs and aspirations', of how the audience was 'the maker of the form', and of how music-hall had always offered 'a great chance to any student of humanity at large'.[8] Even the novelist George Gissing, who was 'no friend of the people' and who was the most scathing critic of so many aspects of the new popular culture, has his fictional *alter ego* Henry Ryecroft recalling the pleasures of having been young in London, of the public houses with their 'pints of foaming ale' and the supper bars with their 'sausage and mash', of the theatres where one could 'roll and hustle with the throng at the pit-door', and of walking home singing as he went. For Ryecroft, like so many others who had worried about culture and the masses, had learnt 'the true instinct of townsfolk' which was to find pleasure in the 'triumph of artificial circumstance over natural conditions'.[9] The 'artificial circumstance' of the theatre and of 'live' variety allowed some middle-class observers a safe glimpse into that 'tumult and promiscuity' which Arnold Bennett found to be typical of American hotel lobbies and which most respectable people took to be the hallmarks of the new city.[10]

The Bohemians thought that they were glimpsing 'humanity at large', the 'throng', but more recently historians have questioned whether that was the case. The theoretical debate has tended to follow Raymond Williams's suggestion that although the urban working-class found in music-hall performers 'their most authentic voice' the halls were not full manifestations of working-class culture but were rather 'a very mixed institution'.[11] They were mixed because although all the vitality, the songs, humour, and much of the idiom came from what E. P. Thompson has described as the traditionally 'rowdy' element in working-class culture these things had now ceased to be spontaneous and informal and had passed into other hands.[12] In their examination of popular culture Stuart Hall and Paddy Whannel were worried by the fact that music-hall seemed to belong far more to the professional performers than to the audiences and that it was individual stars who actually seemed to have created the stereotypes and much of the idiom.[13] A more fundamental objection has been that music-hall and vaudeville were essentially controlled by showmen who were of course entrepreneurs. It was they who controlled the way in which performers, who came largely from working-class backgrounds, developed and packaged popular forms into acceptable acts. The new variety was a carefully edited version of a more traditional and informal entertainment. Whatever values and viewpoints were embodied in the acts would have ultimately been those that were acceptable to the promoters. It was for this reason that the halls were never radical or seditious and that the songs, like everything else that was on offer, were, as Colin MacInnes suggested, 'too inhibited emotionally, too limited intellectually, too commercial in their intentions'.[14] To the Marxist historian Michael Chanan the halls were merely 'tools of commercial exploitation' but a more balanced view would rely on an appreciation of the way in which 'live' variety revealed as much about showmen as it did about 'humanity at large'.[15]

Most social historians have tended to stick with Raymond Williams's argument and have been reluctant to give up the notion that what was most lively and energetic in all that variety came from the working class. Even Colin MacInnes remains convinced that music-hall was 'an act of working-class self assertion' although he concludes his analysis of the music-hall songs with a phrase that should set film historians thinking, for he sees them as a 'sort of bastard folk song of an industrial–commercial–imperial age'.[16] The point surely is that music-hall and vaudeville were transitional forms, transitional, as Stuart Hall and Paddy Whannel suggest, between the genuine folk culture of an earlier age and the mass commercialization of the twentieth century. They were transitional in almost every respect including that of audience composition. The theoretical debate has concentrated on organization and form but it is only more recently that film historians have actually raised the question of audiences. The Bohemians thought that in going to the halls they were confronting humanity, albeit on their own terms. In reality they were confronting those mixed audiences that frequented these theatres. As Robert Sklar has suggested the music-halls and vaudeville were essentially down-town or city-centre entertainments and would therefore be attracting typical down-town audiences, which would consist of an alliance of regulars, casuals, workers, clerks, parvenus, and Bohemians.[17] Music-hall and vaudeville belonged not to 'humanity at large' but to its audience and that audience was hardly ever an exclusively working-class audience. There were working-class regulars but the vast majority of the working class would have been excluded, at least in part by the cost and social ambience of the halls but far more by their geographical location. Something of a myth has developed about the universality of 'live' variety that can be explained in terms of generalizations based on those great centres London and New York, and by the ubiquitous nature of printed sheet music which often used the name of a star as a selling gimmick and which took songs into many pubs and drinking saloons as well as into many homes.[18]

The music-hall and vaudeville were transitional as really was all nineteenth-century popular culture. Through its entrepreneurs middle-class society had made its first approaches to the masses. Popular forms were expropriated and then given back suitably packaged. Everything was aimed at what Henry Ryecroft thought of as 'the host of the half-educated' and was therefore of no real cultural value but the compensations were real. Quite apart from any utility or negative political advantage that came out of popular culture, the important thing was that establishment culture was at least in touch with the masses. Total disaster had been averted, channels of communication had been established, and there were foundations on which to build. There was even, as we have seen, the chance of some vicarious pleasure to be gained from some of the new manifestations. It was into this unresolved but not unsatisfactorily balanced situation that film was introduced, and was immediately identified as something new. A vital clue in this respect was the attitude of the Bohemians and those other refugees from the middle-class world who had found music-hall and vaudeville such an exciting diversion. Almost to a man they were against the new phenomenon of the movies and they made no effort to include them in their 'night-time' world. There was to be no mingling with the throng at the movies. The representatives of the middle classes were quite prepared to leave the movies to the masses. What had arrived now really was mass entertainment.

From the outset it was the sheer popularity of the movies that struck observers. The movies had broken through to a vast new public and everything was on a different scale. Of course the trade papers revelled in hyperbole but the claims that were being made had a greater validity than those that had been made for music-hall. The *Exhibitors Film Exchange* spoke of how movies had brought themselves within 'intimate reach of the great mass of humanity'.[19] The *Bioscope* very much approved of the description of the movies as 'the drama of the masses' and went on to argue that the whole beauty of the movies was that they were for the first time providing amusement, 'the greatest factor in the life of the masses', to 'the millions' who had been 'passed over for so many years and considered of no account'.[20] The numbers were vast and this was very largely because the movies were not just appealing to sections of the masses but to the masses in general. It was the *Bioscope*'s view that for the person 'in search of different phases of human nature there is no better place to find objects of study than to visit a bioscope show'.[21] On every front the movies were cutting into new ground and creating a new audience. In 1908 one reporter found

old men and women whose grey hairs betoken years of life and opportunity for having seen all classes of amusement – seated alongside little folks who have to reach and stretch in order to catch a glimpse of what is being shown.[22]

In that same year another reporter described a Los Angeles cinema in which the audience was largely Mexican, Chinese, and Japanese.[23] Writing in 1928 the American critic Gilbert Seldes summed up the process of how the movies had accumulated their audience as one which

attracted those people from whom no fixed form of entertainment existed, people without knowledge of the language, barred from the theatre, the library, the light magazine, even the burlesque show; those without the slight discipline of mind necessary to follow a play; those too poor to afford vaudeville or the cheap melodrama; city-bred people unaware of the traditions of the cities and the country fair; children, the outcasts and the dispossessed, stragglers in city streets, those whose lives were disorganised so that they had quarter hours perpetually on their hands.[24]

In short the movies had broken through to the masses and had the power to pull in almost anybody and everybody who helped constitute the masses. Seldes marvellously captured the great down-town appeal of the movies when he spoke of the irresistible lure of 'the tinkle of a tinny piano playing a ragtime' which floated 'to the street from a darkened doorway' but the point about the movies was that they were not just a city or down-town phenomenon, they were everywhere.[25] They did not wait for the masses to come to them, they followed the masses and sometimes they were even there first. What was soon being described as 'the industry' boasted that there was a cinematograph theatre in every suburb and in every small town. One never had to go far in search of the movies; like the masses themselves they were rapidly achieving ubiquity.

The movies succeeded because they had gone to the people and had seemingly bypassed every obstacle. The *Bioscope* summed it up nicely: 'No travel, no expense, every comfort and a splendid program is the motto of electric theatres.'[26] In those years before 1914 the movies were a craze and there was constant talk of 'mushroom growth' and of 'epidemics'. In 1907 it had been noted that nickelodeons were opening up on every American street and it was not hard to account for their success. It was true that they only charged 'a nickel, five pennies, a half a dime'. They really were '5-cent theatres' and therefore very different from the more expensive vaudeville and even more expensive theatres. What is more, no special preparation had to be made, no time had to be set aside, programmes only lasted fifteen minutes, and one could enter and leave as one pleased. It was everywhere noted that nickelodeons offered relief to the 'foot-sore shopper' and that these shoppers only needed 'about one minute to find this out.'[27] The craze hit Dallas in 1907 and it was observed that the first audiences were made up of women and children; only later did men follow.[28] But people could go on their own or with groups and families. No special dress was needed and one never had to feel that one was on show or in any sense making a public appearance. The American critic W. Stephen Bush reflected on how the poor and lowly had only been tolerated in the theatre and all too often forced up into the gallery, but the movies had 'emancipated the gallery' and had 'wiped out for ever the odium and ridicule' that had always been shown towards its clientele.[29] To go to the movies was as natural as to walk in the streets and indeed the one was just an extension of the other. The whole process in which cinema audiences were accumulated seemed natural and spontaneous. In 1928 Pare Lorentz was to put the question 'Who goes to the movies in America?' and his answer was 'Everybody.' They went, he suggested, because 'the movie is the most convenient form of entertainment in the world'. For him this convenience has been largely a negative factor for he thought of America as offering no other comparable diversion; there were 'no beer gardens - no public concerts' and the question he asked was 'Who wants to sit at home and play bridge every night?' Lorentz's view was that the movies since their inception had offered cheap and comfortable relief; time had to be killed somehow and one could 'be bored with more comfort at a movie than anywhere else'.[30] This was a very useful corrective to the hyperbole of the trade papers but on occasions even they expressed surprise at the popularity of their industry and were happy to concede that movies were succeeding for very basic reasons. They were just pleased that the movies had become a normal everyday activity. The *Moving Picture World* was glad to be able to quote the New Hampshire reporter for whom the 'nickels' were just like 'a good strong cup of tea and a bit of a gossip' or 'a chat with some good fellow over a cocktail - they rest, that's all'.[31]

In a way the sheer size of the audience that the movies had discovered diverted attention away from any discussion of what the movies themselves actually were. Amazement and congratulation seemed more in order than reflection. In those early days what seemed newsworthy was what was called the movie 'fever'. Cheapness, comfort, and convenience seemed to be the most obvious explanations of the mass response but this was to ignore the films themselves. Nevertheless writers and reporters found it difficult to graduate beyond sociological observation. There were many comments on those women who wore 'the new hipless corsets' and who 'get up in the middle and walk out if bored'; there were frequent references to squalor, aromas, diabolical pianos, and very mixed audiences. From Los Angeles came a report of a film theatre that shared the same building with an undertaker and where the hall itself was squalid and narrow with grease spots on the wall where 'delighted spectators have leaned their enraptured heads'.[32] Whatever the conditions and the nature of the crowd, observers could not fail to see that the movies were being enjoyed. There was occasional boredom, people came and went, there might be a technical hitch but more than anything there was a fascination with the moving pictures and that, of course, was the essence of the experience. Once the pictures moved, then, according to the *Bioscope*

the spectators forgot that they are only looking at pictures and that the acts before them are not actually carried on right in front of them and by real people, and so well are they acted that the absence of spoken words is hardly noticed, and the necessary conversation supposed to be taking place between the characters is carried out in their own minds.[33]

Quite simply the movies worked. Wherever they were shown tragedy was greeted with a silence 'as still as death' leaving just 'the whirl of the machine, stifled sobs and suspicious sniffling'. Comedy produced 'hearty laughter', what James Agee was later to describe as 'laughter as violent and steady and deafening as standing under a waterfall', and it was the sound of this laughter drifting through open doors that was always the best advertisement for the movies.[34] The movies worked, they fascinated, and they entertained. At first they were a novelty and a fad but, perhaps even to the surprise of many in the trade, they were a novelty that did not fade. There was something about the movies although not too many people stopped to ask what it was. Analysis only came later. It was in 1927 for example that Kenneth Macpherson speculated whether those early film audiences had not just been distracted and drawn mindlessly from the streets but rather it might have been a case of 'the people getting in some dim way the fact that there was something under their eyes, a sense of life and expectancy'.[35]

Whether we take Lorentz's view that the masses were bored and ready to be distracted or Macpherson's notion that they had sensed that the movies were at least hinting at new possibilities, it is difficult to avoid being swept along by the romance of those early days. It was one of those moments when we can actually see whole new groups of people just walking into social history. It all seemed so simple. The *Moving Picture World* described how 'the nickel palace of amusement made its appearance with no greater blare of trumpets than the noise of its phonograph horn and the throaty persuasions of its barker' and 'how these came unobtrusively in the still of the night'. What could be easier than to succeed in this business? For its readers the paper listed the ingredients of a 5-cent theatre:

One storeroom, seating from 200 to 500 persons.
One phonography with extra horn.
One young woman cashier.
One electric sign.
One cinematograph with operator.
One canvas on which to throw the pictures.
One piano.
One barker.
One manager.
As many chairs as the store will hold.
A few brains and a little tact. Mix pepper and salt to taste. After that all you have to do is open the doors, start the phonography and carry the money to the bank. The public does the rest.[36]

Things were very simple and this list made that precise point very well but of course this journalist was being somewhat disingenuous as well as cynical. The list of ingredients was deceivingly simple. Storerooms and chairs could be found anywhere but the cinematograph still had to be acquired as of course did the films themselves, which the writer did not even deign to mention. To stress the simplicity of things in this way was really and almost incidentally to reveal the sheer scope and success of the industry. The movies certainly mushroomed as everybody noticed, they multiplied 'faster than guinea-pigs', but they were not a spontaneous creation, a bolt from the blue. The movies were 'for the millions' but they were given to the millions by showmen. This was the most fundamental fact about the movies in Britain and America and it was to remain the most important fact throughout the great years of the cinema's hegemony. It has been said that 'showmanship is the hallmark of the world of entertainment' and certainly from the outset it has been the hallmark of film in the English-speaking world.[37] The triumph of the movies was not an accident or a miracle. There may well have been something lacking in the lives of the millions but that need had to be catered for and the catering was done by the ingenious and indefatigable army of commercial opportunists whose energy and boldness tell us an enormous amount about that age. The romance of the movies was to a significant degree an entrepreneurial romance.

The story has often been told. There was the scientific discovery of the qualities of film, the perfecting of projectors, and then the marketing of projectors and the organization of places of entertainment first in arcades and then in nickelodeons. At every stage new groups of showmen sprang up out of the maelstrom of society. Those who had perfected the machines gave way to those skilled at rounding up the public. Those earlier showmen who had controlled the music-halls and vaudeville thought at first that they could incorporate film into their little empires but they were swept aside by new showmen who knew that there were vast audiences to be captured and that the old theatrical format was far too restricted. The new men knew that film could be shown anywhere, in any old storeroom or vacant shop, and even away from the cities in booths and makeshift structures in fairgrounds, on waste ground, and in fact anywhere crowds were likely to gather. Only gradually did the commercial preoccupation with the projector and the venue shift to a greater interest in the films themselves and then very much the same kind of people who had struggled to control the machines and theatres began to make and distribute the films. It was a dynamic age, an age of opportunity, and the pattern of population migration, income distribution, and increased leisure and freedom that allowed movie audiences to accumulate had also permitted a largely anonymous host of small businessmen to create a new industry and a new entertainment. In time consolidation took place but the industry was created by small men who gambled on acquiring theatres or on making films and who spent days on the road. It was an inexorable social process and almost before the rest of society or history had noticed they had laid claim to the leisure hours of the millions. They had captured the masses. Their triumph was complete for they controlled every aspect of the movies. They had invented a new social custom but they had also annexed a significant part of the working-class experience.[38]

However one looks at the early movies one comes up against the decisive contribution of the showmen, but obviously their role was most noticeable in the way the movies were presented. The movies succeeded because people could just walk in from the streets but from the beginning everything was done to ensure that as many people as possible were brought in. Films could be shown anywhere but the early film theatres very rapidly shunned any initial anonymity. Movies were announced to the world by electric signs, posters, music, and barkers. Managers and proprietors soon realized that if halls were to be half full they might as well be totally full and so every ingenious method was used to maximize attendance. As soon as the industry was conscious of itself a whole stream of advice was directed towards proprietors and they were told how to publicize films, how to gain the attention of all kinds of citizens, and how to eliminate all those petty annoyances and irritations that could upset individuals or whole sections. The new audience was a mass audience but no previous audience in history had ever been given so much careful attention. Comfort was the main aim and in this respect 'fetid air' was a major problem and one trade paper warned proprietors that 'unfortunately there is an odoriferous obnoxiousness about a considerable number of motion picture houses that undoubtedly hinders their profitable operation'.[39] Happy was the proprietor whose cinema was described as a 'parlour-like place under cooling fans'. But whatever problems individual proprietors and exhibitors had the industry was there at hand to proffer advice and encouragement. Very little was left to chance and great attention was given to every detail of publicity so that posters, signs, displays, and press advertisements made the maximum impact. The most common theme in all the trade advice was the need for the manager or proprietor to make himself known to his customers and to gain their confidence. The *Bioscope* explained that 'the public do not like to be treated in a way that seems to be distant or high-handed' and so the manager 'should go among his people and talk to them personally' and he should 'always appear ready and willing to consider a suggestion however trifling it may be'.[40] The point was that managers needed to learn what their audiences wanted but the other value of this familiarity was that any vague and general grumblings could be headed off before they became public. The trade papers not only advocated that managers should take soundings but also practised it themselves and they always encouraged managers to have their own say and to pass on what they had learnt. The manager of the American Theater in Terre Haute, Indiana, stressed that he kept 'in direct touch' with his patrons and that he went into his audiences 'as the pictures were being shown on the screen to listen to their comments'.[41] Getting to know the audience was important but so too was the more formidable task of getting to know the potential audience and advice on this was equally explicit. Early downtown theatres could rely on the casual trade, the 'droppers-in', but small-town and suburban halls had to go after their trade and it was essential that managers acquaint the whole community with what was on offer. The support of the press was seen as being vital and every manager was expected to ensure that he had his local newspapers on his side, but even this was not enough. The *Exhibitors Film Exchange* recommends a 'Neighbourhood Advertising Plan', the essence of which was that every manager would define 'the radius or zone' from which his 'logical business' was secured and that he should then proceed to go directly to the individuals whose patronage he could reasonably expect. The manager was advised to start by walking his zone so as to familiarize himself with it, and then 'scouts' would be sent out to call at homes whilst 'reliable boys' could be hired to 'politely deliver heralds'.[42]

From the earliest days showmen boosted the movies in order to maximize their audience and the whole razzmatazz of salesmanship has become an indispensable part of film culture in the English-speaking world. Because the movies were the first real mass entertainment the showmen realized that the sky was the limit and that there was no possible reason for timidity and restraint. To attract bigger audiences was not just a bonus, it was part of the whole logic of the industry. Showmanship was not just the accidental way in which British and American films were distributed, it was the essence of a whole phenomenon and the films of the English-language world can only be understood in this way. The showmen created an entertainment and annexed an audience in a spectacular initial burst, but, of course, they were not operating in a vacuum and there was one major hurdle that had to be overcome before their victory could be regarded as complete and of permanent rather than fleeting significance. What had to be done was that motion pictures had to be made respectable. The great drive for respectability, which was led by the trade papers and various film industry organizations, really took over the whole publicity campaign and again became almost a defining characteristic of British and especially American cinema. This was a complex story for there were several important reasons why the showmen clambered after respectability. It was in part a question of their own self-esteem. Respectable society and intellectuals had shunned the movies because they saw no need to take them seriously. They thought of the movies as a mechanical novelty, a meaningless and trivial craze which might be allowed to provide a moment's distraction at a music-hall or vaudeville show but which normally belonged to the amusement arcade or fairground. Film was nothing in itself but what had confirmed its worthlessness was that it seemed the exclusive property of a class of showmen who were direct descendants of the old fairground showmen. It was the showmen themselves who defined the place of the movies in the formal and respectable middle-class mind. Their new entertainment was thought of as a slightly hysterical activity organized in a gypsy-like way by men who were, in Bosley Crowther's phrase, 'hobbled by no preconceptions of the canons of propriety and good form'.[43] Not surprisingly it was just basic self-respect that forced movie men to improve their image and to state their claim to be accepted members of the business community. Gradually some progress was made but the personnel of the movie industry in Britain and America have never at any level lost their feelings of inferiority. Motion-pictures have conquered the masses and created many financial fortunes but they have always been largely the monopoly of cultural and social outsiders.

Self-respect was important but there were other considerations. There was the matter of box-office takings and in essence the drive for respectability was part of the attempt to build up larger audiences. The movies had moved from down-town to the suburbs and to small towns and the object now was to capture every section of the masses. The industry was launched by the support of the common people or the 'thick-eared' as they were bluntly described, but after the initial breakthrough it was soon realized that the only obvious way of increasing audiences significantly was by overcoming the objections and suspicions of the respectable. Movies had won a considerable audience but that audience would be permanently restricted if the industry remained at the edge of society proper, if it remained a side-show or an underground activity. The way to greater profitability, then, lay in the direction of bringing in better sorts of people and, to ensure that, a careful eye had to be kept on what was actually shown in the cinemas. Respectable people rejected the movies because they were thought to be trivial but also because they were thought to be corrupting and immoral. The whole atmosphere of the movies suggested 'tumult and promiscuity'. It was widely assumed that motion pictures would be sexually suggestive and probably explicit, the whole tone seemed secular and irresponsible, and few doubted that children and the weak-minded were being pointed towards crime and degeneracy. To a degree, of course, respectable opinion was right. Motion pictures were free to show anything and to suggest anything. There were no constraints and from the outset the showmen were not unaware that many of their patrons had come in search of entertainment that was not entirely respectable. In every city there were cinemas which specialized in what the *Milwaukee Sentinel* called 'immoral, evilly suggestive and crime-inducing spectacles'.[44] Just a merest glimpse at the trade papers reveals the extent to which from the start the movies had to fight against their own impulses and their own logic. They clambered to respectability by continually putting their own house in order, and in a way the battle to bring in not only the middle classes but the religious, the political, and the serious-minded took far more energy and ingenuity than winning that initial mass audience. The struggle was summed up by the *Bioscope*, which pointed out that:

> The great majority of manufacturers and showmen have known all along that clean amusement is what is wanted by that section of their patrons which really matters. They have relegated the questionable film to the zone of undesirables and so, banned by the respectable frequenter of our great picture halls and uncountenanced by the bulk of manufacturers and dealers simply because they respect public opinion, and themselves recognise the evil which would most assuredly be the result of its constant exhibition, the indecent picture is gradually disappearing.[45]

The quest for respectability was very much part of the drive to increase audiences generally and to ensure that motion-picture theatres were not confined to any down-town ghetto but it was also part of an even more fundamental question. Ultimately it was only by becoming respectable that the movie industry would continue to survive as a free entrepreneurial enterprise. It was only by convincing political authorities, the religious denominations, and the agents of respectable opinion that they were responsible citizens that showmen were able to retain control of the highly profitable business that they had created. Given the size of the motion-picture audience it was inevitable that political authorities would become involved in some regulation of the industry even if it was only to be a question of safety and fire regulations, but what made the movies even more into a public issue was that they became a mass activity precisely at the moment when political parties and social agencies were more concerned than ever before with how the masses could be accommodated within cities. A new and distinctive chapter was opening in relationships between the masses, more numerous, more literate, and better organized than ever before, and middle-class organizations and agencies who were realizing more urgently than ever before that new initiatives were needed to bridge the great abyss of class. This new era which opened the century in both Britain and America was to be characterized by an increased politicization of the city as political parties widened their hold, by an increased interest in every aspect of city life, and by increased regulation through political and philanthropic agencies. The movies could not hope to escape, especially as they had accumulated a mass audience in one great swoop that bypassed the schools, the churches, the charities, and all the other traditional agencies of cultural influence. What was frightening was that this new mass entertainment seemed altogether outside the established auspices of middle-class culture and seemed unconstrained by any of the sanctions of proper society. At a time when cities were being reformed and regulated as never before it was inevitable that the movies would be regulated. As mayors, local authorities, government agencies, and social workers made their moves, so there was every incentive for the showmen to put their own house in order. It was very much a matter of life and death as far as the industry was concerned.[46] The showmen hated those whom the *Cinematograph Year Book* always described as 'the Busybodies and Meddlers' and thought of their demands in terms of what the *Bioscope* referred to as 'Prussianism' but in order to keep control of their own industry the showmen accepted many of the standards of middle-class taste and insisted that what they would provide would be for the most part family entertainment.[47]

The movies as a whole had to be moulded to suit middle-class notions of public respectability but meanwhile local battles had to be won in every town and city as sector by sector the wider public was to be won over. The essence of showmanship had become the capacity to build up from one's regular audience, to bring in whole families, to attract women and children, to win over religious families who were normally against organized entertainment, to convince trade unionists and the politically active that a moment's respite was harmless enough, and to convince the respectable and well-to-do that a visit to the movies was not a disgraceful act. The motion-picture industry survived and prospered because this battle was substantially won in the vast majority of communities and especially in the major cities. Long before 1914 the great symbol of the social triumph that the showmen had pulled off was the new purpose-built and well-appointed movie theatre, a structure already far removed from the arcade and the nickelodeon. We know more about movie-going in Chicago than about any other city and this is appropriate for it was in so many ways the symbolic city of those last decades before the First World War. Certainly the battle to give the movies a new respectability received more attention in Chicago than in any other city. By 1907 it was estimated that the average daily attendance in the city's nickelodeons was 100,000 and very naturally local politicians, reformers, and social workers were anxious to assess the significance of this statistic.[48] The showmen followed the debate closely and reacted to every criticism by taking a further step towards respectability and soon the fashionable Loop crowd were as eager to see the movies as were the masses. Smarter and smarter theatres were opened until in 1915 Orchestra Hall itself, the home of the Chicago Symphony, was refitted as a home for 'photoplays'. What was crucial here as far as Chicago was concerned was that it could now boast a movie theatre as good as anything in New York and that the movies had been decisively disassociated from 'immoral' ragtime music by now being coupled with the Symphony. The price range in this new movie venue would range from 10 to 50 cents (10 to 25 cents for matinees) but for this some patrons would also get a twenty-five-piece orchestra. 'Build up to standard, not down to a price' was the motto of the Strand Theater Company, who had now so dramatically brought about the movie's coming of age in Chicago.[49] The same process went on in every town and city; the opening of a prestigious down-town house symbolized a social acceptance of movies amidst the fashionable down-town set but also created new standards and expectations which permeated downwards to other venues and these gradually made it easier for a number of managers to pull in women, children, families, and the respectable classes.

The whole movie industry had become obsessed with achieving respectability by widening the mix of patrons and in the trade papers we see an almost frenetic attention to the small details of improving comfort and achieving the right publicity. In general respectability was achieved and the consequence of that was that the movies had moved somewhat decisively away from the masses that had helped to create the industry. The movies had been born in big cities and had depended initially on the attraction that they held for working people who found themselves crowded either as permanent residents or transients in those cities.

Within a few years the movies had added a significant number of other social groups to its audience. The general social and political advantages of the newly enlarged audiences were obvious but in cultural terms what was really significant as far as the subsequent history of the movies was concerned was that the showmen who made and presented the movies were no longer thinking in terms of a homogeneous or class audience. Every social, political, and box-office consideration suggested to the showmen that it would be unsatisfactory for the movies to remain a merely sectional entertainment. Probably everything in the personality of the showmen and in the nature of business activity itself made it likely that the motion-picture industry would go in search of better audiences but this development was encouraged by a strange mixture of attitudes towards that original working-class audience that had helped create the industry. There was a great fear of the fickleness of audiences, an anxiety that the craze would die and that in particular movies would lose their fascination for precisely those sections of society that had been going to them longest.[50] As the movies desperately sought new audiences we should not underestimate the part played by a fear that mass working-class patronage was just too good a thing to last. Nevertheless this fear was gradually being overtaken by the feeling that the well-established working-class audiences could rather be taken for granted. After all, the kinds of films that they wanted to see and the conditions that they were prepared to accept were now generally appreciated. The showmen were well aware of the general social structure of their respective countries but they were quite prepared, given the obvious appeal of their films, to rely on the common sense and ingenuity of individual managers and proprietors. As far as the working classes were concerned all that was needed was managers who could determine the right mix of films and the right range of prices to suit the specific down-town drop-in cinemas and even more the neighbourhood and small-town cinemas that were now increasingly thought of as catering for 'industrial' or working-men audiences. But any thought or consideration given to working men was only part of a larger strategy of appealing to the public generally. The mass popularity of the movies did not come about because showmen gave no thought to individuating their audiences but rather resulted from an appreciation that the most important thing about the public as a whole was that every section and every group would respond to the appeal of the movies if it could be given access to the right kind of cinema. At one level this meant giving each town or neighbourhood the cinema it deserved and having a range of cinemas in down-town areas. Nevertheless there was within this strategy still a special role for the luxury super-cinemas.

The movies tackled society on the broadest front and refused to be confined to any one social zone but for all that one senses from the trade papers and social surveys that the industry had become preoccupied with its fashionable down-town audiences and that the super-cinemas were thought of as the social cutting edge of the trade. In attracting the fashionable trade the industry was gaining friends who were socially and politically powerful and it was also nicely building up box-office takings for, whilst the better sort of customers attended less often than the workers, they paid considerably more when they did come. What was most important, though, was that these socially more distinguished patrons were indeed creating a fashion; they were sanctioning movie-going not only for other less bold middle-class families but also for all that vast number of people caught in the twilight zone between middle-class comfort and the lumpenproletariat. Families from this range were always in search of respectability and, having followed their betters into churches, lecture rooms, and recreational clubs, they were now being told that a certain amount of movie-going need not necessarily be socially harmful. The best sort of customers were important in themselves but they were more important as the arbiters of social fashion. They brought in their wake a whole range of families who might have been socially ambitious but who were certainly fascinated by the prospect of sharing the movies with even more affluent and glamorous folk. The movies had fought their way out of a corner, leaving saloons, poolrooms, and dance-halls behind, but they had won their way through not so much to middle-class respectability as to classlessness. The big show-piece cinemas were built to pull in the fashionable trade but they were not designed for the exclusive use of a social elite; rather they were provided for all those groups who were prepared to pay money for the movie entertainment that was being provided as part of the delights offered by the down-town city. To attract the best patrons the movie-houses had to ape the conventions and the standards of theatres and opera-houses but very quickly the whole industry realized that the appeal of the movie palaces was not unrelated to the fact that all customers had to be treated the same and so they became temples of a new classlessness. In striving for more respectable customers the exhibitors learnt that it was not just the most affluent who liked to be treated with dignity and style.

The battle for respectability led to better cinemas but it was always conceded that real victory would only come through the production of better films. It was what would be shown on the screens of the new theatres that would ultimately determine what was always referred to as 'the tone' of the movies as a social custom. The initial mass audience had obviously loved short films and especially comedies but there had never been that much attention given to content as novelty value guaranteed that every film would made money. The chaos of the early years meant that in Gilbert Seldes's phrase 'any sort of fly-by-night production company' became a reasonable venture.[51] As the fashionable trade came in so more thought had to be given to subject-matter and to technique and in America this meant that short films had to be replaced or shown in conjunction with multiple-reel films as already pioneered by European film-makers. This switch to feature films inevitably led to a new pre-occupation with fiction and with developing screen fictions that took up the themes and conventions of respectable literary and theatrical tastes. The prestige audience would be won over by movies that could take their place alongside the middle-class novel and play. What was crucial, though, was that this development did not mean that a special category of movies was made for a sectional audience but rather that what was thought of as the 'quality' taste was allowed to shape the general output of movies. Certainly economic considerations were supreme and just as it did not make sense to build cinemas just for the rich so it would have been crazy to make films just for the religious, the doctrinaire, and the intellectual. In 1915 Harry Weiss of Metro Picture Services urged the trade to accept 'Quality' as its watchword but what quality meant for the film industry in questions of both architecture and film-making was standards that would bring in the respectable without prejudicing the masses.[52] The point about quality was that it should not and probably could not be confined. To offer the best was to set a general standard and to create a wider public expectation. Once again the movies learnt that it was not only the wealthy and respectable who liked to think that they were being given the best. The industry built up a new audience not by giving a social elite privileges but rather by suggesting that anyone who had paid their admission price would be given value for money and in particular would be given films that had been made with care and attention.

As quality feature films were produced so the anxieties and introspection could give way to congratulation and to a new hyperbole. The movie theatres were showing well-made and respectable films to a large public that included many of their erstwhile critics. The fictional drama that had seemed to appeal to the better classes was now being offered to a mass society. The industry had responded to the great challenge of a whole era of 'Busybodies and Meddlers' by not only cleaning up minor abuses but by becoming itself an agency of social improvement. For Chicago's *Exhibitors Film Exchange* 'the Meaning of the Movies' was that the benefits and aspiration that had previously been offered by 'a dozen agencies' were now combined in one form for the motion picture was taking over from painting, sculpture, travel, history and so on. For the *Exchange* the motion picture

> brings within intimate reach of the great mass of humanity the vast civilizing influence of the fine arts, presenting each subject in a form stripped of technicalities and intelligible to the average mind. With these facts in mind it is easy to gain the viewpoint of noted producers who maintain that the art of the motion picture is still in the cradle of

its infancy, and as it progresses step by step to maturity, it will wield an influence greater than the press and second only to the pulpit.[53]

Clearly the movies now felt that they could look the reformers of the early twentieth century firmly in the eye and the film-industry boosters were now giving back as good as they were given. The industry's many critics had made great demands and threatened many a crisis but they had not halted the growth of the movies as mass entertainment. The challenge of the reformers had been one great reality but the showmen had always been aware of the other reality and that was that very large numbers of ordinary people, and that included the rich and the poor and people from all nations, were fascinated by moving pictures. They rightly sensed that there was a mass audience waiting to be entertained and so they were given every incentive to hang on to the goose that was laying the golden eggs. Such was the popularity of film and such was the reforming zeal of that first decade or so of the twentieth century that there must have been every possibility that other agencies would take up the chance of producing, distributing, and exhibiting films in their own halls. There was constant talk and frequent illustration of the need for film to be used by teachers, lecturers, trade unionists, preachers, and social workers. The trade papers were always including references to experiments of this sort but it was obvious that these many initiatives came to very little. There was also some possibility that exhibitors would be persuaded that audiences could be attracted to watch non-fictional films of an informative and educational nature. Occasionally the proprietors of some of the quality houses would comment on the successful inclusion of travel films in the programme as it was thought that this would impress the casual respectable trade but far more common was the exhibitor who reported a hostile response to short films dealing with 'industrial' subjects.[54] The Edwardian and Progressive eras were rife with ideas of how film could develop but of all the possibilities the only thing that happened was that the showmen hung on to what they had discovered. They had turned to longer films to attract better audiences and the device of the fiction film not only served to head off the challenge of reformers but also guaranteed an exclusive hold on mass audiences. No organization had the energy to compete with the showmen. Certainly no other organization could challenge the sheer size of an industry that had from the outset relied on economies of scale and realized the logic of a mass audience, but neither was there any other organization prepared to rely exclusively on entertainment, which the showmen had identified as the essence of the movies.

It was the turn-of-the-century city that had created the movies as mass entertainment and the movie phenomenon took much of its tone and logic from that milieu. Paradoxically however the demand for better films saw the American film industry move away from its natural habitat and take up residence in a suburban section of what was essentially a southern Californian oasis. There were many reasons why after two decades of activity the American industry should begin to centre on Hollywood but surely Lary May is right to see the move ultimately in terms of the movies seeking to escape from the constant demands of Progressive America.[55] Industrial America was a pluralistic and highly organized society. The battle to improve the movies had also been a battle in which the showmen had fought to maintain control of what they had invented. The fictional film had guaranteed that the showmen would hang on to their audience. The advent of Hollywood was the symbol of the showmen's victory. In Hollywood they would be able to entertain their vast worldwide audience in relative freedom. Showmanship was to remain as the hallmark of the movies.

2　Towards significance in the silent era

The movies had become a story-telling medium, and, as had been the case with earlier fictional forms such as the melodrama and the 'dime novel', the stories would necessarily have to be given a recognizable social setting. The movies, though, had been born into a far more complex and certainly a more highly politicized era than the earlier fictional forms and many familiar themes, especially those dealing with the problems of wealth or with sudden reversals of financial fortune, would have to be treated more sensitively. The new world was one in which there was an increased emphasis on the social obligations of the wealthy, on the whole question of relations between management and labour, and on the legitimate degree of social and political power that could be exercised by wealthy elites. If the movies were to give their stories a realistic social setting and especially a contemporary setting, and if they were to draw on what had always been some of the major preoccupations of popular fiction, then they would have to define their position carefully with regard to some of the major issues of the day. To the movie producers the problem defined itself in terms of having to retain the loyalty of the masses whilst never questioning fundamental middle-class values and of having to show an unease about certain aspects of the distribution of wealth and social power without ever becoming political or radical. In short the movies had to be contemporary and had to reflect some of the mass anxieties of the age without ever becoming sectional or subversive themselves.

The 'Busybodies and Meddlers' along with the new and better audiences imposed clear constraints on the showmen of the movie industry but all the problems that were posed by society were overcome, and were overcome with such decisive ease that they never again had to be confronted. The solution was relatively easy partly because what was required by society as a whole fitted in very closely with what the showmen believed themselves and partly because the new social awareness was really only a refinement of those old nineteenth-century platitudes that had always underpinned popular fiction. 'From 1908 to 1914 motion pictures preached,' argued Lewis Jacobs, but what the showmen thought best to preach was determined without too much difficulty.[1] A vague belief in the common man and a moral if politically neutral criticism of the abuse of wealth had always been the territory of popular narrative as exploited by religion, legend, folk memory, and popular fiction and so there were lots of safe and suitable stories at hand for the showmen to tell. The showmen were men of their time and they knew how easy it was to tell stories that would be sympathetic to the common man, that would condemn all truly evil men and their agencies, and yet at the same time would do nothing other than confirm existing social values. Nearly everything else was common sense. There was never any question that the movies would become political or radical as the showmen were as opposed to Socialism and labour unions as their fellow American businessmen and, in any case, they remained firmly of the opinion that what they had to give their public was entertainment. Movies only needed to be social when the plot demanded it, and even if some kind of political crisis had to be depicted in a particular story then the attitude or position adopted by the movie would be less important to audiences than the logic of the plot. The movies were telling stories and, of course, there were political values implicit in these stories, but in general the movies were using society rather than engaging it directly. It was the logic of their medium (the camera filmed what it saw) and the need for stories that led producers to film aspects of their times but in the movies themselves the supremacy of fiction relegated society to a background. Feature films, whether drama or comedy, quoted society when it was appropriate or relevant. Society and social issues crept into film as the servant of plot. It was thus in these early years and it was nearly always to remain so.

The early feature films took up society as the situation required. In *The Quarry Man* (1908) a workman is blinded during blasting operations at a quarry; later his wife becomes unfaithful and he is driven to suicide; just in time his wife pulls him out of the river and she now abandons 'the downward path'. Another American film of that year, *A Workingman's Dream*, has a very weary hero who fails to find a job at a factory; he falls asleep and dreams of a Professor Wonderful who offers him instant wealth and a new set of clothes, but he is told that these new gains will disappear if he breaks certain simple instructions; on three occasions he accidentally carries out simple actions which break the instructions and his wealth disappears; he wakes up to see an ambulance taking a worker from the factory - there is a vacancy and this time his application is successful. Of course these films were not innocent but the 'messages' were only a reworking of nineteenth-century exemplars and would not have surprised anyone. Also in 1908 audiences could have seen *Unemployed and Unemployable* in which the central character begins by haranguing a crowd; he is dragged off by his wife and given a whole range of domestic tasks all of which he makes a mess of; he accidentally acquires stolen goods and is arrested; the film ends with this 'lounger' working at last but in the cells. The following year brought *The Miner's*

Daughter in which the heroine deserts her working-man husband for the new mine-owner and his lavish apartment; in time she becomes unhappy but is eventually reclaimed by her husband who storms into a smart reception and virtually throttles the mine-owner. In *Hard Times* (1909) an unemployed father with a dying child smashes a baker's window, is caught by the crowd, and is delivered to the police, who proceed to call in a physician; the working-class family is restored to prosperity and the child to health, and the physician becomes a family friend.[2]

All this was familiar territory but as films became more ambitious so there emerged the possibility of fuller social statement. In 1909 D. W. Griffith directed *A Corner in Wheat* for the Biograph Company and the *New York Dramatic Mirror* announced to its readers that 'this picture is not a picture drama, although it is presented with dramatic force. It is an argument, an editorial, an essay on a vital subject of deep interest to all.' The theme, the *Mirror* went on, 'is the rising cost of living, the inability of the masses to meet the increases and the part played by the speculator in bringing about this unfortunate condition'. The paper praised Biograph for 'having opened up a new vein for motion picture subjects', argued that 'no orator, no editorial writer, no essayist could so strongly and effectively present the thoughts that are conveyed in this picture', and concluded that it was 'another demonstration of the force and power of motion pictures as a means of conveying ideas'.[3] A year later Biograph released *Gold is Not All*, also directed by Griffith, and of this film the *Motion Picture World* said that it would help in 'creating a sentiment that will place a true value upon wealth in its relation to human happiness and its influence upon life'. The reviewer thought that the film deserved 'the highest commendation'.[4] Biograph, it seemed, was giving the public a new social cinema and as the years went by it seemed that D. W. Griffith in particular was just taking the main problems of American society as his subject-matter. Here indeed were ideas and ample evidence that the movies had all the potential to move into a position alongside the press and the pulpit as an agency moulding the ideas and values of the mass public.

The emergence of Griffith as the most important director of feature films in America was related to so many of the forces that characterized the Progressive era. There was a demand for better films and that meant films that would convince middle-class audiences that the new entertainment could aspire to art and be an agency of spiritual betterment. The age was sanctioning a cinema of technical virtuosity and social statement. There were several technical innovations but the spirit of the time made it likely that the man of the moment would be someone in whom technical boldness and artistic pretension would be sustained by the need to preach. It was also inevitable that such an innovator would come from within the industry and be fully conversant with all its conventions.

What elevated Griffith above his fellow technicians was that his sense of what a camera should record and his appreciation that new dimensions of filmic space could be appropriated were given meaning by their constant reference to central themes of American life. He appears to be offering a total cinema in which technique, story, social setting, and spiritual values came together. This was something like the art the Progressive era needed. What is important about Griffith, however, is that his demonstration that feature films could be both art and social treatise was not inspired by any narrow or specific intellectual or doctrinal position. Griffith's breakthrough came almost accidentally as he attempted to forge a career in a new industry about which he knew little. Working alongside other pioneers he was first spontaneously discovering new possibilities in camera technique and then he found that he could equally spontaneously draw on his experiences and his own values. Griffith had come to the movies quite late in life and he came as a man whose varied experiences and whose accumulated opinions, myths, and prejudices had given him a sense of America and of himself as having a place in it. He was the product of an actual family experience; his father had fought for the South in the Civil War and there had been some decline from gentility, but he was as much a product of family myth. The suggestion of a practical background combined with the talk of Welsh and Jewish blood and also with his own striking physical appearance to convince Griffith that he would and should be somebody of significance. He failed as a writer and as an actor but then discovered that the easily acquired skills of movie-making would enable him to become the artist and prophet for which his background had prepared him and for which Progressive America was so eagerly waiting. The scene was set for a movie genius but what was important for the history of the movies was that the genius who emerged to push the medium and the industry into a new era was a self-educated romantic whose values and ideas had not been provided by any distinctive intellectual tradition or urban political party but rather had emerged first out of his Southern, rural, Methodist past and then as he had drifted through a rapidly changing America. The times seemed to sanction important films that would be artistic and socially relevant but America was given films made by a self-made showman with artistic and intellectual pretensions and whose thinking was essentially homespun.[5]

Much has been written about Griffith and his contribution to the movies but the ingredients that made up his genius have never been better identified than in the review Heywood Broun wrote of *Intolerance* when it appeared in 1916. To Broun, Griffith was 'an immature philosopher, a wrong-headed sociologist, a hazy theologian, a flamboyant historian but a great movie man'.[6] Griffith was seduced by his own myth of himself and by the preoccupations of the Progressive era into believing that he was a serious thinker, whereas in truth he was an old-fashioned story-teller who had spontaneously discovered how the technology of film could be used to give stories a tremendous power. There were many traditional features in his films and his whole approach to a story was never far removed from the conventions of melodrama, but what Griffith was able to do was to shift the action of any of his films to whatever chapter of history or social setting that his plot or theme required. It was his sense of history, part romantic, part Christian, and his sense of American society that gave his films their dramatic and visual power. His artistic bravura may well have been inspired by his sense of himself and it certainly encouraged him to become increasingly subjective. His subjectivity, though, was to be his undoing. *Birth of a Nation* (1915) and *Intolerance* (1916) may well have been masterpieces but they were also very obviously controversial and guaranteed to shock sections of the great audience. For film to travel down that road would be to endanger the whole relationship between showmen and their great monolithic audience. Safer ground had to be found and in any case with the coming of war the Progressive demands were being replaced by new constraints. The forces that had called forth a great preacher like Griffith were passing and he needed to be taken out of the limelight. The motion-picture industry moved instinctively against a man whose message aroused dissent and, as we have seen, there were critics who could see even as the films were released that they offered humbug and prejudice masquerading as philosophy. What was inescapable, however, was the impact that Griffith's films had made as films. He was a literary man and he had dreamed of becoming the Shakespeare of the movies, but what he had become in fact was more like a movie version of Dickens. The Victorian novelist had accumulated a simple but coherent view of society but also the genius to tell stories that needed to be firmly set in a fully created social setting. The stories were generally shaped by his values and his literary genius allowed every social detail to be authentic and appropriate. Griffith was never as mature an artist as Dickens and he was the product of the frontier rather than a literary city but he had a social theory of sorts, a gift to embody values in stories, and a mastery of technique which allowed him to make every setting dramatically and socially convincing.

In many respects Griffith was a conventional story-teller and melodrama was always really the framework of his themes. In *A Corner of Wheat* the avaricious speculator is showing his friend through one of his elevators when he receives a cable telling him that he has cornered the world's supply but then in his exultation he stumbles and 'falls to a terrible death in one of his own bins of wheat'. But before we get to this point Griffith has given us what a reviewer describes as Millet-like scenes of rural labour and urban scenes in which great wealth alternates with breadlines and poverty. Griffith's ambition to be both artist and prophet made him elevate melodrama into something fuller in terms of its emotional and social range and the stunning way in which the totally real sense of society sustained his story-line gave his films what appeared to be the power of history and the richness of literature. He knew American society from his days of wandering and he could recreate it effortlessly. In a whole series of urban dramas, of which the best known is *The Musketeers of Pig Alley*, he showed that a society of Dickensian-like authenticity could be created in a film studio. These were simple little melodramas or lessons of everyday life but what mattered most was bringing these gifts for social detail into play in the grander sermons. And so it was that a man who had tried his hand at a whole variety of working-class jobs but who was no friend of the labour unions could, as part of his episodic film *Intolerance*, quite effortlessly recreate a clash between workers and police that is so lifelike as to seem like a newsreel and to suggest that perhaps every subsequent labour riot followed its pattern.

1 *Intolerance*: Griffith's very realistic industrial clash comes as one small part of his great plea for tolerance.

Industrial battles of this sort were almost an everyday event in Griffith's America but here the bloody scenes are staged not as part of a labour or management film but as part of a vast, elaborate, confused, perhaps ultimately nonsensical and certainly eccentric plea for tolerance. The modern or contemporary quarter of *Intolerance* would make an excellent film in its own right but even then the industrial scene would only be part of the scene setting and would fade in the memory as the hero passes from scene to scene in the 'picaresque' fashion of so many movies. Griffith's intention was to condemn the hypocrisy of wealthy do-gooders and just by way of illustration he brilliantly made real the experience of industrial warfare.

Griffith's legacy was a complex one. His great sermons warned of the dangers of being controversial and subjective but confirmed that the movies could greatly increase their emotional power as a story-telling medium by developing a surer sense of society. It was above all his Dickensian capacity to take in social detail as part of a social sense that need not be political that Griffith really passed on to the American motion-picture industry. In this respect he was confirming that what the movies did best was to tell stories as effectively as they could without wandering too far from the values of the old nineteenth-century themes.

Of course Griffith was not the only preacher and audiences were given films that were quite forthright in their condemnation of social vices. One reviewer thought *John Barleycorn* (1914) 'the most powerful moral lesson ever conveyed in films' and stressed how brilliantly the 'selection of types', the 'faithful depiction' of 'the underworld of sea-faring men', and the very smell of the sea that the movie evoked all helped to convey the 'dehumanising effects of strong drink'.[7] Later that year All-Star released *The Jungle* and a reviewer assured readers that the producing company had spared nothing in order to ensure that 'this picturization' would be equal to the novel. All the salient points of Upton Sinclair's story were dealt with in the film: the struggle of immigrant families, the careless methods in the food factories, the strike and riot following a 20 per cent wage reduction, and above all the main themes of the distinction between employer and employed and the 'wide and bridgeless chasm' between rich and poor. The *Modern Picture World* reported that this 'daring' film was doing well at the De Kalb theatre in Brooklyn and that when it opened on Broadway the 'socialist' Upton Sinclair would be present at each performance.[8]

All this was indeed 'daring' stuff and few moviegoers in that 1914–16 period could have failed to appreciate that the messages were coming at them thick and fast as the motion-picture industry tried hard to prove that it was a mature social agency. These movie tracts, however, should be seen in context. Specific lessons were being taught and the abuse of wealth was being condemned but in the vast majority of 'social' films the message usually came wrapped in melodrama. The companies vied with each other to find new settings for the basic story-lines and messages that they had to put over. In 1915 Universal Broadway Features released *Business is Business*, in which an egotistical French capitalist rapidly risen from the peasantry rules over his employees with an iron will until his eventual downfall. At the same time Lasky offered *Out of Darkness* in which a young heiress lives off the profits of a Florida cannery in which hundreds of working-girls earned 30 cents for a 13-hour day at the cutting-tables. The heiress travels to Florida for some yachting but her sloop is run down and sunk by one of her own commercial schooners; she is saved but she has lost her memory; she ends up working on the cutting-tables in her own factory and falls in love with a manager whose previous requests for better conditions she had been happy to ignore. The *Exhibitors Film Exchange* found the theme, which has the heiress played by Charlotte Walker learning 'what life is and what are the actual conditions under which many of her fellow human beings live', plausible and summed up the photoplay as a 'strong arraignment of existing working conditions in certain localities'.[9] A few months later came the California Motion Picture Corporation's *Salvation Nell*, in which we follow the adventures of a young girl from the New York tenements, where her drunken father kills her mother and where all her associates are drunks or wasters, through to happiness in the arms of a Salvation Army major.[10] Meanwhile World Films Corporation's *The Better Woman* has a poor uneducated girl who lives in a mining town cheating her way into marriage with a young engineer and then surviving all kinds of guilt and adventure before proving (in the words of the release summary) that 'a girl, starting life under a heavy handicap, could be worthy of the highest place in the affection of an educated high-bred man'.[11] Metro's contribution to this social cinema came in the form of *The Bigger Man*, which the editor of the *Exchange* described as a 'timely' drama of 'love and labor . . . on the pregnant theme of the relation between capital and labor'. Henry Kolker played the part of a man of the 'working-class' who whilst helping to build a bridge becomes interested in the boss's daughter. During the film the 'workers' demands for increased wages are refused and then follow riots, battles with militia, and eventually industrial peace is restored through the efforts of a young engineer who wins his employer's confidence and the love of the employer's daughter'. The *Exchange* concluded that the production was 'pictorially of merit' but that the battle between strikers and militia was 'farcical, bearing no relation whatever to an actual conflict of its kind'. This critic concluded his review by pointing out to his readers what he thought were the real merits of the film for he had thought of it as being 'neither capitalistic nor laboristic, but a straight-away drama' not at all 'depending on any propaganda to arouse the spectator's interest'.[12]

We should, of course, widen the context even further for, if in the movies preaching usually came hand in hand with melodrama, this should remind us that films were still firmly in the hands of showmen and they were free to use social comment and social settings as they thought best. Progressives and reformers never captured the movies; they merely influenced them in a particular direction, a direction that the producers would appear to be following closely whereas in fact they were really using it for their own ends. The movies were advancing on several fronts and the social theme was but one strand in a more complex whole. Showmen knew that middle-class critics had to be bought off and that topicality could sell films to certain audiences but they also appreciated that audiences were more likely to go to the movies for spectacle, for adventure, for comedy, for sex, to see particular stars, and to be entertained in the widest sense. The need for the movies to preach was very evident in some films but the vast majority of films reflected the styles and themes that movies people were working out for themselves in alliance with their audience as a whole. The young Mary Pickford went into the industry as the Progressive phase approached its zenith, and for Griffith she played criminals and prostitutes; she went on to portray a whole variety of poor hard-done-by girls, many of them immigrants, many of them immoral or pregnant, before in 1916 she played a factory worker in the most memorably titled of all the films of this era *The Eternal Grind*. Of course this film was a condemnation of sweat-shop conditions, and of course it was a melodrama in which poor girls have affairs with the boss's sons and in which the heroine brandishes a gun in order to make one son do the honourable thing but above all it was a vehicle for a star who had already become one of Hollywood's hottest properties. As Lary May has quite rightly stressed a melodrama with a star in the main part is already well on the way to becoming something different. Necessarily the star passes through difficult situations, escapes from dilemmas, and resolves problems. We notice the appalling conditions but not as much as we appreciate the energy and vitality of the star. For Pickford *The Eternal Grind* was a step towards her true screen self, which she was to discover most fully in *The Poor Little Rich Girl* of 1917, a film which satirized the rich whilst it confirmed its star as the richest actress in the world. It also took her a step nearer to Douglas Fairbanks, a former student of a mining school who had strong views of his own on how the movies should depict American society.[13]

Society was there too for the comedians, whose antics were from the very beginning shot against the background of a very recognizable American actuality. Film comedy developed along a parallel track to the feature film drama: the need for better films made feature film producers more ambitious technically and in terms of story and the same forces helped comedy to graduate from improvised shorts to more substantial films. Once comedy was given the incentive to develop it soon leapt ahead of the dramatic film: suddenly there emerged a handful of geniuses and this was not entirely a matter of chance. The comedians were always to enjoy more freedom. Like the producers of filmed drama they relied heavily on nineteenth-century models and conventions but obviously mime, pantomime, and other comic traditions by their very nature could adapt to silent cinema even more effortlessly than melodrama and popular fiction. Once the security of the industry was assured there was every incentive for the comedians to experiment, for comedy relied on movement, gesture, and illusion whilst photography and editing were now opening up all kinds of new possibilities. From the start the new feature film had been saddled with outside obligations; it had to preach or at least uplift, or if it were borrowing from literature it had to satisfy so many knowledgeable readers. At the same time the outside agencies were quite content to ignore comedy, so leaving the comedians to develop their own cinema and not surprisingly it developed as a purer cinema. The comedians then became the classic movie showmen of these early years. Their cinema was purer because they were often more fully in charge of their product than were other film-makers working on serious movies, because comedy encouraged a more direct relationship between technique and content, and because the films were made not for any sectional audience but for the mass audience itself. Even more than most movie men the comedians were men of the people and they sensed what the masses wanted.[14] Mack Sennett had come from a New England working-class background and he had himself worked as a plumber's mate. Chaplin and Keaton came into movies from a vaudeville background in which they had seen poverty and experienced it for themselves. Their knowledge of society had taught these men that there was a huge audience that wanted to laugh and that comedians had to strain every nerve and to try every joke in order to release that laughter. Sennett was the initial genius who taught the others that anything ought to be tried that produced laughter and that the ultimate test was whether any movie actually worked for audiences.[15] The whole world, the whole of society was there for the comedians to plunder. Their own experiences allowed them to take up whatever social reference was needed and if anything the demands of Progressives helped for they allowed age-old traditions of humour to be shaped into what could often appear to be social satire. Comedy had always been anti-establishment but now if the Progressives were happy to see shyster lawyers, pompous and hypocritical capitalists, and venal politicians then so much the better. The jokes could be played out in a fully contemporary setting and could often concern the adventures of very ordinary downtrodden men.

Throughout his career Chaplin took every care to sustain the idea that his life had been a kind of Victorian romance and perhaps if we allow for certain embellishments we can accept this interpretation as legitimate. There seems every reason to believe those 1917 recollections in which Chaplin spoke of how from the moment that he had first seen the light of Brixton he was aware that 'unkind fate must have struck his knife unto me' and of how he had been 'through more hardships and downright poverty than one per cent of the world's worst Jonahs can tell of'. Whilst recalling his early hardships Chaplin also provided a clue as to how he had overcome them for he spoke of how he had 'slaved like a nigger to master the difficult steps that formed the routine of the eight Lancashire lads'.[16] Throughout his early career Chaplin noted the poverty and hardships that were common in society and these observations were fed into his act as he mastered the various techniques of traditional nineteenth-century mime, vaudeville, and clowning. Convention, technique, and an empathy with the popular mind all went into the perfecting of the Chaplin act and it was these things that enabled him to become Sennett's most accomplished pupil and which allowed him to create the cinema's most appealing and most universal symbol. It should also be noted that Chaplin had mastered all the skills of being a showman. He had worked for so many nineteenth-century showmen that he was able to outdo them all. In later days it became fashionable to see Chaplin as a political rebel against Hollywood's factory methods but he is better seen as the last of the old-style showmen offering a highly polished product to the masses that he felt he knew so intimately. He was never happy until there had been a 'successful exploitation' of every one of his films.

The most striking features of Chaplin's film career were the rapidity with which he became popular outside America and the way in which he very soon became a favourite of intellectuals. It became a commonplace for novelists like Arnold Bennett and pioneering critics like Gilbert Seldes to talk of how Chaplin had overcome the limitations of cinema and 'passed beyond the form entirely.'[17] It is not going too far to suggest that it was the fame of Chaplin that first allowed many intellectuals to even broach the subject of film and certainly he brought back the possibility of 'slumming it' that had rather disappeared since the days of music-hall. Seldes, who was to become Chaplin's greatest booster in America as well as his personal friend, wrote of how 'you have to go to squalid streets and disreputable neighbourhoods if you want to see Chaplin regularly'.[18] But more and more intellectuals seemed prepared to take this risk and went on to talk of Chaplin's techniques, his 'dolefulness', his sense of rhythm, and his mastery of myth and fancy. Of course these superior critics disliked the way his films displayed 'the grossest sentimentality', but this was the price that had to be paid for his mass popularity and after all, as William Hunter reminded his readers, Dickens had been far more sentimental for very much the same reasons. In fact, Hunter saw Chaplin as 'the Dickens of the films' and so gave another reminder of how the whole world of silent movies was moulded in the idiom of the great Victorian writer.[19] What irritated Edmund Wilson about Chaplin's more ambitious films of the 1920s was the inclusion of 'gags' and 'low comedy incidents' as if he were trying desperately to hang on to his old mass audience, the clear implication being that Chaplin had now become the property of a more sophisticated audience.[20] In all the 1920s writing on Chaplin, however, we find an emphasis on his humanity and on his sheer ordinariness. To James Agate he belonged 'to humanity: he is one of us', he is still 'a chap', whilst to William Hunter he represented a universal type – 'the downtrodden vagabond isolated and alone'.[21] Writing later, in 1937, J. B. Priestley's main concern was to stress the Englishness of Chaplin (though he did concede that the Chaplin symbol was half-French in inspiration) and he talked of him as being 'the greatest humourist since Dickens' and of belonging above all to London's East End and to 'the swarms of bright-eyed urchins who are thumbing their noses at the nearest policemen'. Priestley had particular pleasure in recalling that moment in *Payday* in which Charlie has to walk home through the rain after foolishly spending his pay and after being pushed out of the last tram; he anticipates his wife's anger and the return to short rations and yet not all is hopeless, something might turn up. Priestley concludes that 'twenty Marxian treatises about the proletariat would not make you feel a tenth of the compassion for the dispossessed urban masses as this bit of pantomime does'.[22]

In 1936 Robert Wagner had maintained that Charlie's pictures are always 'proletarian' but by this time the politicization of criticism had already assured a wider and more varied critical response to Chaplin.[23] Priestly was to recall *Payday* as being a remarkable film but of course it had not been a typical Chaplin film. It was one of the very rare occasions when Chaplin made himself a worker, a member of the proletariat with all the attendant problems of low wages, of dealing with a foreman, and of sustaining a home and family. This was a one-off film for Chaplin and he was well aware that to have sustained that role and that theme would have been to sacrifice much of his great following and to have become an artist with a more sectional support. The classic Chaplin figure was never a worker, never a member of a class and never in danger of being politically motivated and divisive. Chaplin was too much of a showman and too steeped in 'showbiz' ever to fall into that trap. All the nineteenth-century conventions of comedy pointed to the need for universality and in any case Chaplin's own personal inclinations must have pulled him back from being sectionally committed at a time of class warfare. His screen creation was often referred to as 'the tramp' but as Sobel and Francis have suggested the use of this term is as misleading as to call Chaplin 'proletarian'.[24] What Chaplin the showman had done was to create a great screen clown, a clown whose frame of reference was to be emotion

2 *Modern Times*: Chaplin's clown by chance becomes a proletarian rebel.

rather than politics. As Walter Kerr so brilliantly argued, Chaplin's statement was 'philosophical - not social'.[25] What Chaplin had needed was a
clown whose loneliness, detachment, pathos, optimism, indestructibility,
incorrigibility, and vulnerability would allow him to exploit all the

humour and tragedy, love and violence that everyday life offered. He found the identity for his clown not in the figure of a worker but rather in the form of a man whose sensitivity, grace, almost feminine beauty, charm, clothes, and swagger all hint at a better background and perhaps at social and sexual aspirations. From his vast knowledge of that swirling urban society in London and New York it was the type that could be swept up and then knocked back down that Chaplin chose to express the emotions of a whole era. Even then Chaplin avoided being too socially specific, for over and above this there was his own never quite fully adult quality and his essential reliance on mime technique and silence which ensured that he remained a fairy-tale symbol and never became a real-life person. He had created an essentially social symbol but perhaps not surprisingly some critics in the highly politicized 1930s chose to interpret the outer form of his creation in their own way. So many critics wanted *Modern Times* to be a satire on capitalism whereas Chaplin was merely using factory production and the depression as a back-cloth for a series of impish gags. Such was the confusion that *Pravda*'s critic Shumiatski had to remind his colleagues in the west that all of Chaplin's films had depicted 'the tragedy of the petty bourgeoisie in capitalist society'. For Shumiatski the famous scene in *Modern Times* in which Chaplin accidentally finds himself leading a Socialist demonstration showed the comedian remaining 'true to himself' for 'he is lonely - his path has nothing in common with the path of the masses - it is the path of the external failure'.[26] One does not have to agree with Shumiatski's aim of revolutionizing the masses to accept these remarks as a nice corrective to those views of Chaplin as a proletarian and whatever the political reasoning they do offer insights into the psychology and social psychology of the 'little man's' persona. Whatever political positions he was later driven into by a jealous Hollywood, Chaplin as a film-maker was never a propagandist or a preacher. He was always a showman but one whose genius allowed him to become an artist and as an artist he knew that the human spirit was best defended and expressed on the mythic plane. Film was an illusion and, as Charmion Von Wiegard so convincingly argued in 1936, the art of Chaplin was 'built entirely on illusion and fantasy'.[27] Chaplin never used film for some extraneous purpose; rather he fulfilled himself as a cinema artist by using film's own logic and by fulfilling the expectation of that vast audience that had come to accept film as something that worked and as something that offered 'sure-fire' entertainment.

In 1924 Chaplin himself asked the question whether 'the public knows what it wants' and his conclusion was very straightforward. He argued that the public did not stand at the box-office window and demand dramas with happy endings or which mixed pathos and humour, nor did it demand comedy made up of 'slapstick', 'gags' with 'three or so dashes of serious situation and a bit of irony to top off'. It struck him that 'the public has no such specifications' and that their demands were 'negative at best' for it was 'Entertainment' that 'they' really wanted.[28] This was the classic showman speaking and on this occasion he was directing his remarks directly at those intellectuals whom his films had brought into cinemas for the first time. As they became aware of cinema audiences the vast majority of these intellectuals tended not to see them in quite such a negative way as Chaplin. Of course the public only wanted entertainment, but the point for intellectual observers was that the public had only wanted it on their own terms and so the story of film was the story of how the masses had dragged it down to their own level. To Welford Beaton the great weakness of the movie industry was that it had been 'born without reasoning faculties' and had failed subsequently to develop any: since birth, he suggested, the industry had 'allowed the box-office to do its thinking for it'.[29] To talk of the movies then was to talk of the masses. To Gilbert Seldes the movie had 'no fixed form, no standards' and it was the first form (of art and entertainment) to be developed in the era of universal (that is low-standard) education.[30] To the English critic 'HD' the word 'cinema' conjured up memories of 'crowds and crowds and saccharine music and longdrawn out embraces and the artificially enhanced thuds-off of galloping bronchoes' and then again 'boredom, tedium, suffocation, pink lemonade, saw-dust even, old reactions connected with cheap circuses, crowds and crowds and illiteracy and more crowds and breathless suffocation and (in America) peanut shells and grit and perhaps a sudden collapse of jerry-built scaffoldings'.[31] Perhaps part of the fascination of movies has always been that they trigger off so many memories but what is interesting about so much film-making in the 1920s is that movies are so closely associated with that age of the masses that had come at the end of one century and the beginning of another. As Kenneth Macpherson was to note, film always gave evidence of 'its humble Pier Penny Peep Show beginning'. For Macpherson everything about the general run of American movies 'belonged to the 1910 period' when the industry had alighted on a certain type of narrative film as being most suitable for its mass audience. What he suggested was that 'the words nice, nasty, morbid, vulgar, dirty, clean are not words merely, but complete attitudes of mind, complete summaries coded in 1910 language'.[32] It was normally the practice for writers like Macpherson to stress that the movies had grown directly out of the 'dime' or 'yellow-back' novel. For Seldes it was contemporary drama that had been to blame, for it had encouraged the young movie industry to take 'the slice of life' as its subject-matter. But for Seldes too it was 'the times' that had largely been to blame for the infantile nature of the movies. The masses were uneducated and the producers had given them rubbish, but what had really ensured 'the bloodlessness of the American film' was that with intellectuals alienated and excluded there had been 'no intelligent body' to shape the new medium. Speaking for a generation of American and British intellectuals, Seldes condemned American movies for their 'falseness' but saw that it was 'the falseness of the McKinley era', an era when 'the moral and intellectual tone - had not yet become infected with self-criticism'.[33]

It was in the 1920s then that criticism developed apace and it became a socially respectable and intellectual orthodoxy to relate the worthlessness of the movies to the immaturity of the masses. 'Whosoever would have it known that he is not of the common herd', suggested Clifford Howard, 'develops a spleen against the Hollywood movies.'[34] They were seen as an opiate, a worthless retreat from the real world. The mindless sentimentality and inevitably happy endings were seen as a reflection of the popular will. 'For the "thick-ear" has set the standard', said HD; confronted with the screen, 'mind in some way neatly obliterates itself', argued Kenneth Macpherson, and Walter Kron identified 'an absence of taste, conscience, courage and character'.[35] The star system, that 'Hollywood poison', according to Hugh Castle, was seen as yet another concession to the masses, for, as Clifford Howard explained, 'the crowd (and it is the crowd that supports the movies) cannot appreciate entertainment in the abstract, any more than it can thus appreciate art or religion'.[36] According to Howard, 'the public from the very beginning of the photodrama has centered its interests on the personalities of the screen' because 'only through personality can the multitude be satisfied'.[37] The movies had created a false world and what was taken as the ultimate proof of that was the way in which they had failed to deal directly with real Americans and their dilemmas. Seldes pointed out that no encouragement had been given 'to the movie which dealt honestly with life, which created tragedy, which allowed itself a grim and unhappy ending'.[38] What the movies taught Welford Beaton was 'we are not interested in average things, whether animate or inanimate - we are interested in anything in the degree that it is above or below the average'.[39] Writing in 1932 the English critic Bryher asked why it was that the real virtues and strengths and diversity of America had never been conveyed in the movies sent across the Atlantic. The English could have no idea, Bryher maintained, that America had a climate that varied from that of Norway to that of a Spanish summer, that much of America was made up of monotonous stretches of unbroken country, and that there were parts where only Swedish is spoken and others where seventeenth-century English remained almost intact.[40]

The notion that Hollywood produced only rubbish was even more fiercely upheld by British intellectuals than by their American counterparts. The British had added grounds for resentment as the cinema of their own country had been largely eclipsed by that of Hollywood. Most critics had little difficulty in associating the faults of the movies with aspects of the American personality. To condemn the movies was not only to condemn the masses, but to score a few debating points off Americans. The movies were sentimental and adolescent because most Americans were sentimental and adolescent. Occasionally it was conceded that New York had elements of sophistication but it was widely appreciated that film tastes and standards were determined in the populous and philistine Midwest. Hollywood had captured the British film audience and what was worse was that those English films that were made were all too prepared to ape Hollywood conventions. The result was that the real Britain was also never seen on the screen. 'I have never seen Soho on the screen,' wrote Ernest Betts in 1928 and then he added that he had never seen Southend, Birmingham, Chelsea, Bloomsbury, or London suburbia either. For Betts the explanation was simple, for the British were 'afraid to depart from massive but stultifying film values' which the Americans had already built up, and the situation was one in which 'every film producer in the world is mortally afraid of losing that Hollywood complexion, ourselves most of all'.[41]

It was the smart thing to do down Hollywood, but it is not difficult to see that the venom and enjoyment that went into those attacks of the 1920s tell us more about the social values of elites and in particular of intellectuals than they do about movies as such. Many of the critics displayed amazing disingenuousness, not to say hypocrisy. Perhaps they were justified in recalling early days in makeshift cinemas and perhaps they had to mingle with the masses as they went in search of Chaplin movies, but they must have been aware that prestigious down-town and suburban theatres were now largely being patronized, not exclusively by a lumpenproletariat, but rather by a mix of social classes and perhaps above all by young people who were moving up the social scale into more respectable occupations. A more accurate guide as to who went to the movies was given in 1928 by Pare Lorentz, who rather patronizingly suggested that whereas most people went occasionally, the regulars consisted of 'an army of clerks' who not only went but took it 'seriously'.[42] In that same year Welford Beaton argued that it was people like clerks who made up the bulk of the great movie audience and that they went to the cinema for inspiration. In fact, Beaton suggested, the screen had become practically their only source of inspiration:

the discouraged stenographer is inspired by the fact that the stenographer in the picture marries the boss, and the travelling salesman is given fresh hope when he sees Dick Dix or Bill Haines playing a salesman cop the millionaire's daughter in the final reel.[43]

In 1922 the manager of the Grand Theater in DeQueen, Arkansas, explained to the readers of the *Exhibitors Herald* that he was having difficulty in choosing between the easily satisfied 'masses', who just wanted shorts, and the much more difficult to please 'classes', who wanted programmes especially prepared for them.[44] The evidence from elsewhere in America and Britain is that exhibitors increasingly took the masses for granted and were always investing in better and better cinemas so as to hang on to the more respectable lower middle-class audience. Ben Hall has spoken of how in the 1920s the United States 'was dotted with a thousand Xanadus', luxurious cinemas in which people all too concerned with their own improvement could satisfy their curiosity about how other people had succeeded. Hollywood, said Hall, had already discovered people's interest in the rich and 'rags to riches was filmdom's bread and butter'.[45] The content of the films and the increasing splendour of the cinemas both testified to the film industry's improvement. In 1922 the English critic James Agate was reminded of how totally uneducated the average cinema audience was by the fact that a rendering of Mendelssohn's violin concerto between films received very full attention. Agate conceded that one occasionally saw cabinet ministers at the movies, but it was obvious to him that this particular audience had never heard the Mendelssohn, whilst his friend was prompted to comment that it was 'the first time they've ever heard the fiddle'.[46] Seven years later Agate reported on the opening of a new cinema of 'almost Babylonish magnificence' in the London suburb of Brixton, and he drew attention to the running fountain with its goldfish, the marble stairs, the thick carpets, the cushioned seats, the noble organ, and the fact that a full orchestra was to be used.[47] Cinema audiences in the 1920s expected better and better things and cinema-going became part and parcel of their social betterment. In 1927 *Variety* thought Dorothy Arzner's *Fashions for Women*, starring Esther Ralston, 'a corking good picture' and described how 'lovely gowns are in every foot. Ermine negligées; bath in milk, numerous underpanties, chemises and other intimate items, all of which look like a million dollars on the svelte Ralston figure, just round enough.'[48] The picture would, of course, be 'a cinch for exploitation' for it would fit in nicely with 'the usual fashion shows which many of the de luxe houses give in conjunction with the department stores in their cities'; in fact, *Variety* concluded, it 'was probably made with that in mind'.

It was all very well for the intellectuals to associate the movies with the mindless masses, but the masses who went to cinemas in the 1920s were rather different from the masses who had so enthused about films twenty years earlier. The twentieth century had moved on more rapidly than many intellectuals had realized. Daily newspapers were far more aware of how society was changing and in 1929 London's *Daily Express* invited its readers to send in postcards giving their own views on films. This step was welcomed by the *Cinematograph Times*, which could not resist pointing out that 'much of the criticism directed against the art expressed in the cinema originates from the small class not yet accustomed to modern outlook' who assumes 'that no art can exist or progress that does not begin with their patronage' and 'who do not yet appreciate that the masses today are fully competent to judge and to give expression to their own tastes'.[49]

Those who dismissed the movies were also dishonest in the sense that they very rarely conceded that the whole tone of feature films had been moulded by politicians and largely middle-class pressure groups and religious organizations who had ceaselessly clamoured for censorship and for films to be morally edifying and uplifting. Of course it would have been difficult for intellectuals to admit that it was precisely their own condemnation and neglect of films which had removed the one buffer that the film industry could have used to protect itself from the onslaught of 'the Meddlers and Busybodies'. The educated classes had just stood back as the aspiring politician and the over-eager Methodist forced the showmen into a reliance on the melodramatic and the romantic. Only very slowly did intellectuals concede that the movies had been shaped as much by politics as by the showmen. 'Never has an art form been subject to such control,' argued Pare Lorentz in 1930 as he pointed out how the whole industry was 'ruled by fear' and was 'the victim of moral racketeering'. Lorentz wondered whether 'patrons might be made to understand why the movies are so banal and childish . . . if every motion picture theatre prefaced its films with the caption "This picture has been censored by a minor politician or by his assistants"'.[50] In 1929 Kenneth Macpherson talked of the 'doleful and disastrous consequences' of censorship and dramatically made his point by suggesting that censorship was 'England's Prohibition Law'.[51]

What was most disastrous about the educated response to American and British cinema was the way in which good movies or movies that had impressed were conveniently forgotten. Films tended to follow certain broad patterns but the general output was never as standardized as the wholesale condemnations suggested. Hollywood had carried all before it but even the Hollywood product was fairly diversified. From the very earliest days of Hollywood there have been reviews by part-time critics and intellectuals praising particular films for breaking away from the usual formulas. In every year there were one or two very special films which made a real impact outside the regular film audience. The Griffith films and especially *The Birth of a Nation* (1915) and *Intolerance* (1916) were widely debated well outside film circles as, of course, were the films of Chaplin. In general the silent cinema made its greatest impact with adaptations of literary classics and, as we have seen, critics in 1914 thought that the films of *John Barleycorn* and *The Jungle* were in no way inferior to the original novels and felt in particular that the low-life settings were entirely convincing. Similarly in 1925 there was praise for von Stroheim's *Greed*, which was a movie version of the Frank Norris novel *McTeague*. Tremendous publicity was given to the circumstances in which this movie had been made and to the way in which the director had shot some forty reels; 'the eight-hour day for movie fans has not yet dawned' was the thankful comment of Robert Sherwood, but few critics doubted that the film conveyed much of the anger, ugliness, and brutality of the novel.[52] *Exceptional Photoplays* labelled it as 'an uncompromising film' and was quite sure it gave proof that 'motion picture art has by this time attained its majority'.[53] Literary classics were, of course, a highly attractive proposition to the Hollywood studios. To film a well-known book was a sure way to impress the respectable classes and to attract new patrons from the reading public and the familiarity of the title generally helped in exploitation. In particular, the realistic novel had played an important part in shaping Progressive America and the themes of those novels were taken up in Hollywood as the studios struggled to find a formula for fiction films that would be acceptable to the highly politicized cities of the East and Midwest. This Progressive influence lingered on as a minor theme in the cinema of the 1920s and was an obvious outlet for the continental directors who were drawn in by the glamour and potential of Hollywood. The story of foreign geniuses at work in California was a strange and sad one; great men were fascinated by the excitement and power of a city devoted to movies, whilst the studios were attracted by the notion of using these aliens to make profitable and prestigious films. Sometimes the planned movies were never made, nearly always they were botched but nevertheless Lubitsch, von Sternberg, von Stroheim, and Murnau were making films that undoubtedly represented Hollywood's cutting edge into better audiences. If a director's name or even the tag 'distinguished director' brought in patrons then Hollywood's attitude was 'so be it'.[54]

Hollywood hoped that it would use immigrant directors for its own purposes but whatever the frustrations experienced by these foreigners the mere fact that they were working in the American film industry is a reminder that Hollywood was never as monolithic and stereotyped as its critics implied. Hollywood advanced on a broad front and one which inevitably allowed diversity. The main aim was to win new audiences and so there was always room for experiment, especially at the better end of the market. The overwhelming need was just for more films and so nobody really worried if there were a few strange films somewhere along the spectrum and similarly, as there was a need for lots of directors and cameramen, there was no harm in making films which allowed them to gain experience. Occasionally these protégés would come up with a one-off prestige film which could be used to show how respectable and serious Hollywood had become. This is the only way that we can account for the career of King Vidor. In the early days it had looked as if the directors would be the key men in Hollywood and from all over America men anxious to use the format to say something had been attracted to the movies. Nobody became more interested in the fate of these early directors than Scott Fitzgerald, and his unfinished novel *The Last Tycoon* is essentially about how directors were taken over by producers in the Hollywood system. Fitzgerald was fascinated by the director type and in his story 'Mightier than the sword' he offered a portrait of a man who could well have been King Vidor:

> Director Dick Dale was a type that, fifty years ago, could be found in any American town. Generally he was the local photographer, usually he was the originator of small mechanical contrivances and a leader in bizarre local movements, almost always he contributed to the local press. All the most energetic embodiments of his 'Sensation Type' had migrated to Hollywood between 1910 and 1930 and there they had achieved a psychological fulfilment inconceivable in any other time or place.[55]

Vidor was a Texan and a Christian Scientist who first started making his own movies whilst working as a projectionist in what he described as 'the remote part of Texas'. He was in Hollywood by 1915 in time to see Griffith at the height of his powers, and in a sense Vidor was always to remain a representative of the Griffith era; he was to become Hollywood's token Progressive in a period when the main energies of that phenomenon had been exhausted. Vidor was to confess that he had started 'with the definite idea' that he wanted 'to make a film that did not simply come to town to play three days or a week and then was forgotten' and it was always his conviction that the proper subjects for such a film would be the beauty of rural America and the fundamental decency of ordinary Americans. As an apprentice director he quickly defined his own idiom but it took the initiative and the backing of MGM's Irving Thalberg to sponsor his big prestige films. As a child Vidor had hated the Military Academy at San Antonio and he very much wanted to make 'an honest war picture' that would correct the excessive jingoism of the normal Hollywood war film.[56] Many contemporary and subsequent critics have emphasized the extent to which *The Big Parade* (1925) is essentially a piece of romantic escapism but it was the film's thoroughly sensible and balanced attitude towards war that earned it respect from discriminating critics in the 1920s. Robert Sherwood 'could not detect a single flaw - not one error of taste or of authenticity' and he particularly appreciated the absence of 'scenes wherein the doughboys dash over the top carrying the American flag'.[57] The British critic Bryher regarded the film as 'the first authentic comment on the War', praised particularly the depiction of enlistment, and poured scorn on those other British critics who had disliked the film's suggestion that it had been America who had won the war.[58] With *The Big Parade* Vidor won new friends for American films but what had impressed MGM was that the film made money and also pointed to the way in which romance would be coupled with broader themes; there was obviously no harm in indulging Vidor a little. MGM was not quite as happy with *The Crowd* (1928), which was held back for a year and temporarily given a happy ending and which proved only to be as *Kine Weekly* predicted 'a sound box office success' rather than a runaway winner. Not surprisingly this depiction of the humdrum life of a clerk did not capture the headlines in the fashion of *The Big Parade* but with *The Crowd* Vidor again forced the educated classes to take note of Hollywood. *Kine Weekly* suggested that Vidor's realistic and delightful presentation of 'the intimate domestic side of suburban married life' revealed 'his extraordinary knowledge of humanity' and this was the quality that appealed to so many critics.[59] Lorentz spoke of the film's brilliance whilst *Photoplay* suggested that it had come 'as near to reproducing reality as anything you have ever witnessed'.[60] Indeed Welford Beaton, like many other Hollywood figures, thought that Vidor had carried 'realism just a little farther than the public will prove willing to follow' and he brilliantly argued that films had to give hope and to show a way forward, but he did conceded that *The Crowd* was one of the best films ever made and he hoped that it would inspire further ventures into realism.[61] By 1928 Vidor was almost a cult figure amongst movie intellectuals and when he was in Europe in that year all those who hoped for better things listened with interest as he pointed out that independent film-makers and the 'little theatre movement' would never compete with Hollywood and would never break through to the large undeveloped market unless they attracted sufficient investment to improve their product. 'Good films' bringing in 'enormous returns' was the prospect dangled before Europe's intellectuals by the one director whom Hollywood had allowed to experiment with using the new feature-film format to broach contemporary themes.[62]

The praise bestowed on the adaptation of literary classics, the films of the foreign directors, and the role of Vidor always stressed the relative realism of these films compared with the standard product and was testimony to the extent to which the feature film had moved away from the era of social preoccupations when it had been felt that social preaching was the obvious subject-matter for Hollywood. The immediate post-war years had been the last classic period of the film as social sermon and one can almost sense the relief as the studios discovered that social context did not need quite as much emphasis. Throughout the 1920s filmed melodrama continued to use whatever social setting it required and poverty and urban misery were faithfully reproduced whenever necessary as on occasions were the realities of work in coal-mines, steelworks, and more frequently dockyards. But the social setting was now precisely that and not a star feature in its own right. Hollywood had learnt that attractive and in general successful people were better prospects than unrelieved drabness. When the *Exhibitors Herald* described *The Song of Life* (1922) as being 'an appealing and forceful story of life's drab realities' and in particular of 'the dull existence of a track laborer's wife' it was complimenting worthy endeavour rather than laying the foundation for a blockbuster. When in the same issue the journal reviewed *Why Men Forget* we are reminded of just how many social melodramas there were for this film showed a Socialist spokesman being discharged from a factory and 'denouncing wealth in no uncertain terms' before inheriting wealth and marrying a society girl and finally deciding to return to the poor folk from whence he came. 'May interest those who are concerned with the laboring man and his problems' was the critic's judgement but he also added that 'the trite story, the indifferent performances of the unknown players and the lack of new and interesting situations are an almost insurmountable handicap'.[63] The movies had moved away from the slums. In 1927 *Variety*'s judgement of *Rose of the Tenements* was that 'New York's pictorially hackneyed East Side' had been used as the setting for 'a drab colourless presentation offering little in either entertainment or box office value', and that family problems had not been 'dramatized to an extent where the mob can be made to forget the obvious ordinary scheme of things'.[64] In condemning these bad films the reviewers were also revealing just how much the movie industry had learnt.

Hollywood had streamlined its own product and in so doing had alienated the intellectuals. Hollywood's fictional mode seemed worthless to the lovers of the other arts although they were rarely honest about either the problems facing film-makers or their own responses to the diversified output of the studios. Only very gradually did a small number of educated critics come to see that although quite different from the Russian and European film the Hollywood and Hollywood-inspired film had developed its own qualities and that the great mass audience for that kind of entertainment had been responding quite genuinely to positive influence. Perhaps after all, some writers were suggesting, Hollywood was on the side of life. Usually the moment of insight came with Chaplin or with a brilliantly stunning film such as Murnau's *Sunrise* but perhaps it was the quality of the acting which did more than anything to suggest that the feature film had become significant. In 1922 James Agate saw Lillian Gish in *Broken Blossoms* and was in no doubt that 'this plain little American child' had given a performance which meant that she ranked 'with the world's great artists'.[65] Four years later Agate was surprised that the film version of J. M. Barrie's *A Kiss for Cinderella* was so good and in particular that the acting of the American star Betty Bronson had equalled the stage performance of Miss Hilda Trevelyan for what the latter had done with her voice 'this little screen actress does with her eyes, which are the windows of as lovable a soul as was ever born into the world of make-believe.[66] In 1927 Welford Beaton was left in no doubt that the motion picture was 'a throbbing, living, human thing' after Janet Gaynor's performance in Frank Borzage's *Seventh Heaven* and especially by her grief as her husband left for the war; Beaton had cried at the time and even as he wrote the spell was not broken.[67]

Whether through laughter or tears Hollywood was making its mark and confessions were bound to come. As we have seen Kenneth Macpherson had felt that the earlier films had been awful but nevertheless he suspected that 'the people got in some dim way the fact that here was something growing under their eyes', that the movies had 'a sense of life and expectancy'.[68] By what were to be the last years of the silent cinema quite a few critics had become aware of some sense of life in the feature film. 'It is not the least good pretending any longer that the film is a thing one does not go to,' admitted Macpherson, the editor of a journal which in 1928 recommended fourteen Russian and European films but at least in a second category included two films by Cecil B. de Mille.[69] Some contributors to *Close Up* were prepared to go even further. Clifford Howard commented on how Hollywood could ignore all criticisms as 'mere wind' and 'envy' for it had made a success of its own business and it had displayed 'a Yankee genius for sensing the taste of the public and giving the world what it wants'.[70] Meanwhile Dorothy Richardson had suddenly been struck by the thought that the popular insistence of the happy ending was perhaps, however crudely expressed, 'the truth of life' and a tribute 'to their unconscious certainty that life is ultimately good'. During 1928 Richardson became intrigued about the impact of film on the small English fishing village where she resided. She suspected that some aspects of rural life would be lost for ever but at the same time she could see that much was gained. The 'yokel' became 'less of a lout', the dairymaid became 'indistinguishable from her urban counterpart', and in general these 'youths and maidens' were becoming party to 'world-wide conversations'. They were becoming in short 'world citizens'.[71]

3 'The sociological punch' of the talkies

The 1930s was the most crucial period in the whole history of cinema in Britain and America. What was quite decisively determined in those years was the place of film within the respective national cultures and indeed within the even more extensive world-wide English-speaking culture. The American film industry took on a more highly integrated personality and its package of entertainment now universally referred to as 'Hollywood' moved into a position of cultural dominance in America itself and into a position not far short of that in other English-speaking countries. Hollywood confidently made stylish films and presented them to an audience that had become larger than ever. The sheer size of the audience would have made the decade significant but what is of more interest in the 1930s was the way in which responses to Hollywood became more and more complex. In what was to become a highly politicized era in which the most urgent questions concerned the political and economic significance of the masses it was inevitable that there would be a more intensive scrutiny of the role of film and that more demanding questions would be asked of Hollywood. If this was a challenge the American film industry reacted to it in a determined and ultimately triumphant way. This victory was to delight the masses just as it brought little pleasure to the newly energized forces of the political left, but, just as significantly, it was now also an occasional delight to a growing audience drawn from amongst critics, intellectuals, and the more respectable classes generally. All the while Hollywood was winning new friends and gaining a new legitimacy for its methods and style. The English-language feature film came of age in the 1930s first because of its singularity as a piece of entertainment and then because it prompted responses which were important in defining cultural positions generally.

The decade had started disastrously and yet it was out of this very disaster that Hollywood's greatest era was to evolve. What had occurred was an unprecedented box-office slump in which eventually a third of America's movie-houses were to close and giant film corporations were to plunge into debt.[1] The social historian can now fit this slump into the wider pattern of events that was to add up to the Great Depression but at the time motion-picture executives in production and distribution were more given to introspection than to socio-economic analysis. The mood was caught by Welford Beaton in a November 1930 report:

Motion picture lots are rather sad places these days. Every one seems to be wondering what should be done next. Morale is low. Unrest is rampant. Inspiration has gone off-shift. Initiative is lacking. Pessimism spreads into the executive offices where the leaders sit dispirited because they have come to the end of imitating one another without having brought box offices back to life. The industry is in a rut with high sides and its vision ahead blocked by box-office failures.[2]

The consensus was simply that Hollywood had lost track of what people really wanted but there were also a number of other notions. Many blamed the coming of sound not only for its enormous expense and for making producers rely on highly conventionalized and, by their very nature, static plots of theatrical origin, but also for taking all the essential fantasy out of film-going. Some thought that far too many opulent and now half-empty movie palaces had been built for the elusive fashionable trade whilst others detected a more general dulling of the palate as the masses lost their enthusiasm for the old stories and seemed all too ready for something new. The industry had lost its touch and its nerve. Once more, as in the early days, movies were charging around in all directions and not really getting anywhere. The situation in 1932 was best summed up by the exhibitor Ed Kuykendahl who suggested to his colleagues that, 'under the stress of present conditions, all of us are floundering around trying frantically to create a little business'.[3] It was out of this floundering that a new Hollywood emerged.

In the midst of despair the movie producers drifted amongst other things into a new realism. It was very much a drift because there was no one moment of conversion or inspiration and nobody had waved a magic wand. Hollywood had always been prepared to use social realism in the service of melodrama and especially in the service of making prestige films out of literary classics and this practice remained in evidence during these years and led to such notable films as *An American Tragedy* and *All Quiet on the Western Front*. Now there were new forces at work and they tended to lead towards a less traditional form of realism. The coming of sound was probably crucial in this respect as it obviously placed a new emphasis on the contemporary American voice and on contemporary settings, which were in any case cheaper than conventional sets. The new possibilities of sound had been suggested by the great success of that 'gabby' medium the radio which was now helping to give American actuality a new urgency and also by the Broadway stage where the great success of Hecht and MacArthur's *The Front Page* had hinted at the dramatic possibilities of ordinary everyday dialogue. Whatever the wider influences the producers themselves were just experimenting, trying to cut costs and to standardize production, and trying to whip up some interest by injecting a little sensationalism into their films by sailing a little closer to the wind. And so it was that all Hollywood's difficulties led somewhat accidentally to what Ralph A. Bauer has described as a period whose movies 'were perhaps as varied and intriguing' as the movies produced in any comparably short period in American history.[4] All that was needed was for one kind of film to do well at the box-office and a new Hollywood format would be established. It was suddenly realized that films dealing with contemporary city life were doing well and the new realism was born. Meanwhile the country was plunging into depression. Nobody was quite sure what that really meant but if it were to mean that audiences were now ready for films which dealt sensationally with sex, crime, and shady city affairs then that was what they were to be given. It was never a question of somebody saying 'we have a depression, let's give them depression movies' but given the new dispensation it was Hollywood's instinct to come up with just that added edge that the age required in its films.

By 1929 the drift towards a new cinema as being picked up by the critics, who eagerly pointed out both what they liked in the new films and what they thought would be well received by audiences. Frank T. Daugherty was confident that Cosmopolitan-MGM's *The Voice of the City* would please audiences anywhere not least because the director's 'crooks, cops, dips, dope-heads, con-men and gang leaders live and move with startling and entertaining reality'. He was less keen on United Artists' *New York Nights* but reassured exhibitors that if their audiences 'liked jazz, murder, sex and whoopee then this should draw them and satisfy them'. MGM's *Dynamite* directed by Cecil B. de Mille was for Daugherty nothing more than a torrid melodrama of conventional silliness but he knew that audiences would love the tremendous cave-in of the coal-mine. A clear pattern was emerging and in 1930 Daugherty could say of RKO's *Framed* that it offered 'cafes and apartments after the presently accepted modern mode' and 'police autos whining down crowded boulevards, whoopee scenes, police stuff at headquarters, third degree etc., raids and shooting in equal number and of an equal excellence to many already exhibited'.[5] In the same year UA released Howard Hughes's *Hell's Angels*. Writing about this film thirty years later John Clellan Holmes recalled how as an adolescent he had been initiated into manhood by the momentary revelation of 'the soft, white trembling curve of Jean Harlow's breast', but even at the time Welford Beaton argued that it had succeeded at the box-office because 'more than any other picture we have had, it demonstrates that the true mission of the screen is to supply visual entertainment'.[6]

Jean Harlow, alias the teenager Harlean Carpenter from Kansas City, was doing all she could to pull Hollywood out of the slump but in general the more respectable critics were more prepared at this time to hand the plaudits to the male actors, who were seen very much as the cutting edge of the new realism. What Daugherty had liked most about *New York Nights* was the performance of the ex-Broadway actor John Wray as the gangster Joe Privaldi and he told his readers that this characterization would stay with them for months. Wray is first seen being chauffeur-driven in his limousine and from that moment until he lies dying on the floor of a Pullman car with a bullet in his stomach and uttering the words 'Never call a sucker' his performance for Daugherty was one in which he never stepped out of character and never eased his 'taut, cat-like, steel-wire tenseness'.[7] Meanwhile the silliness of *Dynamite* was offset by Charles Bickford's excellence as the condemned-to-death miner, and Wallace Beery was very much the real thing in *The Champ*; for the most part though it was the newcomers who received most praise. In 1931 Welford Beaton was greatly impressed with Fox-Movietone's *Quick Millions* and he guessed it would be big box-office not because it was a gangster picture but because it was 'a good motion picture' and what was particularly good about it was the acting. Indeed for Beaton there had been no suggestion of acting for Spencer Tracy, George Raft, and John Wray had ensured that the movie was 'peopled with human beings'.[8]

Film historians have spent a good deal of time debating the significance of the gangster films and attempting to relate them to the whole ethos of the Wall Street crash and the onset of the depression.[9] At the time both critics and audiences were fairly certain that what they liked about these films was their wit, their tempo, their sensational hints of violence and sex, their authentic urban feel, and the utterly realistic acting. The critics went on praising these qualities but even as they did so they began to have quite serious reservations. They were all too aware of the renewed public campaign for further film censorship but their only response to that was to deplore Hollywood's all too obviously hasty attempt to wrap its gangster and other city films up in some kind of moral message. It was felt that whatever dramatic realism had been gained in the sociological breakthrough was now being sacrificed. In 1931 Dalton Trumbo fiercely denounced the growing trend by first declaring after a whole spate of films such as *The Miracle Woman* that he was 'beginning to weary of the Salvation Army' and then by condemning the practice of sermonizing and adding moral prefaces as 'bad art, bad taste, bad logic and bad box-office'.[10] Just as depressing, though, was the general failure of Hollywood to move on from certain basic themes and situations and there was a new realization of the industry's tendency to just go on duplicating a successful format. Even critics who loved the pace and zest of the new films began to feel that night after night they were just sitting through one long gangster film. What they pleaded for was further experimentation and what they hoped was that the new techniques and acting styles could be extended to other types of films. Their enthusiasm for the gangster film was in part a hope that it would be a transitional form and not an atrophied and unchanging product. As early as 1930 Welford Beaton was indicating the way that Hollywood should develop:

> It should get back to the farm and away from speakeasies, it should give us factories where things are made instead of courtrooms where men are unmade; it should take us into the sweet-smelling atmosphere of small-town houses instead of the polluted air of rich homes of intrigue and infidelity.[11]

Even as Beaton spoke one director was doing his best to harness the new realism to a more rewarding type of movie. King Vidor showed with *The Champ* that he was very much at home in what Hollywood was now establishing as 'the city' but not surprisingly he was also taking up other challenges. His first sound film had been *Hallelujah*, which he had made for MGM in 1929. Many subsequent critics have taken up the point made by radical blacks at the time that this was a romantic and pastoral view of the rural South, but several early critics hailed the film as a brilliantly realistic depiction of a whole section of American society. Welford Beaton thought that its examination of the progress of cotton from field to factory would be of great educational value and he urged distributors to put the film into every motion-picture theatre in the world. More realistically, though, he conceded that as beautiful as it was as screen art it nevertheless belonged to that category of films 'which would not enrich their producers'.[12] The same was true of *Street Scene*, which Vidor directed for Goldwyn–United Artists in 1931. Here again was confirmation for Beaton that Vidor was 'America's bravest director', very much 'a student of the Russian and French schools', but again his great fear was that the film would be a 'remarkable achievement' from every standpoint 'except that of the box office'. On this occasion Beaton thought that the movie would join the list of those that had 'paralyzed the box office' because Vidor had been forced by United Artists to film Elmer Rice's stage play on a very confined studio set, the implication being that this movie of gossip, family disagreements, sidewalk philosophy, and sociological theorizing needed a more realistic and expansive setting.[13] There is, however, just a little disingenuousness in this argument. Other critics praised *Street Scene*: George Blaisdell for instance liked the way in which 'simple persons have come into their own' and *Photoplay* told its readers that here they would find the 'humour, the pathos and the gripping drama' which they saw again and again in their own lives and in their own newspapers, but then it went on to ask: 'Will it be box-office?'[14] Of course Elmer Rice's play had been censored and toned down before coming to the screen but *Photoplay* still needed to ask whether 'the public really wants a true cross-section of life presented as it actually happens'. Intelligent independent critics like Beaton and popular magazines like *Photoplay* knew that Vidor's work was good but they also knew that it was not the answer to Hollywood's problems. 'We hope it goes big,' said *Photoplay* of *Street Scene*, for 'big money on this would encourage more really excellent pictures'. These noble sentiments, of course, were only expressed after the question of whether this was what people wanted had been asked. The essential hypocrisy that has characterized so much modern film journalism was being established.

Vidor was praised even as he was written off as box-office. His sort of realism just could not be expected to compete with that of the gangster film and especially now with that being offered by James Cagney. Just as the critics were beginning to complain about overdoses of city life along came Cagney to inject new energy into the genre and in effect to open up a new era for the movies. *The Public Enemy* broke all box-office records and forced the critics to think again about the new sociological dimension of the movies. Edward G. Robinson had been good in the previous year's *Little Caesar* and there was to be great acclaim for the explicitness of the following year's *Scarface* but it was Cagney's 1931 performance in *The Public Enemy* that occasioned the most significant debate. The film as a whole was quite remarkable with Jean Harlow giving another of her stunning braless roles and with Mae Clark taking a grapefruit in the face in a scene which film historians have interpreted either as an act of sexual debasement or of sexual equality but which contemporary audiences just found thrilling.[15] It was Cagney's acting, though, which was immediately identified as the most significant aspect of the film. Hollywood was just beginning to realize that the old phenomenon of stars might have an added significance in a period of depression and there must have been considerable delight in the studios at the alacrity with which the critics took up the subject of Cagney. James Shelley Hamilton found Cagney's acting 'stunning' and 'remarkable in its vividness and consistency'.[16] The London *Daily Mail*'s Seton Margrave liked this Irish, red-headed New Yorker who was dangerous when roused and concluded that 'in the interests of honesty in talking pictures, Mr. Cagney is welcome'.[17] It was as early as 1932 that Lincoln Kirstein's subsequently very famous appraisal of Cagney as 'the first definitely metropolitan figure to become national' appeared and this particular theme was soon taken up in newspapers through America and Britain.[18]

The Cagney phenomenon was remarkable but it was also very complex and of great long-term significance. Cagney was an authentic city man with impeccable East-Side Manhattan credentials; he was born on the lower East Side but raised in Yorkville and he was fully conversant with the Irish, Italian, German, Scandinavian, and Jewish idioms of his native city but he was also a professional entertainer who graduated through

3 *The Public Enemy*: Cagney, the authentic city man.

vaudeville and song-and-dance routines to being a hard-boiled actor.[19] Soon after making *The Public Enemy* Cagney was to publicize his battle with Warner Bros over the roles he was being made to play and it became very evident that he was a shrewd and realistic businessman who perfectly understood his commercial and artistic value to the studios.[20] On both sides it was understood that Cagney was not just a man off the New York street but rather a remarkable screen performer. The great virtue of Cagney to the Hollywood set-up was that he could realistically depict anger, violence, and meanness without in any way suggesting that he was personally a worthless villain or that the film in which he was appearing was deliberately condoning these unpleasant qualities. The truth was that Cagney was marvellously photogenic and the combination of his looks and his relentless energy made him come alive in his every role. The stunning realism that he offered was not that of any old son of an Irish barman from New York but more precisely his own realism, in part natural and in part perfected by the very conscious application of technique. Once again the movies were proving that they had their own version of what was real. What the cameras were now discovering and what audiences were now reacting to was Cagney's own reality, a unique one-off reality or presence, albeit of the kind one hopes to run into whenever entering a New York bar. Here was a living, walking, strutting answer to Hollywood's prayers, for Cagney's personality served to sanction the suggestions of violence that characterized his films. In social terms these were tough times and certainly there seemed to be a new excitement in the movies. A genre that had grown out of the need for sensationalism did seem to be striking chords at a time of economic insecurity when cities seemed places of dislocation and when, if nothing else, there was a curiosity about how law-breakers operated. Robert Warshow was to argue quite rightly that there must have been much vicarious pleasure in the enjoyment of these films for audiences could watch gangsters break the law, use violence, take risks, and die but were free themselves to leave the theatre safely.[21] In truth one suspects that audiences quite simply enjoyed these films for their pace and wit but Cagney was certainly adding another dimension. It mattered little whether the plot put Cagney in the right or wrong or how the movie ended or whether the action was wrapped up in a sermon. Cagney's impact and the thoughts and feelings that he provoked came directly from his own performance before the camera. Whatever the story-line there was a hero for a new era. James Shelley Hamilton described Cagney's role in The Public Enemy as being that of a vicious, cruel, hard-boiled rat and yet he concluded that we end up sympathizing with him and feeling 'that there was something likeable and courageous about the little rat after all'.[22] In looking for significance some critics took a sociological line but perhaps psychology was a better guide. As early as 1932 Kirstein had understood that Cagney was 'cute, half-boy half-man' and that he suggested nevertheless 'the delights of violence, the overtones of a semiconscious sadism, the tendency towards destruction, towards anarchy which is the basis of American sex-appeal'.[23] Even as he charmed Cagney burnt up a nervous restlessness in a way that would have been very familiar to many of his fans.

Hollywood had always been able to recruit actors who could authentically depict urban working men and by the end of the silent era Bickford and Beery had almost achieved perfection in suggesting that kind of independence that grew out of a tough upbringing and an even tougher manhood.[24] The movies of the depression were not to go after that kind of realism. Cagney's class credentials were as impeccable as those of Bickford and Beery but he was never really to be a worker; he was a city man and it was the pace, wit, style, and electricity of the city that Cagney now seized on as his hallmark. Nature had endowed him with exceptional vitality and both Cagney himself and Warner Bros quickly appreciated how that vitality positively crackled before the camera. In the midst of the depression and a welter of screen bullets and punches Cagney had given a new definition of realism to the movies and this was a definition that Hollywood was delighted to accept. Soon Otis Ferguson was praising the star system for coming up with personalities like W. C. Fields, Jimmy Durante, Mae West, and now Jimmy Cagney, all of whom offered 'the sense of real people' and who were to his mind 'the best and most honest Americans' that he knew.[25]

Not every critic was happy with Cagney and one can sense that the very way in which he worked out his screen identity irritated some people. Frank Daugherty saw Cagney's style as just a logical development from that of other gangster types and identified as the most effective of his 'tricks' the way in which he could suggest that he was 'thinking his own thoughts' and 'reserving his feelings'. To Daugherty this trick ensured that the audience 'automatically became his ally' and it was all therefore very much 'a matter of showmanship'.[26] Of course Cagney was a marvellous showman and that was precisely the point, for audiences had shown a predilection for zest and sharpness and a new kind of urban charm and Hollywood was quite prepared to exploit these qualities in its own way. What really annoyed Daugherty was that critics were applauding *The Public Enemy*, a movie which seemed to him to be just a very well-cut and scripted melodrama that would serve as good 'yokel bait'. In analysing the new acting Ferguson was nearer the mark when he suggested that the movies were now coming up with richer and more vital people but Daugherty's comments serve to remind us that techniques and styles which should have been feeding into a new cinema of experimentation and realism were being used rather to bolster old conventions of melodrama.

The Public Enemy had been a Warner Bros film and that studio soon went on to consolidate its reputation as one specializing in contemporary themes by releasing *I am a Fugitive from a Chain Gang*. It is now generally appreciated that Warner Bros had been particularly badly hit by the depression, largely because of the furious rate at which they had acquired movie-houses in the 1920s. They were now hugely in debt and the standard MGM joke was that the cheap and badly lit contemporary sets were all that Warners could afford.[27] There was slightly more to it than that, though. Most of the theatres Warner had acquired were in what was described as the 'populous East' and especially in Pennsylvania, New Jersey, and New York and it could be claimed that the studio knew and needed to know more about industrial America than some of its rivals.[28] Furthermore there were men at Warners who fully appreciated that a touch of the contemporary might lead to good, entertaining, and successful films. A deliberate Warner Bros policy to produce some social films had emerged and this was encouraged by Jack Warner himself, by his chief executives, Darryl F. Zanuck and then Hal Wallis, by a small team of directors and writers, and even sometimes by individual actors. John O'Connor has described how, following up what was a Zanuck initiative, a Warner Bros team had eventually produced *I am a Fugitive*, a film that outspokenly denounced the Southern chain-gang system by using a true story that had received a great deal of publicity, the studio's gamble on topicality really paying off when the real-life subject of the story was actually rearrested just a few months after the film's release.[29] This was realism with a vengeance; a true story had been used to depict a very real penal practice and the whole thing was very deliberately set by the studio in a specific historical context. Depression audiences were given a hero who first fights in the World War and then finds it difficult to settle back into a factory job; this innocent man is then twice sentenced to a chain-gang, the second arrest coming after a period during which he had succeeded as a respectable businessman; the film ends with him still on the run and having now to depend on crime to keep himself alive. The popular critical response was probably best summed up by Robert Wagner, who gave his readers fair warning:

> Talk about 'roast beef cut thick'. This picture is sorghum and sourbelly, and your enjoyment(!) of it will depend upon your film dietary strength. It is a grand picture if you can stand strong meat. But don't take little Edgar or Vivian.[30]

More thoughtful critics were prepared to hail the film as a breakthrough. To the National Board of Review's William A. Barrett the film had 'performed a service on behalf of the dignity and meaning of the art of the American film' and, with it,

> The American motion picture comes into its estate as a medium for expressing the forces of social behaviour and corrective social thought, of performing the function which intelligent people have been saying it must perform if the screen is to realize its place as a serious art that uses the dramatic materials of our national life and institutions, methods and problems, not thereby to surrendered one tithe of its status as a great entertainment but in order to heighten that status by giving its art a social and more human meaning.[31]

This is a marvellous example of how the new sociological dimension was giving some films a new prestige and a new relevance and thereby gaining Hollywood new friends. There were yet other critics who were all too aware of what was really going on. In his review for *Vanity Fair* Pare Lorentz argued that all the minor characters in *I am a Fugitive* were caricatures and that the film had been spoilt by the director's decision to make the fugitive a hero and to tell the story through him rather than making the actual prison system the central focus of the film. He contrasted this approach with the methods of the best Russian and German directors, who almost certainly would have made a film in which the characters were less important than the system they would be condemning.[32] Lorentz returned to this point a few months later when he was reviewing Fritz Lang's German film *M*. What Lorentz liked about this dramatization of the notorious Düsseldorf sex murderer was that it had all the feel of a newsreel for 'there is no acting in the picture . . . . Never for an instant do you say - ah, what an actor!' His view was that Hollywood could never make such a picture 'simply because in all America you could hardly collect a hundred actors and put them in a picture and keep them from acting'. He still had *I am a Fugitive* in mind and he recalled how in that 'job' (in itself a revealing word) 'every man and woman within a hundred yards of camera range is acting his head off, figuring that he is a Clark Gable, or a Garbo!' Having argued this far Lorentz has to go all the way and he was forced to conclude that there will be no American *M* until Hollywood goes and until 'independent companies allow their directors to do away entirely with actors, and (which is the only sensible way to manufacture movies at all) pick types and faces off the streets'.[33]

There were several weak points in this critique and perhaps at the very least it can be argued that foreign films with social themes always appear to be more realistic merely because the subject-matter and personnel are new. More fundamental is the point that there was an actor, a great actor, in *M*. This was Peter Lorre's first film but he had been acting for ten years in a career which had begun with his running away from home at the age of 15 and which bore many similarities to the careers of other American and European actors who had arrived in Hollywood already. In spite of its loose thinking Lorentz's argument really takes us to the nub of the whole Hollywood system. Whatever the temptation to make films with what Robert Wagner called 'a strong sociological punch' there was never any danger that the studios would move away from what were regarded as the essentials of a Hollywood film.[34] Society was there as a backdrop to drama, melodrama if you like, and that drama could only be presented in terms of individual destinies which had to be resolved satisfactorily in the film itself. Whether it was the coming of sound and the new pace and sharpness that had then ensued, or whether it was because there was a new social awareness as the depression deepened, undoubtedly audiences now appreciated what was thought of as realism. In this situation Hollywood was quite prepared to incorporate into its dramas more realistic settings, more identifiable social problems, and more realistic acting. What Lorentz objected to in American actors both in Hollywood and on the stage was summed up by a director friend of his who spoke of how 'they have no humility'.[35] That was exactly the point. The essence of Hollywood was that it used actors who became real before the camera;

they were not ciphers there to be manipulated by an all-powerful director but they were actors who were able to combine natural qualities and varied skills and techniques in such a way as to create an on-camera identity. The skill of Hollywood was ensuring that the right actor went into the right story. If the actor was real then the film was real and it worked.

Peter Lorre had left the home of his Jewish family in the Austro-Hungarian Empire to become a travelling player at a time when in a different part of the Empire another Jewish family were training their son to join them as travelling players. Paul Muni, though, was to arrive in America some thirty-three years before Peter Lorre and he was to develop his skills in New York's Yiddish Theater. Muni, like his contemporaries Cagney and Edward G. Robinson, went into movies as Hollywood attempted to give a Manhattan sharpness to their product. His style was very different from the others but like Cagney he was a very intelligent actor with strong views and sound business instincts with regard to the films that he should make.[36] In later years many critics were to take up Lorentz's implication that in essence *I am a Fugitive* was a conventional melodrama centred on a romantic hero. Contemporary audiences would have understood that the film appealed to them on that level but were also aware that the tragedy of the film consisted of an ordinary innocent American being hounded by external events and being forced into failure and crime. A European director might have made a film explicitly depicting and condemning the chain-gang system and he almost certainly would have suggested that the system was a metaphor for life itself, but Hollywood had made a more accessible and universally popular film by showing an innocent man hounded by a combination of events and social forces of which the chain-gang was the most obviously dramatic. The very real tragedy was in the fate of one man and what was needed was an Everyman figure who could carry the story by being charming, innocent, ordinary, and haunted and that is what the skills of Muni could give them. Of course he was not a man straight off the streets with 'no humility' but he was a very proud, ambitious, and professional actor who knew very well how to play haunted men. Lorentz might have been very aware that he was an actor, but for Hollywood and its audiences it was Muni's acting that made the whole 'job' permissible, acceptable, intelligible, bearable, and successful.

So there were critical reservations but in general the sociological film was winning Hollywood new friends and helping to fill cinemas. But, critics apart, there were other groups in society far from pleased with these new departures, and the growing publicity given to 'hard-boiled' films now gave new life to the never-ceasing campaign against the movies. Soon there were many echoes of the old pre-1914 complaints. Investigations came hot on the heels of the new sound and realistic films and by the time of *The Public Enemy* and *Scarface* things were building to a crescendo. Hollywood films were now being produced for a society that was debating the impact of film as never before. Publicity was given to academic investigations whilst journals and organizations attempted to direct film-going by informing potential audiences as to which films they should attend and which ignore. Much of Hollywood's mass audience would have been oblivious to this but intelligent and respectable film-goers must have been very aware that society was shaping their film-going. The Payne Fund had sponsored nine investigations in the period between 1929 and 1933 and these observers were all too aware of the impact of the new sociological films and the dangers inherent in further progress in that direction.[37] Dysinger and Ruckwick found that films already carried 'a tremendous sanction' but suggested that with further innovations 'an irresistible presentation of reality will be consummated'.[38] What investigators worried about were the effects on the pre-adult of films depicting 'an exciting robbery, an ecstatic love-scene, the behaviour of a drunkard, and the like'. Blumer suggested that the motion picture held before the adolescent 'modes of living and schemes of conduct' and in a sense organized his needs and suggested lines of conduct, and that this was possible 'for too many of the pictures are authentic portrayals'.[39] The investigators were disturbed by the sheer size of the movie audience, and, thinking of that statistic of 115 million people a week, they asked: 'When has the globe ever known the like?' and 'Who could have imagined a population more nearly, more inclusively, unified by a single agency?'[40] They were concerned most, however, about one section of the mass audience and that was the hard-core army of regular adolescent film-goers who lived in the disorganized city centres, the so-called 'crowded section'. Blumer and Hauser maintained that 'the influence of motion pictures seems to be proportionate to the weakness of the family, school, church and neighbourhood' and that 'persons living in high-rate delinquency areas are most subject to influence by the themes of life treated by motion pictures'.[41] It was in one of New York City's 'crowded sections' that Thrasher and Cressey found that 'the photoplay of *Little Ceasar* seemed to have swept certain groups of boys - like a cyclone, leaving a host of consequences' and came across boys who swaggered, threw mock-punches, dressed, and 'smiled like Cagney' and who went around repeating phrases like 'You can dish it out but you can't take it.'[42]

Amidst the verbiage and jargon of these investigations were conclusions that must have reflected the fears of many respectable Americans, but what is interesting is that the reports were not entirely negative about the movies as such. There was an awareness of the appeal and of the potential of film and a strong stress on the need for film to take up new opportunities by treating a broader range of subjects. Edgar Dale stressed the 'narrow range of themes' in motion pictures and condemned their preoccupation with the rich and criminal. He suggested that a world modelled on the screen pattern would be one with 'no farming, no manufacturing, almost no industry, no vital statistics (excepting murder), almost no science, no economic problems and no economics'.[43] In his study of motion-picture advertising, Charles C. Peters estimated that, in a sample of press advertisements and reviews, adjectives demanding attention, denoting size, and challenging pathos were very frequent whilst 'adjectives denoting reality' formed the least frequent of some nineteen categories. He arranged the pictures used in advertising into some fifty categories and found that whilst a representation of men and women embracing was most common there were no representatives at all of people at work.[44] The movies, as Dr Dale had suggested, had 'the entire world as their range' and yet they had settled for a very restricted section. Investigators were concerned about the exclusion of the normal world and shocked at the preoccupation with aberrant behaviour, but what frightened them most was the failure of the movies to fulfil a clear moral role. If Forman was right in believing that the movies were 'a school, a system of education', albeit as yet 'unlimited, untrammelled and uncontrolled', and Charters could believe that the 'motion picture as such is a potent medium for education', then it was time that something was done.[45] What must have really alerted concerned Americans was Blumer's conclusion that for the most part the movies dulled discrimination, confused judgement, and stimulated random and unchannelled emotions. What Hollywood offered was 'a medley range of vague and variable impressions - a disconnected assemblage of ideas, feelings, vagaries and impulses' and it followed therefore that the movies were 'not endeavouring to provide a consistent philosophy of life'. What troubled Blumer was that Hollywood was 'not seeking to establish any definite set of values'.[46]

What Hollywood had been doing was living off its wits and trying to survive as best it could but it now responded to this challenge not necessarily by taking Dr Dale's 'entire world' as its range but at least by ensuring that there were values in its films. Hollywood produced many films but it was a small town and the industry as we know it was controlled by a handful of men. It was not that difficult, then, for the industry to regain its confidence and composure as certain things became clearer. Most writers have detected a new sense of purpose in Hollywood after 1933 and have related that to a number of factors. The new public concern about the social impact of movies led the industry yet again to put its own house in order by establishing a new Production Code. The inauguration of President Roosevelt and the beginning of the New Deal created a new sense of national purpose and encouraged institutions and agencies to rethink their public role, and however bad things were there was at least evidence that movie-going was surviving as a social activity.

All of these things encouraged the movie moguls to put their faith back into entertainment, to make good movies, and to go out looking for new and bigger audiences. As Robert Sklar has suggested, there was no such thing as a typical depression movie; rather there were a number of formats and an emphasis on production standards and conventions, but now in this new post-1933 dispensation there tended to be far less experimentation. The industry was no longer floundering and there was far less chance of an idiosyncratic, sensational, or outspoken film. With the emphasis switching to control over production, to quality, and to quite massive and well-orchestrated publicity campaigns there was less need to rely on the shock value of a new kind of film. What had appeared as almost revolutionary in terms of content in films made between 1928 and 1932 would now be controlled and integrated into a smoother package. Bauer was to describe this process as 'a counter-revolution' and Roffman and Purdy have seen it as a matter of Hollywood turning 'to the Right'.[47] It remains to be seen whether the changes were that dramatic, but the new dispensation was certainly to mean that sociological themes and realism generally would be handled with more care.

Even in the years of floundering and experimentation, Hollywood had ensured that the use of contemporary settings, themes, and issues had been largely governed by conventional dramatic or commercial needs. What had really occurred was that the Hollywood style had been updated and a large number of films had been located in a more contemporary urban setting. There had been publicity for occasional outbursts of violence and bad language or for shocking displays of sexuality, but there had never really been a significant breakthrough in terms of outspoken social statement. There were obviously some men in Hollywood who wanted to make films with sociological relevance and there was obviously an audience for contemporary films as long as they were made according to the normal dramatic conventions and satisfied more general audience expectations. Roffman and Purdy list a number of new film genres that developed during these years but the vast majority of individual films mentioned did not move very far from what was becoming a stock depiction of the city with its gangsters, 'modern' women, and venal politicians and lawyers. The mastery of a new urban idiom or style was more important than the specific content of any one film, and, as we have seen, anything that departed too far from tradition was not regarded as good box-office. No film received as much publicity as *I am a Fugitive* and that was a film more conventional than most critics suspected and which only attacked corrupt and degrading aspects of the South, a part of the country always regarded as a backwater and therefore as relatively easy game. The use of the terms 'counter-revolution' and 'a turn to the Right' is therefore a trifle misleading and is certainly to misunderstand what had happened in Hollywood before 1933. What happened after 1933 is that sociological and realistic films were now made in a very different Hollywood and national context. In general there was far less emphasis on the city and its problems of law and order, and that particular genre became just one small part of Hollywood's total output. Of course the 'genre' was somewhat doctored now: the forces of law and order had to be given a more positive and heroic role and there had to be far less suggestion of anarchy. There had been some good gangster films but the long-term significance of the genre lay really in its impact on contemporary American cinema generally, for it had taught Hollywood the dramatic possibilities of urban life. Paul Rotha was amongst those who argued that crime films did much to change the whole basis of film technique; now the pace was to be crisper, there was more naturalism, and dialogue was lifted out of the 'doldrums of the photographed play'.[48] There were relatively fewer pure gangster films after 1933 but there were a large number of social or 'social-problem' films although even they remained as only a small percentage of the total Hollywood package. What was new after 1933 in respect of these films was that they were being made for a nation that was experiencing a new politicization and by a Hollywood that was equally trying to redefine its role within the culture. There were obviously men in Hollywood who wanted to use social themes, there were audiences who were willing to attend these films, and there were critics who were prepared to praise and even honour these films. As always, it was Hollywood's custom to work on as broad a front as possible: there should be films for everyone but only on Hollywood's own terms. For the next few years American audiences were shown aspects of their society that they could never have expected to have encountered at the movies and it must have struck at least some members of the public that film-going had become a more serious business. The earlier period had aroused many expectations that America was on the verge of a social cinema, but, as the social-problem films of the post-1933 period came along, critics were to be uneasy about many of their characteristics.

Our Daily Bread was released in 1934 and immediately Otis Ferguson contrasted 'Hollywood's aversion to social content' to 'Mr Vidor's preoccupation with it'.[49] This time Vidor wanted to take up the notion of co-operatives which he had read about in *Reader's Digest*. Thalberg was interested but thought that it was not quite MGM's thing as that studio was moving away from its earlier interest in realistic films towards glossier entertainment, and eventually it was Chaplin who arranged the film's release through United Artists, although Vidor had to mortgage his every possession before firm backing was achieved. Even then the director had to make changes as the backers insisted that the story of an impoverished farmer galvanizing a group of the unemployed into helping make a success of things was combined with a more conventional sex angle.[50] As a result we are given one of the most blatant examples of a blonde floozie being added to a film purely for box-office considerations. Vidor was always to have a special affection for this film but later film historians have had many reservations. They have generally responded to its gentle evocation of rural America but have seen the action as being essentially melodramatic and the politics confused. Roffman and Purdy have quite rightly stressed that Vidor's traditional populism gave him sympathy for the underdog, but prevented him from moving towards any collectivist political situation.[51] Even in this story of co-operation there has to be a hero. Critical opinion has divided specifically over the film's most famous sequence: to save the commune the men eventually come together to dig a canal and as they dig tension is built up by drumbeats and speeded-up photography. To John Baxter this was rather 'solemn mock-Soviet montage' but others have more rightly seen it as a very effective expression of that energy which ordinary people had in abundance but which the America of 1934 so tragically left untapped.[52]

The idiosyncratic nature of *Our Daily Bread* was appreciated at the time of its release and was attributed to the obvious conflict between Vidor's convictions and box-office considerations. Otis Ferguson thought the only real social comment concerned the unemployed and they were rather haphazardly brought together and in any case upstaged by a boy-girl-siren triangle hung on 'the back of such an old love nag as even Hollywood might be ashamed to take out for a canter'. It is interesting to compare Ferguson's reaction to Vidor's film with his reaction at much the same time to the newly released *It Happened One Night*, which Frank Capra had directed for Columbia. He thought that the Capra film had made 'greenish grass grow where there was only alkali dust before' because it consistently preferred 'the light touch to the heavy' and used actors 'who are thoroughly up to the work of acting'. His final reflection was that 'such a picture cannot be defined at all until we find a way of describing whatever it is that makes first-rate entertainment what it is'.[53] William Troy in the *Nation* was similarly unable to find the right words to explain the greatness of *It Happened One Night* and he suggested that 'a good photoplay, like a good book or a good piece of music, remains always something of a miracle' and that 'beyond a certain point the mind is forced to bow down before its own inability to unravel and put together again all the parts of the shining and imponderable whole with which it is dealing'. Troy did, however, use one phrase that went a long way to describe the film's great success, for he spoke of how it illustrated that 'an honest documentation of familiar American actualities becomes in a Hollywood film more absorbing than intrigue in Monte Carlo or pig-sticking in Bengal'.[54] Capra's film was to be one of the most successful, acclaimed, and important films in the depression period because it was firmly set in contemporary America, but not in an America preoccupied with social problems. Whereas Vidor had started out with a theoretical

notion and then wrapped it in a melodrama, Capra had started out with
a fairly ordinary story and then breathed charm, wit, pace, sex, and
reality into it, not least by harnessing the natural talents and showmanship of Claudette Colbert and Clark Gable.[55] This was the entertainment
and the sense of reality that audiences wanted. Otis Ferguson had
immediately spotted the flair of Capra and in reviewing his next film
Broadway Bill he spelt out the lesson that Hollywood was rapidly
learning:

> The industry is at its best when it is dealing with no problems whatever,
> when it is thinking just as little as it can (which is very little), when it
> has got hold of some light empty piece of plot-making, and is putting all
> its marvellous technical resources into building comedy out of likeable
> people and familiar situations.[56]

Ferguson had alighted on what was rapidly becoming Hollywood's
formula for entertaining America through its difficult times. More than
any other film, *It Happened One Night* had pointed the way forward, but,
greatly to the surprise of many critics, problem films kept on appearing.
The greatest surprise came when in 1935 Warner Bros released *Black
Fury*, a movie which depicted in a direct and totally unprecedented way
the impact of a strike on a coal-mining community.

Black Fury could only have been made at Warner Bros, a studio which
had firmly aligned with Roosevelt and the New Deal and which quite
clearly believed that there was a market for films which dealt with topical
issues and in particular with matters of social justice.[57] The impetus for
the film to be made came from Paul Muni, who was always on the look-
out for suitable social themes. While playing in Pittsburgh, Muni had met
Judge M. A. Musmanno, who had written a book on the murder in 1929
of a miner's leader and of the subsequent charges against policemen.[58]
Muni's interest, however, would have come to nothing if there were not
men at the studios who shared his enthusiasm for this potentially
explosive subject. It was Abem Finkel, Muni's brother-in-law, who worked
out a screenplay from the basis of a draft by Musmanno and a melodramatic comedy about Slavic miners by Harry R. Irving, but there were
other supervisors and writers involved and ultimately the vital decisions
with regard to the project would have been taken by Jack Warner and his
senior executive Hal Wallis.[59] A note in the Dialogue File provides a
clue as to why Warner and Wallis were prepared to indulge Muni on this
occasion, for it describes the film as being 'a red blooded drama of life in
the raw, of men of primitive passions made desperate by hunger and
deprivation', 'a tale of strife and conflict, of greed and self sacrifice, of love
and devotion', and 'above all, a stirring plea for human justice'.[60]
Warner and Wallis would have judged that the time was ripe for a film
about human justice, that there would be a market for a film depicting

the problems of a strike in a coal-town and in an ethnic community, and that any criticism of the subject-matter would either be good for business or would be offset by popular and critical acclaim for the acting of that increasingly marketable star Paul Muni. There were considerable dangers in the project, but Warner and Wallis would expect their writers to mould the original story-lines into the Hollywood format and any obvious problems would be worked out with the representatives of the various censoring agents who normally read every script prior to production. 'Abe' Finkel and his colleagues carried out what the critic Abel Green described as the 'canny Burbanking' of the material, but there was still a need for intervention by Breen, who asked Wallis to ensure that the film was not a direct attack on conditions in the mines. In a letter, Breen gave this advice:

> With a view to protecting ourselves against any valid criticism on the part of the organised forces of the bituminous coal industry we respectfully suggest that in scene 61 on pages 26 and 27 you might insert a line spoken by Mike to the effect that while the miners may not have ideal working conditions, nevertheless the working conditions of the coal industry have vastly improved and are getting better all the time.[61]

The writers were able to accommodate such suggestions because the film that they had in mind would be far more a social melodrama and star vehicle than a detailed comment on the mining industry. In their publicity for the film, Warner Bros boasted of the way in which the story had grown out of an actual incident and of Judge Musmanno's involvement in the subsequent litigation, and also of how ex-miners had been brought in to ensure authentic mining scenes. Mention was also made of Muni's great interest in the fate of the Balkan and in particular Slovak communities. 'Muni was and is sociologically-minded,' said the press-book, and 'he had long wished to bring to the American people the picture of these primitive people who worked hard and who died that the wheels of industry might not be stilled'. Muni was obviously thought of as a major selling point and the public were urged to see this latest offering of the man who 'appears in fewer films than any of the big stars'. These lines of advertising were, however, swamped by emphasis on the melodrama, and the Muni posters told prospective customers that 'You'll see Muni let Loose a Blast of Dynamite', 'Her Kisses Made Him - Damned Him - Redeemed Him' and 'They Dug Up Hell Ton by Ton - to Make It'. Exhibitors were advised to invite 'Muni-Mimickers' up to the stage and to exploit the film in the following ways:

> Black is always in fashion for the femmes - which is your cue for tie-up with women's shops. Black shoes, black dresses, black hats, bags can be displayed in windows with the line 'We Call These our "BLACK FURY"

SELECTION BECAUSE THEY'VE CREATED SUCH A SENSATION'.
No need to tell you that display includes stills and theatre mention.[62]

Like the writers, the publicity boys had done their stuff but their combined efforts were not enough. The film was banned in Maryland and Illinois, the New York Board demanded changes, and there was a long debate before it was shown in Pennsylvania, the state that had inspired the film and where Warners had vital outlets. There were powerful lobbies working against the film and perhaps not surprisingly it was given no further publicity in terms of awards or nominations. Jerome Lawrence has suggested that Hollywood 'swept it under the carpet'.[63] Even Muni's name was not enough to sanction this material.

Warner's only chance with *Black Fury* would have been if the serious critics had hailed it as a masterpiece and as a great breakthrough, but on this occasion the critics were all too aware of the stresses and strains that had been created by the processing of an authentic theme into a melodramatic format. Americans knew far too much about the reality of strikes to accept a film in which, in the words of James Shelley Hamilton, 'the trouble arises not from working conditions but from a professional trouble-maker and is solved not according to any principles but by an act of sheer moronic terrorism'.[64] It was obviously dishonest and disingenuous to try to cash in on a film dealing realistically with labour problems and then to hang the whole action on the villainy of professional racketeers specializing in encouraging strikes before helping to break them. It was clear to Hamilton that 'there was never any intention of making a seriously realistic commentary on strike conditions among mine workers, but merely to use such conditions as a vivid and up-to-date background' for a Muni vehicle. As a labour film Hamilton thought that it got nowhere and even as a film about a mining community he thought that 'everything is too neat and tidy and well-ordered to hint at what actual conditions may be'. All we are left with in this critic's eyes is the drama of one simple and honourable man created by what seemed at first a 'carefully studied impersonation' but what became a very moving performance by Muni. Most other critics found that it was a case of the novelty of a labour film and the intensity and charm of Muni's acting being overwhelmed by melodrama, but there was at least one critic who saw *Black Fury* as a step forward. Otis Ferguson was aware that the film depicted a 'phony strike' and that there was no real analysis of labour-management problems but he still felt that it had 'this air of life whatever we may think of its social content'. He was struck by the way in which Muni had depicted the suffering, the bewilderment, and the anger of a simple man, by the way in which the atmosphere and pressures of a strike-bound community had been created, and above all by the reality of the violence, which was a thing 'that shrieks along a man's nerves and settles in his stomach'. He was quite prepared to hail this as a 'great film', for if critics were prepared to lavish that term 'on any half-chewed jumble of stills that comes in from abroad, then I am in favour of loosening up with it on the home front'.[65]

With *Black Fury* Warner Bros had wandered into deep water and there were obviously important lessons to be learnt from the major row that the film had occasioned. The studio could see that labour–management relations were not a suitable theme for feature films and no attempt was ever made to repeat this particular experiment. In *Men of Iron*, released in 1935, Warner Bros attempted to use the steel industry in much the same way as they had earlier used the coal industry. Again the action focused on a strike but this time the melodramatic story, in which all the trouble was precipitated by the boss's nephews and a socially ambitious foreman promoted above his station, was so farcical as to almost sink the film without trace. In several respects, though, the fate of *Black Fury* had confirmed basic Warner Bros notions and they continued to pick up ideas for movies from the daily papers, they went on believing that social melodrama could be profitable, and they had been given further evidence that Muni could win acclaim by projecting himself as a hard-done-by but eventually triumphant saint. With *Black Fury* Warner Bros had just gone a little too far by even referring to strikes and labour problems at a time of mounting industrial tension but the popular and critical reception to the movie showed that the company were not wrong to believe that they had the technical ability and the actors to make films whose reality would be appreciated. The fact that *Black Fury* had been too controversial and yet too muddled to scoop up the prizes did not mean that it was time for Warner Bros to stop being 'sociologically-minded'.

Meanwhile other studios were learning much the same lessons, albeit for somewhat different reasons. If Warner Bros felt some duty to argue for justice in their films there were people in other studios who thought that the vogue for realistic films could be used to condemn radicalism and militancy. United Artists were tempted to point out the dangers of Communism and released *Red Salute*, which dealt with the growing appeal of Communism for student leaders. Of course the message had to be wrapped in a fairly light romantic story but at the time of the opening there was concern that publicity was concentrating too much on the comedy and not enough on the 'timeliness' of the film. One distributor asked for more direct satire to be used and suggested catchlines like 'She was not as red as she painted herself.' Contrary advice came in from Nashville where the film was doing well and where the upshot seemed to be that 'the only way to sell *Red Salute* is as a gay romantic comedy'.[66] In many places the film opened to boycotts and demonstrations but several distributors suggested that these could have been avoided by the use of a more innocent title along the lines of *It Happened in Mexico*. Meanwhile

MGM went even further and harnessed the considerable talents and appeal of Spencer Tracy and Jean Harlow in *Riff Raff*, which attempted to show how simple San Francisco fishermen could be led into militancy by a Communist agitator. Again this film led to boycotts and demonstrations and seemed to confirm that to make propaganda films was to invite box-office coolness and critical hostility.[67]

In 1935 it might have seemed as if Hollywood was moving into a period of labour and political films but such was not the case. A very tiny handful of totally unrepresentative films achieved a certain notoriety but were in general lost sight of as attention focused on better films and in any case they were to represent a dead-end rather than a way forward. Conventional Hollywood thinking in the late 1930s was summed up a few years later by Raymond Moley when he was discussing the general ethics of the Production Code. According to Moley what Hollywood had learnt was that 'when narrative art ventures on the ideological battlefield, it enters a dark and bloody ground' and that the safest bet was 'to stay on the broad highway of pure entertainment'. The most obvious incentive towards entertainment was 'the fact that the industry stands at all times in the presence of a high court with unlimited jurisdiction – the people before the box office' and from that court 'there is no appeal'. What had influenced Hollywood, thought Moley, was the ample evidence that 'the generality of the public takes its movies seriously and is adversely responsive to any effort which offers the least suspicion that they are being used for some purpose other than entertainment' and that in particular 'nothing hurts a picture's chance of success more than the whisper that it contains propaganda'.[68] This was the thinking that led Hollywood to move away from labour disputes and political ideas. For the rest of the decade the working classes were only depicted in a small number of undistinguished films which celebrated or exploited the skills of particular groups of workers. The urge to cash in on contemporary themes remained, however, and another small group of films attempted to dramatize these issues in a way that would avoid the pitfalls of labour films.

Warner Bros remained committed to social drama and their ideas boys eagerly perused the papers for potential stories. The evidence suggests that the writers were already considering a cheap grade 'B' picture about Ku-Klux-Klan and Black Legion activities when the notorious trial of four workmen in Detroit made executions carried out by such organizations a matter of national attention. Warner Bros immediately started a press file on the Detroit hearings and the testimony as well as the photographs of the participants were closely inspected. Legal advice as to what extent the actual iconography and style of the real-life legions could be used was taken at every stage.[69] The eventual movie *Black Legion* followed the detail of the Detroit story in many respects although the idea of a member of the jury actually being recognized as a member of the Legion as had happened in Detroit was dropped. The authenticity of the film was stressed in all the publicity and much was made of the fact that not only had the trial scenes been shot at the same time as the judge was carrying out the Detroit sentences but the film actually used his own words. Of course the studio hoped that the film would succeed as melodrama and much of the publicity stressed its entertainment value. One poster announced that: 'It screams - it screeches from the screen - the shock-packed sensations that blazed a trail of headlines America will never forget - filmed by Warner Bros with all the fire and fury of *G-Men* and *Fugitive*.' Exhibitors were advised to have hooded figures with torches in their lobby and even to consider on opening day having 'a comedian carried out of the theatre on a stretcher by two hooded figures, and into an ambulance', the stunt to be pulled 'every hour or so'.[70] Such crassness was inevitable but for all that the Warner Bros team had come up with a powerful film. The production team, which again included writers Robert Lord and Abem Finkel, had made a film which depoliticized the Legion by making its motive force sheer racketeering rather than political control and by making the violence and executions personal rather than political but nevertheless they had come up with a realistic depiction of how a weak man could be drawn into a recognizably Fascist organization. The Warner brothers themselves were vehemently against racist organizations and they could be proud of the movie. The publicity spoke of there being no lesson in the film: Bogart was quoted as saying that 'if there is one thing that has no place in theatrical show it is an attempt to preach', but no member of the audience could miss the point of this film. The depiction of the Legion itself might not have been truly authentic but what gave *Black Legion* much of its initial impact was that the story with all its political message and melodrama was very firmly set in a very real community of American working men. The press-book heralded *Black Legion* as the 'Truest To Life Film Ever Made' and if this claim was meant to refer to the actual Detroit trial it was to the settings of the film that the most audiences would have applied it.

In the photograph that the studio had acquired the four men brought to trial in Detroit look out at us almost belligerently announcing their status as ordinary guys; they wear poor suits and no ties, they are unshaven, and they clutch their hats.[71] The script file described how the movie would show the impact of a coercive group on 'an ordinary man' and would be set in what was interestingly referred to as 'a lower middle-class suburban neighbourhood of an industrial town'. The synopsis continues:

Frank Taylor is an ordinary American workingman. He is in his early 30's, fairly good looking, generous, kindly but very ignorant about sociological matters. He works skilfully with his hands. Thinking irritates and confuses him. Inevitably he harbours most of the prejudices, dislikes etc., of the uneducated ordinary man. He is employed in a big automobile factory and is at present making a nice wage, although he and his family suffered considerably during the depression. The few conventional and pitifully inadequate ideas he has about government, politics and such subjects he derives from the cheapest and most sensational newspapers. He doesn't even really read the newspapers with attention – except the comic strips and the sporting pages. In other words, Frank is adult in years and appearance but his mind is that of a 14 year old boy. There are millions of Frank Taylors in the United States. They constitute the rank-and-file ready to follow sheeplike after any crackpot fanatic who promises them something for nothing.

Frank has been married about 10 years to Ruth and adores her. Ruth comes from about the same social stratum as her husband and has had very little more education, yet she is instinctively smarter than he. Her sex has endowed her with a natural realism, patience and understanding that her husband lacks. She teases Frank 'Honest to goodness, sometimes I think you're just a big baby' and she is correct.[72]

Robert Lord's basic story-line provided a marvellous portrait of an ordinary worker and a very telling 'explanation of the roots of political prejudice' but these details had to be made real on film. The actual movie starts with a stock all-purpose flash of a steel-mill although the subsequent factory shots are quite obviously a Burbank studio. More important in suggesting realism is Taylor's neat suburban home and cheap car, which would have surprised British workers and American workers living in coalfields and Eastern industrial areas but which nicely reflect conditions in prospering auto towns. The home is modestly plain inside with the radio as the only luxury and the Taylor family conversation is punctuated with constant references to the hardships of the depression, the debts that had been accumulated, the struggle to get the mechanic's job in the factory, and the need for Frank to get the foreman's job if there is to be further improvement. The whole setting is thoroughly authenticated and everything leads nicely into Frank's deep resentment as a worker of Polish extraction gets the promotion that should have been his. Ultimately, though, all of this setting and development depended on the acting and this is where Warner Bros could really score. 'We cast for type not names' said director Archie Mayo and it was this that clinched the film's impact. Mayo went on to explain his selections:

Erin O'Brien Moore looked 'earthy' to me and I knew that she would not squawk about not being able to use make-up and wear Orry Kelly creations. Bogart, of course, had worked with me before in *Petrified Forest* and I couldn't see anyone else for the role of Frank Taylor.[73]

4 *Black Legion*: Bogart ensures that 'Frank Taylor is an ordinary American workingman.'

This was Bogart's seventeenth film (*The Petrified Forest* had been his eleventh) and one of the first in which he gave some indication of his range. Perhaps it is hindsight which has allowed us to understand fully the sheer technique that went into Bogart's acting but many people at Warners could see Mayo's point that he was just the type of actor needed to breathe life into the kind of story that the writers were making into a speciality. It was acting of this quality that brought the company's films alive. James R. Silke was to refer to how Warners offered 'heroes made from life' and Janet Graves has explained how the rigid financial limits imposed at the studio placed a premium on good dialogue and good acting. It was, she explained, 'a man's studio, a writer's and an actor's studio' and out of this combination came that formula that was so 'stridently American'.[74] We can add that it was 'stridently American' because it was realistically American. James Shelley Hamilton thought *Black Legion*

was an exceptional film precisely because it was 'one of the best exposi-
tions of what genuine Americanism is and is not what the screen has
produced'. What Hamilton could see was that the talents of Warner Bros
had combined to produce a film that was not so much about the Legion
as 'about the kind of short-sighted, uninformed and well-enough-meaning
men who have to be given an understanding of what democracy really is
so that they will not go on and on providing tools for such legions'.[75]
Warner Bros had once again profitably combined instruction and entertainment but as was so often the case it was the way in which they had
used an actor that made the movie work in both respects.

Not that the film worked for every critic. Otis Ferguson was not entirely
convinced by *Black Legion* as he thought it too gloomy (with appeal only
for the 'O'Neill audience'), too jerky in its action, ultimately too indecisive
and somewhat lacking in political specifics. In truth what really shaped his
view was the comparison between Mayo's film and *Fury*, which was
released by MGM at much the same time. Several films of the 1930s were
to deal with the very real and widely condemned phenomenon of lynching
and in 1935 MGM had finally allowed their imported genius Fritz Lang to
make this story after several years of waiting. Lang's film was immediately
hailed as a masterpiece especially with regard to its frighteningly real
depiction of the prejudices and hysteria that lay waiting to be released in
a typical Midwestern town. Even this product of genius was flawed as it
trailed away into melodrama but for a fleeting moment Hollywood was
shown what could be achieved if its resources were used as the basis for a
director's cinema. Of course Lang's movie was far more interested in
psychology than sociology but there were other differences too: *Fury* was a
one-off movie whereas the more pedestrian and less ambitious *Black Legion*
was part of a continuing Hollywood tradition. The first half of *Fury* was
virtuoso cinema, whereas *Black Legion* was part of a developing movie
culture. In this respect Ferguson thought that the Warner Bros film was
a good indication of what could be achieved by Hollywood when it tackled
social problems honestly and he summed it up by returning to one of his
favourite points about Hollywood that 'even half a loaf on the national
stomach is at least nourishment taken in'. Ferguson had developed this
notion of 'half a loaf' in reply to those left-wing critics who condemned both
Hollywood's lack of political detail and its slickness. What the *New
Republic* was calling for was a fuller appreciation by the left of what
necessarily constituted entertainment and of what Hollywood had actually
achieved. The radicals were also concerned about detail whereas Ferguson
could see that 'movie people tend to understand things in surface terms'
and that their 'command of surfaces is supreme'. What Ferguson had found
and what the left just could not see was that when Hollywood really tried
they produced a thing that ought not be pedantically analysed for 'the
thing exists by itself for its moments on the screen, unquestionable'.[76]

For a variety of reasons and motives Hollywood had floundered towards some kind of realism. That shift of emphasis had created amongst many people an expectation of a more fully developed social cinema. Throughout the 1930s Hollywood was to make films condemning various abuses and malpractices in the American system and there were always to be films which clung to the conventions of the city film as they had emerged in the early part of the decade. In general, however, the various studios were happy to move into an era of more varied entertainment. The political and social context and the popular mood seemed to demand an upbeat cinema but this cinema was not to be a cinema of fantasy or make-believe but rather it was a cinema created in the image of its audiences. The times had called for a certain mood but it was the genius of American cinema that it could harness the talents of actors and actresses whose every word and gesture rooted the films in the society for which they had been produced. People went to the movies for many reasons but not least because they wanted to see stories which starred very real and very attractive Americans. The Hollywood formula guaranteed entertainment but it was essentially the actors who gave film audiences precisely the authenticity and reality that they required. What 'sociological punch' had amounted to was that actors could still make films work.

4 'The propaganda mills of the 1930s'

In the 1930s, the decade of the depression and the New Deal, American intellectual and cultural life was to be dominated by the reactions of writers, artists, and young people to the fate of ordinary Americans and to their struggle to survive and to organize. These various reactions came together to form what Robert Warshow has called the 'popular front culture', and it was very much this culture that formed the touchstone of intellectual judgement as America moved towards involvement in the Second World War.[1] The movies were to be influenced by the emergence of this new set of cultural and critical values but to a much lesser extent than other American cultural and art forms. The system of control at Hollywood effectively sealed off the movies from many cultural and political influences but, in any case, the studios had recovered a good deal of their confidence and to a considerable if not total extent were sure about the kinds of films they should be making. Meanwhile the intellectual and political leaders of the new cultural dispensation had much to say about Hollywood as they attempted a full-scale explanation of the role of the movies in American life. Those for whom politics were the main consideration denounced the financial forces that controlled the studios while less politicized observers regretted the extent to which Hollywood stood outside the cultural main stream. There were to be many savage denunciations of the motion-picture industry during these years but Hollywood not only survived all this but did so very much on its own terms. Moreover, for all its iniquities, Hollywood not only held most of its popular audiences but also retained a capacity to fascinate, even to attract, and certainly to surprise its most outspoken critics. Hollywood hung on to its own identity and contributed to American and world-wide culture on its own terms and that achievement had to be accepted and perhaps even respected.

The alignment of intellectuals and workers that was to be the basis of 'popular front' culture was probably born in Harlan County, Kentucky, in 1931 when a delegation led by Theodore Dreiser and including John Dos Passos and Sam Ornitz went to investigate the treatment of political prisoners during the coal strike.[2] In the 1920s writers had responded to individual events such as the Sacco and Vanzetti saga and the struggle at Passaic, New Jersey, but what was new in the early 1930s was first the deepening depression and then a growing concern and the harnessing of that concern by the Communist Party, by the John Reed clubs, and by other radical organizations.[3] Throughout the early 1930s as unemployment grew and huge protests were organized in cities throughout America, culminating in the great marches on Washington in 1931 and 1932, so a new radical politics was born and intellectuals were drawn into that politics in a totally unprecedented way. All over America young writers, artists, and students found that almost for the first time they wanted to read about the working class, to write about them, and to join with them in demonstrations and protests. This new cultural energy created a new literature, a new criticism, and new art forms, it gave intellectual backbone to the American Communist Party, and it saw the emergence of a whole spate of new organizations that attempted to feed ideas and enthusiasm into American life. At first it was the vitality of the organized left that was most in evidence, but with the coming of Roosevelt, who to a certain extent had depended on intellectual endorsement in the election of 1932, cultural developments rested on an interplay between intellectuals and agencies established by the New Deal. In artistic terms the first impetus had been towards a new literature: Jerre Mangione points out that there were already eleven identifiable proletarian novels by 1932, but by the mid-1930s most of the energy seemed to be going into organizations, conferences, and agencies.[4] The intellectual capital of the new phenomenon was New York City, which was to become more dominant now in American cultural life than at any other time before or since: the intellectual core was provided by the small magazines such as the *New Republic, New Masses*, and *Partisan Review*, and the intellectual cutting edge came in the form of the Federal Theater Project. With the plays of Clifford Odets being produced on Broadway and with plays like Albert Maltz's *Black Pit* and Archibald MacLeish's *Panic* being put on at the Civic Repertory Theatre and at Brooklyn Labor Theater and then being analysed in journals like *New Theatre*, New York became very much the cutting edge of a great breakthrough in drama but in fact reports of new theatres and new productions were coming in from all over the country. What was really exciting was that dramatists and their companies were actually coming into contact with new working-class audiences and in particular with trade union audiences. The spirit of 1935 was nicely captured in a report by Alice Evans:

> I saw a thousand workers from the silk and dye mills of Paterson, New Jersey, pack the Orpheum Theatre there for the strike benefit program presented by the New Jersey Section New Theatre League sponsored by the American Federation of Silk Workers. Against the gaudy curtains of a converted burlesque house, three dramatic groups presented plays that dealt mainly with trade union problems ranging from *Laid Off*

by David Pinski, to *Waiting for Lefty* both given by the Newark Collective Theatre, and including *Exhibit A* presented by the Bayonne Theatre Against War and Fascism, *The Union Label* by the Paterson New Art Group.

The most exciting thing about this program with its high points of audience participation during *Union Label* and *Waiting for Lefty* was that silk workers *liked* it, and their enthusiasm was contagious.[5]

Throughout these years intellectuals were discovering Marxist theory and the possibilities of social art but at the very same time they were finding that there was a proletariat and a proletarian energy in their own country. They were learning for the first time that America was a pluralistic society and it was for this reason that so much New Deal art and literature just celebrated very ordinary but newly perceived aspects of the nation. At the 1936 American Writers Congress, which was to end with the very respected novelist James Farrell calling for the singing of 'The Internationale', delegates had been told by Meridel Le Sueur that:

There is only one class that has begun to produce mid-Western culture and that is the growing yeast of the revolutionary working class, arising on the Meseba range, the wheat belt, the coalfields of Illinois, the blown and ravaged land of Dakota, the flour mills, the granaries .... It is from the working class that the use and function of native language is slowly being built in such books as those of James Farrell with the composition and the colloquialism of the streets of Chicago; of Jack Conroy with his worker heroes going from the auto industry in Detroit to the coalfields; of Nelson Algren, of the worker-writers in the *Farmers Weekly* and the *Western Workers*.[6]

The novelists and dramatists always received the most attention but from the very earliest days of this cultural dispensation independent film-makers had been attempting to create a new social cinema. It was the way in which the newsreels had ignored the great unemployment demonstrations of March 1930 which first led to the activities that were to develop into the Workers Film and Photo League and that organization in turn was to inspire several attempts to create a new tradition of films which would document working-class and labour struggles in America.[7] Throughout these years films were made and shown to working-class and intellectual audiences but the films of the league, of Nykino, and of Frontier Films were ultimately not as important and influential as the emergence of a new and more general film culture. What was to be vital in this respect was the way in which a new tradition of serious and radical film criticism had emerged so that a regular analysis of Hollywood and foreign movies became a fully integrated aspect of the new intellectual journalism that was characterizing the whole era. For the first time film became a significant element in a cultural critique of America, and, in fact, good films were not only talked about for now they could be seen in a new type of theatre. Again New York City was very much the centre of things and the ease with which the best Soviet, continental, and independent films could be seen at the Acme Theatre on Union Square, at the New School, and at a growing number of commercial venues meant that the new critics could address their remarks to an increasingly well-informed audience that was providing the base for a new movie culture. Meanwhile things were not entirely hopeless outside New York and journals like *Film Front* and *New Masses* eagerly reported the activities of the Cinema Guild in Detroit and of the New Film Alliance in a number of other cities.

The enthusiasm for films to be made and for a more varied programme to be shown was always there but in truth film was to remain a very junior partner in the new cultural network that was being forged. The passage of time has allowed a more critical evaluation of all the artistic achievements of the 'popular front' era and we can see now that social themes were not as typical as once thought, that audiences, membership, and readership were always small, and that much that was initially hailed as great has turned out to be fairly mundane. We can also see that it was perhaps misleading to take the vitality of Manhattan as being typical of the nation. What we are left with now are some stunning photographs, some evocative novels, and a number of plays that authentically captured 1930s dialogue and anxieties.[8] At the first of those American Writers Congresses that witnessed the high point of enthusiasm for proletarian literature Jack Conroy declaimed that the writer's task was 'to vivify the daily struggles, the aspirations, triumphs, despairs of the future masters, the workers' but we can question now the extent to which that task was achieved.[9] To reassess 'popular front' culture in this way is both to make more intelligible and to put into perspective the relative failure of independent cinema in that period for quite clearly too much fuss has been made of so-called achievements in other areas. In fairness, though, it must be conceded that at least an expectation of breakthrough in literature and a renaissance in drama did seem to be under way. With regard to film the difficulties and obstacles were all too obvious. It was appallingly difficult to make independent films and there was little chance of any meaningful commercial distribution. In time New Deal agencies were to show an interest in documentary film but only in a very limited fashion and obviously there was not going to be any real challenge to Hollywood. What was really horrific, though, as far as radicals were concerned was that the great audience that was needed to sustain film had already been lost, mainly because it was so set in its ways. The new class of left-wing and radical intellectuals could edge towards a new literature, a new journalism, and a new drama because in a way they were filling vacuums, but what chance was there of making any impression in a movie world so dominated by Hollywood? There was, then, relatively less activity and expectation with regard to film but there was also a more tangible obstacle to react against. Not surprisingly hostility to Hollywood became one of the touchstones of the new culture. Everything was done to destroy that philistine empire which had annexed the very American people that the intellectuals now wanted to claim as their own.

The general reaction of radical intellectuals to Hollywood began with the notion that the studios were in effect controlled from Wall Street and that it was the 'financial wizards' of the Chase Manhattan and other banks who had determined the values and ethos of the whole movie business. Added to this was a contempt for the hypocrisy of the Hays Office and the whole Production Code, which were meant to defend morals but which were thought of as using a moral stance to sustain a very effective political censorship. Time and time again the left-wing journals showed how a blind eye had been turned to the gangsterism and sexuality which the Code was meant to outlaw whilst all suggestions of political radicalism were banned. Not surprisingly the vast majority of Hollywood films were thought of as being trivial and worthless. At the opening of the decade it was the prolific Marxist critic Harry Alan Potamkin who was doing most to educate magazine readers into a more socially aware criticism of films and he talked of how Hollywood had become preoccupied with 'the restless rich' and in particular with 'the love irritations of those who were born to the purple'. Potamkin went on to speak of the increasing glibness of the Hollywood movie, of 'its brilliant superficial polish that seemed to suggest that rich people actually behaved in this witty way'.[10] Meanwhile other critics referred to how films based on scripts by Hecht and McArthur had 'an aura of seeming brilliance' and to how the movie *I Live My Life* had a 'flashy high-tone' which it used to depict 'as lovable a family of multi-millionaires as can be seen in a year of fantasies'.[11] In an article he called 'Luck comes to the proletariat' Louis Norden explained how movies seemed dedicated to the 'gospel of Saint Success' and how a new preoccupation with lotteries was yet another example of how sudden riches tended to come to any film hero originally placed in a lowly social setting.[12] One critic spoke of the power of Hollywood films to 'disarm' and of how *Romance in Manhattan* was characterized by a 'perfumed atmosphere'.[13] The immensely popular film-maker Frank Borzage was described as a 'sentimentalist and tear-jerker' and as a 'sugarcoated director'.[14] This framework of responses covered the great majority of Hollywood films; they were thought of as slick and meaningless entertainment running along well-established and endlessly repeated lines. To this extent the new radicals of the early 1930s would have received much support from the educated classes generally but a number of critics were now going far beyond this bland discussion of Hollywood as they developed a more full-blooded political critique.

The real fear that emerged in the 1930s was that Hollywood was going Fascist. Now the urgent concern of left-wing critics was to explain those political steps being taken towards Fascism that had seemed to follow on from the growing links between California, Wall Street, and politicians in Washington and to identify precisely the growing number of Fascist values within the movies themselves. As early as 1930 Potamkin had been warning about right-wing values in Hollywood films but it was the accession of Roosevelt which suggested that a drift towards dictatorship and a Fascist-type regime was not out of the question.[15] In 1933 Potamkin in reviewing *Gabriel Over the White House*, a fantasy about a crook who becomes President, explained that it had been made by the Hearst wing of MGM and then went on to show how Hearst and other right-wing newspaper owners were building up Roosevelt into a 'benevolent dictator' whilst they were also glorifying Mussolini.[16] In 1934 Potamkin suggested that 'every reactionary agency and institution in our society has its hand or wants its hand in the movie' and he called on the left to build up an alternative movie culture.[17] The first issue of *Film Front* referred to an 'unprecedented advance in political guidance over the industry by the Federal Government' since the start of the New Deal.[18] Left-wing critics retained a deep suspicion of Roosevelt's links with Hollywood and especially with Warner Bros, but William Randolph Hearst remained far more the danger figure, especially after he transferred his interest to Warner Bros. The fact that Hearst's mistress Marion Davies had been given one of the two bungalows on the Warner Bros lot was taken as one of the most frighteningly political developments of the period.[19] By 1935 there were constant references to Hearst's growing political influence in Hollywood and to Hearst and Warner's support of what were thought of as Fascist movements in America. *New Masses* headed an article 'Heil Hearst' and *Film Front* referred to 'the propaganda mills of Hearst and the brothers Warner'.[20] Suspicion of Hollywood was now at its height and Irving Lerner (writing as Peter Ellis) saw RKO's decision to distribute *March of Time* newsreels as an unfurling of 'their true flag the swastika'.[21] In particular the favourable depiction of the demagogue-broadcaster Father Coughlin created a new fear that he had now become the man of the moment for the film magnates. The greatly respected Carey McWilliams told the readers of *Nation* about various paramilitary groups in Hollywood in an article he called 'Hollywood plays with Fascism'.[22] At the same time Jay Rand told the readers of *New Masses* about the activities of those he described as the 'Hitlerites in Hollywood': Victor McLaglen's light-horse troop had received much publicity but far more sinister were police preparations, including the issue of pistol permits and gold badges to Hollywood personnel, the press campaign, and the type of film now being inspired by the Hearst-Warner axis.[23]

There were two aspects of this new politicization of Hollywood that concerned the left. First there was the growing number of films in which armed forces were depicted and praised. It was obvious in this respect that Washington was working hand in glove with MGM, Warners, and the other studios and the intention was quite clearly to build up the military in preparation for another war. In 1934 *Film Front* reported that when *Here Comes the Navy* was being shown in Detroit the theatre owners had enlisted the support of the Naval Reserve Band, the Sea Scouts, a sound truck, and a cruiser which sailed past the waterfront and beach areas with banners for several days, all with the purpose of whipping up war hysteria.[24] Films like *Annapolis Farewell*, which had obviously been made with the full co-operation of the navy, and *Here Comes the Navy*, *Flirtation Walk*, *Devil Dogs of the Air*, and even that comedy of Anglo-American relations *Ruggles of Red Gap* and many others were all seen as part of a drive towards militarism and to war.[25] The movie *Red Salute*, which was an attempt to warn students against red organizers, was seen as a direct response to the recent student peace strike which students at Hollywood's near neighbour UCLA had been prevented from joining.[26] Jay Rand also noticed that the Paramount child-stars Baby Le Roy and Virginia Wendler had been made honorary members of UCLA's graduating class of 1934 and concluded that this was an indication of the 'future cultural level if the rest of the country goes fascist'.[27]

Just as serious as the warmongering films were the anti-red and anti-labour films which were now thought of as being typical of Hollywood. *Riff Raff* was always seen as the worst example of 'Hearst's viciousness', but a whole clutch of films, including *Frisco Kid* and *Barbary Coast*, were seen as attempts to warn audiences against red propaganda and industrial militancy and to argue the cause for vigilante action in the face of danger and agitation. Film audiences throughout America would have been aware of growing industrial unrest and of the increased appeal of labour unions but what left-wing critics urged their readers to remember was that Hollywood films were now being produced in what was probably the most class-conscious and political state in America. The politicization of Hollywood films had come about because of growing political and industrial unrest throughout California and indeed in the studios themselves. First there had been the 1934 gubernatorial campaign in which Upton Sinclair had promised to 'end poverty in California', then the mounting unemployment throughout the state, then the bloody clashes between vigilantes and migrant labourers in the fruit-growing and farming areas, and finally the great general strike on the San Francisco waterfront. The class war was being fought with a vengeance in California and red propaganda seemed to be ubiquitous. It had even come to the studios and the activities of the Screen Writers Guild of Communists and the film-based labour unions seemed to be bringing the class war into the motion-picture industry itself. According to Jay Rand 'the Californian capitalists' had 'the jitters' and were mobilizing all propaganda organs against radicals: there was even talk of a black list to remove the radicals from the film industry.[28] Undoubtedly the San Francisco waterfront had provided the biggest shock and with the constant fear of further general strikes along the entire pacific coast it was perhaps to be expected that anti-red and anti-labour union venom should be poured into *Riff Raff* and those other labour films. The readers of left-wing journals were warned about these very obvious propaganda films and urged to organize boycotts and demonstrations. It was more important, though, that they should be warned against the propaganda somewhat more discreetly contained in precisely those films that many other film critics were hailing as important because of their social content and their realism. It became essential for audiences to know that Hollywood could be politically reactionary at the very time that it was seemingly breaking new ground in terms of artistic and social awareness. At first *Film Front* had argued that the film companies had turned to films about the workers as audiences were tiring of the 'sex-pap'. They considered this a 'Canute-like gesture' to deal with discontent and denounced the depiction of the workers as 'either a cog, a peasant-like creature, a person at the mercy of the elements, a down-an'-outer with comic possibilities or a boor'. The new type of movie was full of 'falsehoods and half-truths about the workers' and sometimes even worse than that.[29]

Wider audiences would have thought of King Vidor as being an accomplished and socially sensitive pioneering director but throughout these years he was to be a major target of the left. As was so often the case it had been Potamkin who had first sounded the warning by writing of 'the pretences to social themes' in *The Crowd* and *Hallelujah*, and of the latter he had suggested that 'its attitude was that of the white American towards a disparaged people'.[30] There was now a new understanding on the part of the left of the whole position of blacks in America and in 1936 Herbert Kline in calling for better plays about negro life quoted Langston Hughes's remark that 'in one sense, Negroes have always known Fascism'.[31] Meanwhile Vidor had made *So Red the Rose*, which according to Arthur Draper deliberately portrayed 'the Negro masses of the South as stupid sullen rioters'.[32] Draper noted that Vidor had handed over the film to producer Douglas Maclean, who was also a Southerner and this perhaps was why the Negroes were depicted as a threat to white supremacy at a time when they were joining up with white labour both in the Sharecroppers Union and in the steelworks and coal-mines of Birmingham. Vidor's conservatism was generally known but nevertheless even on the left there remained a certain admiration of his skills. The pattern that emerged was one in which he was praised for his technical ability and sensitivity but then taken up for the political implications of his films and for his concessions to box-office. In reviewing *The Wedding Night* John R. Chaplin praised Vidor's 'amazing sensitivity' and especially his handling of Gary Cooper and Anna Sten although he thought that ultimately the social theme was sacrificed to the love interest and he also took the opportunity of the review to suggest that Vidor had 'not intended *Our Daily Bread* to become a film with Fascist implications'.[33] The dilemmas of the left with regard to Vidor were perhaps best summed up by Irving Lerner (Peter Ellis) when he reviewed *Our Daily Bread* for *New Masses*. His review is full of praise for many of Vidor's attributes: he is spoken of as 'one of the few sincere and honest directors', not at all 'fascistic' like Walter Wanger, who had made *Washington Merry Go Round*. Like his hero Chaplin he is thought of as having 'an inherent sympathy for the underdog', and *Our Daily Bread* is described as depicting 'a definite sympathy for the mass, a faith in the success of co-operation and unity of workers'. For all his praise, however, Lerner is still forced to conclude that the movie is 'confused and reactionary' and that Vidor himself, 'like many confused and well-meaning Liberals', had fallen for 'Roosevelt's demagoguery' in respect of 'back-to-the-land for prosperity'.[34] The left was happy to conclude, then, that Vidor was too simple a man for the times in which he now found himself. His small-town sense of individualism and human sympathies were almost irrelevant in the days of general strikes on the waterfront and armed battles in the fruit-growing valleys.

There were other heroes who had to be brought down to size. Paul Muni had become for many people the cinematic symbol of the depression and his carefully selected social-conscience films had earlier been praised as pointing the way to a more mature American cinema but left-wing critics could easily relate his films to the general Hollywood scheme of things. *Bordertown*, an intense melodrama set in the north of Mexico, was well received by many critics for the way in which it indicated social unrest but what Irving Lerner saw was 'a warning to the proletariat (especially to the non-Nordics) not to mix with the respectable Californian Nordics'.[35] In *Film Front* Phillip Russell suggested that as the Paul Muni character achieves some success in the movie one could 'hear the rumble of his doom' for 'the brothers Warner are not going to let a Mexican get away with that high and mighty stuff for long'. For Russell the movie had portrayed the Mexicans in 'the time-hallowed Hollywood tradition', that is, 'as an uncultured inferior lot', and the whole moral of the exercise was that 'Mexicans and foreign-born' should 'keep to your own side of the fence'.[36] But of course it was with *Black Fury* that Muni had most fully subscribed to the new Hollywood politics. In *New Theatre* the movie was reviewed by Albert Maltz, whose play *Black Pit* was playing to great acclaim at New York's Civic Repertory Theatre. Maltz welcomed the attempt by a film company 'to dramatize directly the conditions of an industry and the events of a strike' but criticized the failure to depict the real squalor of a mining town, the omission of all the ways that companies used to cheat the miners' families, the many technical errors most of which served 'to prettify the life of the miner', and above all Hollywood assumptions that 'strikes are started by racketeers, militant workers are paid stool-pigeons, strikes are unwarranted, miners are stupid sheep' and that 'mine operators are fairplay boy-scouts who counsel their hired thugs not to use violence'. In *Black Fury*'s version of the class struggle, concluded Maltz:

> Everything that has been the basis of a thousand better strikes is omitted; everything that might picture the true life of the miner is distorted. Instead we get a picturesque background, a trite love story, a vicious and phony strike, and a ridiculous, impossible, terroristic solution.[37]

Whatever Muni's original intention had been Hollywood had come up with a highly fictionalized depiction of a labour struggle. In *Film Front* all was explained by a film technician who wrote from Hollywood to say that 'Hays snipers' had been on the Warner lot and made it clear that Muni's film was not to depict rank-and-file militancy but rather should be a 'tirade against unionism and strikes'.[38] Warner Bros had learnt their lesson well for in the following year Robert Stebbins was to say of *Men of Iron* that it 'even exceeds *Black Fury*'s insults to the American working class'.[39]

By 1935, then, it was generally accepted in left-wing circles that Hollywood had become a propaganda agency and whenever it dealt with social themes it did so in such a way as to reflect the values sometimes of Washington, nearly always of Wall Street, and more often than not the views of Californian business interests, who were thought of as having some Fascist sympathies and who were in general horrified at the advance of radicalism in their own state. What left-wing critics hoped was that audiences would think of films in terms of the national political context and in particular of the political and industrial context in California.

In 1940 the literary critic Edmund Wilson undertook a survey of a group of writers who had made California the setting for their novels. He was to argue that as California 'had always presented itself to America as one of the strangest and most exotic of our adventures' it was not surprising that so many writers had attempted to come to terms with this new phase of experience. As Wilson examined Californian writing two themes were to emerge. He could see that many writers were fascinated by Hollywood and the film community and were beginning to use them as the basis of novels. Some of these writers actually worked in the studios and some of them were even developing a literary style that reflected the influence of the movies. He could also see that Californian writing had been characterized by an interest in labour struggles which could be explained by the fact that 'in our century the labor war has been fought out in California more nakedly and savagely than - except for the more primitive parts of the South - perhaps anywhere else in the country'. California had seen struggles involving the Wobblies, the Vigilantes, the fruit-pickers, and workers on the waterfront, and in all of them blood had been wrung. Not surprisingly, perhaps, the labour cause had been 'dramatized with more impact' by West Coast writers than by those of the East. In earlier days there had been Frank Norris, Jack London, and Upton Sinclair, whilst more recently James M. Cain, John O'Hara, Hans Otto Storm, and John Steinbeck had all taken up the theme of the Californian class war.[40] Wilson's essay is a useful reminder of the context in which we should examine the Hollywood movies of the 1930s for he was to depict a state that was a political and industrial powder keg and also one in which there was considerable literary activity. The movies were being made in the midst of this political maelstrom and mini-literary renaissance and yet what influenced left-wing critics was that film audiences generally just treated the movies as entertainment and were both oblivious and apathetic with respect to the political background.

Wilson saw a California in which writers could hardly avoid being drawn towards the world of movies and he was fascinated by those writers like James M. Cain, Horace McCoy, Richard Hallas, Budd Schulberg, Scott Fitzgerald, and Nathanael West who worked for the studios and yet who went on writing novels some of which dealt with Hollywood itself. This attempt by Wilson to integrate Hollywood into an analysis of Californian culture provides a clue to some important points about Hollywood. Writers were drawn to Hollywood like moths to a candle and they travelled to fabulous California, that state which Theodore Roosevelt had described as being 'West of West', to earn incredible salaries and of course to win new audiences for their work as they helped to improve the general level of movies. It was a time of depression for writers as well as for everyone else and it was not surprising that they were drawn to what was not only the one growth industry but also a cultural activity. What was perhaps more surprising is that Hollywood attracted writers not only from the West itself and from the vast Midwest but also from that New York City which had become the great centre of a distinctive cultural renaissance of its own. What Hollywood knew, suggests Fred Lawrence Guiles, was not only that 'talent was a purchasable commodity' but that 'every mortal being had his price'.[41] Once Hollywood identified a talent that it could use it knew that the right offer would bring in the great writer who might feel that his genius could transform the movies or the radical who would have dreams of making Soviet-type films in America. The most startling Hollywood acquisition was Clifford Odets, described later by Guiles as that 'stormer of the capitalistic barricades' and 'spokesman for the casualties of the crack-up of our own economic system'.[42] Odets was the hero of the New York left for he had made it on to Broadway. He went in search of new and bigger audiences and he was to remain for five years in Hollywood fascinated by its glamour and, according to Harold Cantor, by the power of the tycoons.[43] As Odets and other radicals went west so the unbelieving critics back in New York checked to see whether the inspiration and insights that had thrilled New York audiences could be made to work in Hollywood. When *The General Died at Dawn* appeared in 1936 the National Board of Review's James Shelley Hamilton found it to be good melodrama but he did not think that it had needed an Odets to write it. He contrasted the generally unexceptional nature of the movie with 'some of the high-falutin speeches' Odets 'occasionally breaks out with' and concluded that 'his trip to Hollywood appears to have profited nobody but himself'.[44] Sam Ornitz was another New York radical who went to Hollywood, where it was hoped that his writing would make *The Man Who Reclaimed his Head* into an attack on the manufacturing of munitions but John R. Chaplin could see that any debunking of munitions was counterbalanced in the eventual film by distinctive Hollywood trade marks such as a love story which was used to provide the motivation for a vital murder.[45] Meanwhile Harry Carlisle made the opposite journey from California to New York to explain what was happening. He suggested that Hollywood was decaying but that it retained 'extraordinary power':

and it takes writers daily, even those who have signed protests, even those who have come out and actually protested and participated in a certain amount of struggle - it takes those writers and it pulls them away from us, so that even the most revolutionary of them begin to waver and their creative powers and talents are drawn into support of capitalism.[46]

From California John R. Chaplin described how the Hollywood system operated on those who thought that they could change it or take advantage of it and explained that it could only be understood from within its midst.

There are writers with courage, writers with intelligence, writers with amazingly well-founded political views who come out here. But the small-town atmosphere, the manner in which everybody knows everybody else's business can be sensed only on the spot. And the hugeness of the industry is so crushing that only a fool would try to buck it unless organized into a powerful mass body.[47]

Chaplin's view was that the arrival of newcomers like Odets and Ornitz was adding to what was 'a great undercurrent of advanced thought' at Hollywood but that all these various individuals and groups who wanted to change the system would never get anything done until they organized in such a way as to defeat the blacklisting of trouble-makers.

We can see now precisely how prescient were Chaplin's remarks for whilst Hollywood went on buying talent and even witnessed the emergence of some organizations there was never really a movement strong enough to challenge the ethos the tycoons had created and certainly not influential enough to create a new kind of film. The writers were kept on the fringe of the movies and there was never any real possibility that film would become part of the cultural response to Californian reality in the same way as those novels discussed by Edmund Wilson. The most remarkable feature of the 1930s was the way in which the movie moguls isolated the production of movies not only from a turbulent America and an explosive California but also from the representatives of alternative cultures and politics who had even penetrated into the studios themselves. There was, as John Chaplin explained, a lot of talent and intelligence in Hollywood, and there was, as Ceplair and Englund have more recently demonstrated, a growing political base as the Communists, guilds, and labour unions recruited in and around the studios.[48] The descent of intellectuals on Hollywood is a romantic story and the struggle to take radical politics into the studios is a stirring tale but what remains amazingly true is that in film terms nothing was achieved. The period became one of utter frustration for radicals as they confronted a production system that had promised so much but which was in reality entirely beyond their reach. Joris Ivens, the great Dutch filmmaker, visited Hollywood in 1936 and contrasted the triviality of American films with the real-life drama that was going on in Southern California itself, where 3,000 Mexican fruit-pickers were on strike.[49] In 1938 the American film critic and film-maker Pare Lorentz praised the educational movie *Men Make Steel* but could not help being struck by the irony that after ten years in which 'we have been thinking a great deal about the facts of this country - of its land, its social and economic problems and about its great factories' the fact was that 'no movie company has even attempted to use the actual drama of our national life as photographic material'. What was clear to Lorentz was that 'Hollywood doesn't know anything about the United States.'[50]

Could it have been otherwise? To a considerable extent the answer to that question was provided by the writers themselves for with all the film outlets blocked they had to fall back on their traditional skills and cinema's loss was literature's gain. The frustration of those years has come down to us in novels which amongst other things stress just how monolithic and impregnable the Hollywood system was. Two short novels by Nathanael West and Scott Fitzgerald are usually taken as the best expression of how sensitive intellectuals responded to the singularity of Hollywood. Neither story attempts to portray the full social and political drama of California but rather to concentrate on individuals as a way of pointing to broader themes. West's *The Day of the Locust* is a psychological study that looks at the failure of Hollywood's hangers-on and contrasts the myths of the movies with the emptiness of the lives lived by the masses. The novel ends with a frightening depiction of mob violence and hysteria and this led Edmund Wilson to comment that 'of such mobs are the followings of fascism made'.[51] It is interesting, though, that West should move from the lives of frustrated individuals into a surrealistic coda rather than into the real-life politics of Los Angeles and California. By contrast Scott Fitzgerald's *The Last Tycoon* is really a layman's guide to the kind of genius and talent that ruled Hollywood and an attempt to understand these things on their own terms. Part of Fitzgerald's argument is that the tycoons like Monroe Stahr just knew how to make movies whilst on the East Coast people were only interested in the stars and in superficial things and so 'they never see the ventriloquist for the doll'. In his notes for this unfinished story Fitzgerald went on to complain that:

> Even the intellectuals, who ought to know better, like to hear about the pretensions, extravagances and vulgarities - tell them pictures have a private grammar, like politics or automobile production or society, and watch the blank look come into their faces.[52]

Stahr had mastered the grammar and everything else that went into the making of movies and Fitzgerald's point is that nobody else in the studio, no director or writer, was able to do that. Stahr understood fully what movies were, that it was a matter of taking 'people's own favourite folklore', dressing it up, and giving it back to them, and that could be perfectly well achieved from the isolation of Hollywood: all other matters were extraneous.[53] Such was the isolation of Stahr that Fitzgerald is content only to hint at the drama that was going on in California itself or at the politics of the lesser studio mortals. For a moment we are given a fleeting glimpse of the larger realities when Brimmer, a *New Masses*-type radical, is brought to meet Stahr, but Fitzgerald loads everything in his hero's favour. The meeting ends in violence but only after Brimmer had admitted that he has some respect for Stahr's paternalism and Stahr has lectured at length on the professional shortcomings of directors and writers. Fitzgerald's fascination with personality prevented him from bringing Stahr face to face with political reality although in real life for all their isolation Hollywood tycoons would have had to confront it on a daily basis. Both West and Fitzgerald had thought that their own literary skills and the nature of Hollywood itself necessitated a mythic and symbolic approach but less ambitious writing could equally depict the frustrations of those who wanted to see a rather different motion-picture industry.[54] Like West and Fitzgerald Horace McCoy worked as a screen writer and his 1935 story *They Shoot Horses, Don't They?* marvellously captured the anguish of the many ordinary people who drifted from small towns into Hollywood only to experience failure. His hero Robert Syverton dreamt of the movie that he would really have loved to make if only he could have become a director. It would be,

> Well like a two- or three-reel shot. What a junkman does all day, or the life of an ordinary man - you know, who makes thirty dollars a week and has to raise kids and buy a car and a radio - the kind of guy bill collectors are always after. Something different with camera angles to help tell the story.[55]

Many people had gone to Hollywood wanting to make this kind of film only to discover that the studios had their own ideas. Many of those who were frustrated were radicals with a real knowledge of American actuality but their experience was of no avail. In his 1938 story *I Should Have Stayed at Home* McCoy actually depicted political conversations amongst Hollywood writers as they debated the rights and wrongs of union matters in the studios themselves. A writer who was a veteran of labour struggles, who had 'scars on both shoulder blades from carrying banners in the Sacco-Vanzetti case - and in thousands of other picket lines too', is dismissive of the so-called radicalism of the new 'parlour Communists' and 'social climbers'.[56] We are nearer here to the actual politics of Hollywood than in any other novel but what is interesting is that the hero of this story is not anticipating films about junkmen but just hoping that a great novelist will come along to do justice to the lives of 'the twenty-thousand extras in Hollywood'. Literature not film was the only cultural hope and even then it would be a novel about failure in Hollywood rather than about the political drama of Los Angeles and California. It was to be many years before a writer was to think of putting Hollywood into its full Californian context.[57]

The Robert Syvertons, then, did not make their films and in general they had little impact on the films that were made. The Syvertons that made it into the studio did create guilds and unions and a new political consciousness that saw Hollywood radicals link up with wider political movements and help to break down some of Los Angeles's isolation. What they did not do, however, was to create any alternative film culture within Los Angeles itself. What independent cinema there was in America was based in the East and relied very heavily on radical initiatives from New York and political patronage from Washington.

There was plenty of intelligence and radicalism in Los Angeles but the very nature of the community and the singularity of Hollywood prevented the emergence of any organization that could provide the basis for a different kind of film. What was lacking was a sufficiently well-organized working class within the city itself and also the kind of intellectual subculture that had created an alternative theatre in New York. An appearance by Paul Muni at the Pasadena Playhouse was hardly the basis of a cultural renaissance. In other words Los Angeles was not New York and that was precisely why the movie moguls had gone there. They had created their own environment, their own oasis, and no invasion of ambitious Robert Syvertons, of major writers, or of East Coast Communists was going to make any headway against a town that the movie bosses and their henchmen had always had sewn up. As Scott Fitzgerald knew Hollywood was 'a mining town in lotus land'.[58] The great struggle to unionize Hollywood in the 1930s was a dramatic story but it was bound to be an unreal struggle given the isolated and suburban nature of Los Angeles. For a while in the 1930s the Communist Party gave a unity and sense of purpose to Hollywood radicals but in a way this unity was artificial and the Party was really a substitute for the kind of indigenous politics and culture that should have been developed. The hollowness of what was going on was revealed in the total lack of impact on the movies themselves. The nature of industrial relations was changed but all the screenplay writers and their associates did nothing to create a genuine base for 'popular front' culture in Hollywood. As Ceplair and Englund have shown Hollywood made only one movie that can be described as a 'popular front' movie in any political sense but what was worse was that all the radical intellectuals in Hollywood were unable to create a film institute, a cultural journal or tradition, a local legitimate theatre, or anything that could challenge the moguls.[59] The political success of the 1930s was the Screenwriters Guild, but in cultural terms there was complete atomization as Scott Fitzgerald well knew.

Things were different in New York. The very nature of the movies was a product of Los Angeles's sun-drenched blandness whereas the various energies of New York were fuelling a more dynamic culture. The New Yorkers who went west to change things were never heard of again but back on the East Coast itself the vital questions could be asked. As the great fight to establish collective bargaining went on in America's industrial centres independent film-makers attempted to put together a film record but as far as commercial cinema was concerned intellectuals and radicals just had to be content with developing a more sophisticated response to Hollywood itself. In terms of film the main achievement of the 'popular front' decade was the growing complexity of film analysis, which meant that Hollywood films were now far more fully debated within the culture and that ideas about films fed into a wider debate about America itself. The new levels of awareness in film analysis were very much in evidence in the responses to Chaplin's *Modern Times*, which was released late in 1935. Several critics saw this film as the high-water mark in Hollywood's rising tide of realism and thought that the most important thing about the film was that it should have been made at all. In *New Masses* Robert Forsythe commented on how 'for the first time an American film was daring to challenge the superiority of an industrial civilization based upon the creed of men who sit at flat-topped desks' and concluded that what made the movie epoch-making was that 'with the distributive machinery in the hands of the most reactionary forces in the country there is no possibility of honesty in films dealing with current ideas'.[60] What Forsythe and many others wanted to praise above all else was the obvious honesty of Chaplin. But these were indeed modern times and Chaplin was not going to get away with just making an honest and funny film, especially on a subject such as work. Chaplin himself intervened in the promotion of his film to suggest that it was 'without a doubt the best comedy' he had made so far as well as the one which would have 'the greatest success'.[61] However, a New York that was acquainted with *Pravda*'s view that Chaplin's films, including his latest, dealt with the 'tragedy of the petty bourgeoisie in capitalist society' and revealed that 'his path has nothing in common with the path of the masses who are being rapidly revolutionized' was obviously a New York that was going to have much to say about *Modern Times*.[62] In *New Theatre* Charmion Von Wiegard brilliantly argued that the movie was flawed and confused and that it was neither just a comedy, as the distributors and popular newspapers suggested, or a really significant social satire, as many radicals were suggesting. What had gone wrong as far as Von Wiegard was concerned was that Chaplin had taken his tramp figure from the old world of illusion and fantasy in which he had innocently reflected everybody's failures and introduced him into the very real world of factories and labour demonstrations. The accidental way in which Charlie finds himself leading an unemployment demonstration was funny enough in itself but given the personality that Charlie had developed for himself it could lead nowhere and least of all bring about a change in Charlie himself. Von Wiegard concluded that 'his wistful but optimistic romanticism is as out of date in the world of today as was Don Quixote's tilting at windmills'. The times were no longer innocent and 'the lonely little individual was too lightweight a character to tackle the issues of the day'. 'Against the background of modern times,' Von Wiegard suggested, 'a hero cannot be the pure clown.'[63] As Otis Ferguson argued, '*Modern Times* is about the last thing they should have called the Chaplin picture' for it was really a silent movie using old techniques and old jokes. It also relied on Chaplin's old persona and, as Ferguson reminded his readers, 'on the screen he is only partly a citizen of this world' for 'he lives mostly in that unreal happy land – where kicks, thumps, injustices, and nowhere to sleep are no more than a teasing and a jolly dream'.[64]

In a critical climate that was all too aware both of the theoretical significance and the actuality of the proletariat Hollywood's best-known maverick had shown that he was no more able than other Hollywood producers to come up with a realistic portrait of American workers. Chaplin had failed to depict 'a citizen of this world' but that at least was something that other Hollywood producers could do. During these years in which radical critics denounced either the triviality or the Fascism of Hollywood they could also on occasion find things to admire. As always Hollywood offered a range of films and retained its capacity to surprise. In 1935 Irving Lerner quite liked John Ford's *The Whole Town's Talking* for, while its message that 'you can still become wealthy and famous in this great country of ours' was 'asinine', it was still put over with 'a smoothness and a humour that was disarming'.[65] At the same time *New Theatre* liked *Alibi Ike* because it retained much of the charm of Ring Lardner's original story and because Joe E. Brown was 'perfect' as the baseball pitcher.[66] The following year Lerner described *The Story of Louis Pasteur* as 'a step forward, a small but welcome one'. He did not think that this medical film was as good as John Ford's *Arrowsmith* or MGM's *Yellow Jack* but it conveyed 'its message with signal maturity' and owed much to Muni, who not only suggested the film but contrived to display that he was an actor 'of real theatrical culture'.[67] Meanwhile Robert Stebbins was greatly impressed by Howard Hawks's *Ceiling Zero*, which retained much of the drama and 'bawdy' humour of Frank Wead's play. What Stebbins particularly liked was that the retention of the unhappy ending meant that 'for once the peculiar egocentric, anti-social character that is Cagney's creation received proper solution, when as the philandering aviator, he falls to a spectacular and well-chosen death'.[68]

The pattern of the 1930s was one in which a much fuller analysis of Hollywood films combined abuse with praise for individual films which displayed honesty or more commonly were characterized by an unusual sharpness or energy. Abuse was at its height in 1935 but thereafter there seems to have been some acceptance on the part of radicals that Hollywood was not going to make movies about the militancy of the rank and file and, as the studios seemed to be giving up on the worst type of propaganda film, there was a tendency to discuss the Hollywood product in a slightly less frenetic way. It was now more generally accepted that there were Hollywood conventions and that Hollywood films had to be approached on their own terms. It was partly a matter of Hollywood's old ability to disarm but there was also a realization that at least there were now better films. As the radicals and their associates were demanding a more realistic cinema Hollywood had moved towards its own definition of realism and that definition was one which showed that whilst the producers did not show steelworks and coal-mines, nevertheless they did, in contradiction of Lorentz, know something about America. As the decade moved on critical attention focused on the films of Frank Capra. The great success of *It Happened One Night* had taken Hollywood by surprise and it was film audiences themselves who had stumbled on the charm and vitality of that film. In the following years, though, Capra was regarded as the man of the moment and given every encouragement. The radicals had called for realism whereas the producers knew that audiences really wanted entertainment. In general they wanted to produce escapist films but obviously there was a great market for contemporary films that were not in any way depressing or mere propaganda. The scene was set, then, for Capra to become 'the film-maker laureate' of the New Deal and to suggest that for all its faults America could still be great if it relied on the old virtues of personal integrity. Capra was Hollywood's answer to the New York intellectuals and his films challenged them to come to terms with his view of America. What ensued was a fascinating debate in which the official, populist, and New Deal myth of America ran straight into the collectivist notions of New York but out of this there emerged a fuller and somewhat more sympathetic understanding of how Hollywood films worked.

James Shelley Hamilton thought that there might be some substance in the satire of *Mr Deeds Goes to Town* but was far more struck by how a fairly crazy 'Saturday Evening Postish story' is made to work by Capra's technical skills and sense of style. Capra's gift was 'for warming up a plot with a good-natured spirit, disguising its frailties with all sorts of human and amusing by-play and keeping the whole thing plausible and pleasant by a genial semblance of common sense'. For Hamilton, Capra was a master of pace and his magic weaved 'a spell of likeableness and plausibility'.[69] Robert Stebbins, however, decided that 'for Hollywood *Mr Deeds* is a tremendous advance'. He concedes that the movie was 'pure wish-fulfilment' and would serve like all of Hollywood's products to 'dull the militance of labor' but he could also detect a 'sincere and understanding awareness of the world's ills'. Hamilton had only given a passing mention to the film's social content but Stebbins used his review to draw special attention to John Wray's performance as the dispossessed farmer. He praised the scene in which Wray's farmer meets Mr Deeds as a well-conceived and well-acted dramatic moment but what struck him more was that 'for the first time in the movies we have been given a sympathetic, credible portrait of a worker, speaking the language of workers, saying the things workers all over the country say'.[70] Just as Stebbins had been struck in 1936 by the pioneering qualities of *Mr Deeds* so in 1939 Patterson Murphy was greatly impressed by Capra's *Mr Smith Goes to Washington* and he hailed it as a movie that went 'beyond entertainment' to become 'a pure lesson in civics'. Murphy thought this the best film he had 'ever seen about American democracy' and in true Capra-like style he concluded that it was 'one of the great triumphs of the democratic method that such a film of self-criticism can be made and universally shown in our land'. At the same time Murphy had reservations about the film and in particular he suggested that Capra had shown problems and depicted dilemmas rather than offering solutions. What Capra had done was to fall back on his old trick of 'a single Galahad's heroism' but Murphy would have been happier with a fuller statement of how Americans could regain control of their government and 're-establish the full meaning of our citizen government'. In other words he thought that the dramatic crisis in the film needed to be solved 'through a people's rather than an individual's action'.[71] For Murphy, Capra's refusal to point to the need for a political solution was a blemish but for Richard Griffith it ruined the movie for it showed that a director who had started out as an original was now just happy to confirm what was a prevailing popular myth about the nature of America. Griffith's own view was that 'individual idealism is no solution for any practical problem' but was rather 'the totem people worship when every other way out cuts across their thinking habits'.[72]

Many critics agreed with Otis Ferguson's view that Capra's best film had been *Mr Deeds* and that thereafter the movies became too schematic. Ferguson could see that what was important about Capra was his style rather than his message and he had praised *Mr Deeds* as 'a humdinger and a beauty' precisely because it was 'like all motion pictures - literally too much for words, more to be seen and heard about'.[73] It became Ferguson's view that at some point during the production of *Mr Deeds* 'Mr Capra began to leave this world' and by the time of *Mr Smith* he fully agreed with Alistair Cooke's view that Capra 'had started to make movies about themes instead of people'.[74] The whole point now, however, was that there were many movies that were 'too much for words'. Capra had shown the way and others had learnt the lesson that style and mood were all important. As he praised *Mr Smith* Murphy referred to 'the complete flowering of a style' and 'company cohesion' and he suggested that these had become the hallmarks not only of Capra but of a whole genre of films. Producers had learnt how to use actors in a natural way and learnt also the importance of 'good-heartedness' and about not taking things too seriously.

In general Hollywood had not taken things too seriously in the depression and had concentrated far more on entertaining the nation. It was the sheer quality of films as entertainment that allowed the motion-picture industry to build up its audiences. The New Deal obviously helped to remove many of the fears that had haunted both Wall Street and Hollywood in the early years of the decade. Hollywood recovered confidence and also realized that there was not quite the need for the anti-red overkill of 1934 and 1935. In fact the New Deal even sanctioned films like those of Capra which radiated an upbeat pride in democracy and in the capacity of ordinary Americans to overcome problems by relying on good old-fashioned virtues. With its confidence returning and its mastery of pure entertainment assured Hollywood felt able to channel the progressive and even radical values of some of its employees into realistic and political films. There would not, of course, be any films dealing directly with the great labour struggles of the day and the protests of Catholics in Boston and other cities at the showing of *Blockade* showed the dangers of broaching in however bland a fashion a subject so controversial as the Spanish Civil War.[75] Nevertheless there seemed no danger in making serious films on certain well-defined but broad themes and indeed there seemed every possibility that such films would do well at the box-office in certain areas. Hollywood as always could interpret every change in public taste, however small, and was well aware of how international developments combined with continued problems at home to produce a new seriousness amongst a significant section of the public. Intellectuals like Archibald MacLeish were praising those directors who 'believed that the movies were old enough to accept the adult responsibilities of art and to present the world as it really looks rather than as it appears through the gilt glasses of an adapted best seller'.[76] Even more important though was the growing influence of those organizations which were attempting to build up more discriminating audiences. This was very much the era of Better Film Councils and of the National Board of Review, and in 1937 an Organization of Film Audiences was formed in an attempt 'to influence film production'. The specifications of this new body were 'to curtail production of anti-labor and pro-fascist films' and 'to promote the increase of cultural, instructive and anti-war films'. The Organization intended to use its weekly bulletin and local chapter to endorse whole-heartedly films like *Black Legion* and *Fury* and to give added publicity to films like *Winterset*, which apparently was 'doing spotty business' probably because it was 'a highly cultured film'.[77] Hollywood could see that there was an audience for better films and if that audience were to include some of the 26 million adults who never went to the movies then there was every justification in making a handful of films for them.

There can be no doubt that in these years Hollywood made many new friends as movies were made that broke down the hostility that many educated and respectable people still had for the whole world of movies. In some ways 1936 had really been the turning-point and the National Board of Review felt that films like *Mr Deeds*, *Pasteur*, *Fury*, *Modern Times*, *Winterset*, and *Ceiling Zero* indicated not that a new epoch had dawned but at least that American cinema was entering a period of 'post adolescence'.[78] The following year brought *Black Legion*, *The Good Earth*, and Paul Muni in *The Life of Émile Zola*. All the time a new kind of audience was being built up. Capra was bringing in new people as was the new Cagney persona and after *Angels with Dirty Faces* there must have been many who saw for the first time the truth of Otis Ferguson's statement that when Cagney spoke one never stopped to question 'that it is the living truth spoken through him and not a line rehearsed'.[79] When United Artists released *Dead End* the National Board of Review asked New York City's Tenement House Commissioner to review it and he hailed the movie as he had hailed the original play as a marvellous exposure of 'the horrible influences surrounding the children of the slums' and as a good example of how the best propaganda has to work as effective drama.[80]

What happened in the next years was that growing international tension encouraged Hollywood to go on making serious films and even to make films that contrasted American democracy with the evils of other political creeds. In allowing these films to be made Hollywood was reacting to the seriousness of a section of its audience, to the evidence that in general audiences were declining, to the pressures from writers and directors within the studios, and finally to the prompting of Washington and the Hays Office, which now saw very clearly the need for propaganda films. The last years of peace were to see yet another clutch of films which won considerable praise from intellectuals and the film audience organizations. By this time even the radicals were finding films that could be taken at least a little seriously. In early 1940 James Dugan wrote an article for *New Masses* which he called 'Changing the reel' and in which he spoke of a new 'Progressive period'. He was careful with his judgement and he stressed that he was talking about only 'a handful of films', that none of them 'was free from contradictions and front office interference', and that in most cases laudable ideas had been 'poorly executed'. Nevertheless he felt that 1939 had seen the realization of 'the long campaign of Hollywood's progressive film makers to bring reality to the screen' and that *Juarez, Confessions of a Nazi Spy, Boy Slaves, Young Mr Lincoln, Back Door to Heaven,* and *One Third of a Nation* were all evidence of 'honest motivation'.[81] Of course the left was not entirely happy with Hollywood and as the European war got under way a new campaign against the film studios was launched. Whatever credit Hollywood had gained by becoming anti-Nazi was surrendered by its becoming promilitary. Charles Glenn urged the readers of *New Masses* to note that Hollywood was not only still anti-labour but was now frantically drumming up anti-Soviet and anti-Nazi feeling so as to speed up America's entry into the war. He reminded people of how close Warners and the other studios were to Washington and he saw the hand of Roosevelt in what was now happening.[82] James Dugan also pointed to the growing number of pro-British films and warned of 'the Hollywood–St James axis'.[83] Better films there might be but Dugan's warning was that Hollywood should never be regarded as 'an idiot child' and that Americans who did so could soon be laughing at their 'own funeral'.[84]

It was in this context that Fox released *The Grapes of Wrath* and then a little later *How Green was my Valley*, both of which proved that films of social realism could do well at the box-office and bring in new kinds of audiences. These films were inspired by Darryl F. Zanuck, who in many ways had created the first bout of realism almost a decade earlier. What Zanuck sensed was that the political and social climate was right for movies that admitted that there were serious problems but that there was no real threat to America as long as faith was put in the ordinary American and in particular in the ordinary family unit. Steinbeck's novel was the perfect material for Zanuck and his team for the emphasis of the story was on people rather than on politics and it had been written very much under the influence of the movies. As Edmund Wilson noted at the time Steinbeck had drawn heavily on Pare Lorentz's documentary style and on Hollywood conventions and so it was not surprising that the story 'went on the screen as easily as if it had been written in the studios'.[85] Of course Zanuck had to insist that his writer Nunnally Johnson and his director John Ford play down some of Steinbeck's radical implications and this was done by altering the role of the camp and leaving the Joads not as potential labour organizers but rather as spokespeople for the Americans as a whole.[86] So instead of a story that pointed towards a Socialist solution Zanuck offered a film that was more or less straightforward New Deal propaganda and one that was aimed at the largest possible audience rather than just a section. The movie was consciously created as a monument to what America had just been through. It was brilliantly photographed in the documentary style that 1930s America made into an art form, it chose rural America both as a symbol of what had gone wrong and as the ultimate source of America's strength, it made it very clear that America was a place of violence, meanness, and suffering, and it quite unashamedly used a whole range of sentiment and emotion to suggest that the family was everything and that the individual American had saintly qualities. At every stage the movie impressed by the way that technique enhanced content and throughout it surprised audiences by how little it had diluted Steinbeck's indictment. Edmund Wilson could immediately see that this was 'probably the only serious story on record that seemed equally effective as a film and as a book' and James Shelley Hamilton thought that 'it proved that Hollywood can lead the world in serious as well as merely entertaining pictures'.[87] To Otis Ferguson it seemed as if it was 'the most mature picture story that has ever been made, in feeling, in purpose and in the use of the medium'. To Ferguson this was a 'show for the people': it was 'more than their show than any show on the face of the earth'. He thought that there was 'no country in the world where such a film of truth could be made today' although he confessed that he 'still didn't know how they did it, though its possibility had been latent in Hollywood for years'.[88]

The Grapes of Wrath was made because it was sanctioned by

Washington and by the box-office and because it did not necessitate any significant extension of the Hollywood idiom. Henry Fonda's Tom Joad was there to reassure not to anger Americans and, as Edwin Locke suggested, the Joad family was well chosen because 'most people already feel that something should be done about the migratory workers'. He speculated that the picture could 'stir up bad blood in the more backward parts of the country' but that it was 'unlikely that the reaction will be violent or widespread'. If anything Locke thought that 'like many other middle-class philosophies' the ending of *The Grapes of Wrath* would move men 'to the endless and overgrown paths of acceptance'.[89] What Locke and others could see was that Hollywood had learnt to make great films on its own terms. In *Of Mice and Men* United Artists offered a film that again used a Steinbeck novel to make a film about people described by Hamilton as 'universal in their humanness' although once more it dealt not with industrial workers but with somewhat bizarre migratory farm workers.[90] With *How Green was my Valley* Zanuck did at last tackle an industrial theme but in transferring the action to a mythical Shangri-La he ensured the exclusion of even the limited labour content that there had been in the original novel. Zanuck had made it clear that he did not want a 'labor' story and so this story of Welsh coal-miners became just a hymn of faith in the American family.[91] As Cecilia Ager spotted, the coal-mine and its related dreams of disaster and unemployment were only there for pictorial effect for the movie was not interested in economic factors. Above all the movie was about 'the strength and character and beauty in the faces of the people'.[92] Ferguson agreed and confessed that the picture 'as a whole is nothing so much as a return to the gone days of boyhood – with the family bickering and eating its healthy fill under the big and final fellow at the head of the table'. He thought that there were good things in the movie and that these good things had been made real because they had been 'worked over by men who had an abiding interest in people'.[93]

It is fitting that we should quote Otis Ferguson at this point because as the war approached no critic in America had such a balanced view of Hollywood. Throughout the decade he had joined his fellow New Yorkers in looking at Soviet, British, and documentary films and had seen things that he liked in all of them and yet he refused to subscribe to any cult that was based on them. Many of these films had their moments but for him they did not compare with the best of Hollywood. The beauty of Hollywood films was that they were popular and in general they were popular because they had life in them. As he reviewed *How Green was my Valley* the keywords that came into his mind were 'real' and 'people' and so for Ferguson it was Hollywood's ability to go on making films that were real and were about real people that was the essence of its genius. To Alfred Kazin, Ferguson 'was one of the real roughs of the Thirties': he was an ex-sailor, a jazz fanatic, a real resident of Manhattan, and he was always 'sour on intellectuals'.[94] He was indeed a plain American and one who, as we have seen, as early as 1934 had confessed that Cagney, Durante, Mae West, and W. C. Fields were the 'best and most honest Americans' that he knew.[95] Like the majority of his fellow countrymen Ferguson had the gift of knowing just precisely what the movies really were and like them he had been able to derive some enjoyment in what had otherwise been a miserable decade.

More than any other critic Ferguson had urged audiences to settle for Hollywood's half a loaf, to enjoy Hollywood on its own terms, and yet for all his independence of spirit he too was a man of his time and his intellectual judgement was affected by wider developments. Earlier in the decade he had loved Cagney, Mae West, and the Marx Brothers, and yet later he could talk of *The Grapes of Wrath* in such glowing terms. In the mean time the combined impact of the Production Code and the New Deal had forced Hollywood to bring to a halt any experimentation and to fit its films into more limited moulds. Now the evidence suggested that audiences were tiring of that mould and so Hollywood's response was to borrow some of the concerns and some of the iconography of the radicals and of New Deal artists. They did so in such a brilliant way as to give America a film that was immediately and widely hailed as the depression's greatest work of art. As Robert Warshow was to suggest judgements such as these reveal the extent to which in the 1930s radicalism had 'entered an age of organised mass disingenuousness'.[96] At first, Jack Conroy and his friends had called for writers and workers to come together: subsequently in Detroit and in Pennsylvania the workers went on with their fight but intellectuals and radicals settled for that poetic vision of rural America that constituted 1930s documentary style. For a while Hollywood nodded in that direction but Otis Ferguson and other Hollywood fans knew in the depths of their hearts that through its mastery of people and reality Hollywood could do much better than that. The actors Jimmy Stewart and Henry Fonda were very much the frontmen of the new cinema but surely it had been Cagney who throughout the decade had represented Hollywood at its best. In 1937 Ferguson suggested that Cagney's

> half-pint of East Side Irish somehow managed to be a lot of what a typical American might be, nobody's fool and nobody's clever ape, quick and cocky but not too wise for his own goodness, frankly vulgar in the best sense, with the dignity of the genuine worn as easily as his skin.[97]

Of course audiences never saw Cagney as a factory worker or a labour organizer but that was not Hollywood's way. Cagney was only an entertainer but he still conspired to have a little more life in him than was ever to appear in the novels, plays, and documentaries that were meant to herald a new age. The tycoons and the masses were not quite as prone to mood and fashion as were some other groups. They had seen no reason to abandon their faith in individual solutions and in 1939 the producer Walter Wanger could suggest that, amongst other things, 'the American screenplay presents a perpetual epic of the ordinary unregimented individual'.[98] There were times in the 1930s when that had seemed a somewhat superficial approach and then there had been other times when it threatened to give way to something rather more sinister. On reflection, though, Wanger's little bit of Hollywood hype is not a bad explanation of how film producers saw their work and of why they were able to give so much pleasure to so many people.

5 'The faintest dribble of real English life'

In Britain there has always been a lively and contentious debate on the role and significance of film but those who have followed the debate must often have experienced *déjà vu* for in truth the same themes have kept on emerging throughout the whole history of British cinema. Basic texts which neatly sum up all the dilemmas that have characterized the production of feature films in Britain can be selected from almost any year of this century. We could select, for example, G. A. Atkinson's remarks made in 1927 at a time when the introduction of the quota system to control the entry of American films was being widely debated. Atkinson began his article by the kind of devastating dismissal of British films which has consistently featured in this kind of analysis. He argued that 'if British film production were to die tonight it would leave the world nothing by which to remember it'. He suggested that the plain fact was that British cinema audiences were under 'the spell of the American film', in spite of the 'prolonged campaign against it', although he conceded that the British exhibitor was very much 'the slave and chattel of American masters'. All the evidence suggested that British audiences had failed to support the domestic production of films, and Atkinson concluded that if there were large audiences for British films then they were not amongst those already attending cinemas. It was not difficult for him to explain this preference for American films:

> The simple truth about the American film as a whole is that America has found in the motion picture a definite medium of natural expression which is a contribution to the common stock of nations not less worthy in kind than German music or Italian art or British literature .... The American film stands in the main for the American spirit, a certain joyousness, optimism, youthfulness and determination, which cannot be regarded as an undesirable contribution to the universal stockpot.

For Atkinson the great question was whether Britain could make some kind of cinematic contribution but he had serious doubts about the wisdom of 'blundering legislation' aimed at the production of 'compulsory films' and he was also critical of those British producers who 'have shown no vision higher than a desire to imitate American methods'. He thought that a national film school would help but in the meantime he was forced to conclude with a judgement that was to reverberate through subsequent decades. His view quite simply was that 'the British spirit has not yet found national expression on the screen'.[1]

The debate on the quota was perhaps the first occasion when the general significance of film in British life was fully discussed and it was in the years that immediately followed that film began to achieve some kind of tentative place within the culture.[2] At every stage the promoters and advocators of film had to fight against an intellectual and social snobbery that had designated the cinema as worthless. The main mouthpiece for this attitude was the *Observer*'s St John Ervine who saw film as a threat not only to his beloved theatre but also to the general level of intelligence of humanity as a whole. He loved to quote the observation of a cinema proprietor in Newcastle upon Tyne that 'the average picture is intended for unintelligent young women of eighteen' and he added his own judgement that 'pictures were mere herd-stuff; a pish-posh for people with proletarian minds'. The last phrase was significant for Ervine had the intelligence to realize that the people with 'proletarian minds' were 'not all in the working class' and he instanced a duke of his acquaintance who had 'the mind of a bottle-washer'.[3] Films were thought of as fodder for the mindless and what was worse was that they were produced and marketed by showmen, by cultural outsiders who tended to be of rather dubious ethnic origin. There was no denying the popularity of film but it was not difficult to explain the appeal of something that had been carefully planned with the masses in mind. In particular it was obvious that the Americans had mastered the medium and could effortlessly make films that were slick yet facile, shiny yet shoddy, and emotional yet superficial. The hallmarks of Hollywood were thought to be the clever but ultimately unsatisfactory 'wise-crack' and the total mastery of 'sentimental sham emotions'. As the Hollywood style became more obvious there was often a grudging recognition of the techniques involved but these were never mistaken for significance and not untypical was the comment of one critic that the director Raoul Walsh had a 'genius for endowing the obvious with brilliance'.[4] Throughout the 1930s many people retained this hostility to the pictures but perhaps in general the opponents of film moved away from Ervine's extreme views that films were for 'nit-wits' and towards Seton Margrave's view that what Hollywood specialized in was 'hokum', which involved the skilful manipulation of emotions in a superficial, sentimental, meaningless, but not totally unlikeable way.[5]

In many quarters it remained fashionable to dismiss Hollywood but what was really happening was that an increasing number of critics and intellectuals were beginning to share that taste for Hollywood that the British masses had been the first to acquire. In 1927 Atkinson had detected many positive qualities in the American film idiom and at the same time L'Estrange Fawcett had argued that 'you may not like American films but you cannot possibly disregard them' for 'they are vital' and 'force themselves on your attention'.[6] As critical support for Hollywood films developed, so 'vital' became a favourite word and it was soon joined by 'gusto' and 'tempo'. In 1934 Arthur Dent pointed out that 'America prefers pictures with a fast tempo' for pictures with quick action are a better reflection of their hectic model of life'.[7] In 1936 J. B. Priestley commented that 'American life has a quicker tempo than English life' and was more dramatic 'just as the screaming American police car is more dramatic than its Scotland Yard equivalent'.[8] Priestley was a key figure for, whilst other writers like Edgar Wallace and Hugh Walpole had gone to Hollywood to partake of its bounty without surrendering any of their contempt of film as such, Priestley was determined to understand film on its own terms. He had major reservations but he gradually succumbed to the charm of film and in so doing he greatly helped to sanction the cultural acceptance of pictures in Britain as a whole. He reported that Hollywood itself was an isolated, artificial, and provincial place and not surprisingly in its films there was 'only a thin overworked seam of real life' but nevertheless Priestley did not make the mistake made by so many intelligent people who 'have always tended to underrate Hollywood'. He detected 'genuine artistic impulses' but more than that he just knew that Hollywood had the power to entertain and he confessed that it had supplied him 'with at least 9/10ths of the good entertainment' he had been given in picture theatres. What Priestley had done was to look at a phenomenon that entertained 20 million people a week in England and his conclusion was that it would be stupid to 'despise the actual medium'. He warned his fellow intellectuals that they could no more stop the masses going to films 'with a few cultured sneers than you could stop Niagara by telling it that it was in bad taste'. To Priestley the movies were a 'huge spontaneous world movement' and he quite honestly confessed that he 'saw more in it to wonder at than to despise'.[9] By 1937 and 1938 other critics and writers were finding that they could admit to an enthusiasm for films and even for Hollywood films without being dismissed as morons. In 1938 the novelist Elizabeth Bowen wrote a marvellous essay in which she captured precisely that combination of surrender and curiosity which was enabling an increasing number of people to be entertained by films without being made to feel guilty. Following a decade in which so many intellectuals had only found it possible to rave about Soviet or continental films, Bowen openly admitted to being elevated by glamour, to being dazzled by the 'stars' ('They live for my eye'), and to enjoying the 'family-feeling inside a good film', the way in which 'the world it creates is valid, water-tight, probable'.[10]

What Bowen's quite excellent essay revealed was that educated people were attempting to understand feature films on their own terms and in particular this understanding was being extended to film's treatment of reality. There was a growing appreciation of Hollywood's humour and of its ability to produce first-rate musicals but this was the 1930s and not surprisingly it was Hollywood's capacity to convey what were taken to be the realities of everyday life that now impressed and helped more than anything to build up the middle-class audience. Hollywood's first bout of social realism had shocked many in America itself but it really came as a bolt from the blue for English audiences. At first some critics dismissed much of this realism as melodrama and sensationalism but all the time there was a growing appreciation of the way American films and in particular American actors were quite effortlessly depicting authentic scenes. As early as 1932 Seton Margrave had welcomed Mr Cagney 'in the interests of honesty in talking pictures' and by 1937 Richard Carr was talking of Cagney as 'one of the most significant of modern film actors' and of the way in which 'all the features of the American urban type' were to be seen in his acting.[11] It was that great clutch of realistic films that were sent over in 1936 that finally made British critics face up to Hollywood's assault on the real world and even critics on the left began to find things to admire in American films. In the *Daily Worker* there was praise for the way in which *Oil for the Lamps of China* touched 'the fringe of reality'; *Mr Deeds* was described as 'one of the most brilliant films we have seen for years'; *Fury* was praised for proving 'the tremendous force for progress that the cinema can be without in the least sacrificing entertainment value'.[12] In reviewing *The General Died at Dawn* the critic Trevor Blewitt admitted that 'whatever else you may say of Hollywood you cannot accuse it of not being on the spot'. What Hollywood was now offering was probably best summed up by Blewitt for this article, on a film which vividly depicted the lot of Chinese workers and which had been written by Odets, was headlined: 'Films cash in on reality'.[13]

All of this of course was in marked contrast to British cinema. It is not difficult to detect pronounced anti-Americanism in much of what many British intellectuals had to say about Hollywood in the 1930s, but at least the fervour that went into denouncing American sentimentality and 'the accents of the Bowery' was moderated by the realization that British films were of even less cultural significance. The great irony as many critics saw it was that British films were poor precisely because they attempted to follow the Hollywood model rather than trying to achieve a distinctive identity. In 1933 Eric Knight's argument was that 'we have wasted too much time attacking Hollywood' whereas the time should have been spent in creating a more independent cinema. For him Britain's commercial cinema was, 'to its shame, even worse than Hollywood' and he condemned both Hollywood and Elstree together.[14] Throughout the decade British films were always bracketed with American films and always suffered in the comparison. It was always felt that Hollywood's films were getting better and that British films were being left behind largely because they were less real and less vital. In 1930 Ernest Betts had written an article which he headed 'British films discover England'. He had praised films like *Murder, Loose Ends, Escape*, and *Blackmail* for the way in which they illustrated that British films had 'discovered the England of real people, familiar streets, the shops and houses, and glowing pleasure-haunts of our own cities'. Betts had suggested that a whole new phase of prosperity had begun for British films and that this was the result of the British studios at last knowing what they were talking about: 'they are talking about us' for now 'we welcome ourselves in that pleasing mirror, undisturbed by the caricatures and crudities of the older film fiction'.[15]

That headline 'British films discover England' was to be used over and over again in later years as individual films made some sort of break-through but the truth was that for the rest of the 1930s critics were to bemoan the absence of the British people from British films. Betts had got it wrong: there was to be no 'pleasing mirror' and the caricature remained. Critics knew what the difficulties were – they knew all about censorship for example – but still they wondered why the Americans were able to do so many more exciting things. Many of them were prone to criticize particularly the writing of British films for whilst they could detect some small improvement in the technical quality of the home product they frequently commented on the lack of good stories that came out of the British studios. More commonly they discussed the shortcomings of British actors and in particular they suggested that too many of the techniques and accents used by actors and especially actresses owed rather too much to London's West End. Writing in 1933 Charles B. Cochran described the natural behaviour of Hollywood actors and suggested that 'too often in British films the characters are obviously acting' and 'acting on a scale and with a tempo which in the conditions of the theatre might appear natural and right'.[16] In 1938 the *Daily Worker*'s Jane Morgan wrote of the need for 'actors who have not had every spark of humanity ironed out of them by the strange conventions of the West End stage' and reminded producers that 'absurd caricatures' would not be accepted by audiences that had never been to a West End play.[17] It was quite remarkable how quickly the critics of the 1930s came to realize the importance of film acting; hence their praise for George Raft, Cagney, and the other American pioneers. In this respect they soon came to appreciate the value of the star system. At first they had taken that to be part of the Hollywood 'hokum' and razzmatazz but then they saw that it was precisely the stars that made American films work. In 1934 the *Daily Film Renter* congratulated the British studios on the way they were beginning to use the 'star system' and instanced the great box-office appeal of Jack Hulbert and Cicely Courtneidge but in the years that followed the old question 'Where are the British stars?' was often asked.[18] In 1938 Ian Dalrymple admitted that 'we haven't the acting personalities to persuade the mass-audiences to support us' and Victor Saville confessed that 'we haven't the stars here yet'.[19]

There were many discussions of the shortcomings of British films and it is interesting that in general critics placed far more emphasis on cultural factors than they did on censorship or on the growing permeation of the British film industry by American interests. But whatever the reason it was clear that more and more people wanted to see 'themselves' in British films. When Maurice Orbach spoke at the formation meeting of the Workers Film Unit about the need for 'the making of films in this country with the punch and power of Eisenstein' he was speaking for many people outside the left-wing organizations in his audience.[20] In that same year of 1936 one of Britain's best provincial film critics Frank Evans (in reality Ernest Dyer) of the *Newcastle Evening Chronicle* strongly criticized Lord Tyrrell of the British Board of Film Censors, who had recently condemned the 'creeping of politics into films', and he asked whether the cinema was 'to have no Galsworthy or Shaw or Wells'. It was Evans's view that only when 'the cinemas become to us what the Areopagus was to Athens or the Forum to Rome' that the country would be civilized and he suggested that it was time to 'bring in the real world to redress the balance of the false'.[21] All the time the comparison was made with Hollywood. In 1938 the *Daily Worker* published a long letter from a David E. Thomas, who argued that 'the chief reason ... for the conspicuous lack of success which attends most British films lies in their remoteness from the lives of the people' whereas American films were 'not afraid to pillory any aspect of American life that suggests itself'.[22] At the same time the paper's film critic Jane Morgan reported that it was 'the unanimous opinion of our readers on British films - that they are in the main tedious, with no interest and little entertainment value for the ordinary cinema-goer'. Amongst concrete suggestions that the readers had made was one calling for a British *Dead End* dealing with juvenile unemployment whilst others wanted semi-documentaries dealing with shipyards and mines of the kind that 'the USA was so good at'.[23] Even *The Times* took up this theme and contrasted British films with Hollywood's lack of reticence and preparedness to 'sacrifice natural pride for verisimilitude where social matters were concerned'. Indeed it seemed to this observer that Hollywood took 'a special delight in publicly washing the dirty linen of America in the cinemas of the World'.[24]

Respect for Hollywood's social honesty increased and British films were made to seem all the more inferior. These were constant themes by 1938 but what is interesting is that the debate amongst critics and intellectuals rarely widened out. There was little inclination to discuss censorship or financial control and there were not many reactions to the broader cultural points made in 1936 by Priestley when he suggested that he did not think 'that English working-class life provides as good film material as American'.[25] The restricted scope of this whole debate almost suggests a degree of disingenuousness but certainly it provides valuable insight into the cultural and film values of Britain in the 1930s. Perhaps more than anything it indicates the extent to which Hollywood was setting standards and determining the levels of expectation as far as feature films were concerned. We can see this most clearly in the reactions to what we may term the growth of an independent film culture within Britain itself. This independent film culture was really made up of quite distinct organizational developments. First there was the network of film societies and intellectual film journals with their passion for Soviet and continental films and their distrust of Hollywood. Then there was the British Film Institute, which was in favour of encouraging a wider range of films and in particular wanted to see film achieve respectability within the educational system. At the same time the 1930s saw the development of a Socialist film movement in which a number of organizations attempted to make newsreels and documentaries and to secure a wider distribution of Soviet films especially to working men's and labour clubs and to independently run cinemas. Finally there was that group of British filmmakers who, inspired by John Grierson, had begun to make documentary films for a variety of sponsoring organizations. All of this added up to a considerable amount of activity and it quite definitely contributed to a significant and distinctive British concern about film. Concern is the right word for the people involved in all these organizations took film very seriously and regarded the need to change fundamentally the existing dispensation as a matter of some urgency. The members of all these organizations believed that film was too important to be left to showmen, that Hollywood although it could occasionally make an honest film was basically insincere, shallow, and possibly dangerous, that film could aspire to art as some silent films and many Soviet and continental films had indicated, and that the mass audience needed to be weaned away from the showmen and offered more serious and instructional films.[26]

There was a lot of concern but in truth mainstream commercial cinema and the mass audience were little affected. All these organizations were active enough but what they contributed to British life were subcultures rather than anything really significant. They allowed a small number of people to become active in independent film-making and distribution and perhaps most importantly they allowed a meaningfully large number of people to see foreign films. What they could not do was to influence in any way the British film industry in terms of either production or distribution. All the evidence suggests that producers and distributors set their minds firmly against any concessions to those independent lobbies and they did this feeling confident that it was they who really knew what audiences wanted. Their credo was that there was no room in the cinema for propaganda, very little room for instructional material, and not much room for the documentary depiction of reality. The views of British exhibitors were best summed up in 1936 when the officers of the Cinematograph Exhibitors Association (CEA) gave evidence to an official committee. Mr Fuller, the general secretary, suggested that no documentary film 'has ever set the Thames on fire' whilst he dismissed the BFI as 'a bunch of half and halfers' who were no good at education or entertainment. Mr Fligelstone the president of the CEA, stressed that the public would never come to the cinemas to be educated and he seemed quite happy to accept Mr Guedalla's recent definition of a documentary as a film in which 'machinery was photographed upside down!'[27] Allied to the strong belief that the public preferred American films to British films, these remained the firmly held convictions of British showmen throughout the whole period and all the efforts of the more serious-minded hardly concerned them at all.

What is interesting is the way in which this general acceptance of the Hollywood dispensation amongst British showmen gradually permeated what we may call critical opinion. This being the 1930s obviously a good deal if not all of the independent film activities were inspired by Socialist, radical, or popular-front-type values. In terms of actual film the independents achieved very little but they did create a pattern of expectation. Their own newsreels and even the commercially sponsored documentaries were not widely distributed but what they were contributing was a potent argument that films ought to be more serious and more realistic. The most important thing about independent film activities in the 1930s was the way in which they created a new climate of opinion with regard to the role of film within society. In 1934 D. F. Taylor had identified what he described as 'The new sociological cinema' and he argued that cinema as a whole, including feature films, 'is shaping towards its ultimate realisation as a social service'.[28] In those years the arguments of the documentary film-makers were more important than their films. John Grierson's message was that film-makers had to 'exploit the powers of natural observation, to build a picture of reality, to bring the cinema to its destiny *as a social commentator*, inspirator and art', whilst Paul Rotha's conviction was that 'a film is good, if, and only if, it represents the fundamental realities of today – and a fundamental reality of today is the urgent need for social reform'.[29] These were powerful arguments in the days of mass unemployment and Fascism but they were being put forward in a context in which there were very concrete film realities. What happened in Britain was that these demands for a realistic and progressive cinema merged in the minds of many people with an acceptance of those Hollywood conventions which had so obviously won the approval of the masses. By 1938 it was generally appreciated that there would never be a mass audience for propaganda, educational, or even poetic or didactic documentary films but at the same time there was a growing belief that Hollywood had mastered the art of injecting reality into entertainment film. There was a growing enthusiasm for elements of reality in films but also a realization that the feature film generated a degree of vitality and satisfaction denied the documentary. Feature films had their own life and this was the way towards realism. Most critics would have gone along with Graham Greene, who denied that it was 'the critic's business to assist films to fulfil a social function', and would have argued rather that it was the critic's job to detect whether a film had life and whether it worked on its own terms.[30] There was much praise for the documentary films made by Grierson, Rotha, and others but they were never seen as an alternative to Hollywood and it was not only in New York that critics made qualifications in their tributes. *Sight and Sound*'s Arthur Vesselo was often concerned about the mix of art and propaganda in these films and also their reliance on clichés such as factory chimneys and operators on their way to work.[31] Like Vesselo, J. B. Priestley basically liked the documentaries but he refused to treat them as something sacred and precious. He thought of them as films made by people of a certain background who were offering not British reality but their own version of that reality and it was a version that was 'highly-coloured', 'romantic', and 'picturesque'. It seemed to Priestley that the film-makers had not come to terms with British reality to anything like the same extent as his fellow writers and dramatists and he refused to put them on a pedestal. His judgement was that 'they entertain - they move - but they have not been more nakedly truthful than the rest of us'.[32]

The extent to which most critics shared Priestley's view is indicated by the almost total exclusion of the documentary film, and indeed of the whole independent tradition, from the general debate on the strengths and weaknesses of British cinema. Most critics agreed with the industry and the public that the feature film was the thing. What was even more remarkable, however, was the exclusion of many British feature films from their consideration. Rather like Hollywood the British film industry had throughout the 1930s produced a wide variety of films in the knowledge that different types of films would ensure the continued patronage of different kinds of audiences. The British industry was operating on a considerably smaller scale but it was faced with the same problem of ensuring a continuous stream of films so that regular attendance could be maintained. British producers, though, were faced with the additional complication of having to fulfil quota requirements. What is interesting and revealing about the range of British films is that intellectuals and metropolitan critics were quite prepared to ignore totally all but the best and most expensive British films. Hollywood had captured the

British market and was very effectively securing financial control of much of British production and distribution but it had also by 1938 more or less completely won over British critical opinion. Apart from the out-and-out adherents of Socialist, Soviet, and documentary films the leading critics and moulders of opinion had come to believe that it was the Hollywood feature film that was pointing the way forward. Their own experience suggested that the CEA was quite right to stress that British audiences did not like British films and they came to share the view of producers like Korda that it was only by producing films that were as well written and as well made as those of Hollywood and which would therefore incidentally be acceptable to American audiences that British cinema would come of age. Secure in this conviction they therefore chose to ignore all the cheaply made British films and discussed them either as quota quickies or, to borrow the language of the trade papers, as 'fill-ins for the industrial halls'. In the process they chose to ignore a whole genre of indigenous comedy that in reality contributed an important element to British cinema.

From 1931 on the Lancashire *comédienne* Gracie Fields was making films which relied very heavily on her authentic working-class charm and talent. There were occasions (notably in her 1934 film *Sing as we Go*, which dealt with the closure of a mill) when she threatened to become a political symbol of working-class independence but, as Jeffrey Richards has very convincingly argued, what British producers did with Gracie was to channel her authenticity away from a class and into a national appeal.[33] Her work was best summed up by Graham Greene, who found that her films all seemed designed to show both 'a sympathy for the working class and an ability to appeal to the best circles' and their implication was that 'unemployment can always be wiped out by a sentimental song' whilst 'industrial unrest is calmed by a Victorian ballad, and dividends made safe for democracy'.[34] Nevertheless she had provided the first real example of a British star who achieved fame by harnessing her own working-class vitality rather than by acting out caricatures. Similarly another Lancastrian, George Formby, took his working-class accent, vitality, and irreverence into films in 1934. His films too strayed near the political, especially *Off the Dole* made in 1935, but, as with Gracie Fields, his plots never really amounted to a serious statement and the challenge to authority tended to come in the attitudes shown to and remarks made about the rich and perhaps above all from the sheer natural cheekiness of the star.[35] These music-hall stars had been put into films to make money but the evidence suggests that even the producers were surprised at quite how much money was made and at how popular the stars themselves became. It seems as if the producers were a little ashamed of what they had created and they conspired for some years to disguise the success and even the existence of this indigenous cinema. The truth was that

producers were under the influence of American standards, were transfixed with the notion of breaking into American markets, and were afraid
of what pro-American critics and West End audiences would think. By
1937, however, even American observers were noticing the box-office
appeal in Britain of home-grown stars, and, following a *Motion Picture
Herald* poll in which Gracie Fields came third after Shirley Temple and
Clark Gable and George Formby came fifth after Gary Cooper, the writer
Terry Ramsaye could not help noticing that Britain now had stars with
'a drawing power equal to that of Hollywood's most famous personalities'.
He was particularly interested in the appeal of Formby, whom he described as having 'a purely British value at the present time, and to some
extent a localized value even in England' but as none the less representing in England 'something rather like that for which Will Rogers stood
in America'.[36] At the same time Aubrey Flanagan reported to America
that with an 'insistence on the purely native scene and purely native
humour' in this brand of national comedy 'Britain has ever been on the
safest ground' but his accompanying remarks provided a valuable insight
into how the industry itself was thinking. Whatever the success of Fields
and Formby it was Flanagan's argument that the genre of what he described as 'vaudevillean *mélanges*' was not the way forward for the British
industry. He referred to 'the clusters of unambitious renter-sponsored
pictures aiming at a family audience, sentimental essays woven around
the titles of the older ballads, lachrymose and shoddily concocted concessions to the moronic and matronly' and showed that these films were
'among the modest money makers and seldom in the red'. Nevertheless
they were not the way to fame and fortune and Flanagan suggested that
'making down-to-earth pictures for the British masses', and he instanced
John Maxwell's work at Elstree, was a sign of an inferiority complex
which made producers think of their films as 'British films', instead of as
films.[37] Whatever the appeal of a Fields and a Formby the British film
industry could not rely on them alone to retain audiences, and films had
to be made that did well in America. The fact was that Elstree, Denham,
and the other studios had to compete on Hollywood's terms.

The industry knew that it was 'not economic to depend on the British
market alone' and that Fields and Formby could not become the models
for an indigenous cinema but what was strange was that the critics were
quite prepared to go along with that judgement, albeit for their own
artistic reasons. It is true that many of the critics were quite out of touch
with what provincial audiences liked or even saw and that they based all
their notions about public taste on what they saw in London or on what
producers told them. That there was some popular disquiet abut this is
suggested by the way in which some respondents used Sidney Bernstein's
1937 questionnaire to argue that critics should review those films on
general release and not those on show in the West End.[38] Like most

critics P. L. Mannock usually gave little attention to domestic comedies but in 1938 he very revealingly told *Daily Herald* readers that they might be surprised to know that there were parts of the country where Formby, Will Hay, Sandy Powell, and Stanley Lupino were more popular than the Marx Brothers and other 'quick-fire American wise-crackers'. Mannock argued that in the silent era British comedy had been ignored, that the coming of sound had allowed music-hall humour and routines to be transferred to film and that several comedians were now mastering the new challenge. Having 'surprised' his readers with all this information, though, he still concluded that 'even now the British screen can hardly claim to have discovered a really big talkie comedian': Mannock like so many of his colleges was firmly for the Marx Brothers.[39] Even at this distance one can sense how embarrassed the critics were by those British films that they found to be provincial, cheaply made, rooted in music-hall rather than cinematic conventions, and perhaps, above all, just silly. We can detect the note of apology even in the writings of John Grierson, who praised American realism and then said of Britain that it offered 'musicals and farces galore, but there is all too little of the real thing'.[40]

London-based intellectuals just did not take 'music-hall' films seriously and did not regard them as contributing anything meaningful to the development of cinema. Grierson's dismissal of Gracie Fields, whom he described as 'doing her Saturday night turn in a Lancashire parlour', came in an essay which illustrated as much as anything else how total was Hollywood's victory. Grierson was dismissive not only of British comedy but also of the efforts of directors who had attempted to make sensitive films about British working-class life. For several years John Baxter had been attempting to show that Hollywood's way did not have to be the British way but, just as the leading critics had always been happy to ignore *A Real Bloke* and other films, Grierson was only prepared to mention in passing Baxter's 'sentimental to the point of embarrassment films' although he conceded that at least they dealt with 'real people's sentimentalities'. In this essay at least, Grierson allied himself with those critics who chose to forget the constraints of censorship and the box-offices as he suggested that the failure of the British to break through to cinema realism was essentially a cultural failure.[41] Yet it was now generally accepted that American culture had allowed that breakthrough. What was needed was for the technical expertise that at least some British studios had acquired to be put at the disposal of the same kind of well-written and realistic stories that Hollywood was now coming up with. The British domestic comedies and dramas of the 1930s were an irrelevance, a cul-de-sac, and it was felt that the time had come for British cinema to enter the main stream. As was so often the case the situation was best summed up by J. B. Priestley as he called for the British studios and the documentary film-makers to pool their talents. What he wanted to see was a 'strengthening and thickening of the ordinary British film' for:

> Nearly all our films are much thinner in their social texture than the French films and the better Hollywood products. They seem to be taking place in a kind of vacuum or in a world peopled sparsely by a few anxious character actors. When they show us an England, it seems to have been taken from a few issues of the *Sketch* and *Tatler* and a collection of Xmas cards. Only the faintest dribble of real English life is allowed to trickle into most of our films, from which everything not of immediate entertainment value has been so carefully removed that most of the entertainment has vanished too.

What Priestley wanted was that 'the caliphs' of the British studios should put their equipment, actors, and expertise into the hands of those documentary men whose work had been characterized by enthusiasm, zest, a social conscience, and a knowledge of the English scene. His prescription was clear and precise:

> If the Arabian Nights caliphs could have left the Savoy Grill and these earnest young experimenters could have marched out of Soho Square and both parties could have met, somewhere near Haymarket, then British films might have entered a new and glorious life.[42]

So sure was Priestley's sense of Britishness in the 1930s that even as he wrote this passage the caliphs were at last thickening their films by using some of the documentary techniques and themes to make their films more real. But Hollywood remained the main model and it was in all probability direct American intervention that now provided the direct financial and artistic inspiration. All the while American executives and artists had been flooding into the offices and studios of the British film companies. In 1937 Aubrey Flanagan had described this migration as a veritable Armada and had suggested that in some studios it was 'as easy to purchase an "Old Fashioned" as it is a mild and bitter'.[43] The key year was 1938 because the new Quota Act encouraged American companies to go into production in Britain itself and from that time on there was a far greater American influence over the kind of films made in the British studios. In a sense Hollywood and Wall Street had come to Britain and what we see is an emphasis on films that would do well in America and also the introduction into Britain of categories of film that already had been established in America. Critics and intellectuals had created the expectation but ultimately it was the Americans who pushed British cinema through the cultural block that had prevented the making of realistic and, in particular, social-problem films. Suddenly there was a new pride in British films and we can trace the mounting enthusiasm in the reception given to individual films. Victor Saville was a director who had always attempted to make films of the same technical excellence as Hollywood but what was notable about his 1938 film *South Riding* was that considerable care had been taken over the telling of a political story and that there was a realistic treatment of social problems, especially inadequate housing. The *Daily Worker*'s Jane Morgan was furious that Winifred Holtby's Socialist novel had been turned into 'national Government propaganda' by using paternalistic benevolence as a solution and she dismissed the film as 'a barrage of nonsense' but other critics found that here at last was an intelligent and well-made film dealing with what could be recognized as social issues.[44] In the same year there was praise too for *Pygmalion*, with P. L. Mannock even suggesting that 'how to speak English is a subject of greater interest now than when the play was written'.[45] Interestingly, both films initially did well in New York and forced the critics there to pay increased attention to British films.

The real turning-point, however, came later that year with the opening of *The Citadel*, an event which really marked the arrival of the social problem film in Britain. P. L. Mannock hailed this adaptation of A. J. Cronin's novel as 'by miles the best film of medical life ever made' and he had no hesitation in stressing the extent to which it was an American achievement. He found it quite remarkable that 'a picture so authentically charged with British atmosphere, feeling and spirit', could be produced in a British studio by an American company, MGM, and by a Hollywood director, 'the brilliant King Vidor'.[46] Certainly the hand of Hollywood can be seen throughout this film; it can be seen in the technical excellence, in the quality of the writing, which had been a team effort, in the authenticity of the dialogue, for which Emlyn Williams had been partly responsible, in the authentic medical details, which were partly the work of a technical adviser, and in the acting performance of Robert Donat, who was in the process of being built up as a British star in the Hollywood mould.[47] But if Hollywood methods had given the film its power they had also contributed to its shortcomings for, as *The Times* suggested, 'the last part of the film is marred by an unsatisfactory mixture of melodrama and loose argument'.[48] *The Citadel* was very much a Hollywood-type social-problem film. It was a searing condemnation of private medicine and, as *Film Comment* was later to suggest, its use of an American idiom made it far more outspoken than any purely English-made film could have been.[49] From America too came its highly inaccurate depiction of mining trade-unionism. The opening sequences of the film were indeed pure documentary and there was an authentic enough feel for the strange landscape of an isolated coalfield but nothing could be allowed to interfere with Vidor's main theme that Robert Donat as the young doctor had to be in turn disillusioned, corrupted, and redeemed. The film was about a hero's struggle to fulfil himself and so in true Hollywood style it only visited the mines for its own purposes. The miners are shown as a stupid peasantry whose ignorance and suspicion merely support a medical racket. We have been taken, as *Film Comment* was to suggest, more into the Bible belt than into the highly politicized South Wales of contemporary reality. The death of a child is God's will, black lung is caused by local mists, scientific experiment is the work of the devil, and our young hero is faced on all sides by popular prejudice. 'Did anyone ever try to help the people and the people not object?' asks the doctor's wife, and this of course was the pure gospel of Vidor and one not unacceptable to the Hollywood and Wardour Street moguls. *The Citadel*, then, condemned a racket and exalted a hero but in so doing it fudged every political issue; in particular mining trade-unionism had been dismissed as a restrictive guild or syndicate and therefore as an obstacle to individual fulfilment. For all that, though, the film still offered enough for Alan Page to tell *Sight and Sound* readers that it was 'the best British made film I have seen this year, if not at any time'.[50]

Both *South Riding* and *The Citadel* had shown that popular, radical, and yet thoroughly respectable and tasteful novels that appealed to the middle-class and the better sort of working-class readership could be used as the basis of prestigious films that would do well both at home and in America. Now the search was on for suitable material and as *The Citadel* was being made so work was under way on another Cronin novel, *The Stars Look Down*. The rights to this story had been acquired by Isadore Goldschmidt, who had appreciated both the popularity of the novel and the power of its theme. He told reporters that 'a Cronin book sells well because it contains truth that cannot be hid' and that 'the material that Cronin gave them to work on is of the richest'.[51] Again the greatest care went into the writing of the script and into the making of the film. Years later Carol Reed, the director of the film, confessed that he had simply taken the novel as suitable material without any particular concern about its theme or its message that the mines should be nationalized and he simply added that 'one could just as easily make a picture on the opposite side'.[52] Yet at the time the company aimed at what was thought of as being a new realism for British films and sought to make considerable publicity out of the fact that location shooting was being done in the North (albeit in the more picturesque Cumbria rather than in County Durham) and that coal and pit-ponies had been brought into the Twickenham Studios to add authenticity to one of the most expensive sets ever built in Britain.[53] During the shooting a journalist asked Carol Reed how he was going to deal with the 'Socialist impressions of the book', and, although he gave Alison Smith 'a quizzical look', his answer was a little less disingenuous than his later comments for his line was that 'we're portraying people who - whether you agree with them or not - might naturally be expected to be in favour of nationalizing the mining industry' and that 'to omit or misrepresent that viewpoint would twist the story'.[54]

What happened of course was that a British company who had first hoped to make the film in 1936 now sensed that both the censors and audiences were ready for more realism and that any suggestions of radicalism could only give the film more punch at the box-office. And so it was that British film-goers were given a film that depicted the miner more fully than in any previous film. The early part of the action dealt explicitly with the consequences of a three-month strike occasioned by the men's refusal to work the dangerous Scupper Flats seams and the film ends with the drama and tragedy of the inevitable disaster consequent on the working of those seams. Between the two sequences comes the film's most dramatic moment as the miner's son Davy, played by Michael Redgrave, addresses his fellow university students in a debate and argues the case for nationalization by stressing that coal was not invented by man but put there for the benefit of the nation; as Davy speaks images of his old colleagues at work in the pit are superimposed over his face. This is one of the most stunning and effective sequences in the history of British cinema and it was almost inconceivable that it could have been made at any time before 1939. As it was, the film was held up for some time and not released until the outbreak of war. The mining scenes were authentic, the touch of radicalism was quite bold, and the *Spectator*'s Graham Greene justly concluded that this was 'a very good film', in fact he doubted 'whether in England we have ever produced better', and he suggested that it stood comparison with *Kameradschaft*.[55] In the opinion of the *Daily Express* the film was '100 per cent - if you can take it'; the people were real people and there was 'a grime of coal dust in every foot'.[56]

The *Manchester Guardian* found that *The Stars Looked Down* was 'a grimly honest film' and then added the comment that 'it has taken a long time for the British film to catch up the American' in putting working people and their lives on the screen.[57] This, of course, was very much to the point for once again Hollywood was the model and there are several features in the film which indicate that it was made with American audiences in mind. The film opens with a narrator who speaks in a curious mid-Atlantic accent and who in telling us about the work of 'simple working people' uses the phrase 'the same the world over' twice. He also tells us that the miners are 'often without a spokesman'. At the end of the film he returns, not to urge us to vote Labour, but rather to speak of 'darkness', 'fulfilment', 'the unconquerable spirit of man', and 'purging the world of its ancient greeds'. The highly organized Miners Federation of Great Britain, who had long advocated nationalization, must have been surprised by all of this as well as by the actual depiction of trade-unionists in the film. Early on there is a very American-looking playboy of a union leader urging the men to work the dangerous seams and, not surprisingly, a heckler shouts at him that 'You know what you can do with the unions.' Later in the action Davy appears before the union executive to make another of his great speeches, in which he eloquently outlines the dangers of Scupper Flats but the executive members, who had been made to look remarkably like a board of directors, rejected this argument, attributing it to personal animus, and they move on to discuss the trivial matter of painting a branch headquarters, so making themselves accessories to the disaster that follows. The whole treatment of the union is very American in tone although it must also have reflected that prejudice against the miners which many middle-class people in Britain had shared since the 1920s. The very success of the miners in organizing had made them into a corporate entity and a vested interest and so in Carol Reed's film the call for nationalization is not allowed to become a working-class political cause but is rather a metaphor for individual fulfilment. The union is not something on which a new society can be founded but rather a reflection of the self-interest inherent in the old order and therefore a part of the very self-interest that our Christian saint of a hero must transcend and overcome. In the *Tribune* Elizabeth Young had no difficulty in identifying this advocacy of nationalization coupled with a condemnation of trade unionism as 'totalitarianism' and 'fascist'.[58] There were to be other less sophisticated criticisms of Carol Reed's film and especially of the acting. Some critics thought that the Hollywood-inspired notion of using a star like Michael Redgrave had not worked in this instance and in general they rather missed authentic North-East accents. There was uniform praise for Emlyn Williams, who was by now well known in New York and who was contributing so much that was good to British films at that time, and because of him the film is often described as being about Wales. There was praise too for Margaret Lockwood as the young girl on the make who latches on to Davy and tries to steer him away from politics and into bland respectability. She tells Davy to 'Give up this silly thing about miners. Nobody's got any patience with that these days. Don't waste all your lovely brain on that.' Graham Greene could talk of comparisons with *Kameradschaft* but in truth what life and authenticity *The Stars Look Down* has comes far more from Emlyn Williams's brilliant creation of Joe, the ex-miner who is after 'big money' and will cut any corner to get it, and from Margaret Lockwood's working-class chiseller, who tells Davy that she 'was born to be a lady', than it does from the mining scenes. A particularly well-written script allied to extremely professional acting ensured that it was the social melodrama that provided the insights into the real nature of the depression rather than the superficially more dramatic story of Davy and the tragedy of Scupper Flats.

MGM must have hoped that Carol Reed's film would make money in America, although they subsequently worried about its radicalism and held it up for two years. When it did appear *Liberty Magazine* rather

5 *The Stars Look Down*: Redgrave as working-class leader and saint.

ironically commented that 'this smashing film of Cronin's five year old novel of the Welsh coal-fields' could never have happened in Hollywood.[59] Things were obviously happening in British cinema but nobody could have been as surprised as British audiences themselves. For years their cinema had ignored contemporary problems and then suddenly as war approached they were given two films that dealt not only with working-class communities but with the miners, that most highly politicized and emotive section of the whole labour movement. And there was more to come for in 1940 Michael Balcon's Ealing Studios released *The Proud Valley*, which not only dealt directly with the opposition of the miners to a pit closure but also starred Paul Robeson, the well-known Socialist activist. This was all too much for Graham Greene, who complained that:

No picture of a mining district ever seems to be complete without a disaster (we have two in this picture): the warning siren is becoming as familiar as the pithead gear shown against the sky – and that has joined the Eiffel Tower and the Houses of Parliament among the great platitudes of the screen.[60]

Michael Balcon knew that his studios could not compete with Denham and Pinewood in the international market and Ealing was already concentrating on low-budget British films. None the less the same methods were used in the production of *The Proud Valley* as in *The Citadel* and again Hollywood standards can be detected. A team of writers worked on an original story called *David Goliath* which had been written by Bert Marshall and his wife Alfredda Brilliant of the Unity Theatre; the successful Welsh playwright Jack Jones was brought in as an actor and to contribute original dialogue, and South Wales was combed for supporting actors and technical advisers. And, of course, an American star was brought in to play the vital role of the black sailor who wanders north from Cardiff in search of a job. Paul Robeson was already known in South Wales, where he had appeared in concerts to raise money for the Republican cause in Spain, but in pre-release publicity he stressed that he had been drawn to the film not by what was described as its 'slightly pink tint', but more by the opportunity to play the part of a kind, generous, and likeable negro.[61] The preparation was extensive and careful but necessarily this was going to be a rather different film from its two predecessors. It was going to be expensive, it was going to be far more Welsh in idiom, and initially it was going to be far more radical, for it was to end with the miners taking over the closed pit and running it themselves. In the event this ending was changed so as to include the coming of war and the sending of a delegation to London which successfully persuades the company to reopen the pit now that the country needs the energy.[62] From the beginning the story was one that combined a radical critique and prescription for action with a good deal of sentimentality and that was precisely the kind of film that the 26-year-old Penrose Tennyson, ex-Etonian and descendant of Macaulay and Tennyson, proceeded to make. *The Proud Valley* is a curious mixture of realism and stereotype, of radicalism and soap opera, of innocence and sharpness. It is a sentimental, lyrical, and, of course, musical tribute to the working class made essentially by outsiders who attempted to convert a political and industrial drama into a warm folk-tale. There is no trade-unionism on show and all the bright ideas came not from any organization but from David Goliath's young friend Emlyn, but the miners are real people, we do see them producing leaders and choosing delegates, and by the end of the film there is a sense that the men themselves and their community constitute a real and perhaps irresistible force. Reactions to this film will always be essentially personal and will depend on how people react to the stage-Welsh idiom, to what John Osborne has described as Paul Robeson's role as a 'Blakean figure of goodness', and to the quite clever device of using choral singing as a metaphor for class solidarity.[63] The most dramatic moment of the film comes when the miners' choir is rehearsing *Elijah* in the unfortunate absence of their bass soloist; suddenly and fortuitously from the street below comes the marvellous voice of an itinerant black sailor singing 'Lord God of Abraham'. That moment is the litmus test of the film, one either weeps or groans. Not surprisingly Mr Robeson's 'big, black pollyanna' with all the accompanying 'sentimental optimism' did nothing for Graham Greene, who was also not very struck by an ending of 'patriotic speeches and crisis posters and miners dying for England'. Dilys Powell would have preferred the original ending but still found it an honest and warm film and far more moving than *The Stars Look Down*. 'Welsh miners come into their own' was the headline used by the *Picturegoer*, which argued that 'when British producers get down to the essentials of life they appear to be more successful than in any other medium'.[64]

Within a year and a half a lot had happened in British cinema and it is not going too far to suggest that these three mining films represented the beginning of a more adult approach to the making of feature films. The main basis for this change was a new chapter in intellectual fashion, which was itself part of a new set of political circumstances. It was altogether appropriate that films about mining were to be the main symbol of cinema's new role within the culture. At the time of the general strike in 1926 British miners had stood alone and had been dismissed as unconstitutional extremists by most intellectuals, who rather shared W. H. Auden's view that the strike was not to be taken seriously.[65] A contempt for militant miners remained a distinguishing feature of much polite society in the Britain of the 1930s and was best summed up by Evelyn Waugh when he said of one of his heroes that he was usually spoken of in terms 'normally reserved for the mining community of South Wales, as feckless and unemployable'.[66] The 1930s, however, had also seen both the emergence of mass unemployment, especially amongst miners, and the new threat of fascism. As important sections of the intelligentsia now became politically interested in Socialism and in the proletariat for the first time, so the miners, whether at work or out of work, became the classic embodiment of the values on which a new politics would be based. Writers like George Orwell and J. B. Priestley spelt out that the miners were the all-too-forgotten base of British civilization and Alberto Cavalcanti and other documentary film-makers established shots of miners at the coal-face or searching for coal on slag heaps as the central monochrome image of the depression.[67] The miners were to the mythology of Britain's depression what the sharecroppers were to America's.[68] As war became a distinct possibility and both the unions and the Labour Party showed signs of revival, so the intellectual concerns with miners and urban workers generally were taken up by other agencies and became part of a general political climate which politicians, newspapermen, and film producers had to recognize. These were the changes that led to a new British cinema but the kind of films that had emerged by 1940 still owed more to the inspiration of Hollywood's social-problem genre and to the direct involvement of American money and personnel than to any indigenous cultural or political factors. MGM and Wall Street had played a greater part in British cinema's coming of age than had *The Road to Wigan Pier.*

6   'The wartime drama of the common people'

In the Second World War the two great democracies of Britain and the United States had to harness their full resources and the energies of all their people to defeat the aggrandisement of totalitarian powers. The great struggle to sustain the war effort necessitated a new sense of national identity and a new appreciation of the responsibilities and possibilities of democracy as well as a new understanding of the way in which these things should be articulated and communicated. In a war involving all the people it was inevitable that the vastly popular medium of film would play a crucial cultural and political role. In the 1930s politicians and censors, film producers and directors, and critics and intellectuals had all in their respective ways arrived at a point where they could see that the social content of feature films was a matter of the utmost significance. Influential critics had created the notion that the English-language cinema could only really achieve greatness by dealing more directly with the lives of ordinary people. Politicians were very aware of the forces attracting films towards realistic subjects but were determined that films should not expose their vast and impressionable audiences to political ideas. For their part film producers were quite prepared to indulge those directors and writers who wanted to create a more maturely realistic cinema as long as their films eschewed all controversy, conformed to well-established plot conventions, and retained box-office appeal.

The actuality of war did not so much create an entirely new set of circumstances but rather offered new opportunities in which all these existing expectations and notions suddenly became more relevant and urgent. For the first time politicians became aware off the positive rather than negative potential of realistic films and producers not only sensed that a box-office bonanza was in the offing but that co-operation with governments and a cultivation of patriotism would bring the official recognition and respectability that the industry had long sought. Meanwhile a section of film-makers and critics hoped that the new sense of democracy at war would at last allow film to deal more fully and openly with all those social realities that it had ignored for almost a quarter of a century. In the event the Second World War was to generate a tremendous amount of creativity and a very new social sense amongst British and American film-makers but ultimately politicians and producers retained the upper hand and, as always, they ensured that realism was defined and worked out on their terms. The English-language feature film was given a new dimension by the war but at the same time it remained subject to the conventions and principles upon which it had been established.

The coming of war provided drama enough for the British film industry. For two years the industry had struggled to survive a financial crisis which had threatened to close down most British studios and then just as a certain amount of confidence was returning there came what was thought to be the further disaster of war. Anticipating aerial bombardment the Government closed down all cinemas and that, many people thought, was that. In fact the Government order was soon reversed and gradually it dawned on producers that there was still going to be a need for a British film industry.[1] Things could never really be the same again; now there would never be the possibility of a Hollywood developing either along the Thames or to the north of London for some studios were already closed and personnel drastically cut back. Meanwhile for that trimmed-down industry which survived there was plenty to do and a vast audience to be entertained.

At first it was the new opportunities for documentary film that were most obvious, for right from the early days of the war the Government revealed its intention of making use of the non-fiction skills that British film-makers had acquired. Quite simply the Government now stepped in to take over the role that a number of official and commercial agencies had earlier fulfilled and it became the sponsor of a whole new chapter in documentary film-making. On the Government's part there was a full appreciation of the power of the film as a source of both inspiration and information and there was also an awareness of those polls and surveys suggesting that people were feeling in need of more information and more hard news. The first official films were ready within a few months of the outbreak of war and by 1940 the renamed Crown Film Unit of the Ministry of Information was building up a team of film-makers to make training films and a variety of documentaries for cinema audiences in general.[2] Soon films depicting the involvement of the British people in the war effort became a standard feature in most film programmes. There were short films conveying information or explaining jobs that had to be done and also more ambitious films which depicted military actions by concentrating on particular units and groups and which, in some instances, took the form of dramatized documentaries with prepared scripts and with the characters played by actual serving men and women. As the war continued it became clear that the Government had in fact created a whole new kind of British film and there was both popular and critical acclaim for this breakthrough. In May 1940 the *Documentary News Letter* expressed pleasure at the Government's initiative and at the way in which the public itself was showing so much interest 'in the wartime drama of the common people'. It particularly appreciated the way in which the use of 'real people' in the telling of stories had helped to overcome the traditional artificiality of the British cinema.[3] There was widespread pleasure at the freshness and authenticity of British documentaries. Writing just after the war the critic Dilys Powell recalled that she had always found pre-war documentaries to be honest and worthy if somewhat lacking in humanity whereas the wartime documentaries had immediately struck a new note. In particular she had found Harry Watt's 1941 film *Target for Tonight* to be a turning-point:

> The actors were serving airmen, the dialogue was simple, realistic, ironic in the English manner .... But somehow imagination had irradiated a plain story of the everyday experience; the audience, excited and moved, shared the adventures of these young airmen who fought for them in such solitude and against such odds: there was a new genre in the cinema, a fact, a fragment of actual life which still held the emotional tremor of fiction.[4]

Powell went on to describe how in 1943 and 1944 London audiences had been stunned by the brilliance of Soviet documentaries but she had felt that British films like *Desert Victory* and *Burma Victory* could now stand comparison. Then in 1945 came the Anglo-American *The True Glory* directed by Carol Reed and Garson Kanin and this, Powell felt, had left the Soviets far behind. The great virtue of this particular film was that it brilliantly depicted 'the common experience of an army of human beings' and Powell concluded that the technique of 'letting the fighting man speak for himself in his own accents' had made the film into not only a 'historical document' but also 'a human document'. This praise was echoed not only by other British critics but also in New York and Hollywood itself, where there was a very real appreciation that British documentary techniques had opened up a new chapter in film-making. Film historians too have fully appreciated the importance of what had happened to non-fiction films in wartime Britain and Richard Meran Barsam has spoken of the way in which that moving and eloquent 'record of British unity, patriotism and humanity in time of peril' added up to 'an extraordinary achievement'.[5]

It is difficult to argue with the notion that the wartime documentaries provide one of the great moments in British film history and to this day they not only provide a wonderful record of the war effort but also retain the power to move anyone who either lived through that period or grew up when the war was still part of living memory. In a way the films themselves were so much better than anything that had gone before and they have become so much a part of a certain kind of nostalgia that it is difficult to think objectively about them. The film historian, however, should note one or two points with regard to the often very remarkable films. It should be remembered for example that they were not always so well received by contemporary audiences as they were by intellectual critics and subsequent historians. Dilys Powell shared the *Documentary News Letter*'s enthusiasm that audiences were enjoying films of actuality and she recalled with pleasure how she had gone to an isolated Welsh mining town and seen how 'at the end of the day's work, miners and their wives sat rapt and silent through a documentary record of the making of an airscrew'.[6] One suspects that in this recollection Powell was developing a somewhat romantically exaggerated myth of the war years for other observers noted that even less provincial audiences sometimes had difficulty with realism. In 1941 Ernest Betts spoke to Charles Kohn, the manager of the Granada Woolwich, who reported that film taste was now being made in the air-raid shelters and that the mood there was against war films and in favour of escapism.[7] In 1943 Roger Manvell reported that audiences had been greatly embarrassed by documentary films and that in particular 'people who see themselves in a documentary nearly always laugh their heads off'. His argument was that audiences were so used to the conventions of melodrama that anything which smacks of real life really disorientated them and he found that this was true especially of violence or of actors trying to use everyday swear-words. In the feature film *In Which We Serve* the actors had sworn and so a taboo had been broken, a convention of accepted artificiality had been smashed and the experience, said Manvell, was rather 'like taking your uglier underclothes off in front of a comparatively well-dressed assembly'.[8] In his 1948 account of London cinemas during the war Guy Morgan not only recalled that war subjects were unpopular until 1942 but concluded that 'the British public, as a whole, has never been cajoled into loving the documentary'. Morgan excepted *Target for Tonight* and *Desert Victory* but maintained that in general all the 'Herculean efforts' of the Ministry of Information had not been able to counter the public's intolerance of war films.[9] One senses that in the war the new film genre provided immense satisfaction for many film-makers and critics but that the exhibitors and public, whilst being respectful of the best, were for the most part unenthusiastic. There was always a desire for hard information but once that had been given audiences wanted to turn away from the war and be entertained. Several observers noted in particular that there was a strong popular dislike of anything that appeared to be propaganda, although in this respect Ministry of Information films were never put in the same category as those feature films which had been given a rather crude and obvious message. Throughout the war there seemed to be a dislike of films which attempted to deal with what were called 'social developments'.[10]

This last point is interesting because it is obvious that only a small percentage of wartime documentaries dealt specifically with social developments. The main theme of these films was a people at war and that meant inevitably that groups in society were examined from a particular standpoint. The bulk of the films depicted fighting men or workers in key wartime industries and civilians were only brought in to show the tremendous resilience and indefatigable energy of ordinary people at times of crisis.[11] In the majority of films what audiences saw was precisely the kind of national identity and public mood that the Government sought to encourage. As the *Documentary News Letter (DNL)* argued far too many documentaries had only 'a purely ephemeral how-the-wheels-go-round interest' and were propaganda only for bureaucracy: 'with a few small changes (such as different uniforms) they'd do equally well as German or Japanese propaganda'.[12] Whatever freshness real people brought to even the average documentary it was only the exceptional film that broke out of the official mould. What was possible was suggested by three 1943 films. Humphrey Jennings's *Fires were Started* used 'real people' to tell the story of the blitz and in particular to record the contribution of London firemen. The *DNL* found that the film was characterized by 'the best handling of people on and off the job that we've seen in any British film', that it offered 'maybe for the first time - proper working-class dialogue', and that all in all it was 'a fine and fruitful record of a way of living and doing a job that *did* work and of a discipline that came from the job itself',[13] Jennings had indeed made a marvellous film, certainly one of the best films ever made about the process of work and also about London, but the *DNL*'s reviewer quite rightly draws our attention to one or two moments that indicate precisely why and how the film was made. *Fires were Started* was an official film and throughout there is an exaggerated emphasis on how all the classes came together in the London fire service whilst the film ends with the rather crude and over-simplified proof that fire-fighting was worthwhile as the munitions ship sails safely out of the docks. The *News Letter* also spotted three or four occasions when 'with somebody playing the piano or reading or reciting poetry' Jennings had gone 'all arty for a moment'. We are reminded that British documentary rested on a pact between Civil Servants who wanted to maintain national morale and a group of film-makers who had their own distinctive view of the people. Jennings was a left-wing poet and artist whom the war had allowed to bring to fruition his view of the English people as a civilized bulwark against the offence of Fascism and ignorance.[14] It was his love of the cultural and Socialist values inherent in working-class life that inspired his films and allowed him to choose those telling details and revealing moments that it became important for his camera to record. Before his early death in 1950 Jennings had made a number of films but by far his best work had come in *Fires were Started* and then in his other film of 1943 *The Silent*

Village, which he made as a tribute to the people of Lidice, who had been the victims of a Nazi massacre. To depict the impact of Nazi occupation Jennings chose the inhabitants of a small Welsh-speaking mining village and his choice was quite inspired. Cwmgiedd was a picture-postcard village that was more rural than urban. Jennings found the local miners' leader to be 'a tremendous Tolstoyan figure of a man' and he was over-whelmed by the miners' love of education, of Socialism, and of boxing, and the way in which all of them knew more about the Soviets than they knew about Surrey. What Jennings had found was real enough but Cwmgiedd was far from being a typical working-class community. It was rather the perfect discovery for a man in search of a Tolstoyan peasantry. *The Silent Village* is a wonderfully moving hymn of praise to an essen-tially pastoral community and in this case real people were acting out and confirming one intellectual's private vision. At the very time he was making this film Jennings spoke at a seminar on documentary film and in his remarks he conveyed all the enthusiasm of the 1930s intellectual who had just discovered the people and at the same time revealed a good deal about the relationship between film directors and the people:

I have found people extra helpful and extra charming in war time. They are living in a more heightened existence and are much more prepared to open their arms and fall into somebody else's.

To that extent they are walking the same way that we are, to that extent they are better film material, and the emotion that they them-selves are feeling is part of the emotion that we indeed are always attempting to use and to propagate about life.[15]

Jennings's films were very personal but for all his belief in the poten-tial and beauty of the working class his filmic vision of it was not really very different from that of the general run of Government films in which happy people went about their tasks with perhaps only the occasional grumble as they worked for the good of all and for an eventual victory. Far more challenging was Paul Rotha's *World of Plenty*, which was also made for the Ministry of Information in 1943. Film historians have rather criticized Rotha's examination of the world's food crisis for its somewhat pretentious, slick, and diffuse assemblage of statistics, graphics, interviews, and discussion but at the same time they acknowledge the power of his argument that massive State intervention was needed both to regulate food distribution and to plan the post-war world.[16] Contemporary critics were far more struck by the way in which film techniques had been used to convey a point of view for here at last was a documentary that broke away from an uncritical and sentimental celebration of the war effort. The *News Chronicle* thought it 'as dramatic as any thriller'; the *Evening Standard* thought it revealed 'the whole art of advocacy'; *The Times* found that it treated a complicated problem seriously whilst keeping 'expectant and amused the spectator's pleasure-loving eye'.[17] To the *New Statesman* the film was 'much more than a first-class documentary'; it was also 'a political event' and that, of course, was precisely what Rotha had intended and what several other documentary film-makers would like to have done if they had been given the chance.[18] There was to be a handful of subsequent films which looked forward to a post-war welfare state, notably Rotha's own *Children of the City* and *Land of Promise*, but there was never really a political cinema in Britain in the Second World War. Of course in Government films we see people at work in factories, shipyards, and mines but we never see these people on their own terms. In 1947 Doreen Willis looked back over the preceding few years and acknowledged that documentary films had 'helped to orientate people to the complex workings of industrial society while assisting them in the fight for a better deal' but she also argued that the definition of their work normally used by the film-makers, namely, the 'creative interpretation of actuality', should have implied more 'than photographing sweaty faces, slum housing and the gyrating of machines'. What she found 'almost breathtaking' was the ease with which an organized audience of eight million trade-unionists and nine million co-operative families had been ignored.[19] The war had allowed the filming of ordinary people, had given a few artists the chance to indulge themselves, and after lengthy battles had even allowed political statements about housing and food, but what it had not done was to allow an independent documentary cinema. The Government had largely used documentary for its own purposes and as yet the labour movement itself continued to show no great interest in using film as part of its own propaganda. The war had given documentary film-makers new opportunities. They had moved from the sidelines into the mainstream and their films were more widely seen and greatly praised than ever before but, to the real disciples of the faith, all the wartime publicity had really disguised the fact that there had been no real breakthrough in terms of documentary's real purpose. Rotha's judgement was that 'the purpose of the documentary idea so clearly defined in the 1930s became lost during the war, for, however good some of the films were technically, there had been no 'real common policy' except that films should be made in what was allegedly 'the national interest'. What was vital to Rotha's concept of documentary was 'social good purpose' and that, of course, he took to mean rather more than sentimental patriotism.[20]

There was praise for British documentary but, delighted as people were to see ordinary people in British films, one suspects that such films were more often regarded as being worthy rather than startling or even entertaining. And in any case feature films were always thought of as being more important. The general view was nicely summed up by Dilys Powell when she argued that 'ultimately it is on the quality of its entertainment films that the prestige of a national cinema must rest' for 'we judge a country's literature not by its text books . . . but rather by its imaginative works'.[21] With the release in the early months of the war of *The Stars Looked Down* and *The Proud Valley* there was every expectation that British cinema was progressing towards a much fuller and more sustained social commentary. In confirmation of this 1941 saw the appearance of John Baxter's *Love on the Dole*, a film that the censors had on several occasions blocked before the war, and the first of Baxter's films to receive any widespread publicity.[22] In fact it is difficult to think of a British film that received quite so much initial praise as this film version of Walter Greenwood's original novel and Ronald Gow's subsequent dramatic adaptation. It was highly praised by the *Spectator*'s Edgar Anstey, who later chose it as his film of the year, and a reviewer for the Rank Organization hailed it as a 'first-class British production'.[23] It was interesting that this Rank reviewer had no doubt that the film would do good business and the mood of those days was even reflected in his suggestion that the 'good title' had been an 'undeniable pull'. He described the film as a 'poignant drama of the industrial depression' and 'a moving tragedy of environment' but without any hesitation or further explanation he went on to say that it held 'great entertainment values and strong human interest'. What critics liked about *Love on the Dole* was its unrelieved realism. Anstey found it so real that he had difficulty in believing that 'it came out of a film studio' whilst *Kine Weekly* described it as a 'documentary of compelling power' which 'told the truth honestly' and which depicted authentically 'the working and living conditions in a typical drab pre-war English industrial town'.[24] Quite unusually for a British film the critics went on to praise the way in which the acting had sustained the realism. What had been vital in this respect was spotted by the *New Statesman*'s William Whitebait, who commented on Baxter's use 'of a new set of actors (always best in a film of this kind)' whose performances were 'striking, while never showing tuppence-coloured against the penny-plain background'.[25] There was acclaim in particular for the 20-year-old Scottish actress Deborah Kerr, who played the part of a girl whose father and brother were unemployed and whose whole family was being forced into grinding poverty. The climax of the film was probably one of the most shocking moments that British audiences of that period had ever seen for the young girl goes off to become a bookie's tart so as to improve her family's fortunes. Perhaps no single dramatic development so effectively conveyed the despair generated by 1930s poverty and although Deborah Kerr had many of the usual vocal limitations of young British starlets she was, on this occasion, able to convey an intensity and an anxiety that earned real conviction. Ernest Betts praised her performance and urged a more general acceptance of her own advice to other actors and actresses that one should just 'be yourself'.[26]

6 *Love On The Dole*: The intensity of Deborah Kerr suggests that British realism had at last arrived.

Baxter was praised for having so effectively depicted working-class life but what critics liked even more about this film was that it constituted an argument. For Edgar Anstey *Love on the Dole* was clear proof that there was free speech in wartime Britain but furthermore it demonstrated 'that the one inconceivable war aim would be a return to the status quo ante'.[27] Here was a powerful manifestation that the British people were fighting not only to defeat the Nazis but also to banish for ever the poverty of the last decade. 'It is in many respects a direct challenge to democracy,' said *Kine Weekly* but then went on to explain that the film was not just crude propaganda. What the journal described as 'axe-grinding' had been avoided because the facts had been 'faithfully' presented and the story had been told honestly and sensitively.[28] The truth that no 1930s film had even been allowed to tell was now acted out in such a way that almost everybody could acknowledge the power and inevitability of the argument. The praise was not just for a realistic British film but for a film that could effectively use a social drama to sustain a clear point of view and it was that which made this such an exceptional film. *Kine Weekly* concluded that the film was a 'documentary of compelling power' but also of 'urgent provocation'. The journal's argument was that Baxter was an artist and that his skills had transformed 'sociological melodrama' into a statement of artistic and social truth. What it liked in particular was the film's sense 'that life goes on' as well as its final assertion that there was indeed hope: this was truly a 'profound kaleidoscope' and the entertainment was surely of 'Dickensian stature and humanity'. Later British audiences were quite able to appreciate the honesty and social starkness of *Love on the Dole* but they were also more likely to notice that it was a low-budget film, an almost pre-television studio drama, and to feel that it was based very much on classic nineteenth-century melodrama. The high praise of contemporary critics was very much a reflection of their surprise that Britain could come up with such an outspoken condemnation, albeit of a set of circumstances that was rapidly disappearing, and also of their deeply held conviction that the film was pointing out the way in which British cinema should develop. Above all British films were becoming significant. Ernest Betts contrasted Baxter's film with the latest Bette Davis vehicle, a version of Somerset Maugham's story *The Letter*. The Hollywood film was a 'cracking good film', a smooth classic melodrama that was 'first-class entertainment', but to Betts it was of 'no significance while *Love on the Dole* blazes with it'. His summing up of *The Letter* was that 'in these times we can't be bothered with potty little murders like these' for what British people wanted and what British producers should be making were pictures like *Love on the Dole*, which had depicted 'the nation showing fight, a much grander, more human fight'. It was not often that British critics could use a native film to do down Hollywood and one can still appreciate the relish with which Betts wrote in 1941.[29]

Baxter's film was singled out for special praise but it was also taken as the pick of a bunch of more significant and more social films. Anstey put *Love on the Dole* alongside *Major Barbara* and *Kipps* as evidence that British films could compare with Hollywood's best and that a 'form of national expression' was being evolved. He had used the phrase 'a deeply moving social study' to describe *Love on the Dole* and like so many critics that now became the formula that he wanted to see repeated. The arrival in 1942 of Hollywood's *How Green was my Valley* which showed 'the quality of ordinary people' and which was a reminder 'of many powers that the cinema normally left unused' was further evidence of the way in which the film should develop. What was especially pleasing was that the public seemed to like these new social dramas. Bill Thornton, the manager of the Odeon Leicester Square, reported that *The Stars Look Down* had broken all records at his theatre and he was confident (somewhat mistakenly as it transpired) that *Love on the Dole* would go on to do the same thing.[30] All forces seemed to be moving in the same direction for the director Michael Powell told Ernest Betts that his colleagues in the film industry were not prepared to work on 'tuppeny-halfpenny subjects about blondes and jazz and what happens down Argentine way' and that they would be off to do war work if they were not given films that meant something, that were 'real'.[31] Perhaps the mood of 1941 was best summed up by a conversation Ernest Betts had with the directors Leslie Howard and Anthony Asquith. Both men admitted that the film industry was in a difficult position for as yet there was no real evidence that the Government had realized how important film could be in the war and neither was there conclusive evidence on whether audiences wanted realism or 'the tinsel of make-believe'. On the whole Asquith was taking the war pretty coolly and he was sure that the entertainment film would take 'propaganda and documentary themes' in its stride. But Howard was obviously quite beside himself with joy at the new prospects that were opening up. For years, said Howard, he had been making films about other people's ideas but now he was making films according to his own ideas: in fact, he argued, there was going on a great conflict of ideas, so 'why can't the cinema join in this?' Both men, said Betts, were demanding quality instead of trivia, both thought that 'the proper job of film' was 'to tell the whole world the sort of people we are', and both thought that it was 'time we had a sort of social significance on the screen'. 'In short' concluded Betts, 'they want the cinema to grow up.'[32]

Looking now at this enthusiasm of 1941 we can only conclude that there must have been considerable disappointment during the years that made up the rest of the war. There was to be warm praise for individual films which concerned themselves to a greater or lesser extent with ordinary people but it can hardly be argued that feature films entered into the great conflict of ideas or grew up in the ways that directors like Howard and Asquith wanted. In particular there was no serious attempt to build on the foundations that had been established by *Love on the Dole*. In 1941 *Kine Weekly* had suggested that it was John Baxter's childhood experience of the industrial North that gave him his insight into the working class but it must be admitted that even his subsequent work was never as satisfactory as *Love on the Dole* and it certainly received far less attention. *The Common Touch* was a very strange and somewhat confused allegory that was meant as a tribute to 'the humble people of our great cities' whose courage and endurance had become the basis of national survival. The story is simply crazy and the middle-class characters are hopeless caricatures but there is a wonderful range of working-class, or rather lumpen, cockney characters who give the film a real ballast. Again we are more in the world of Dickens than the contemporary East End. Perhaps to outsiders ordinary Londoners can indeed seem to be very Dickensian but to limit a tribute to city-dwellers to essentially nineteenth-century stereotypes is only a limited form of realism. Edward Rigby was a marvellous cockney type and his final prediction that the post-war world would be like 'Heaven on earth' was genuinely moving but on the whole the film was somewhat contrived and sentimental. Edgar Anstey liked Baxter's 1942 film *Let the People Sing*, especially for the way it communicated something of the nature of British democracy for we are actually shown debate, disagreement, and dissatisfaction with the police, but he also admitted that it was 'an insubstantial little piece of Priestley parochialism'.[33] *The Shipbuilders*, released in 1944, offered a much fuller picture of working-class existence. Edgar Anstey praised it for depicting many aspects of Glasgow life such as the dereliction of the shipyards, the meanness of the streets, the domestic consequences of unemployment, the impact of the blitz, the catharsis of football, and above all the home and work routines of working-class families. Nevertheless he also thought that the film had serious weaknesses for it was not smoothly constructed, it was sentimental, and above all 'the economic issues were simplified down to a point at which one is left feeling that every feat of economic and sociological organisation can be achieved by kindness'.[34] There is no hint in the film of Clydeside's traditional militancy and sophistication and the argument that the whole community should concern itself with strengthening the shipbuilding industry is made in sentimental rather than political terms. Baxter was indeed sentimental but to look at his career is to be reminded of Nicholas Pronay's point that as far as British feature films were concerned censorship was always the first reality.[35] The long-standing objection to films dealing with industrial relations had been somewhat relaxed at the start of the war but was then reinforced with equal effect. As Pronay and Jeremy Croft have argued British censorship was always informal rather than systematic but it was no less effective because of that and the wartime practice of Government control over the allocation of film stock was used to ensure that films 'impregnated with propaganda messages' received the fullest encouragement.[36] John Baxter was indulged and his talent for using the working-class idiom was restricted to a number of sentimental tales which were never regarded as major films. The prestige films were those in which all classes and all sections came together to sustain the war effort.

The reputation of British cinema during the war rested on a small number of films which without in any way endangering morale nevertheless depicted the war and the involvement of ordinary people in what was taken to be an honest way. In retrospect we can see that many aspects of the war were neglected – for example the blitz was one very obvious omission – and there was never any attempt to tell the whole military and social truth, but there were sufficient integrity and vitality in the films to convince contemporary audiences and critics that British films were worth while. Very crucial in this respect was the way in which film-makers avoided crude propaganda and did not attempt artificially to implant messages in feature films in the way that, much to the annoyance of British audiences, Hollywood persisted in doing. Equally important, though, were more positive factors. What happened in effect was that the studios did not opt for total realism but rather managed to develop conventions and a style that conformed very closely to the contemporary idioms of ordinary British people. What was vital was the contribution of actors and writers. Early in 1942 Edgar Anstey argued that 'screen-acting must be above all a pursuit of naturalism' and added that 'British acting, like British production as a whole, has gone on steadily overhauling Hollywood'. With George Carney's performances for John Baxter very much in mind he suggested that 'the most pronounced advance has been amongst the small-part players where British production once was weakest'.[37] This became something of an orthodoxy and critics and trade papers frequently spoke of 'brilliant characterizations' and 'fine portrayals'. With the parts of ordinary people being written a veritable repertory company of British actors, many of them new, now emerged to flesh out films and to give them a new freshness. There was always special praise if the actors in any film were totally unknown but even the old faithfuls were thought of as bringing reality to the new British cinema.

All of this contrasts very markedly with later responses that were to stress the shortcomings of British acting and characterization at this time. Many later audiences were to find these films disappointing precisely because the acting seemed so conventional and the characterizations were largely based on stereotypes. The phrase 'repertory company' is almost a give-away because that is precisely how many later observers have thought of wartime British actors. They were in Charles Barr's phrase 'a working-class stock company' and they turned up in film after film to play wisecracking cockneys, dour Scots, garrulous Welshmen, down-to-earth Northerners, or country bumpkins.[38] Sue Aspinall has even suggested that it was 'the unfamiliarity of middle-class writers, directors, producers and actors with working-class life' that led to the dependence on 'familiar stereotypes from comedy or music hall'.[39] What we need to do here is to reconcile the views of those who either at the time or since enjoyed British wartime acting with the views of those who have been all too aware of caricature. We should remember that the contribution of the writers was as important as that of the actors. What they did was to invent dialogue and a conversational style that obviously avoided anything that was overtly political or controversial but which nevertheless suggested that ordinary people had lives and values of their own, that they were not just going to be cannon-fodder, that they were not push-overs, and that if there was such a thing as Britishness then it was precisely here in the spirit, humour, and slight irreverence of ordinary people that it was to be found. British film-makers undoubtedly aimed at a new naturalism in their films but what realism they achieved depended more on the way that individual actors and especially comedy actors made use of dialogue rather than any great breakthrough in acting technique as such. There were far more natural and sincere performances than in the past but it was the wit and vitality of the more theatrical performers which gave the films their edge and which stayed in the memory. The new naturalness was very worthy but it was the coming together of old music-hall acting and good lines that made British films more real.

It was at Ealing that they specialized in this new British idiom and where they were in time to create a new kind of film. In the 1942 film *The Foreman Went to France* the story tells of an ordinary workman who goes to France to rescue some vital machinery. This is a wartime adventure film and it is fascinating that the whole action rested on the exploits of very ordinary people and that they were allowed mild criticism of official bureaucracy and red tape. The whole impact of the film, though, depends not on the story itself but rather on the acting, on the dialogue, and especially on the playing of Tommy Trinder as the wisecracking cockney. The Rank reviewer referred to 'the comedy flashes' of Tommy Trinder and 'flashes' is the right word for the authenticity and vitality of this and so many of these wartime films depended more often on asides and wisecracks than on the story as such.[40] There was certainly a commitment to naturalness but very few films were prepared to go all the way in that direction. To depict ordinary people was to risk staleness in a film. Ealing's *San Demetrio London*, which was made as a tribute to the merchant navy, was perhaps one of the most honest films made in the war for it was a drama based almost exclusively on the experiences of working-class people. The film is certainly interesting inasmuch as it quite clearly suggests that ordinary people could be heroic and that they could take initiative without official prompting and meddling but the social historian can only wryly reflect on the ways that the people were only allowed to display these sterling qualities within a tightly controlled wartime situation. Certainly *San Demetrio* is the story of an ordinary bunch of civilians but they come to us contained within their merchant navy roles. Furthermore this film did reveal the danger that what was ordinary could all too easily become mundane and mediocre and here the low-key natural acting is only acceptable because of the suspense and melodrama inherent in the wartime story. What was questionable was whether this ordinary and almost anonymous acting could be used as the basis for social melodrama. In 1942 Frank Launder and Sidney Gilliat made *Millions Like Us* as a

tribute to ordinary people at home and in particular to the women working in munitions factories. The Rank reviewer thought that it presented
'telling realisations of wartime conditions' and that it was a picture which
'pulsates with the very spirit of wartime Britain'.[41] The spirit of the
people might have been suggested by the posh voices of the starlets in
their upper working-class home, or the hopelessly exaggerated acting of
an apparently wealthy socialite and a poor Geordie girl, or even by the
almost painful ordinariness and baby-talk of Gordon Jackson's airman
hero but audiences would have been far more convinced and entertained
by the humour and asides. At the start of the film the audience was asked
to recall those pre-war days when eggs came out of shells and the Government only took some of your money; later we see a member of the Home
Guard taking a drink to 'fortify himself' and someone comments 'that's
the only fortification we've got'; the father eats a sausage and comments
that 'What's in this sausage is a mystery, and I hope it's not solved in my
time.' The film has some good serious moments such as when Megs
Jenkins reflects on how the wartime hostel used by the factory girls was
so much better than conditions in the mining districts just a few years
previously ('It's took a War to do it, but if somebody is going to develop
a social conscience I'm not going to sneeze at it'), but in general it was
the wit which gave the film its edge. We see the ubiquitous Basil Radford
and Naunton Wayne laying mines on a beach and Wayne comments 'we
must remember not to bathe here after the War'. That was the stuff of
British realism.

Towards the end of the war Sidney Gilliat made *Waterloo Road*, a film
that was very much about 'the people' and in particular 'the little people',
as Alistair Sim refers to them in the opening shots. Sim plays the part
of a doctor who doubles up as narrator and his whole point is that in the
war 'the little people' had their battles too. The film is a very creditable
tribute to ordinary people and certainly it deals very directly with the
way in which several different groups had become disorientated by the
war. The working-man hero admits that he was 'doing nicely before the
War' and before he was called up: he had been working in a locomotive
repair-shop but he had set his heart on becoming an engineer and on
taking his wife to a new house in the suburbs well away from the
working-class Waterloo Road. His wife too had seen her ambitions
frustrated by the war and Alistair Sim warns that women become
rebellious if their 'beaver instinct' was denied. Most spectacularly the film
admits that there was a group of 'spivs' in the country who had dodged
the war and spent their time in bars, pin-table saloons, at the pictures
'picking up a few hints from Victor Mature', and 'jitterbugging at the
Alcazar' with the wives and girlfriends of serving men. According to Sim
'these people would swear away their own grandmother for a packet of
Woodbines'. It was certainly a strikingly frank film and it had a real sense

of place – it was very much a London film – but that hard-earned authenticity was inevitably diluted by some traditional British faults. John Mills is acceptable as an ordinary soldier only because he is totally lack-lustre and he uses a kind of intense earnestness as the basis of his realism. He is totally mismatched with Joy Shelton, who is very sexy, but, as was so often the case in British films, she is too posh and harsh for the family context in which she was placed. Stewart Granger is suitably oily as Ted Purvis the spiv but as an ex-fighter he sports a nose that had never been punched and at the end he collapses into smiles and sentimentality and so surrenders any real edge that he had earlier struggled to achieve. Nevertheless the film retains its authenticity by the acting of some of the lesser characters and by its mastery of cockney humour and idiom, and in particular a pub scene which uses good music-hall patter keeps us squarely on terra firma. In the pub the song title 'La donna è mobile' is instantly translated to 'Woman is mobile' and is therefore authoritatively attributed to the Minister of Labour, Mr Bevin. Pretty girls apart, and it is the lovely Jean Kent who really steals the movie, it was the writers who gave so many of the films their real edge.

The approach to realism was a matter of convention and technique. What critics liked best were the films which showed ordinary people becoming fighting men or putting up with the ordeals of war. Both Noel Coward's *In Which We Serve* and Harry Watt's *Nine Men* were highly praised but it was Carol Reed's *The Way Ahead* which was immediately acclaimed as the most successful British war film. What Carol Reed and his writers Eric Ambler and Peter Ustinov had attempted to do in *The Way Ahead* was best summed up in the press-book's assertion that wars were not won by strategy and production but also by 'men and women'. This was going to be 'a plain tale of typical Britons of this generation who were called from the plough, the bench, the office: the man with the white collar, the man without a collar' and so on. Just like the film itself the advance publicity aimed to cover every angle and to appeal to every section: 'Yesterday he was your husband, my son, their brother, the man next door, the chap over the way, that lad from the village.' What audiences would be shown was the way in which 'a travel agent's clerk, a boilerman, a road-house playboy, a Welsh rent collector, a Scottish labourer, a shop assistant, a businessman with nervous indigestion, a man who wanted to go into the Navy, and other relevant characters were made into soldiers. An important clue to the production team's approach was given in the reminder that 'when the British civilian goes to war he takes with him those qualities of rueful pessimism, of humour, and of broad humanity which makes him in the end one of the most formidable fighting men in the world'. There had been much talk of 'Tommy Atkins'; 'Well,' said the press-book, 'here is his film.'[42]

Those were ambitious intentions and claims but the film was one that more than lived up to its promises. It stood out from other British films because of its tantalizing, somewhat ambiguous, and controversial ending and because the whole quality of the writing seemed so much better. David Niven was joined by a platoon recruited from the usual repertory company but that definitive cockney Stanley Holloway and his gang were now given a script that had all the wit and irony of a Hollywood film. C. A. Lejeune thought that the film had 'a real script', that the dialogue had a 'cutting edge', and she found the whole thing startling. She knew of 'few films that can bring the audience on such close human terms with the people on the screen . . . . *The Way Ahead* actually plays and talks like life.'[43]

It was generally agreed that *The Way Ahead* was a great film but the very positive response to the film raised several questions. In a sense the very praise given to Carol Reed's film came as a reminder of how inadequate most British films were. At the end of the war British critics were still complaining about how badly written most British dialogue was and C. A. Lejeune, for example, was still emphasizing how much young actors could learn from the way in which someone like Cagney could convert a poor part into an exuberant and ingenious creation. Furthermore the success of a film that dealt with ordinary people in a military context now posed the question as to whether the same kind of success could be achieved with post-war domestic subjects.[44] When she first saw *The Way Ahead* Miss Lejeune wondered whether the film people were now thinking seriously about what she described as 'the gravest reorientation in history'. Her hope was precisely that 'they will apply to the adjustment of a nation at peace the same specialised attention they have applied to the encouragement of a nation at war' and that someone was 'planning a film to show how a good soldier can be turned back into a good civilian'.[45] Here was the clear implication that showing ordinary people at war was perhaps a shade easier than depicting them coping with everyday life. Much the same implication was to be found in Dilys Powell's post-war reflections. She was, as we have seen, greatly impressed by Britain's wartime films but she knew that what had happened was only a step towards maturity and towards realism. For Powell the war films had been uneven but they showed 'a movement towards a national subject'. What the war had done was to 'set the English film on the path in which masterpieces may be created'.[46] Much the same view was expressed by the *Documentary News Letter*, which argued 'that we have not yet succeeded in making the British film industry a medium of expression of the British people and the British view, though it is nearer to it than at any time before'.[47]

During the war the actual content of feature films suggested that film could well develop into an indigenous 'medium of expression for the British people' but there were other factors that made for optimism. The quite tremendous popularity of the cinema was providing much food for thought at a time when there was of necessity a new interest in the whole phenomenon of national identity, mass culture, and public morale. Before the war the masses had gone to the pictures, intellectuals and Socialists tried to organize the showing of better films, and a few critics and social observers had begun to think about films more seriously, but that very much was that. What happened during the war was that there was a filling out of film's role within British society and culture, both films themselves and film-going were taken more seriously by critics, politicians, and social observers, and a debate emerged in which facts, theories, and new developments were fully analysed. It was to be in the five years immediately after the war that the debate on film in Britain became a matter of the utmost political and cultural significance but it was during the war that interest first developed and possibilities were first understood.

Quite basic to this fuller understanding of the significance of film was a new awareness and appreciation of film audiences themselves. Before the war questionnaires had made their appearance and there had been a good deal of rhetoric about the impact of film on young children but in fact the mass audience had been very much taken for granted by almost everybody. In the early months of the war Leonard England of Mass Observation looked at audiences responding to the new documentary films and wondered whether 'the increase in such films will increase the amount of cinema response and turn the cinema-goer from a passive creature into someone more alert and civilized because the new film subjects are more near to everyday life'.[48] A wider range of films might well have breathed more life into audiences but the significance of this somewhat patronizing observation is that it reminds us that film audiences became more alert very largely because more people, and that included politicians, producers, exhibitors, critics, and social scientists, suddenly decided that they were interesting and important. Mass Observation had been interested in cinema audiences for some time and in particular had used its intensive study of 'Worktown' (Bolton) to build up a detailed picture of who precisely went to the cinema and what it was that they wanted to see when they got there.[49] With this expertise it was not surprising that Mass Observation was greatly amused by the Government's panic at the start of the war and continued to be shocked by how little the Ministry of Information's Film Department actually did and especially by its taking no steps at all to check up on the effect of its own films. Mass Observation leaped into the gap and was soon accumulating massive amounts of information about film audiences throughout the country. There was always something rather ludicrous about the way Mass Observation's observers noted every cough, yawn, jeer, and snore as they dutifully visited all kinds of cinemas and in their reports one can

find abundant quotations to substantiate any theory one cares to choose
for there were old ladies who loved American gangster films and young
people who preferred British comedies and so on. There were many
different types of film-goer and each cinema certainly had its own distinctive audience but even then tastes could change very quickly. In
November 1939 the manager of the Classic Tooting told Mass Observation
that his strategy was 'to keep putting on films, some are flops, some are
OK. Then you work on the good ones', but he wryly added that 'it is the
turn of the card – which way the people act'. Like all exhibitors he had
studied his audience and he had his own pet theories: in his suburban
middle-class audience there were many women so war films were out but
adaptations of books were very much in ('good readers make good
patrons') although the success of *Pygmalion* he attributed largely to the
great interest in the moment when the actress says 'no bloody fear'.[50]
The great audience was indeed pluralistic and there was a whole gamut
of responses to any particular film. Formby and Old Mother Riley were
loved in Bolton and hated in Surrey, and somehow most audiences seemed
to have the knack of laughing at the wrong moment, and of jeering at the
moments of greatest suspense; some films were accompanied throughout
by full audience participation, others were greeted with total indifference.
The evidence was confusing and fascinating but perhaps out of millions
of details some kind of picture began to emerge. Audiences were quite
prepared for the truth and for basic information but they did not want
propaganda, either in newsreels or in feature films. At first there was an
interest in war subjects but then audiences tired of them. At every point
and in nearly all cinemas people wanted first and foremost to be entertained, they wanted good films. There were still many who preferred
American films, but there was evidence that interest had declined in
certain kinds of American films whilst there was considerably more
enthusiasm for the best British films. Many sections of the public seemed
more interested in realistic films or in films that dealt with familiar and
recognizable subjects but that did not mean that they wanted grim or
unhappy tales. *Love on the Dole* had been hailed by the critics but it was
a box-office disaster; everybody knew that *Mrs Miniver*, made in
Hollywood as a tribute to the British people, was somewhat dishonest and
unreal but it was one of the biggest smash-hits of the war. It was often
the case that what critics liked cut no ice with the public and at the
King's Hall, Penge, an observer was watching *Citizen Kane* when he
overheard three women speak:

> 'Funny picture isn't it.'
> 'Peculiar'
> 'What's it all about?'[51]

In 1941 *Picturegoer Weekly* presented Mass Observation with over 1,500 readers' letters, amongst them a contribution from S. A. Girling of Norwich, who recalled Ma Joad's declaration in *The Grapes of Wrath*, 'They can't lick us 'cause we're the people' as one of the great moments in cinema history, and also one from J. Chambers of Wombwell, who thought that the film had been rather boosted by the critics whereas in fact 'it only aggravated the painful realities of everyday life'![52]

As the war progressed so more and more information about audiences became available. The Ministry of Information itself used the Wartime Social Survey to acquire a detailed knowledge of film-going. It would have noted that whilst 70 per cent of adults sometimes went to the cinemas there was within that larger audience a distinct section of true film enthusiasts, and that the lower paid and least educated went more often than the higher paid and better educated. It would have particularly noted the argument that the cinema could be a valuable public medium in that its publicity reached 'some of those groups in the population which are less open to the influences of other media - women, the younger age groups, the lower economic groups and those with elementary education'.[53] All these facts were of interest to the bureaucratic mind but meanwhile the most important and exciting revelation thrown up by the wartime observers was that there was now a new popular enthusiasm for British films. Of course the overall situation was complex but the pattern that emerged was that, whilst there were still many Hollywood enthusiasts, audiences in general had become more irritated by Hollywood excesses in the spheres of propaganda, sentimentality, violence, slang, and patriotism. As far as British films themselves were concerned it was clear that the old music-hall stars like Formby and Old Mother Riley had retained their popularity and even won through to new audiences, but this information was thought less important than the fact that both critics and audiences were now enjoying prestige British productions. Audiences, it was true, still preferred entertainment and escapism but they also seemed ready now for more serious stuff. Perhaps the most encouraging thing of all was they now liked British stars, often preferring them to their well-established American equivalents and, what was crucial, these home-grown stars now tended to be serious actors and actresses rather than the old music-hall stars. *The Bernstein Questionnaire* of 1946-7 gave dramatic proof of these trends although it is interesting that Hollywood films were still far more highly praised for their technical qualities.[54] From all sides the evidence seemed to suggest that film was going to play an increasingly important part in the lives of the people, and especially in the lives of 'impressionable people', and that at last audiences were responding to both British stories and British stars. There seemed to be a strong argument for and every encouragement for the British to take film more seriously: certainly audiences seemed poised for some kind of domestic breakthrough.

The British film audience was really discovered during the Second World War and so too, in a way, was the British film industry. At the time of the quota legislation in 1927 and 1937 there had been major debates on the domestic film industry both in Parliament and in the trade papers but there had never really been any public interest in the politics and finances of the film industry. Audiences were certainly far less concerned than the exhibitors or critics whether films were American or British, the public never showed any interest at all in the interminable arguments in the trade papers, and, of course, they never read the credits on pictures once they had taken in the names of the stars. Korda had become something of a figure for a while but in general the British public had shown no interest in producers, in the personnel of Wardour Street, or in that steady colonization of the British film industry by Wall Street. Things had changed in the war and certainly there was far more awareness now of movie politics. Audiences tended to notice now whether films were British or American and they were picking up some echoes of the trade and political debate. Not everyone would have followed the whole story but certainly it was now fairly widely appreciated that J. Arthur Rank was moving into a position of some supremacy in the British film industry. The emergence of the Rank empire was already beginning to cause panic on the left and amongst those who would rather have seen the British industry established on the basis of small studios, but in government circles and amongst some critics Rank had been identified as precisely what was needed to provide the basis for an internationally prestigious British cinema. Rank was creating a Hollywood-type structure and at the same time establishing links with Hollywood and Wall Street themselves. In effect he was guaranteeing that British films would be made according to higher technical standards and that they would then do well in America. In 1946 Frederic Mullally wanted to expose the dangers of what Rank was attempting but he was all too aware of how the country as a whole had fallen for 'the fairy story which presents Rank as a doughty crusader bent on a large-scale invasion of Hollywood's own American territory'. He blamed Fleet Street for conspiring in the projection of Rank and suggested that most editors 'have simply been overawed by the stature of this great film emperor'.[55] To most people, however, everything seemed to be coming together, the stories were better and so was the acting, audience appreciation was there and so too was the commercial potential. It seemed almost inevitable that an age of masterpieces was about to dawn.

If the Second World War had given the British film industry a subject it presented Hollywood with a further opportunity to enhance its prestige and to claim recognition as a national institution. Hollywood had used the depression of the 1930s to establish its seriousness, its political reliability, and its respectability as an organ of cultural expression and it soon appreciated that the war would allow a further definition and development of its national role. Certainly the war might see the loss of some of Hollywood's international markets but new markets would be developed at home as the studios developed even closer links with Washington and became thought of even more as the official arbiters of those values that were fundamental to America. The war necessitated a vast mobilization of manpower and resources and Hollywood lost no time in becoming an integral part of the whole process. No section of the community could rival Hollywood in terms of the energy invested in the buying of bonds, the film companies made their resources and personnel available for Government and military films, and quite obviously the studios themselves prepared to make feature films that would both entertain the masses and let them know what America was fighting for. The war started badly for America but there was soon a good deal of optimism within the film community for it appeared that wartime business would be profitable and that relationships with Washington would be harmonious (there being no question of Government control), and writers and directors were optimistic as there seemed every possibility that the war would occasion more serious and more realistic films. As Ceplair and Englund have shown the war quickly benefited Hollywood's sizeable radical community, who now came out of the cold to team up with the rest of the industry to make films about America at war.[56] In America, as in Britain, it was quickly appreciated that the war had brought one great benefit and that was an improvement in popular taste. In *New Masses* Paul Trivers and Robert Rossen claimed that audiences had matured and that they were now responsive to 'responsible' films.[57] In many quarters there was an expectation that war would now allow the movies to deal more fully with the real issues that concerned ordinary Americans.

The war did bring the whole film industry nearer to the American people but, of course, it was to do so very much on official terms. In general there was no relaxation of that careful censorship which had outlawed from feature films any mention of day-to-day political and social issues. Labour was as militant as at any time in American history and so obviously there could be no films dealing explicitly with industrial relations just as there were no films dealing with the plight of America's Japanese community. Behind America's military effort there was an enormous industrial mobilization which finally brought the depression to an end and launched a new era of prosperity; the war, it had been suggested, was really won in the factories of America. This was a dramatic chapter in American history but for the most part Hollywood was not interested in making the details of factory production into a major motion-picture theme and, on the whole, the feature films of the war years were less realistic and less concerned with social issues than had been the films of the 1930s.[58] It was only occasionally and, one feels, with a sense of duty rather than with any fervour that tributes were made to the home front. *Pittsburgh* may well have been intended as a 1942 tribute to coal-miners and steelworkers but it was really a full-blooded melodrama and a star vehicle for Randolph Scott, John Wayne, and Marlene Dietrich. One British reviewer predicted success for this film at the box-office because 'human interest is well to the fore' and 'there are smashing fights', but it was the way in which the film ended with the coming of war and with the two male antagonists agreeing to work flat out to break production records that presumably pleased the authorities.[59] *Joe Smith, American* was made as a tribute to factory workers and as a reminder of how vital aircraft production was in the war effort. The details of factory life and more especially of home life were realistic enough to make this an effective film but interestingly enough the story concerns itself not with factory matters but rather with the kidnapping of Joe by Nazi spies. Hollywood had been prepared to make a tribute but only if the story measured up to its own melodramatic notions. There were to be other quiet tributes such as *Steel Against the Sky* (1943), which honoured bridge-builders by transferring what was quite obviously an old western-type story to an industrial setting. In general it remained true that feature films ignored industrial subjects and reviewers were forced back on just praising the momentary glimpses of reality that crept into the occasional film. In 1943 *The Hard Way* told the story of a girl's successful career in show business but it began with a few shots of a Pennsylvania mill-town and James Agee, who was always on the look-out for realism, reported that he had been 'all but floored – with gratitude'. He now looked forward to film-makers using 'this country as it ought to be used in films and as it has scarcely been touched'.[60] In 1944 King Vidor fulfilled one of his ambitions by making a film about the making of steel but although there are some fine industrial shots in *An American Romance* the vast majority of critics felt that any edge that the film had in social terms was just killed off by the way in which the film came out as a hopeless piece of propaganda for the American way of life. One has the feeling that if Hollywood had to deal with domestic matters then in general it was happiest with suburban life. *Since You Went Away*, made in 1944, showed Claudette Colbert and her two daughters coping with life during hubby's absence in the war. This was America's home version of *Mrs Miniver* and it was to be one of the most profitable films of the war years. At one point Colbert of all people goes to work as a welder in a shipyard but the film is far more convincing in its portrayal of suburban rather than industrial matters. Bosley Crowther thought that its characterizations were 'authentic to a degree seldom achieved in Hollywood' but other critics were more aware of being manipulated.[61] The film combined both melodrama and sentiment with realism and James Agee very perceptively spotted that

David Selznick had thereby invented a style that would 'dominate Hollywood for the next ten years'.[62]

As in Britain the genre of wartime documentary allowed ordinary American citizens to appear before the cameras. In fact it can be argued that Britain was very much the model for throughout the war American critics lavished tremendous praise on the British documentaries that were being shown in New York and elsewhere and those film directors like Frank Capra who had been recruited by the US government to make official films were very well aware of Britain's pioneering role in this kind of film activity. The American documentaries of the Second World War were extremely effective and important films. The Government's recruitment of top Hollywood directors allowed the documentary format to be snatched away from the romantics of the 1930s and to be used to deal with a less sectional reality. In the *Why We Fight* films troops were shown how film could be used to explain political and social issues whilst in combat films 'reality' was given a new urgency and immediacy. Of course, these films were propaganda and their half-truths and sentimentality indicated all too clearly that they were under the control of the official mind. In the *Negro Soldier* there was no mention of racial discrimination in civilian America and the commentator did not even explain that there was also discrimination in the forces themselves, whilst John Huston's *The Battle of San Pietro* dealt so explicitly with combat losses that it was not shown until after the war. Nevertheless there was a maturity and urgency about many films actually shown which seemed to suggest that American cinema was entering a new era. In truth this dimension in documentary film-making was very much dependent on the military imperative of war itself as was indicated by the relative neglect of wider social and domestic issues. Short films were made on civilian themes and *Steel Town* (1944) even briefly referred to the steel strikes of the 1930s but these films made little impact and were far less widely seen than the military training films.[63]

What the war did more than anything, of course, was to give Hollywood a new fictional genre. Between 1942 and 1945 Hollywood produced many war movies although it is important to note that a large number of these films did not do particularly well at the box-office and in general war themes were less popular than escapist films.[64] In terms of structure what was most interesting about the new war movie was the extensive use of the platoon format. The platoon was the basic unit of America's fighting forces in the Second World War and Harry Brown's novel *A Walk in the Sun* conveniently brought to Hollywood's attention a device which allowed it to celebrate the role in the war of the ordinary guy. The platoon became a basic component of American narrative cinema and in film after film either an utterly professional or a hopelessly neurotic sergeant was put in charge of a group of very ordinary Americans whose appearance and whose names telegraphed that they had been chosen to represent the various ethnic groups or particular cities or regions that made up the country as a whole. This new platoon format undoubtedly allowed the American feature film to move nearer to ordinary people and it gave a new sense of everyday reality and of familiarity to the movies.[65] This was most noticeably true when relatively unknown actors were used as was the case in the best of the war films *The Story of GI Joe*, a movie based on the experiences of journalist Ernie Pyle, who had insisted on unknown actors and had then approved the selection of the minor key actor Burgess Meredith to play himself. The platoon format seemed to be sanctioning a more natural acting style but in reality, of course, what it did was to offer new opportunities to actors who could breathe life into the essentially caricatured or token roles they were offered. What Hollywood needed was not unknown anonymous faces but rather actors like William Bendix who were themselves just larger-than-life ordinary guys. With actors like Bendix available there was no need for Hollywood to forget everything that it had learnt about the need for actors with real vitality.[66]

The platoons were allowing ordinary Americans to see themselves or their selected delegates on the screen and at the same time these films gave hope that Hollywood was moving towards a point when it could deal with everyday American life in general. It was this hope and expectation that lay behind the enthusiastic response that was given to the best war films by critics such as John T. McManus, who said of *GI Joe* that 'this is the real stuff'.[67] According to screen-writer Philip Dunne the trend was 'obviously towards greater realism, towards a more frequent selection of factual American themes, towards the theory that motion pictures should not only entertain and make money but should also give expression to the American and democratic ideals'.[68] More perceptive observers, however, might well have had reservations even over and above the obvious suspicion that this new realism, rather like the advances in documentary, was totally dependent on the fortuitous circumstances of the war. For one thing it was clear that the new interest in the ordinary GI was all too often an interest in his psychological state rather than in his reactions to his home environment or in his social and political views. As Colin Shindler has shown many movies presented the GI as a frightened homesick 'kid' although this type did rather give way in time to the weary disillusioned veteran.[69] In general there seemed to be far more interest in the ordinary GI as the subject for a study of anxiety or guilt or confusion rather than in the ordinary person as the basic component of a political democracy. It was as if Hollywood and its writers and directors knew that there was going to be far more mileage in the dramatization of psychological disorientation amongst ordinary people than in the dramatization of everyday social reality. This was obviously in part anticipation of what censorship would allow but it was also based on an understanding of what constituted the best dramatic possibilities. In particular there seemed to be real possibilities in the theme of the returning servicemen. The comic genius Preston Sturges saw the tremendous possibilities of taking an apparent hero, who is in fact an army reject, back to his home town but his *Hail the Conquering Hero* was not going to be the typical or the most widely publicized end-of-war film. The emphasis rather was to be on the psychological trauma of the returning veteran. Disorientated heroes were not only forced to come to terms with a society that had gone on living normally without them but often they had to come to terms also with their own disablement. It was the blind John Garfield in *Pride of the Marines* and the armless Harold Russell and the alcoholic Fredric March in *The Best Years of Our Lives* who pointed to what were to be new themes in American cinema. *The Best Years of Our Lives* was an appropriate film to end America's participation in the war and to point to a new post-war dispensation. It was designed by Samuel Goldwyn to be a great film and a great film it certainly was.[70] James Agee was well aware that it was a somewhat pat, timid, and even deceitful film but he none the less found it 'pleasing, moving and encouraging' - a 'great' film which showed 'what can be done in the factory'.[71] *The Best Years* was an immediate success and soon became a much loved film but, as early as 1947, the director Abraham Polonsky was making the point that the movie had shown far more interest in the banker Stephenson (played by Frederic March) than in the working-class Fred Derry (played by Dana Andrews).[72] The film presents us with an ex-soda jerk who had been converted by the war into a bombadier and we see him returning to a society that has no job for him - but, argued Polonsky, the film-makers could not sustain their interest in this working-class character and they made a film that concentrated rather on the problem of the rich, 'the social strata least affected' by the war. Polonsky identified the scene when we see Derry sitting in the nose of a scrapped bomber and reflecting on the ironies of the war as a genuine moment of social commentary but in general the failure of the film to sustain an interest in Derry's predicament was ample confirmation that 'the movies just seem to find it impossible to deal with people who work for their living in factories and on farms'. In part Polonsky's argument was countered by Richard Griffith, who explained that the greatness of the movie was ensured by the way in which it offered only 'partial and temporary' rather than 'generalized or abstract' or 'economic and social' answers and solutions to personal dilemmas. Its emphasis on drink and sexual fidelity rather than on unemployment meant that the film was not emotionally tied to the precise social circumstances of the era in which it was made. What Griffith was arguing was that Hollywood had used the contemporary trauma of demobilization to make a commercial success of a film dealing with mid-life crises rather than a documentary on precise social problems. In other words Hollywood had universalized from a set of specific dilemmas. Samuel Goldwyn had made a great film but he had also marked out the territory in which he thought Hollywood could do best. In 1945 Dorothy Jones commented on how the war had allowed Hollywood to gain 'immeasurably in social awareness' but now Goldwyn and other moguls were showing how that awareness was to be deployed.[73] Hollywood's subject was not going to be society as a whole and certainly not that sector in which people worked. The way ahead lay in the suburbs and the best bet for the movies was the anxieties that those areas generated. So began what Griffith himself described as a 'dense engagement with the psychological facts of American life'.

7   The post-war age of anxiety

The war had sanctioned films about everyday life and ordinary people and in so doing had effectively clinched the argument that left-wing intellectuals had been making in the 1930s. The critical orthodoxy in those years had suggested that the English-language cinema would only come of age when it was capable of dealing directly with social issues. Necessarily the war years had seen a concentration on military matters but that was sufficient evidence to confirm that the true destiny of film lay in the direction of the documentary of fictional treatment of actuality. Critics responded now to the cessation of hostilities by assuming that the time had come for a fully social cinema. By 1947 Dilys Powell had become the official spokesperson for Britain's better class of film-goer and in a BBC talk she spoke of how the artist in the cinema was asking 'for the film which grows strongly and naturally in its own soil, which has not to be forced, which is not a manufactured product but something springing from the lives and hearts of the people who produce it'.[1] In the following year America's most respected critic James Agee admitted that he found it 'hard to believe that absolutely first-rate works of art could ever again be made in Hollywood' but if there were they would 'most probably develop along the directions worked out during the past year or two; they will be journalistic, semi-documentary, and social-minded, or will start that way and transcend those levels'.[2]

The kind of cinema that critics wanted had been indicated in the best of the war films but even more it was being demonstrated by the Italians. In the immediate post-war years Italian neo-realism was acclaimed in London and New York and spontaneously identified as the beginning of a new era. Critics sometimes had reservations about particular films but in general they were just charmed by this new genre and they developed a real affection for this kind of film-making. James Agee did not like the idealization of the priest and of the Communists in Rossellini's *Open City* but he had no doubt that the acting of the Romans and especially of Anna Magnani 'somewhere near perfectly' defined 'the poetic-realist root of attitude which the grand-trunk of movies at their best would have to grow'.[3] So good was this acting that in Pauline Kael's recollection 'many Americans used to slick war films thought *Open City* was a "document" and mistook the magnificent Anna Magnani, Aldo Fabrizi, Maria Mistri and the other actors for non-professionals'.[4] A year later De Sica's *Shoeshine* came to New York and Agee found it to be 'one of the few fully alive, fully rational films ever made'.[5] Meanwhile in London the British critics were getting just as excited as they went to great lengths not only to praise the Italians but also to spell out the lessons that British filmmakers needed to learn. What *Open City* had demonstrated convincingly to D. A. Yerrill was that 'true realism' lay not in 'the sentimental recognition and expression of circumstance, behaviour or surroundings' but rather in the way in which an artist had carefully composed a total experience to which 'everything, every character, every movement' contributed. What Yerrill wanted his fellow countrymen to note was that Rossellini's realism had not consisted of distracting shots of Rome's ruined streets but had rather concentrated on the essentials in such a way that 'we have lived with the people in the film, we know them'.[6] In 1948 the critic Richard Winnington saw Rossellini's *Germany, Year Zero* and concluded that the director was 'the brightest thing that has happened to cinematography in perhaps two decades'. What he welcomed was the way in which Rossellini had refuted 'every canon of established film making' and repudiated 'its monumental elaboration'. The Italian director's secret was that:

> He affirms the cinema as well as life. His realisation is that if you look closely enough into a person you discover his world; his dedicated purpose is to document the individual and his method is ceaselessly to reveal that individual in his own environment by an ever-moving camera.[7]

All of this was in contrast to the British scene and Winnington, who had met Rossellini, reported that he 'like some of us, is astounded at the failure of British films to document or even touch a climatic period of British industry'. At one swoop Rossellini and De Sica had transcended the whole debate on the relative qualities of documentary, semi-documentary, and fictional films by blending the techniques into a new kind of feature film and it was the fervent hope of many critics in London and New York that the Italian example would be followed.

Both Yerrill and Winnington had spotted that the real charm of neo-realism lay in the way that the film-makers looked at people rather than in the shots of real streets and places, but there was no doubt that the sense of the outdoors contributed greatly to the freshness of these Italian films. Perhaps some critics appreciated that with the great shortage of studio space the Italian directors had been virtually forced out into the streets but whatever the cause there was a very obvious contrast between the real locations in Italian films and the studio-bound elaborateness of so much of the British and American product. Of course the war had weaned many directors away from the various studios and so there was some expectation that the Italian breakthrough could be emulated at home. In America especially there were encouraging signs. King Vidor for example had been so struck by the panoramic view of Gary Indiana's industrial scenery as glimpsed through a train window that he was inspired to make *An American Romance* (1944), which contained some of the most dramatic footage ever seen in an American feature film. Then with the appearance of Louis de Rochemont's *The House on 92nd Street* (1945) and *Boomerang* (1947) it really seemed as if American movies were moving in the same direction as Italian cinema. In 1947 Edgar Anstey critically assessed the 'New realism in feature films' and he pointed to these *March of Time*-inspired movies as evidence that realism had arrived in 'the country richest in the tools of artificiality'. What he liked about them in particular was the emphasis on the 'unhistrionic level of day-to-day events' and the way in which Hollywood contract players like Lloyd Nolan and Dana Andrews had been used in a thoroughly naturalistic way.[8]

With hindsight we can see that de Rochemont's films were not typical and did not represent the beginning of a new kind of cinema, but at the time they did seem very much part of a new swing towards realism. Movie after movie seemed to be confirming a Hollywood commitment towards various forms of realism and not surprisingly it seemed as if there was a general inclination to pick up and then build on the particular kind of realism that had been achieved in the 1930s. Audiences could hardly fail to notice that Hollywood once more seemed preoccupied with social problems, and movies such as *The Lost Weekend*, *Crossfire*, *Gentleman's Agreement*, *Pinky*, and *Lost Boundaries* seemed to indicate that the feature film format could be used effectively to combine drama with a warning of the dangers of alcoholism, anti-Semitism, or racism. Even more noticeable was the way in which Hollywood had retained its interest in New York and in big cities in general and it was the dominance of the city-based film which suggested more than anything that contemporaneity and realism were to be the way forward. Audiences were to be taken back to those city streets that they had been shown in the 1930s but now there were to be new techniques that made possible even greater authenticity. A key film was Robert Rossen's *Body and Soul* (1947), which had John Garfield playing a fighter from the slums in such a way as to suggest that Hollywood was seriously looking at how the lessons taught by Odets and the Group Theatre, which Garfield, of course, had learned at first hand, could be used again as the basis for a new cinema.[9] Stephen Belcher identified this movie as a return to the old 'tenement' genre but suggested that it went 'deeper into its milieu'.[10] In fact it seemed now that the tenement milieu and the city milieu generally could be convincingly depicted in almost any Hollywood film and it was very much in these years that a mastery of the urban idiom became a central feature of American cinema. American movies had always based much of their appeal on their urban quality but in these years after 1945 a new depth and definition was given to this tradition. Whenever required a Hollywood movie could depict the opulence, sophistication, wit, and freedom as well as the violence and squalor of the city. At the time it seemed as if location shooting was becoming an essential part of Hollywood's urban preoccupation but we can see now that New York footage was far less crucial than those new lighting and studio techniques that effortlessly created a very real imaginary city. Even more decisive was the contribution of writers and especially that of the 'hard-boiled' crime writers. In particular these were to be the classic years of Raymond Chandler and James M. Cain and in truth these novelists-turned-scriptwriters emerged almost as God-given gifts to Hollywood at this time.[11] Their mastery of dialogue and sense of place had made them natural film-writers even before they became scriptwriters but what was essential was that their themes of sex, violence, and crime, and even more their mastery of language, allowed Hollywood to make films that always suggested that they were thoroughly contemporary and real although, in fact, no great sacrifice had been made in terms of subject-matter. Hollywood had made it clear that it regarded realism as a matter of style. The definitive film was *The Big Sleep* (made in 1946) whilst Humphrey Bogart was certainly the most influential actor but thereafter countless American movies and especially, as time went by, 'B' movies moved effortlessly through an endless city of apartments, bars, nightclubs, railroad stations, and car journeys, and at every point both male and female leads and all their support players never ceased to speak snappy and witty city-talk. For many film-goers throughout the world this had become the only authentic and meaningful setting for films although it was not until 1957 that this audience was to finds its spokesman. In his critique of what he called America's 'underground films' Manny Farber spoke of how 'the average gun film travels like a shamus who knows his city and likes his private knowledge'.[12]

Meanwhile the British film scene also seemed to be moving towards realism and towards the consummation of a social cinema. The documentary films of Humphrey Jennings and especially *The Cumberland Story* of 1947 suggested that non-fiction films would still be playing an important part in British cinema whilst in that same year Roy Boulting's *Fame is the Spur* made it seem as if there was going to be a return to the 1938-9 tradition of feature films based on bestselling socio-political novels. Even more encouraging was Ealing's *It Always Rains on Sunday*, which struck many critics as something of a breakthrough for not only had it achieved an authentic East End idiom but it did that rare thing for a British film of combining human interest and excitement in such a way as to offer both 'entertainment for the masses' and 'special delight for the discriminating'.[13] The trade described the film as 'strong', which indicated that it was dealing in tougher and more basic emotions than was the norm and what was crucial in this respect was 'the strong natural performance' of Googie Withers. All this was taken as evidence that British studios now had the potential to turn out the kind of contemporary and sophisticated drama that had become a Hollywood trade mark.

In both America and Britain Italian neo-realism had appeared to critics as a full confirmation of all their critical expectations and it was now widely assumed that the techniques of realism would be refined and that the English-language cinema would move towards a social cinema. Critics were sitting back and waiting to be overwhelmed by realism. They were to be disappointed and the more discerning amongst them could soon see that neither the American nor the British studios were attaching priority to social subjects. As always, exhibitors were to be offered a wide range of films and specifically social films were to constitute only a minor strand. On the face of it the film world almost seemed to be perversely going against the only logical and natural way ahead but those who interpreted developments in that way were rather forgetting the unusual circumstances of the immediate past. In the depression left-wing intellectuals had aroused certain expectations to which, at least in part, producers had seemed to respond whilst in the war, of course, film had inevitably become caught up in a wider national and democratic rhetoric. Film was now free of those broad cultural influences but there remained other constraints and, as always, critics were often slow or unable to appreciate that specific context in which feature films were made.

In America the new post-war cinema was largely shaped by political considerations and straightforward censorship prevented there being any breakthrough as far as labour films were concerned. As had been so often the case it was another chapter in the career of King Vidor which had indicated the way things were going. Vidor had envisaged that his *An American Romance* would be a celebration of the steel industry and of American industrial enterprise as a whole. As we have noted the movie that finally emerged in 1944 included some of the most dramatic industrial footage in the history of feature films, but it had also classically illustrated how confusing and conflicting intentions could blunt an American movie. Vidor's original script had included a sitdown strike but that had been removed at the request of the Office of War Information. In any case it seems as if Vidor himself was really more interested in what he wanted to depict as the epic career of the character Steve Dangloss, the European immigrant who rises to become an industrial magnate, than he was in the welfare of the workers. Certainly labour confronts capital in this movie but only to buttress the conflict between father and son. We are back with the great melodrama of the

American dream with heavy industry providing a dramatically novel setting. The film might well have been of major interest in telling us more about Vidor's concept of America, but MGM ensured that it was as much their film, first by denying him the stars he had wanted, and especially Spencer Tracy, and then by cutting thirty minutes from the final print. By this time the irony was that the director's own experience of Midwest roadshows had persuaded him that audiences could get bored with industrial sequences whereas the studio much to Vidor's annoyance, actually cut the scenes of human drama.[14] Obviously things were not going to be easy and straightforward for directors with social vision or with an interest in everyday issues. As a matter of fact things were going to be worse than anyone could ever have imagined.

The post-war years saw some great industrial conflicts in America as labour and capital fought for position in industry after industry. Throughout 1948 and 1949 the pages of *Box-Office* and *Variety* carried many complaints from exhibitors as strikes seriously affected local box-office takings. By October 1949 *Variety* had detected a pattern in which cinema attendances soared during the first week of a strike and thereafter progressively declined. With the miners having been out for five weeks and the steelworkers for over two weeks the trade could only look with despair at takings not only in the cities of Detroit, Pittsburgh, Gary, Youngstown, and Bethlehem but throughout wide areas of states like Pennsylvania, West Virginia, and Alabama.[15] If only through box-office receipts then the film industry knew all about industrial tension and it was not really surprising that there were no great initiatives to make films on that particular subject. This prejudice against labour films was fuelled, though, not by events in Michigan and Pennsylvania but rather by struggles a good deal nearer home. In fact the whole mood of post-war Hollywood had been determined by an event that had occurred at Warner's Burbank studios in October 1945. A strike had been called by the Conference of Studio Unions (CSU), which by this time had nearly 10,000 members, but Warners had gone on using scab labour. When pickets appeared at Burbank the studio had hired 'bully-boys' and police dogs, and issued steel bolts, hoses, guns, and tyre chains to their own private police who were going to help the regular police to break through the picket lines. There was fierce fighting but the lines had held and indeed the whole strike was to be a success for after eight months the workers gained a 25 per cent wage increase. Not surprisingly, though, Jack Warner came out of this a changed man and, as James R. Silke has suggested, it is not difficult to see this as having ended the period in which Warner Bros made films in praise of the 'little man'.[16]

Both at that time and subsequently public attention quite naturally focused on the dramatic House Un-American Activities Committee (HUAC) hearings in which various individuals and especially the

Hollywood Ten reacted in various ways to what was a public inquisition but, as Ceplair and Englund have argued, the hearings should be seen as the sequel to a massive battle in which Hollywood had in effect defeated radical trade-unionism.[17] Between 1945 and 1947 Hollywood had fought and won a battle that ensured that it remained a company town. The studios had broken the hold and crushed the CSU whilst at the same time sanctioning and promoting their own company union, the International Alliance of Theatrical State Employees (IATSE). Having defeated independent and radical unionism on a mass level the film companies could afford to be less concerned about the Screen Writers Guild and left-wing intellectuals but now the impetus was coming from Washington. As American xenophobia developed apace ambitious politicians wanted to put the screw on Hollywood and make a public display of ensuring that the nation's entertainment was not sullied by Communism. At first the studios were reluctant to co-operate: they wanted to avoid staff disruption and legal problems over contracts and in general would have preferred to handle things without external interference. In the event it was to be a matter of public hearings and, of course, the producers had no alternative but to co-operate. There was a sad inevitability to the whole saga of the hearings and in particular to the fate of the famous ten, a sad inevitability that was to characterize so many of the public debates and trials of the cold war era. As Ceplair and Englund have reminded us many of these men were, or had been, Communists and supporters in name at least of Stalin and so in any public interrogation all that really remained to be determined was their degree of personal integrity and dignity. The HUAC hearings are of more interest to psychologists than they are to social historians and it is a great and very revealing shame that the image of Hollywood in the late 1940s that has come down to posterity is that of the witness baring his soul and not that of the battle fought at the Burbank gates.[18] The very public rout of a group of talented, honourable, but ultimately misguided men must be seen as a footnote to a wider story in which a company town had been re-establishing its hegemony. More important than the hearings was the black list but even that was of less significance than the way in which the studio chiefs had eliminated the whole institutional base of political pluralism within the Hollywood community.

Communists and radicals had failed to make any really significant contribution to the content of feature films during either the favourable intellectual climate of the 1930s or the favourable political climate of the war and so it is hardly surprising that there was to be so little social comment in films in a new era in which political radicals were not only on the defensive but fighting to save their jobs. The new mood of America had created a new sensitivity in which it was quite obvious that writers and directors were having to think very carefully about every political nuance. The tale was told that when in 1948 United Artists released a film version of William Saroyan's play *The Time of Your Life* one piece of politically dangerous dialogue had already been removed: audiences were never to hear Cagney respond to a barman (who wanted to know what he was going to do with the water melon he had just acquired) with the words: 'What do you think I'd do with it, sell it for a profit?'[19] This typically snappy Cagney manifestation of impatience had to go because it might have seemed like a Communist sentiment. Clearly this film like every other had been checked to ensure that it was politically sound but it is interesting to note that *Box-Office* still wondered whether the movie's 'blend of life's seamy-side philosophy and cynicisms' would be annoying for 'rank-and-file' ticket-buyers.[20] Suddenly there were so many things to worry about with every film and in fact the new political dispensation had coincided with a massive collapse of Hollywood's confidence.

After the extremely successful year of 1946 Hollywood had entered a period of crisis in which it was known that costs were soaring and audiences declining. There was also the legal challenge to the whole structure of the Hollywood empire which culminated in a Supreme Court decision, the outlawing of monopolies, and the loss by the studios of their highly lucrative control of the exhibition side of the industry. To an extent previously unknown Hollywood was confused about the fundamental and related questions of who exactly went to the movies and what it was that the audience wanted to see. In an article which considered whether this was 'the end of an era' and whether 'the motion picture industry may be turning a historic corner' *Fortune Magazine* wondered why it was that so many films no longer had 'an authentic relevance to the age', and why was it that *Top Hat*, for example, spoke the language of 1935 better than *When My Baby Smiles at Me* speaks 'the language of 1949?' One of the most interesting features of this lengthy examination of Hollywood's dilemma was the way in which it communicated the industry's growing dissatisfaction with the role of critics. It showed that many critics now felt that the movies had lost their 'magic touch' and yet *Fortune*'s correspondent in general accepted the industry's view that critics had really lost touch with the public. What had particularly irritated Hollywood was 'the high praise given to foreign films' and also the 'fatuous and indiscriminating way' that some critics had of 'praising any picture with a reform theme or documentary style'.[21] Critics, it appeared, were no longer speaking on behalf of that mass audience that Hollywood wanted so badly to understand and they were calling for movies to be made that quite obviously would have only a limited appeal. The influence of those critics had been confirmed in an investigation carried out by a body representing the rural exhibitor. The Allied State Organization canvassed exhibitors in thirty-two states and reached the conclusion 'that the movie industry in striving to appeal to the tastes of sophisticated Broadway audiences and to win the plaudits of professional reviewers is sacrificing its reputation as a mass entertainment medium'. The great danger as Allied saw it was that 'the motion picture will become class entertainment' and it felt that it had to spell out that 'the public goes to the movies for an emotional experience' and that 'John W. Public in his search for realisation and entertainment is not a serious-minded individual'. The reports also indicated the danger of making films that would alienate significant sections of society: for five years films had been glorifying Catholics and Jews and yet the vast majority of Americans were Protestants. There were too many 'psychological stories' and too many 'crime and blood and thunder stories', which inevitably upset local pressure groups, and certainly stories which 'bring forth stark dramatic reality' should be avoided as they would arouse demands for local censorship.[22] Hollywood's identity crisis had become very public but as the issues were debated in well-researched articles and reports it was clear that the studios were not merely going to concede to the critics by creating a minority cinema of social seriousness and at the same time they were going to go all out to find out precisely who their real audience was. There began the fullest investigation there had ever been into the nature of the movie-going public and the industry was to use those findings to ensure survival. Hollywood would save itself by making movies for precisely those groups in society who went to the cinema most.

The social content of American feature films was being determined in the context of the loss of confidence and the new emphasis on evidence research. In Britain this very same issue of the social content of feature films was to be come a fundamental strand in an even deeper crisis and in an even more crucial cultural debate. Box-office was not an immediate problem in Britain for the people were going to the pictures as never before and it was in many ways this boom that prompted many people to believe that the time had come to determine more positively what it was that this vast audience actually saw. In those immediate post-war years there seemed a possibility that two lines of expectation would converge. The first expectation was cultural and aesthetic and it consisted of that confidence on the part of critics that the war had allowed British cinema to come of age and that it now had the potential to eclipse Hollywood as far as domestic taste was concerned. In the volume of *The Penguin New Writing* that had appeared in 1944 a 'Film Critic' had neatly summed up the mood that was to prevail for the first few years of peace by anticipating films that would 'reflect our national consciousness and aspirations' and would encourage audiences to sustain that reflection of Hollywood's 'sordid Shangri-la-ism' which had begun in the war.[23] What critics most wanted to see now were films that would be, in C. A. Lejeune's words, 'fine pieces of native work'.[24] Requests for this kind of film now became a constant refrain, 'a parrot cry' as one critic saw it, and one feels that never before can film-makers have been given such full and precise advice. Certainly there can never have been such an obvious degree of critical expectation.

The second line of expectation was commercial. At the end of the war it had occurred to some producers and politicians that the time had come to protect and boost the British film industry in such a way as to make it less necessary for exhibitors to rely on the Hollywood product. In fact the war years had already seen a reduction in the number of films sent over each year but in 1946 there were still 342 American films as compared with 83 British. An official investigation in 1944 had urged whatever Government would be in power to retain something like the quota system of the 1930s but had also warned that there would have to be major changes both in the financing and distributing of British films if any effective challenge to Hollywood was to be mounted.[25] In the event the challenge of helping to establish an altogether more ambitious film industry fell to a new Labour Government and the great tragedy in the history of British cinema was to be that a Government which reshaped so much of British life was never really able to deal effectively with the question of film. One has the distinct impression that there were no real enthusiasts of the cinema in the Labour Government but at first they could see that there were real prospects of achieving a breakthrough especially as J. Arthur Rank, who now owned a third of British cinemas and about 60 per cent of the industry as a whole, was now promising that the domestic industry could come up with sufficient films to rival Hollywood both at home and abroad.[26] Bland speeches were made but then economic realities began to bite. In the second half of 1946 the country had spent £124 million on American goods and 7 per cent of that had gone on films. During the general financial crisis of 1947 the Government imposed a 75 per cent duty on the value of all imported films. Nobody in the industry had been fully consulted about this extreme increase and so in the months that followed the Government had to be educated into the realities of the movie business. On the one hand there were British producers who now had to explain that they did not have the resources to produce sufficient films and on the other hand there were American executives who now made it clear that the Government had rather over-simplified the distinction between domestic and foreign films. The politicians now realized that the so-called British film industry was really an Anglo-American industry and so a scheme was devised that allowed American film companies operating in London to retain moneys that would have gone as duty for reinvestment. There was also the further realization that British exhibitors would inevitably have to rely on large numbers of American films: the new quota requirement that 45 per cent of films had to be British was soon reduced to 30 per cent.[27] All that survived from this sad story, in which Labour had, according to Paul Rotha, 'tinkered with the industry's problem', was the new National Film Finance Corporation which would help subsidize independent productions.[28]

Britain's film crisis had been much gentler than that which occurred in America: there were no battles at studio gates, no hearings, no public confessions, and no arrests, but nevertheless it had been a crisis that plunged everybody who thought and cared deeply about film into the deepest despair. The whole saga of this sudden and very dramatic crisis, which had for a moment rather surprisingly placed film at the centre of British politics, provided a huge and very depressing process of education for critics and intelligent observers alike. It was clear now that there was no escape from Hollywood or rather from the tenacious financial hold of Wall Street, and what was really frightening was the irony that this reassertion of America's stranglehold had come at the very time when the overall Hollywood product was thought of as being in decline and moving away from British interest in terms of content. In 1947 Penelope Houston noted Hollywood's 'headlong fall into mediocrity' and analysed the 'degradation' that was sweeping through the studios as part of 'a last tremendous flourish of inanity'. It seemed to her as to so many other British observers that 'the wall insulating Hollywood from life grows even higher'.[29] All of this was bad enough but what really intensified the gloom and alarm was the growing realization that in their own way British films were just as cut off from life. A great opportunity had presented itself and collectively the British had been unable to rise to the occasion. Endless meetings and reports had produced no great political initiative and no new economic formula. The politicians had been unimaginative and perhaps even treacherous but the real failure had been artistic. The British film industry had just failed to produce the truly national films of quality that had been so eagerly anticipated. Of course there had been an improvement but what that improvement had amounted to was an occasional and one-off masterpiece usually based on a literary classic. The growing feeling was that these so-called 'prestige' films did not add up to a total British cinema. Throughout the period of the Labour Government the two most common complaints were first that the two most prominent producers Rank and Korda seemed entirely concerned with aping American production values so that their films would do well in America and secondly that, prestige films apart, the general run of British films were both cheap and mediocre. In this latter respect the views of critics coincided with those of many ordinary film fans. In Britain too these were the classic years of audience research and in all the many investigations into what 'Mr and Mrs Ninepennies' wanted it is interesting that the new respect for some British films and stars had not eliminated a traditional prejudice against all those trivial comedies and melodramas that were thought of as being 'quota quickies'. With all too many categories of film the term 'British picture' was thought of as a disparaging remark and even a warning. Indeed so complete was the disappointment with the general run of British films that even the most left-wing and nationalistic critics occasionally praised the quality of Hollywood's entertainment. All the evidence surveys confirmed that Hollywood still had its natural constituency in Britain and the majority of critics on very many occasions begrudgingly became part of it.[30]

What had happened in these years was that the showman had triumphed, albeit at the behest of the censor and the banker. The movies in Britain and America were to be about entertainment of a prescribed sort. It was now up to intellectuals, critics, and political radicals to rethink their position and to come to terms all over again with a mass medium that was as far removed as ever from their influence. It was in these bad years that new ways of thinking about film were to develop and in time the debate was to broaden out considerably but for the moment all that critics could do was to find crumbs of comfort in the occasional film that hinted at what might have been. The basic criteria of judgement remained the same and were conveniently summarized by James Monahan, who argued that 'the British tradition of film-making is sturdiest and most British' when there was a strong element of 'documentary' and that element he defined as a 'relation between the behaviour of human beings and the real circumstances of this modern-existence'. In particular Monahan felt that 'good work' would ensue if directors and film writers were to 'modestly adapt the life around their own back-streets into the terms of the cinema'.[31]

Very occasionally this instruction was followed and usually the outcome was greeted with approval if not always with total satisfaction. In many ways one of the most remarkable films of the period was Jill Craigie's *Blue Scar* of 1949, which attempted to convey the reality of family life in the South Wales mining valleys as well as the quite complicated response of the miners to the coming of nationalization. Initially the film brilliantly succeeds in capturing the warmth and intimacy of everyday life in a mining community but then it collapses into a badly edited *mélange* of sentimental melodrama and hurried political statements. A generation later the film is of enormous interest to historians but at the time reviewers could only reflect on its box-office limitations. The critics like the film but could well understand why the three major circuits were reluctant to release it. Milton Schulman speculated whether the British public would 'pay to see a film that deals honestly and intelligently with an important aspect of British life' whilst the Rank reviewer concluded that whilst it would 'appeal to the more thinking types who like natural realistic drama' it would not be 'strong box-office for all classes'. Very few reviewers were prepared to take up the issues that Craigie had raised but as Fred Majdelany very pertinently argued 'the mere fact that a film eschews glamour and has a working-class background does not automatically impregnate it with virtue'. He found *Blue Scar* 'dim, a little amateurish and not particularly entertaining' whilst Milton Schulman, who very much wanted the film to do well, nevertheless thought the cutting was 'crude', some of the camera work 'amateurish', and the plot 'artificial and forced'.[32]

Jill Craigie's experience in 1949 illustrated that it was not quite enough just to go into the back streets. Distributors had standards both in terms of production quality and entertainment value and those had to be met before there could be box-office take-off. Just a couple of years earlier Roy Boulting had been taught a very similar lesson. Far more money had been spent on *Fame is the Spur* and far more care had been taken to ensure that it was a big film but there had still been problems. What Boulting

7 *Fame Is The Spur*: As a Hunger March is enacted in Uxbridge in 1947 it seemed as if the Boultings were returning to what British films had promised in 1939.

had done was to go back to the 1938 formula in which a genuine star (Michael Redgrave again) was used to bring to life a bestselling novel in which one man's dilemmas were set against a background of working-class life. The film is one which can but be of great interest to social historians for not only did it contain some of the most convincing documentary-type scenes of working-class politics to be found in any British feature film but it also graphically dramatized some of the dilemmas which have occurred in the careers of nearly all leading Labour politicians. What is interesting now is that Boulting's insights into the fundamental ambiguities of the Labour Party came at precisely the moment when the Labour Government was coming face to face with the realities of political power. There is a lot to think and argue about in *Fame is the Spur* but clearly the whole time-scale and range of action make the story far more suited to a five- or six-part classic television series of the 1980s than a two-hour movie of the 1940s and in any case the evidence suggests that the markets were not yet ready for a public seminar on the question of whether success spoils Labour politicians. The Rank reviewer thought it 'hardly a picture likely to appeal to everyone' for the story 'seems long drawn out and much of the political talk seems of little avail these days'.[33]

One obviously had to be very careful with those stories set in the back streets and in general experience suggested that political messages ought not to be too strong and that they certainly should be securely packaged in a format that would guarantee entertainment. An indication of what might be acceptable was provided by the 1950 film *Chance of a Lifetime*, which tells the story of how the owner of a small engineering works who was constantly frustrated by the sheer pigheadedness of his workmen finally hands the whole enterprise over to them. In running the works the workers obviously learn valuable lessons and by the end of the film the owner is back, new ideas are being implemented, and successful export orders are contributing to the national economic well-being. Contemporary critics were delighted that such a film had been made at all. Lindsay Anderson was well aware that it was a very slight film ('a sketch rather than a document'), that it was essentially 'a sentimental comedy' and 'an affable little sermon on the virtues of tolerance, co-operation, and mutual goodwill', but he felt far more compelled to stress the film's remarkable qualities. He stressed how exceptional it was that a film should deal with labour relations, he was delighted with the location shooting, which had taken the company to a real factory and above all he was thrilled with the 'liveliness and lifelike-ness' of its cast, in which fresh talent had been mixed with non-professionals.[34] The Rank reviewer agreed that 'absolute authenticity' was the keynote of the film and he also stressed that the acting was 'entirely natural and convincing'. What was crucial for the distributor however, was that the film was not in any way politically dangerous or controversial. It was stressed that the film had made 'no attempt to enlarge its appeal with trimmings', in other words there was 'no attempt at glamour, love interest or sensation', but at the same time no antagonism would be aroused for the theme had been handled 'honestly and sensibly', it maintained 'a firm grip of the interest', and it therefore worked as entertainment.[35] *Chance of a Lifetime* had emerged as one film which effected a compromise between the expectations of the critics and the demands of the distributors. It had done this by returning to the social message of the war years and to the milieu in which the actor-director and writer Bernard Miles had been at his happiest. The message here, as in the war, was that the nation does best when the classes pull together and learn to overlook respective deficiencies. It is fascinating to the historian that a working-class theme should only be allowed to return to the screen in the form of this message but what is also very apparent now is that the working class was having to pay a price for any screen prominence that it was given. Surely most audiences today would find the depiction of workers far less convincing than Anderson suggested: most of the actors look quite out of place, both in the pub and in the factory, and the impression that they are slumming it is suggested by the difficulty that they have with accents. But what is far more noticeable today is the lengthy and sustained going-over the workers are given before they are allowed to learn their lesson. The first part of the film constitutes a considerable indictment of the British working class and its trade-union representatives: the owner says of them that 'the only time I see them looking keen is when they're queuing up for their pay packets'; later he complains, 'I'm fed up of hearing what you are entitled to: what am I entitled to?' and when confronted with workers' control the union representatives are thrown into total confusion and can only reflect that 'We're used to fighting bosses', soon 'we'll be out of a job'. It is wholly in character with the film's general view of the working class that during the period when the works is under control of the employees new suggestions put forward by an able young engineer are firmly opposed by one of the two worker-directors. This young engineer is played by Kenneth More, who provides by far the most convincing performance in the whole movie. In trying to evoke that atmosphere of class co-operation that had characterized the war Bernard Miles had succeeded only in caricaturing the workers but he had at least allowed Kenneth More to suggest that there was a class of eager young professionals ready to make their mark in British society. Certainly *Chance of a Lifetime* suggested that British cinema might be on safer ground with that class than it was with the workers.

In producing *Chance of a Lifetime* Pilgrim Films had strayed into territory that was now thought of very much as belonging to Ealing. At the end of the war nobody had appealed more for films to be made that would present 'a complete picture of Britain' than Michael Balcon. He had wanted films that would deal with every aspect of British political, cultural, and industrial life.[36] In the years that followed Balcon and his team at Ealing set out to produce films that would be good, entertaining, and thoroughly British, both in their command of social detail and in their dramatic idiom. So successful was Balcon that soon the British press was totally intrigued by his whole approach and many articles were written stressing the vital ingredient of team work and also noting the importance of good stories. It had become so common to point out that British films were badly written that now, almost for the first time ever, the press enjoyed publicizing the role of T. E. B. Clarke, who was identified as Ealing's most successful writer. It was pointed out that Clarke knew a bit about life; he had been to Cambridge but he had also been to Australia, worked as a journalist, and served as a wartime policeman, and, what's more, he travelled extensively by public transport, which was, of course, 'the way to meet people'. Here at last suggested the *Daily Herald* was a British writer who could get beyond stereotypes and offer something different for 'his feet are on the ground. His stories spring from the lives of ordinary people. His characters are as robust as those of Dickens.'[37] One senses immediately that there was enormous national pride in what Ealing had achieved and reviewers had no hesitation in using the name of the studios as a hallmark for very funny and very British films. It is also very interesting to note that critics began to have reservations as soon as Ealing moved even slightly away from what was thought to be a well-established pattern. It had soon been appreciated that Ealing had come up with a fairly consistent version of Britishness and critics soon expressed disappointment if they suspected that films were departing from that version for the sake of the American market. Ealing had created a pattern of expectation: we know, Kenneth Tynan wrote in 1951, that

> there probably will not be a hero, or that, if there is he will be slightly comic if not downright weird, that we shall not spend much time in the boudoir, or the countryside, that we shall see a good deal of the Civil Service, the police force and the small shopkeeper, and that the theme will be the bizarre British, faced with yet another perfectly extraordinary situation.[38]

All this, of course, was far removed from the back streets that some writers thought that British films ought to be visiting. Ealing had indeed responded to the challenge of 1945 but it had done so on its own terms. In 1950 Sir Michael Balcon spoke of how Ealing films would always succeed if they retained that quality of being stamped by 'personal signatures'.[39] What Kenneth Tynan found to be novel about Ealing was that it presented the rare phenomenon of a studio with 'a point of view'.

Certainly for the first time ever both critics and audiences knew that the name of a British studio meant something but they were probably less interested in the point of view than in the general ambience of the films. What 'Ealing' meant to most people, then as since, was a number of sophisticated social comedies and in particular the indication of a new tradition of comic acting, especially in the creations of Alec Guinness, whom Tynan had already identified as 'a waxen poker-faced Chaplin'. We now know that here was indeed an Ealing 'point of view', that what was bizarre and eccentric in British life was being celebrated at a time when it was felt that centralized bureaucracy and the demands of an industrial society were threatening to take over, but contemporary audiences had been less concerned to work that position out than they had been to welcome a very clearly defined comic world. The team at Ealing had created a fictional world out of its own experiences and then made that world work in cinematic terms by bringing together good stories and good acting. Writing in 1951 Tynan fully appreciated that what Ealing offered was 'an exceptional middle-class man's view of the middle class', but for audiences that mattered less than at last a British studio had created genuine entertainment by adapting the British dramatic idioms to the demands of the cinema. For audiences and critics alike the most successful Ealing films were the pure comedies in which any social view-point was well disguised or only gently hinted at. Following the great success of that definitive Ealing film *Kind Hearts and Coronets* there was a much cooler reception for *The Man in the White Suit*, a film in which the Scottish-American director Alexander Mackendrick set out to satirize all those obstacles and blockages which prevented dynamic progress in British industry. There were some critics who could see that with this film Ealing was winning through to more serious ground - a *Manchester Guardian* critic, for example, spoke of it as the studio's 'bravest adventure' and as a film that had come close to the 1930s work of René Clair in combining hilarity with social observation - but for most audiences and critics the basically serious notion of the film had blunted the comedy and they had to content themselves with yet another great Guinness creation.[40] What was wanted were further episodes of Ealing's world of comedy, and a greater receptiveness to new ideas, not sermons on the need for social co-operation.

The world that Ealing had created was greatly admired for its total Englishness but it was none the less thought of as a fictional world. Consequently, far less attention was given to Ealing's more realistic films, to Ealing ventures into the back streets. Certainly there had been a good deal of praise for the realism of *It Always Rains on Sunday* but thereafter the majority of critics almost seemed to acquiesce in the acceptance of straightforward social realism as a more secondary genre in Ealing's output. The general feeling was that, however worthy the intentions, the final outcome was never fully satisfactory. James Monahan thought *Dance Hall* 'failed unaccountably in its attempts to catch the atmosphere of the palais-de-dance' which is 'such a conspicuous element in the social life of so many of the typists and factory girls of Britain', whereas later observers would almost certainly find that director Charles Crichton had brilliantly succeeded in recreating the dance-hall atmosphere but had failed rather in finding actresses who could convincingly play factory girls.[41] Ealing had the same problem with *Pool of London*, a film which was praised by the *Daily Worker*'s Thomas Spencer for the way it had created an authentic London docks atmosphere and for the realistic way in which it told one story of the West Indian seaman who comes ashore to meet a girl. For Spencer, though, this was to be yet another British film spoilt by the need to conform to American conventions, for the story of the black seaman is soon eclipsed by 'cops and robbers' scenes in which an American character looms large and at the same time he was far from happy with the acting of another British actress. His feeling was that

> if Ealing learnt not to pull their punches, not to build films with British settings round unattractive American personalities and not to fob off garden-suburb types like Susan Shaw as the 'personification of the working girl' they might make a film equal to our best.[42]

Meanwhile those flawed films could never rival what were thought of as those perfect comedies. The one exception to this pattern was *The Blue Lamp*, which Basil Dearden directed for Ealing in 1950, for in this case there was unanimous praise for the way in which London locations had been used and the very real atmosphere of the streets and pubs around the Edgware and Harrow Roads had been captured. Monahan spoke of the 'impressively understated' way in which the work of the police had been depicted but what made this one of the most memorable films of its era was that it had depicted the murder of a London bobby and that it had sharply defined the contrast between ordinary settled British family life and the threat of the criminal elements on the streets. Even Honor Arundel in the *Daily Worker* thought that the film's realism 'whets the appetite for more' although she could never have guessed how popular London police melodramas were actually to become in the English canon. What she could see, though, was that this breakthrough into realism had come in the form of a tribute to and a eulogy of the police. Of course the Metropolitan Police had co-operated fully with Sir Michael Balcon in the making of this film: 'We have been told so often that our policemen are wonderful', reflected Arundel, 'that it is not surprising that someone should have made a film to prove it once and for all.'[43]

The truth was that by 1951 nobody really expected major works of social realism from British studios. Of course there was always a warm welcome for the minor works that attempted to take up social themes but they tended to be regarded with a certain amount of curiosity. In 1952 a Rank reviewer praised the realism of Philip Leacock's *The Brave Don't Cry*, which told the story of a Scottish mining disaster. For this reviewer the acting was 'so good that many of the players could well have been pitmen before they took up the acting profession' and so all in all it was 'an unusual picture'.[44] In the same year there were some favourable comments for the more natural scenes in *The Happy Family*, a comedy which dealt with the demolition of a cockney home. Kathleen Harrison was especially delightful as a very natural cockney mum but for the Rank reviewer Stanley Holloway's dad somehow never seemed real, 'perhaps because of a variable and unidentifiable accent'. The warning that this film was better suited for 'Cockney audiences than provincial' was an indication of how distributors were likely to react to films that were too firmly set in a regional or subcultural idiom.[45] It was now widely appreciated that the more prestigious British films would be set in an altogether different world, a world that was best summed up by the *Daily Worker*'s Thomas Spencer in his review of the 1951 film *The Franchise Affair*. He warned his readers 'not to be put off by the middle-class conventions' of this film and reminded them that 'the unfortunate fact is that the lives and problems of the gently nurtured are what British film-makers do best'. The consolation for Spencer, and it was the same consolation treasured by so many other film-goers as they watched so many other British films, was that 'there was not a hint of American vulgarity' in *The Franchise Affair* and 'these days that is something'.[46] The British had settled on a predominantly middle-class and socially safe cinema, especially as far as the prestige films were concerned. As early as 1947 Lindsay Anderson had taken a critical look at the new reputation of the British cinema and had been forced to fall back on Virginia Woolf's concept of 'middlebrowism', which implied a 'picture of geniality and sentiment'.[47] In this middlebrow world of British films, in which literary adaptations were so often the stand-by, there were occasional successes when all the conventions seem to work but more often than not films were characterized by what Gavin Lambert summed up as an 'atmosphere of mediocrity' and an 'ultimate dullness'.[48] All too often the *New Statesman*'s William Whitebait found that the 'dead hand' of direction produced a 'flatness' in British films and he concluded that 'if national boost is the American foible, ours is theatrical blight'.[49]

As critics were resigning themselves to the comfortable world of British cinema perhaps the most outspoken blast came from the American writer Richard Griffith, who had been asked by Paul Rotha to bring up to date his volume *The Film Till Now* which had first appeared in 1929. It was Griffith's frank opinion that there was still no fully British cinema and that the promise that had been suggested in a handful of wartime films had been squandered. According to Griffith British cinema had failed because writers, directors, and producers had not attempted to find stories 'out of the living experience of the British people'. The frightening fact was that 'British fiction films by and large seldom have anything to do with significant life anywhere' and Griffith argued that the main reasons for that were 'the policies of American companies in their British activities, the odd cosmopolitan character of British studio personnel', and the association of realism with the alternative form of documentary. What Griffith quite rightly emphasized was that the whole commercial and artistic structure of the British industry prevented it from embracing Britishness in the way that so many critics had expected. In all those prestige films that really mattered Britishness would necessarily be defined in American and international terms. In fact Griffith was not entirely pessimistic for from his 1949 perspective it seemed to him that the country undoubtedly possessed 'the intellectual and emotional resources' and was 'undergoing the experiences which could make her the leader of the film of reality'.[50] At this point, though, Griffith was probably not fully attuned to the cultural scene in Britain and in particular to the place of film within the culture. In part the studios were responding to a popular need and in part they were responding to a certain relaxation in the cultural pressure as far as content was concerned. When in 1950 Alan Ross looked back over the years since the war what he remembered most as far as films were concerned was the way in which 'a bewildered rather apathetic public sought an outlet for its enthusiasm in fantastic demonstrations at film premières'. Those were the years of austerity and there was a noticeable 'lack of social functions' and so suddenly stars like Margaret Lockwood, Anna Neagle, Ann Todd, Stewart Granger, and Michael Wilding were invested with an immense national significance. Glamour, romance, and sentiment seemed to be the order of the day as far as the film companies were concerned. And really who were the intellectuals to say anything different? It was for Ross 'a time without novelties and frills, a time when "culture" seemed a luxury, and a time when so many writers quite deliberately turned away from the mass theme and general social optimism of the last decade'. Literature, said Ross, took a 'turn to the Right' and 'the Marxists shut up shop'.[51] Of course they had not shut up shop as far as film was concerned and throughout these years writers on the left were always to provide the fullest critique of Rank, Korda, and indeed Balcon, but these supporters of a more truly British cinema had no real influence at the studios now and they were exerting no real pressure on any key groups in society. A certain intellectual consensus had been lost and in a situation in which politicians had no real interest in film culture the showmen and financiers had been allowed to create their own film world.[52]

British critics were far from happy with the domestic film scene but in these years they continued to have slightly confused responses to Hollywood. There was always plenty of sharp anti-Hollywood invective, especially on the left. By 1951 Oliver Martin was of the view that 'film-writers and directors have nothing to say' and that was because those who had something to say 'have gone soft, or been dismissed and jailed, or become routine hacks or had the spirit pressed out of them'. Martin maintained that workers in the American film industry were 'entirely dependent on the caprice of millionaires'. His colleague Thomas Spencer saw the situation as being even more sinister: he continually condemned the growing number of American war films and was always keen to detect a McCarthyite influence on the content of feature films. In early 1951 he angrily complained that 'the way films are going these days suggests that we shall soon have to get permission from the Un-American Affairs Committee before we can go to the cinema at all'.[53] What was interesting, however, was the frequency with which initial anti-Americanism often tapered off into admiration for a particular film or for Hollywood's technical excellence. In early 1950, for example, William Whitebait of the *New Statesman* fired off a lengthy tirade against the way Hollywood films formed an 'unbreakable shop-window' for 'USA Incorporated'; it was 'self-advertising' all the way, 'American boost, American romance, American cliché, the American way of life'. This is what he had to encounter every week and then just as he was 'tumbling into complete Americophobia' along came a film like Joseph Losey's *The Dividing Line* (*The Lawless* in the USA), which faithfully depicted Mexican fruit-pickers in California, or Clarence Brown's *Intruder in the Dust*, which had a 'conviction of life and place'.[54] Of course there were not to be many more opportunities for Losey in Hollywood but nevertheless throughout the 1950s there were always to be American films of this sort to which the British could respond with enthusiasm.

Meanwhile in America critics on the left were mounting their own verbal campaign against a Hollywood from which they had been so dramatically and effectively excluded. One of those who had been driven out of Hollywood was John Howard Lawson, who long before he became one of the famous 'Hollywood Ten', had achieved eternal fame by having written *Blockade*, which had been thought of as one of the few serious Hollywood films of the 1930s. On his release from prison Lawson published *Film in the Battle of Ideas*, which was intended both as a Marxist critique of Hollywood and as a programme of action. He began by denouncing the Hollywood product, condemning in particular the way in which in war films like *Steel Helmet* 'the "mad-killer" of gangster pictures finds a mission on the Korean battle-front' and so 'his insanity becomes patriotism'. Lawson was convinced that the declining film audience was a product of 'cynicism and apathy' and was sure that the people of the country had seen through 'the fraud perpetrated on their screens'. Of course he was particularly concerned about America's working class and he wondered about the implications for the whole labour movement of the fact that movies continually suggested that 'working-class life is to be despised' and that 'workers who seek to protect their class interests are stupid, malicious and even treasonable'. The situation in America was that 'workers and their families see films which urge them to despise the values by which they live and to emulate the corrupt values of their enemies' and so Lawson went on to demand 'a broad movement to improve the content of commercial motion pictures' and in particular to ensure an 'honest treatment of working-class themes' and 'an interpretation of history that accords to facts and avoids . . . insults to popular traditions'.[55]

At very much the same time as Lawson was writing another member of the Hollywood Ten was actually in the process of implementing those very ideas. The director Herbert Biberman had gone to Silver City, New Mexico, together with his blacklisted wife, Gale Sondergaard, to make a feature film about the experiences of the largely Mexican miners who belong to Local 890 of the International Union of Mine and Smelter Workers. The producer Paul Jarrico and director Biberman explained that the miners and the families were playing themselves and that their film *Salt of the Earth* would 'illuminate the truth that the lives and struggles of ordinary people are the richest untapped source of contemporary American art'.[56] Biberman stressed that the film was 'made to be seen' and was meant 'to be useful to working people, to inspire them, to create greater solidarity among them'.[57] Everything about this film, including the enrolment of so many blacklisted names, was a direct challenge to the whole Hollywood ethos and not surprisingly, as *Hollywood Review* reported, Hollywood 'disassociated itself quite gratuitously and somewhat frantically from the whole project'.[58] During the making of the film considerable opposition had come from Hollywood's major union the IATSE, which was now very much a company union (nevertheless the film had been made by a fully unionized crew), and after the completion of the film Roy Brewer, West Coast head of IATSE and president of the Hollywood Motion Picture Alliance, was one of those fêted at a much-publicized ceremony in Silver City for their work in combating the influence of a 'Communist' film.[59] There was a well-orchestrated campaign against the film. In the House Congressman Jackson warned that 'if the picture is shown in Latin America, Asia and India it will do incalculable harm not only to the United States but to the cause of free people everywhere' and in the Catholic magazine *The Sign* the film was described as an 'anti-American diatribe' in which 'familiar Communist lies and clichés have been dusted off and utilized'.[60]

Salt of the Earth became quite a *cause célèbre* as its distribution difficulties were publicized and when critics actually got to see the film

8 *Salt Of The Earth*: For blacklisted film-makers the members of Local 890 played
themselves.

they were often surprised, as was Bosley Crowther, to find that it was 'in
substance simply a strong pro-labour film with a particularly sympathetic
interest in the Mexican-Americans with whom it deals'.[61] That was
exactly right for, while the film has a highly professional finish and is
characterized by quite stunning monochrome photography and some very
fine female acting, the men are rather ponderous and lack-lustre and
there is far too little background information and wider explanation. In

a lovingly photographed New Mexican landscape a stark elemental miracle play is acted out with each distinct episode involving quite sharply defined groups. What is on offer is not a full documentary of a working-class situation but rather an artistic idealization of a peasantry at the point of industrialization. But it was a film about workers and about the violence with which companies and the police responded to industrial action and it was therefore precisely the kind of film that Hollywood was not offering its mass audience.

In recent years nobody has written more intelligently about the Hollywood of the 1950s than Peter Biskind, and his overall view is that for Hollywood the prosperity of those years had made 'class struggle obsolete'.[62] The witch hunt and the black list had driven radical directors and writers away and now the keynote was to be entertainment. As far as films dealing with society were concerned there were perhaps as many as two hundred films like *My Son John* which were specifically made as anti-Communist propaganda but more important and far more widely seen were thousands of films which examined all the social and political dilemmas of life in a pluralistic but now largely suburban and corporate society. Almost effortlessly Hollywood had assembled a repertory company of actors and put them into a fictional world in which all the tensions arising out of family, community and corporate life could be examined. In any particular film the main character would be strong or weak or the crowd would be strong or weak depending on the particular dilemma being highlighted. In all of this, though, there was no room for class criticism or for collective action. The emphasis was on the individual and his or her own story, with society as a whole there as a back-cloth. The ethos that Hollywood created was one inspired, as Biskind argues, by the corporate liberalism that dominated Eisenhower's America and so Marxism was neutralized and discontent was always seen as 'a psychological, individual issue, not a social or class issue'.[63] Even at the time the more perceptive critics could see that movies had somewhat redefined their place within the culture. The expectation had been that movies would become more documentary; in fact they had become more psychoanalytical. The technical excellence was as apparent as ever, and totally acceptable and very appealing actors peopled a somewhat idealized but nevertheless very recognizable version of American society, but the films were now quite clearly fictional and melodramatic. What now intrigued many critics were the patterns and myths that formed the basis of the fictions. The mythical world of the movies was there to be read and interpreted. 'The movie theater', Parker Tyler had already spotted, had become 'the psychoanalytical clinic of the average worker's daylight dreams' although as far as content was concerned that worker was almost exclusively thought of as a citizen of the suburbs and that industrial America that King Vidor had glimpsed through the train window was never depicted in the movies.[64] 'Symbols are a dime a dozen in Hollywood's storehouse' was how Manny Farber summed it all up and he speculated that many spectators probably felt that they 'were caught up in the middle of a psychological wrestling match'. For Farber reality had disappeared 'in the fog of interpretation'.[65]

Farber was writing at a time when critics were being forced to rethink the whole position of movies in American culture. The starting-point for the debate had been provided by the left-wing novelist James Farrell, who in the 1930s had very successfully depicted a working-class world in his *Studs Lonigan* trilogy and who now emerged as an outspoken critic of the movies. He found that almost all Hollywood pictures were characterized by 'an inner emptiness' and he suggested that they were part of 'a tremendous commercial culture' that had developed 'as a kind of substitute of a genuinely popular, a genuinely democratic culture'.[66] What happened next was that in responding to Farrell writers like Gilbert Seldes, Dwight Macdonald, and Robert Warshow began to work out the role and values of what was thought of now as 'popular culture' and in particular began to evaluate Hollywood's contribution to that culture.[67] In much of this evaluation Hollywood just stood condemned for the triviality and artificiality of its product and there was a general feeling that something had been lost in the relationship between film-makers and their audiences. As early as 1947 Robert Warshow had argued that 'the chief function of mass culture is to relieve one of the necessity of experiencing one's life directly' and that the great problem had become one of regaining 'the use of our experience in the world of mass culture'.[68] As these critics of the 1940s and 1950s attempted to analyse mass or popular culture it was noticeable that they often took steps to distance themselves from what they thought of as the 'popular front' culture of the 1930s. They were all too well aware of how left-wing views of that period had created a whole pattern of expectations about movies and that those expectations had lingered on long after 1945. But as Gilbert Seldes made clear most critics no longer believed that the arts had any mission as such. They were not necessarily looking for any message or sermon in the movies, but rather they just wanted to work out the role of the feature film and its interaction with elements in American society.[69] 'The movies are a part of my culture', said Robert Warshow, and as a writer on film he was at his happiest when he could show that films were 'an important element in my own cultural life, an element with its own qualities and interesting in its own terms and neither esoteric nor alien'.[70] Whatever else they were the movies were still American, they were still popular, and they continued to operate in that paradoxical way which allowed them to have a life of their own at the same time as they fed off real elements in American life.

In a sense this question of how films related to American life was the most perplexing one for the critics of the 1950s to answer. In her pioneering anthropological study of Hollywood Hortense Powdermaker had referred to that 'surface realism' of film which tended to 'disguise fantasy and make it seem to be true' but in their hearts most writers knew that the question was more complex than that.[71] Perhaps nobody worried away more at this problem than the critic Manny Farber, who was very much aware of the decline in Hollywood but also of the way in which in many movies, and they now tended increasingly to be 'B' or genre movies, there was still that reflection of language and vitality of city life that had first appeared in films in the early 1930s. Indeed it can be argued that it was almost impossible for any film to come to terms with American society other than in modes established by the 1930s. Even in the general run of films that critics like Farber so disliked for their 'overtones of meaning' and for their psychological rather than narrative thrust there were 1930s influences at work. Farber attributed what he called 'the new Worried Look' of films and their obsession with 'conscience, regret, guilt and frustration' to the fact that so many directors had 'got their higher, and highest, education in the New York of the latter 1930s' and so had 'never lost the obsessive need to "improve"'. These directors, said Farber, had lost their radicalism but retained their earnestness and the result was a cinema characterized by a bleak misanthropy, by 'social significance gone sour'.[72] Almost as Farber was writing preparations were well under way for the one film which more than any other illustrated the way in which the 1930s were haunting the American cinema of the 1950s, for in *On the Waterfront*, as Peter Biskind was to argue, director Elia Kazan was to harness 'the methods of the 1930s to the ideology of the 1950s'.[73]

There were many things about *On the Waterfront* to satisfy all those film-goers who were nostalgic for the 1930s. The publicity stressed that 'the entire picture was filmed on location in the areas of the Port of New York' (although quite understandably Hoboken New Jersey had been used rather than Manhattan so that the famous New York skyline could be kept in camera) and that for the most part the crowd was played by actual longshoremen, who had needed 'no coaching' for the scenes depicting the infamous shape-up in which labour was recruited and which had only very recently been made illegal in New York.[74] In the 1930s social-problem style it was stressed that the movie was based on Pulitzer prize-winning revelations in the New York press and had been inspired by the experiences of Father Corridan, the tough waterfront priest who was on record as saying that in the port of New York where he had grown up one either became 'a gangster or a priest'. Of course Father Corridan had been brought in to coach Karl Malden, who had been chosen to depict him, and, what is more, in the film Malden was actually to wear the Father's hat. In the time-honoured way exhibitors were urged to 'turn your lobby into a real waterfront' and were reminded that two records of harbour sounds were available to clinch the atmosphere. Everything had been set up for a totally convincing and dramatic exposure of the corrupt connections between the mob and the waterfront unions, but Kazan was not just going over old 1930s territory for in what he very much wanted to be a film of his time he wanted to equate the corruption of the unions with Communism and he wanted to sanction fully the behaviour of his hero, who finally decided to tell all. In Biskind's memorable phrases *On the Waterfront* was a 'child of HUAC' and the central character Terry Malloy was 'the informer as hero'. The film was Kazan's statement about his own experiences as an informer.[75]

It is hardly surprising that this combination of authentic locations and intensely personal political statement made *On the Waterfront* into the most passionately debated film of the whole Cold War era. Much of that debate concentrated on what has been termed the film's political ambivalence, whether it was in fact a right-wing or a democratic–liberal argument that was being put forward in what was quite obviously meant to be a political allegory. The majority of critics and film-goers, however, were less concerned with allegory and were far more aware of the film's dramatic and visual power. This was realism in a form that no other film of the era had offered. The final product was a total justification of using a real story and setting it in its proper location. Elia Kazan subsequently explained the dangers of making a true story surrounded by the workers whose lives were being filmed: he was going to be beaten up outside a bar until rescued by a longshoreman who went on to beat up his threatening colleague; 'the atmosphere was that violent', there were things he could not tell – about having to pay people off and so on. 'We were right in the midst of life on that picture', Kazan concluded, 'and it shows doesn't it?'[76] Of course it shows and that accounted for much of the film's power. But not for all of it: for the actual locations and the real longshoremen were also helped by the actors and it was they who really made the film so memorable. Kazan knew all about the dilemma of leaving an organization to which one had passionately belonged as well as circumstances in which one would inform on former associates and so he could invest his film with dramatic moments of truth, but actors were needed to make those moments work, and those actors were available in that very New York Group Theatre with which Kazan had worked since the 1930s; just as in the 1930s when Hollywood wanted what it thought of as realism it had to turn to Broadway and to the acting academies of New York City. The style was slightly different now, there had to be far more anxiety, far more anguish, far more theatrical power, but still the right actors were there. Kazan was not inevitably infallible but he got there in the end for he came up with Lee J. Cobb and Rod Steiger and with Marlon Brando, who was on his way to becoming the greatest screen actor of his generation.[77]

9 *On The Waterfront*: Terry Malloy walks away from union corruption and Marlon Brando walks into our cultural history.

It was precisely this sense of having experienced a new kind of acting talent that made *On the Waterfront* such a memorable film for so many individual film-goers. What they could see was an actor working from within to create a total character, a man who in Biskind's phrase was 'a brooding, inarticulate, violent, lumpen or laborer' and yet one capable of sensitivity, of feeling, and of occasional moments of revealing confession as he moves towards his ultimate political understanding and redemption.[78] Pauline Kael was later to comment that 'actors before Brando did not mumble and scratch and show their sweat'; Brando, of course, had sweated in previous films, most memorably in his performance as Stanley Kowalski in *A Streetcar Named Desire*, but Hal Hinson is surely right to argue that in that earlier film Brando's performance had been essentially theatrical and that he had concentrated on creating what was in effect a symbol of raw masculine power.[79] Now in *On the Waterfront* he creates a real character who fully inhabits the story that is being told. It is true that not everyone was immediately won over to this new 'method' acting. Manny Farber always preferred a more traditional, more dignified, more professional American male hero and he was not too keen to have 'skin-pores, weaves of cloth and sweaty undershirts' thrust before him. Of Brando's performance in *Streetcar* Farber had said that he conveyed passion 'by stuttering the first syllables of his sentences and mumbling the rest as though through a mouthful of mashed potatoes, a device that naturally forces the spectator to sociological speculation'. Farber wanted what he called 'male truth' but he was always somewhat put off by Brando's 'liberal knowingness'.[80] For many other people, though, it was the truth of Brando's acting that made him seem to be very much an actor for their times. He appealed most strongly to precisely those who were attempting to understand and to give analytical expression to the feelings that existed below or behind the façade of Eisenhower's suburban and corporate America. Norman Mailer was attempting to understand the role of the rebel, the outsider, the 'white negro' as he called him, the hipster, and it is not going too far to assume that he had Brando, the actor who was to become his friend, in mind when he set out to define some hip characteristics. In a footnote Mailer noted that 'the hipster has that muted animal voice which shivered the national attention when first used by Marlon Brando' but earlier and without using the actor's name Mailer had suggested that 'the language of Hip is a language of energy, how it is found, how it is lost'. For Mailer the hipster listens for an 'inner unconscious life', for the God 'which is located in the sense of his body' knowing that 'there are no truths other than the isolated truths which each observer feels at each instant of his existence'.[81] It was to be many years later that Mailer was to return to the subject of Brando, seeing him then as America's 'greatest actor' and as 'the raucous out-of-phase voice of the prairie'.[82]

As Mailer and other writers on society attempted to work out the exact credentials of America's rebel elements they necessarily came up against the question of how the hipster related to the old bedrock of the proletariat. Mailer suggested that 'the hipster comes out of a muted rebellion of the proletariat, he is, so to say, the lazy proletariat, the spiv' and then years later in his essay on *Last Tango in Paris* he completed his judgement that Brando was America's 'greatest actor, our noblest actor' by adding 'he is also our national lout – could it be otherwise in America?' Jack Kerouac would probably not have put it quite in that way but just like Mailer he had been quick to look up Brando on arrival in Hollywood because *On the Waterfront* had appealed just as powerfully to him as a writer concerned with the meaning of rebellion in America. Kerouac was always anxious to distance himself from Mailer's existential musings but what is interesting is that unlike the Brooklyn intellectual Kerouac had come from a working-class town and had grown up surrounded by 'mill-rats' as they were termed. It was said of the creator of the 'beat' generation that the mill workers of Lowell had left their mark on him for it could be seen in his 'workingman's stride, head down, hands in pockets'.[83] It is interesting to note that for years Kerouac, who was always proud of his French ancestry, had idolized that great representative of the French working man Jean Gabin, but now in Brando he had been given an authentic American hero, and of course, a hero sprung from that real America out west. As Mailer, Kerouac, and others had attempted to give meaning to those life styles which challenged post-Hiroshima America, so they had been driven away from the traditions of European Marxism and the New York-inspired 'street socialism of the 1930s' and into a fuller understanding of native American idioms, especially in terms of jazz and black culture.[84] The crucial significance of Brando was that he represented all the passion and emotion that operated in a tension with the official version of America. Brando, Pauline Kael was to argue, 'represented a reaction against the post-war mania for security' and became 'the major protagonist of contemporary American themes of the fifties'.[85] This new protagonist, this new social hero, was not, however, a factory worker confident in his collective identity and standing as the unchallenged head of a normal family household but was rather an outsider, an anti-social rebel whose motivation came from social and sexual anxiety rather than from class conflict and who was certain only that solutions would have to be found in personal terms and in the company of other outsiders. As always the golden rule applied and American actors only became socially significant by establishing personas that were recognizably everyday-American but now, as Joan Mellen later argued, 'where men were concerned the American film turned inward'.[86] 'We all contain the culture of our country in our own unused acting skills,' claimed Mailer, and during the 1950s it seemed to many people that as Brando developed his skills so the basic anxieties that characterized the reality of their lives were made more intelligible.[87]

In the early 1930s those gangsters who had brought real American vitality to the screen always had to suffer in the end but audiences always remembered their initial 'brio' rather than their ultimate demise. Similarly new audiences recalled the fascination of Brando's dilemmas rather than what Biskind calls his ultimate 'socialization'. It was the same with James Dean, that other great screen hipster, for, as Joan Mellen has reminded us, his films usually ended with rebellion failing and with what she calls the sanctification of authority.[88] It was the very expression of confusion and then the powerful indication that things could only be worked out in personal and not social terms that really counted. The American cinema had forced its way into a new era of cultural relevance by remaining true to its own cultural conventions and by rediscovering the extent to which the camera could seek out personal qualities that were basic to America. Those qualities did not necessarily have to be basic for all Americans because Brando and Dean were essentially cult figures whose full meaning was only appreciated within subcultures. In the past Hollywood had never been too interested in subcultures but in this respect too new lessons had been learnt. In particular the film companies had learnt that there was now a giant teenage audience and also a growing audience for intelligent films. The demands of youth and of thinking people now had to be met.[89] If there were actors and films who could satisfy both those audiences then perhaps there was much to be said for allowing films to be socially relevant once again and for giving one more whirl to the old idea of stars. Now that even intellectuals and trade unions seemed less concerned with class war perhaps there was no harm in giving exposure to a new generation of working-class heroes.

8 British working-class heroes

By the mid-1950s British cinema had clearly been driven very firmly and decisively into a cultural cul-de-sac. A set of conventions had been established which produced films that were often very polished and entertaining without ever really being significant in cultural and especially in social terms. As far as critics were concerned the situation in 1956 was very perceptively summed up by the novelist and critic Gavin Lambert, who at the time was teaching film at UCLA and was therefore well placed to contrast the British output with that of Hollywood. What struck him most forcibly was that what he called 'the social film', which was 'such a vital tradition of American film-making', had by contrast, 'never flourished in Britain'. In part he was prepared to blame the old documentary school for not giving a firm lead, for their films had often been remote from their human subjects and had tended in any case to be more 'about objects' such as trains, boats, and fish. What 'realistic style' there was in British cinema tended to occur as background to the melodramas of Hitchcock and Balcon but in general Lambert was of the view that British film-makers did not give their films a meaningful social direction. He instanced the way in which David Lean's *Great Expectations* and *Oliver Twist* could display 'impeccable taste and surface' and yet remain essentially 'inorganic' because of a failure of vision which denied the films any of Dickens's own 'social indignation'. It was precisely in this respect that Lambert found the comparison with Hollywood instructive for whereas American films were quite prepared to confront social problems British films refused to acknowledge that such problems existed and became very evasive if controversial subjects were broached. Films crossing the Atlantic, then, tended to convey rather different messages for whilst 'to an English audience the plain-speaking of American social films' came as 'a shock and as a relief' English films struck Americans as being 'deeply reassuring' because of their 'quaint conservatism', their lack of 'real protest', and their suggestion that the most important things to be worried about were 'old railway lines' and 'contraband whisky'. From his Los Angeles perspective Lambert could see a British cinema that 'reflected a closed society, unfriendly to change and regarding self-criticism as rather bad form' and he concluded his piece by confessing that he found the British film-makers' dislike of commitment both mysterious and maddening.[1]

In London meanwhile commitment was becoming the hallmark of some of the more influential critics for this was very much the era of Lindsay Anderson and Penelope Houston, who were using the pages of *Sight and Sound* to give a new political and cultural sophistication to the old message that British films would only get better by becoming more realistic. In effect Anderson and Houston were in the process of creating a new left-of-centre film consciousness in Britain and it can be argued that the way in which they approached films in the mid-1950s was to establish patterns that were to be followed by a subsequent generation of thinking film-goers in Britain. Their very serious and always socially-minded approach to films was to alienate or amuse many other critics and perhaps the American critic Pauline Kael was one of the first to point out their excesses. She was struck by the way in which English critics 'are always pecking away at failures of conviction or commending a show of conviction' and she was greatly amused by the way in which these critics would react to a film according to its social setting: films that dealt with the rich were seen as evasive whilst *Marty*, a 1955 film which simply and naturally told the tale of a Brooklyn butcher, was noticeably overestimated. In particular Kael had been somewhat put off by Penelope Houston's tone and when Houston praised the acting of some newcomers as 'purposeful' the American critic suggested that she sounded 'a bit like a high-minded social worker addressing her charges'.[2] There was certainly a good deal of pretension and political self-righteousness in this new school of British criticism but nevertheless the scene was being set for new departures in British cinema. Anderson, of course, was more than a critic for he was to be the main inspiration of Free Cinema, that movement which gave new life to the tradition of documentary film-making in the 1950s. Free Cinema was important in that it reminded a new generation of film-makers that there were other Britains waiting to be filmed but at this stage what was probably more crucial was that both Anderson and Houston were constantly drawing attention to the undoubted power of the American film. They never ceased to hammer away at the political dangers and intellectual immaturity of much of the Hollywood product and yet not at all infrequently they found themselves fascinated by either the poetry or the dramatic intensity of individual films. For Houston *On the Waterfront* had been just a 'melodrama with a stiffening of serious ideas' but she was well aware that Marlon Brando's playing had given the film a distinction and a relevance that it would not otherwise have had; in effect he had given the film 'a wonderfully firm centre'.[3] In what was to become a notorious article Lindsay Anderson wrote at length about *On the Waterfront*'s 'badness' and in particular about the 'fascist' implications of its last sequence where the dockers sheepishly follow their new hero back to work but Anderson too had been somewhat transfixed by the 'rare poetic power' of Brando. 'No actor can give a film poetic validity on his own', concluded Anderson, but that sentence rather limply followed the references to Brando's 'enormous passionate honesty' and his 'beautiful sensitivity' which 'shines out like truth itself in all this falsity'.[4] The political purists would have nodded their agreement with Anderson's political denunciation of Kazan's film but the majority of film enthusiasts would surely have been glad to have been reminded of Brando's sheer cinematic power. Behind all the verbiage and attitudinizing there was now a clear recognition that it was precisely this kind of cinematic power that British films lacked. As early as 1952 the English critic Richard Winnington had written about 'the terrific Brando', about his 'sullen glow' in A Streetcar Named Desire, and about his 'power' which transcended acting in Viva Zapata.[5] Throughout the decade British critics were coming to realize that there could only be a fully social cinema in Britain when there was a new style of British acting.

As a number of influences combined to take British cinema into a new era it is fascinating to note that the traditional film-makers were quite prepared to move into the sphere of social relevance on their own terms. In fact throughout the period since the war John and Roy Boulting had always attempted to give their films a certain social edge. We have already seen that their Fame is the Spur (1948) was a serious attempt to examine some of the Labour Party's dilemmas but there was also other films like Brighton Rock (1947) and The Guinea Pig (1949) in which they used the actor Richard Attenborough to convey some sense of the violence and resentment that was thought to be typical of a new kind of juvenile. Occasionally as with Brighton Rock the critics would note that a certain atmosphere had been created but on the whole these films were regarded as being rather worthy and theatrical melodramas in which the acting had been rather strained. The Boultings had also developed a brand of comedy which attempted to satirize various aspects of British public life in an extremely light-hearted and somewhat farcical way. Many aspects of British society were fairly easy game and the Boulting comedies dealt with them in a mildly amusing and almost totally inconsequential way but as they approached the slightly more controversial subject of industrial relations it was perhaps inevitable that their film would occasion some debate. I'm All Right Jack (1959) is a film that displays so many of the faults that have characterized British cinema as a whole. Like other Boulting comedies it has an insubstantial feel to it, it has no real body or texture, and the music, the cutting, and especially the acting of Ian Carmichael all suggest that one is looking at a comic or a series of cartoons rather than dealing with real people or a real situation. Quite rightly the critic William Whitebait dismissed the notion that the Boultings had achieved a position of 'detached satire' for what we are offered is really a series of sketches in which, as Whitebait suggested, the humour emerges rather mechanically from a very obviously prepared script.[6] What we have, then, is a collection of jokes, some of them visual, such as the news-reader's message that 'With victory came a new age' being followed by Victor Maddern's V-sign, and many of them given added power because they are delivered by familiar but very well-cast comedy actors: the line 'We have chaps here who break into a sweat when just standing still' is funny in itself but it becomes quite memorable when hissed out by Terry Thomas, that quite definitive ex-officer turned low-level manager. The one-liners are good, they come thick and fast, and they hit out in all directions ('I imagine you'll just supervise - after all you were at Oxford'), but steadily the barbs at the union's expense accumulate and it becomes clear that the real villain has been identified. We are shown a card-playing work-force regularly taken out on strike by a union (membership of which is 'not compulsory but you've got to join') that is led and personified by its shop steward Fred Kite played by Peter Sellers. Kite is a great comic creation and it is he that gives the film its biting edge and lifts it above the ordinary. The clues were all in the script (Terry Thomas's Major Hargreaves refers to him as 'the kind of chap who sleeps in his vest - a real shocker'), make-up played its part by adding the Hitler moustache, but the brilliance came in a performance in which Sellers conveyed the total humourless-ness, the intellectual pretentiousness, the unthinking sloganizing and pro-Soviet sentiments, and the sheer destructive arrogance of a politically committed trade union official, beautifully and precisely located in a social position well above his proletarian rank and file and just below the lower manager.

The genius of Sellers ensured that *I'm All Right Jack* would be a great box-office smash. British Lion had some problems in the mining districts of South Wales where there was political opposition to the film but elsewhere there was an entirely enthusiastic and spontaneous response: 'the public have a wonderful nose for smelling out what they want' commented a spokesman for the company as he noted that 'word of mouth' was doing his advertising for him.[7] In the newspapers of the left there was a good deal of dismay at the film's viciousness and cynicism and especially at what were thought of as the rather gratuitous and throw-away racist remarks of Kite and some of the workers. But other critics could see that the film was both very funny and a very accurate reflection of how many people saw trade unionism in 1959. The film itself had depicted the way in which television was now reporting industrial disputes and at the same time had fully confirmed the impression of wildcat union irresponsibility regularly offered in news broadcasts throughout the 1950s. Certainly Sellers had modelled Kite on one or two real-life union officials who were constantly appearing before the cameras at that time. Roy Boulting was on record as saying that he and his

10 *I'm All Right Jack*: The bloody-mindedness of trade union power; Peter Sellers as Kite.

brother enjoyed 'making fun of the Establishment' and 'the trade unions are part of the Establishment'.[8] In a year in which the Conservatives had won their third consecutive general election this was precisely the way that many film-going electors would have thought of the unions. The Boultings had certainly latched on to a winner in hitting out at trade union arrogance but, of course, the writing of both Frank Harvey and John Boulting and then the general direction of the film had ensured that what was on offer was both funny enough and traditional enough to pass as conventional entertainment whatever the politics of the audience.

In a way the film received a more balanced reception in those parts of America where there was already a growing appreciation of English comedy. Selected American audiences had developed a taste for genteel English satire and for English comic acting and they were now delighted and a little surprised that those gifts had been applied to industrial relations, a subject which in many cases had become less topical and controversially dangerous in the American context. On the whole Pauline Kael found the satire of the union practices rather 'affectionate' and she was somewhat surprised by the hostility that had been shown by the English left-wing critics. Penelope Houston thought the film had been made 'from no standpoint' and was obviously the work of 'sour Liberals'. Kael's reaction to these and other remarks was an understandable reflection that here 'the critic's jargon is not far removed from the shop steward's'.[9] What had happened was that the Boultings had produced an amusing film, albeit a film with one great acting performance, entirely within the conventions of British cinema. Quite obviously there was now an audience for that type of comic sketch both at home and abroad but for others the Boulting format still represented a very inferior kind of cinema. Of course all the committed critics fell into the trap of Kite-like responses to jokes about what had become political sacred cows but more fundamental and crucial than that was their wider argument that true cinema had to amount to more than caricature and public-house humour.

The limitations of traditional British cinema were also very evident in *The Angry Silence*, which was made in 1960 by Guy Green. To a greater extent than almost any other British film there was an attempt here to convey some of the passion, mood, and dilemmas of a typical strike. Atmosphere was quite obviously going to be of the essence with this film and in this respect there were considerable successes: the locations are right and the structure and pace allowed the development of quite considerable tension, both between the hero and the rest of the work-force and between the private home life of the hero's family and the wider public world. The story is about a workman who refuses to join a strike and so is 'sent to Coventry' by his work-mates and we are invited without reservation to take the hero's side as he is subjected to all kinds of pressures; we see the strain on his pregnant wife and his two children, and eventually how he loses an eye whilst his son is partially tarred. The film ends with a full exposure of just how weak, foolish, and childish the work-force had been. Of course this was an attempt to capture something of *On the Waterfront*'s qualities within the British context and quite obviously the fact that the film sides with the individual man of integrity against the unthinking mob occasioned precisely the same kind of political objections that had greeted both Kazan's and other American films. But once again the straightforward political points were less important than the cinematic ones for what was really wrong with Green's film was that it sacrificed its authentic locations and occasionally authentic dramatic tension by becoming exaggeratedly melodramatic. At the start of the film an unidentified but quite obviously Communist agitator arrives to stir up trouble and we are quite gratuitously informed of the film's political standpoint, but thereafter the emphasis on the heroic stance of the main character seems less an illustration of a legitimate point of view and more an excuse for melodramatic tension as we see him subjected to violence not only from ordinary workmen turned into a baying mob but also from delinquents with flick-knives. The logic of the action is dictated by the need for frightening scenes rather than by the social and political situation and as Ernest Callenbach pointed out the workmen never meet together to argue over the rights and wrongs of the closed-shop situation; in fact there is no real explanation of the hero's position and even the existence of the union as such is only raised towards the end of the film. Pier Angeli is very beautiful and moving as the hero's wife – here we have femininity of a far more intriguing and challenging kind than that offered by English starlets – but again one senses that the hero has been given a very beautiful Italian wife in a purely gratuitous attempt to heighten the tension. Ultimately, however, the film is melodramatic because the hero is played by Richard Attenborough. It was Raymond Durgnat who pointed out that British film-makers of the 1950s were obsessed with juvenile delinquency, the one bit of social tension that they could inject into their dramas without offending the consensus, and Attenborough was the classic delinquent actor who at first looked young enough to play juveniles and who later could be let loose in parts of neurotic and over-tense adults.[10] C. A. Lejeune thought that Attenborough was good in his cockney part in *The Angry Silence* but in adding that he had somehow managed to make it distinct from 'his other Cockney parts' she was really giving the game away.[11] The whole film was really a vehicle for an actor who was thought of as one of the leading British actors of the day and one who specialized in roles in which he was alienated from the crowd, and yet Attenborough was not interesting and original enough to sustain a story independently of melodrama. As Norman Cecil suggested Attenborough was 'not a prepossessing actor', he had a limited range of 'acting devices', and was blessed only with 'a round face, cow-like eyes and bantam fortitude'.[12] The traditional British cinema of the 1950s had once again exposed its real nature. It had come up with an anti-union film but only within a format in which a strike had been used as the basis of a melodrama and it had centred the action and based its supposed message of the dignity of the individual on an entirely theatrical and unrealistic acting performance. Once more there had been a fear of dealing with a real situation and with a real person.

C. A. Lejeune had not at all enjoyed *The Angry Silence* and in fact 'the harsh and ugly story' had left her with the firm determination never to have anything to do with industry even if she had 'to rusticate with half-an-acre and a cow'. Indeed she wondered whether industrial workers and

11 *The Angry Silence*: Protection for the British Terry Malloy; Richard Attenborough shows 'bantam fortitude'.

their wives really wanted 'to see films about industrial workers and their
wives' and whether it was not really the case that they went to the cinema
precisely to get away from industrial disputes. This distinguished and
venerable critic need not have worried for the film companies had no plans
to submit their audiences to a regular diet of films about industrial
disputes and in that sense *I'm All Right Jack* and *The Angry Silence* stood
very much on their own. In the meantime, though, there had been a
commitment to a programme of films with industrial settings and,

although in some quarters the Attenborough film was associated with what was being identified as a 'new wave' in British cinema, in fact things were already moving in a slightly different direction. The new interest in industry had less to do with tense melodrama but rather grew out of a wider range of forces. Almost inevitably the inspiration for the new kind of cinema came from outside the industry itself and it need not surprise us that of all the strands within British culture film was to show the most reluctance to give up the norms of the early 1950s. As even mass taste began to change and as the film industry discovered that there were many young and intelligent film-goers so now film-makers found themselves having to run very hard to catch up with young writers, with the theatre, and with television.

The 1960s was to be a controversial decade and cultural historians will always debate the meaning of what happened in Britain in those years. There need be less disagreement however about the years immediately preceding that hectic decade for it is clear that in the second half of the 1950s significant sections of British society were growing dissatisfied with the middle-class culture as defined by popular writers and artists, by theatres, and by broadcasters.[13] Young people were both responding to new American music and creating their own musical scene, whilst an increasing number of college-trained intellectuals were beginning to look for something more challenging in their leisure-time activities and in the books and journalism they read. What is important here is that within these broad social changes a new brand of essentially autobiographical writing developed in which poets, novelists, and playwrights attempted to trace the tensions first between themselves and their own family and community background and then between themselves and the values of the increasingly suburban conservative consensus, all the while adhering to colloquial and authentic patterns of language. Quite suddenly there were writers saying that they were what they were because they came from particular backgrounds, ones that had received very little attention in British culture, and that in one way or another those backgrounds and then their subsequent experiences had given them an energy and a confidence that they now wanted to feed into a new national debate. Over a period of four or five years people who read books, who went to the theatre, or who most probably just read the *New Statesman*, the *Sunday Times*, or the *Observer* knew that there were new British voices who were somehow or other challenging the cultural norms. Already there were attempts to define the new era, to pin it down with slogans like 'the angry young men', and to work out its precise commitment to Socialist principles or existentialist philosophies, but on the whole it was still the general impression of vitality, of individual energy, and a new range of language which really conveyed itself to the wider body of onlookers. There was just a general feeling that a generation of educated Britons had been given their own spokesmen.

Of course the film industry was always ready to turn to well-publicized literary successes and now there was the additional incentive that the young writers had clearly pointed to the existence of a new kind of audience. It was time for British films to reflect the new mood and new energies but first some different conventions and modes of operation had to be established. Inevitably there were false starts as film companies took hold of literary successes only to succeed in reducing them to the crass and bland levels of run-of-the-mill films. The problem that film-makers faced was that of introducing some kind of edge or social anger into films whilst hanging on to the format that would entertain the mass of ordinary film-goers. It would in any case have been difficult for any British director of the mid-1950s to have captured the tone of metro-politan and Oxbridge incredulity that Kingsley Amis had juxtapositioned with provincial pretension and absurdity in his 1954 novel *Lucky Jim* but by any standards the film version made by the Boultings in 1958 is bad. In their usual way the Boultings had settled for caricature and farce: the action takes place in an entirely studio-bound artificial world and all sense of place, time, and character is sacrificed so as to ensure blandness. What is now almost unbelievable is that *Lucky Jim* was filmed almost two years after the great theatrical event of the decade, namely the first night of John Osborne's *Look Back in Anger* at London's Royal Court Theatre. Only a small number of theatre-goers would ever have seen Kenneth Haigh's performance as Jimmy Porter at the Royal Court but across the nation many people got to know about it because critics like Kenneth Tynan immediately identified Jimmy Porter as the spokesman of a signifi-cant and identifiable group in British society. The play, said Tynan, 'presents post-war youth as it really is, with special emphasis on the non-U intelligentsia who live in bed-sitters and divide the Sunday-papers into two groups, "posh" and "wet"'. It's appeal, he argued, would be to a minority but to a minority almost seven million strong, 'which is the number of people in the country between the ages of twenty and thirty'.[14] Quite simply Jimmy Porter was venting his anger on behalf of an educated generation that wanted to see some sense of meaning and purpose injected into Englishness now that the empire had passed away and who wanted to be allowed to use their own values and talents so as to forge a new cultural and political debate. Jimmy suggests that people like him were often thought of as getting their cooking from Paris, their politics from Moscow, and their morals from Port Said, and he should have added their cultural and musical inspiration from America although he reflects that 'it's pretty dreary living in the American Age - perhaps all our children will be Americans'. Whatever the truth of this analysis the main source of his anger is a concern for Englishness and how that can be worked out in terms of his own energies. For the new generation that was, and was to remain, very much the heart of the matter and it was this concern that was to inspire so many writers over the next few years. It was precisely this concern that film-makers now had to capture in their own product.

The original reviewers of John Osborne's play had not been slow in identifying the American influences. In the *Daily Worker*, 'P.G.' suggested that it was 'the kind of play Tennessee Williams might have written if he had spent a month of rainy Sundays in Birmingham', whilst in the *Sunday Express* Derek Monsey provided a wonderful example of how insights can be born out of cultural antagonism when he argued that 'what Marlon Brando's script writers have done for the inarticulate American moron, Mr John Osborne has attempted to do in *Look Back in Anger* for the over-articulate English phoney intellectual'.[15] That evening spent at the Royal Court had reminded some critics at least of the way in which American films had been pointing and British film-makers would certainly have taken the point that recourse to American idioms might be the only way in which the new anger could be brought to the screen. What happened now was that a sequence of films appeared in which new aspects of British society were offered instalment-like to audiences and in which some element of anger was communicated. In a way the process was very much hit or miss because starting from the premiss that it was desirable to film a particular play or novel there was no guarantee that the adaptation, the acting, or the directing would adhere to the spirit of the original or be meaningful and memorable in cinematic terms. Success or failure might come in quite unexpected ways. Tony Richardson's 1959 film of *Look Back in Anger* was an accomplished film that was certainly far more demanding and challenging than most other British films and it is not surprising that it was not a great success at the box-office. It was, as Pauline Kael stressed, very much a talking film; it prompted her to acknowledge 'the glory of talk' and to give thanks for 'rhetoric', and to that extent the Osborne position was fully communicated.[16] There has always been a critical debate in Britain as to whether Richard Burton was the right choice to play Jimmy Porter for the purists thought of him as being too old (he was 33 whilst Jimmy was meant to be 25), too theatrical, too Hollywood, too physical, or too Welsh (critics tending to forget that Osborne was half-Welsh and had even included a Welsh character in the play), but there is no doubt that Burton convincingly depicted anger and resentment especially in those scenes where he is denouncing his wife's upper-middle-class and imperial background.[17] Meanwhile Gavin Lambert thought Burton 'electrifying' and he was particularly struck by Jimmy Porter's reference to his wife's 'Mummy' for to Lambert the British middle-class Mummy was one of the great reference points of the culture and 'the most damning thing that one can say about most British films is that they're made for Mummy'.[18] Certainly Burton successfully identified the enemy and made his points count but he was not the right man for the part. Probably in 1959 there was nobody who could have done it better but his problem was not that he was old but rather that he was too patrician to play successfully a social rebel: his classical features and ecclesiastical voice had robbed him of his impeccable working-class credentials and he was already in a league where he could only play kings and emperors. But for all Burton's power it is interesting that he did not totally dominate the film. The original play had indeed been entirely Jimmy Porter's but in the film he only claims part of our attention: not for one moment do we believe that Burton himself is playing the trumpet but jazz is firmly identified as the music of a rebel breed, the performances of Mary Ure and Claire Bloome made femininity into something more challenging, more vulnerable, and sexual than it had ever been before in English films, and above all perhaps there was a very real sense of a recognizable England in the location shots. Lambert commented on the 'superb evocation of London suburbs' and in particular it was obvious that the market-place, the railway station, and the pubs were very real places. This was unmistakably and unashamedly an English film.

Exactly the same was true of Jack Clayton's 1958 film of John Braine's novel *Room at the Top*. This was to be a commercially successful film because it dealt realistically and maturely with the subject of sex in a provincial English town. The whole power of the film came first from the suggestion that a sexual affair could be enjoyed even in the industrial North and then from the suggestion that an ambitious young man would abandon a fascinating mistress in order to marry a rich man's daughter. Again the locations were exactly right but what was far more crucial was that Simone Signoret's performance as the careworn and very moving mistress constituted a display of sexual and emotional frankness that was quite novel in British cinema. In a sense the depiction of the male hero Joe Lampton was a little less important for he was really meant to be something of a cipher, somebody who realized that his progress from a working-class home through lower middle-class respectability and anonymity as a clerk to eventual career success depended to an extent on the emasculation of personality. Seen in this way the casting of Laurence Harvey was absolutely right for as one later critic was to comment the part 'perfectly matched the cold arrogance of his screen personality'.[19] Harvey certainly offered a frightening version of a deliberately manufactured man for which his own career had perhaps ideally prepared him but if his Joe Lampton was an accurate enough comment on what was a real social phenomenon in England it was altogether too stark a performance to become the basis of any kind of mythology outside the film itself. There were thousands of real Joe Lamptons but not all of them were quite so much like the tailor's dummy or, to use the word that David Thomson was to apply to Laurence Harvey himself, 'the zombie' that we were offered in this film.[20]

Quite obviously British cinema was waiting for its own Brando, for an actor who could embody social anger and yet combine it with some indication of his own confidence and vitality. More than anything else the British cinema screen was crying out for an uninhibited display of masculine energy, preferably from an actor untouched and unprocessed by traditional Home-County and film-studio blandness. It was very revealing that the two most interesting and culturally challenging male roles to have come up in the British cinema since the war had been offered respectively to the son of a Welsh miner who had gone on to become the greatest Shakespearean stage actor of his day and to a Lithuanian who had grown up in South Africa. For a number of entirely different reasons neither Richard Jenkins nor Larushka Skikne had it in his power suddenly to use the cinema to speak for a whole generation. It is at this point that one becomes aware of all the problems of class, community, and religion in British life and of finding actors who could retain traces of cultural authenticity from their backgrounds and yet remain attractive and intelligible as they were exposed to wider audiences. As British directors contemplated this problem they were given a very good lead by Joseph Losey, who was now making a series of films in London in which he was using Stanley Baker to provide an element of class tension. Losey had always been interested in the notion of the working-class guy who carries something of his background with him into a wider world as was beautifully illustrated in his 1951 Hollywood film *The Prowler* when the face of the Los Angeles cop, played by Van Heflin, lit up with delight as he realized that the lady on whom he had called might have remembered him as a young basketball star in their Midwest home-town. Now Losey wanted Baker to display all the class and sexual arrogance of a Welsh miner's son as he came up against social privilege, authority, and affectation. Basically *Blind Date* (1959) and *The Criminal* (USA *The Concrete Jungle*) (1960) were melodramas in which Losey's attempt to incorporate some of the virtues of American genre films was somewhat negated by elements of pretension and by self-conscious acting of a traditional British sort, but certainly as the police inspector in the earlier film Baker's Welshness nicely heightened the social and sexual tension.[21] At the end of *Eve* (1962) Jeanne Moreau looks at Baker, who is now playing a fraudulent working-class novelist masquerading as a personality at the Venice Biennale, and dismisses him as a 'bloody Welshman' and that of course was the problem for British directors could not go on just using 'bloody Welshness' as the only vehicle for social anger. As for Losey himself, subsequent interviews were to confirm that he had never renounced the radicalism and approach to class that he had learnt in the New York of the 1930s and which had led to his blacklisting, but it is interesting that, apart from *King and Country* (1964), in which Tom Courtenay played a working-class lad shot for desertion during the First World War, he was

12 *Blind Date*: For Losey, Stanley Baker brought to the British screen working-class manners and sexual arrogance.

not again to concern himself with either direct political messages or working-class themes. He was to explain this in terms of his finding the conflict between the middle class and the aristocracy more complex and therefore more interesting than that between the middle and the power-less working classes. On the whole he thought 'it would be pretty hard to find a worker with the preoccupations which most bourgeois artists are deeply concerned with' for whilst there were 'unhappy' and 'angry' workers it was 'hard to find a neurotic worker'.[22] So as Losey found that he and his writer Harold Pinter shared a fascination with 'class dynamics' they were able to produce two of the most sharply observed stories of class in England without any direct reference to the working class. In *The Servant* (1963) the whole world of a young aristocrat is taken over, degraded, and destroyed by his man-servant Barrett, a role in which Dirk

Bogarde conveyed all the insidious and obsequious cunning of the servant class, whilst in *Accident* (1967) not a little of the fascination in a very complex film arises out of the artistic, professional, sexual, and basically class rivalry between Bogarde and Stanley Baker, Losey's two favourite British actors, who were here recapturing for the camera their real-life hostility.[23]

Meanwhile in 1960 that long-awaited quality of 'bloody Englishness' was at last captured in cinematic terms in a film version of Alan Sillitoe's 1958 novel *Saturday Night and Sunday Morning*. In the previous year Karel Reisz had made *We Are the Lambeth Boys* for the Free Cinema and already he had shown that his Central European, English boarding-school background had given him insights into the particular vitality and disrespectfulness of working-class lads. His documentary had shown many of that genre's old faults - quite commonplace English phenomena for instance are explained as if the commentary had been written for visitors from another planet - but we are introduced to very real and natural Londoners and there is one superb scene as the youth-club members return from a cricket game against a posh school: as their lorry passes through the West End our working-class heroes sing: 'We are The Lambeth Boys' and barrack lookers-on just to let them know who precisely were travelling through; silence returns only as they cross to the council flats and poor terraces on their side of the river. Such minor acts of class rebellion were the very stuff of English life and it was precisely that tone of what Alexander Walker called 'truculence' that was the essential element in the artistic and popular success of *Saturday Night and Sunday Morning*.[24] Excellent location work was now becoming the hallmark of the new British cinema and Reisz's opening scenes in the factory rooted his film in an industrial community in an almost totally unprecedented way. Of course there are hints of music-hall in some of the support playing and in truth much of the plot was extremely skimpy and the hero's main antagonist is only a plump street-corner gossip, but what gives the whole enterprise ballast are the locations and also the two portraits of very different working-class women by Rachel Roberts and Shirley Anne Field. There was not a hint of caricature or affectation in Robert's platitudinizing housewife and Shirley Anne Field confirmed that the age when working-class glamour was entrusted entirely to middle-class starlets was really over. The women needed to be good so as to provide the right tension for Albert Finney's bravura performance as the factory-hand Arthur Seaton. This was Finney's first major screen role; he had trained for and achieved early success on the stage and his declamatory style remained essentially theatrical but now he gave Reisz a performance that succeeded totally in cinematic terms. Finney was later to talk of his debt to Brando and in particular of the way he had learnt to use the telling gesture but what was crucial in his depiction of Arthur Seaton was his sheer magnetism.[25] Finney himself was independent, surly, powerful, and northern enough to express all of Arthur's rebelliousness and bloody-mindedness and yet he could also charm his entire audience by the very obvious relish with which he wrapped his mouth around Northern vowels and with which he enjoyed every meal, drink, and woman who came before him. 'Most of us know someone like Arthur', said the *Daily Worker*'s Nina Hibbin, and certainly there could have been no fuller depiction of the way in which most working-class lads thought of themselves.[26] No wonder that Pan printed a large number of paperback copies of Sillitoe's novel, put a drawing of Finney on the cover, and co-operated with British Lion in the biggest tie-in and joint promotional campaign that the country had ever seen.[27]

As the critics sought to identify the qualities of *Saturday Night and Sunday Morning* Hibbin suggested that it was a film 'that talks to us in

13 *Saturday Night and Sunday Morning*: Albert Finney as the worker who won't be ground down.

our own language – it is the best, most accurate and profoundest film that has yet been made in England – here at last', she concluded, 'is a film which, not only in the contemporary fashion, is about the working class, but also of and for the working class'. Such enthusiasm was a worthy tribute to the way in which Reisz and his team had completely mastered the Northern idiom but in a sense Hibbin and many other contemporary critics had missed the point. In his novel Sillitoe had sought to express the thought-process of a worker in essentially literary terms and in order to do this he drew on his own experiences as a factory worker but he was doing so in his new guise as a well-travelled and ambitious writer. Sillitoe himself had left the North far behind and it was that which helped him to distance Arthur from the rest of the work-force, from his family, and from his neighbours.[28] It was precisely the point that Arthur was better than anyone else that Finney had so brilliantly picked on and used as the basis of his performance. Of course he gets his come-uppance – rebellious heroes always do – but only in the most minor way: his already-married mistress becomes pregnant, he is beaten up in a far from convincing fight, and finally he has to settle for marriage to his girlfriend. Certainly there was a good deal of comment about the last moments of the film when Arthur and his girl look at the rapidly expanding housing estate where they will live; he throws a stone and is mildly admonished but promises that 'It won't be the last one I throw.' Has Arthur been tamed? Of course he has for that's the way of life, but one can guarantee that audiences were less concerned about that ending than critics and they would have forgotten too about all those earlier set-backs he had received. What would be remembered was that initial effusion of energy and arrogance. Arthur is the man who voted Communist in the last election but only as a way of saying a plague on all your houses for he had been under age and had used his father's vote; of course he hates foremen but at the same time flaunts his pride in his own ability to be a successful worker and therefore a high earner, but above all he is just different from and better than anyone else and especially his fellow workers, who 'got ground down before the War and never got over it'. At the very outset Arthur has established that his whole philosophy is best summed up in the phrase 'don't let the bastards grind you down' and he warns 'I'd like to see anybody grind me down'. Whatever happens in the subsequently rather predictable and silly story we know essentially that Albert Finney will never be ground down. We accept him as a genuine worker but we can appreciate fully why he was so much better than the rest of his mates and why inevitably he must move away from them. The degree to which he fascinates us is the extent to which he must move away from the world that moulded him. And so Sillitoe, Reisz, and Finney had at last succeeded in giving cinematic expression to the kinds of confidence, arrogance, and vitality that allowed a talented worker to begin to change himself into something different.[29]

Saturday Night and Sunday Morning had above all succeeded in mythologizing that crucial moment when the successful person comes to terms with what was best about the family and community whilst at the same time appreciating that his individuality and talent would now have to be tested in a wider world. It was a moment very new in British cinema and yet on which the whole mythology of America and the very different tradition of acting had made into a basic convention of Hollywood's films. Amongst those who noted this new direction in British films was the American sociologist Herbert J. Gans, who was interested in the cultural and class differences between English and American films. Gans had examined the frequently made accusation that American films were essentially 'models for the middle-class life-style' but his conclusion was rather that Hollywood portrayed 'people with working-class traits' who were seeking a middle-class life style and who quite crucially were able to do that 'without having to resort to middle-class methods like "proper" behaviour, education, status and rationalism'.[30] At last the British had learnt this lesson. We are interested in Arthur Seaton not because he is a worker but because he is an exceptional worker who will obviously go places, but even more we are interested in Arthur Seaton because he comes in the form of Albert Finney. The crowds turned up in their thousands because they had been told that at last there was a British actor who had not emasculated his personality in acting school and who knew that to convey reality you had to be far from ordinary. British cinema had made its most powerful statement about the working class by discovering a new kind of hero.

In the early 1960s it often seemed as if British film crews had more or less taken up permanent residence in the industrial North as all the much publicized plays and novels of the period were turned into films. No other film had quite the impact of *Saturday Night and Sunday Morning* and certainly nobody emerged to challenge Finney's position as the darling of the moment. There remained the fascination of actually seeing the industrial North on film and often the location shots were the most memorable of a particular film; certainly Halifax was the real star of *Billy Liar*, photographed by Denys Coop for John Schlesinger in 1963. Within the industrial context each film developed its own mood and style and at the time one came away remembering the rather fussy pretentiousness of *The Loneliness of the Long Distance Runner*, the tedium of *A Kind of Loving*, and the unrelieved gloom of *This Sporting Life*. There was now a general sense that the documentary nature of these and other films was well sustained either by well-established professionals (Trevor Howard as Mr Morel was by far the best thing in Jack Cardiff's 1960 version of *Sons and Lovers*) or, more usually, by a new school of actors although nobody seemed to have quite that full-bloodedness that Finney had displayed. Rather it was a question of taking more minor delight in a range of different qualities. There was the remarkable way in which Tom Courtenay could suggest vulnerability, resentment, resilience, and a tendency to anarchy as the introverted loner; there was the utter charm and naturalness of Rita Tushingham which allowed her to inject memorable magic into the sordid world of A Taste of Honey; there was Laurence Olivier's haunting evocation of music-hall in The Entertainer; there was what one reviewer called Ian Hendry's 'terrific' caricature of a salesman in Live Now, Pay Later; and perhaps most memorably of all in Lindsay Anderson's 1963 film of David Storey's novel This Sporting Life Richard Harris and Rachel Roberts succeeded in conveying the powerful way in which a whole range of emotions could be experienced even in a drab provincial world.

For all its sense of professional accomplishment and whatever the moments of genuine delight, this new wave of British films could not go on for ever if only because the particular chapter of literary endeavour of which it was essentially a reflection had already come to an end. In truth the culture as a whole was moving on and now as young people, artists, and intellectuals sought to celebrate Britishness there was less interest in contemplating the old provincial milieus which so many of them had left far behind. Both audiences and critics had tired of the proletarian settings and were almost certainly beginning to share the kinds of reservations that the American-based Englishman Vernon Young had experienced with A Kind of Loving: Young had commented on the 'deadly, patient accuracy' with which director Schlesinger had 'exhumed every shop-worn brutality of instinct and reproduced the excruciating syllables of a populace'. To Young this technique had amounted to 'a kind of loving' but in essence all it had achieved was 'a competent naturalism' and there was 'never more style than the absence of it' in the subject dictated.[31] It is important to read the American critics on that wave of British working-class films because they were in an excellent position to spot their qualities, and especially the extent to which they could surprise, whilst at the same time they were able to see more objectively than British critics those shortcomings that prevented the films from being truly great by international standards or from becoming really influential within their own culture. Even as early as Saturday Night and Sunday Morning Elizabeth Sutherland had identified problems that were to remain characteristic of the genre when she suggested that Reisz's film ultimately lacked 'the magic of the unsaid' and offered nothing 'to make you shiver': for her Reisz had illustrated 'the curse of so-called "realism"', he had 'made illusion real' but not 'really significant', he had made a film that was 'more than documentary' but 'less than art'.[32] What Young, Sutherland, and others could see from the beginning was that, whilst there had been a British breakthrough, it was only a breakthrough into a new kind of worthiness. The sheer professionalism of cameramen and actors had allowed the mastery of a new idiom but that idiom was being used only to reflect the energies of an earlier group of writers. The films had been made at one step and several years removed: meanwhile those writers had gone on to the next stages of their careers and they were already tackling different and equally real challenges. That left a clutch of British films that had only proved that they could record a range of emotions and feelings within a 1950s industrial context. Of course various kinds of 'anger' had been expressed but what in turn angered the American critics was that the film-makers seemed incapable of developing that already old-fashioned social and cultural position into a fuller and more responsible statement. In America it often seemed as if what the British liked best about their new cinema was precisely Young's notion of the 'loving' way in which provincial working-class life had been captured on film and even if protest was shown there had been no real attempt to follow that through in cultural terms.

In remarkably perceptive observations Dwight Macdonald had already expressed his amazement at the general phenomenon of English literary anger. For the American critics the whole new British fascination with the working class just seemed like a reprise of what New York had been though in the 1930s, but on reflection he did admit that in America as compared to London 'The Enemy looks very different'. Macdonald's concern was with the growth of what he termed 'masscult' and 'midcult' and in that England which the angry young men were railing against he, for his part, could detect all the defences and safeguards that were needed to defend high culture. Young British writers were not yet in a position to appreciate this point and hence their different perspective: for them there was too little democracy, for Macdonald too much; they saw cultural divides as 'relics of a snobbish past' whilst he saw them as dikes against cultural corruption; 'they see standards as inhibiting, I see them as defining'; and 'they see tradition as deadening, I see it as nourishing'.[33] Of course it was to take the British quite a few years to catch up with this debate but here we have some indication of the level at which British cinema and criticism should have been operating. At this stage it would be fairer to remind ourselves of some of Pauline Kael's more general observations. In her initial response to the new British realism Kael was often in danger of caricaturing political and artistic attitudes but she was surely right to stress that 'the notion that working-class life is reality' made sense only in a very crude way and that there was every reason why art, including film, should go on to look at equally 'real issues' confronted by 'the desperate and dissatisfied offshoots of industrialism - those trying to find some personal satisfaction in life or in art'. She then went on to comment on how claustrophobic the new films were and this led her to reflect on whether 'the main difference between the English working-class and the American working-class experience

may be the miracle of space' for 'our space and the privacy it affords us
. . . . allows for day-to-day freedom of thought and action'.[34] These are
important points which need fuller comment but suffice it here to note
that American critics had fully appreciated at the time how limited and
parochial the British achievement had been. We are drawn back to the
significance of Finney's performance in *Saturday Night and Sunday
Morning* for perhaps he alone had suggested that there were energies that
required more space and that would pose questions outside the narrowly
traditional proletarian world.

The conventions and prejudices of both class and West End theatre had
traditionally defined the qualities that leading British actors had been
expected to possess but now Albert Finney had shown that producers and
directors could successfully experiment with a new type of actor. It was
no longer necessary for passion, appetite, and enjoyment to be held in
check, the camera was no longer afraid of robustness and charisma, and
the English language no longer had to be enunciated solely in the accents
and style of minor Civil Servants. The cinema at last recognized that
there were other British modes of behaviour and of speech and at last
began to appreciate something that Hollywood had always known, and
that was that individuality in cinema terms was often best provided by
actors who even as they trained and began their own social ascent nevertheless retained much of their own adolescent identity as well as
something of their working-class or regional idiom. Of course this was a
lesson that British culture as a whole was learning in the 1960s and these
were the years in which television personalities, politicians, academics,
writers, designers, and photographers clung on in a wholly unprecedented
way to their regional accents and identities. Whatever the lasting value
of what was achieved in Britain in the 1960s that new sense of the country as being made up of a number of regions remained a revolutionary
fact. Certainly there was no transfer of resources or of political power
away from the dominant Home Counties but now at least talented individuals from wherever were invited to succeed on their own terms in their
own way. Now too there were television companies, newspapers, and journals who no longer patronized the regions and regional identities but who
rather took these things seriously. Quite simply the message of the 1960s
- and, for all the propaganda and hype, it remained a fundamentally
valuable and liberating one - was that you could be talented and
successful although you came from an unfashionable region or working-
class community. What remains true and crucially important was that the
areas of success remained circumscribed. Certainly fortunes were made in
these years but it was fundamentally cultural rather than industrial or
even entrepreneurial vitality that was being celebrated. The talented
British had chosen the arts in the widest sense to be their special area of
excellence and it should not surprise us that, as the world and especially

America became fascinated by 'a swinging London' and by 'a trendy Britain', there almost seemed to be something 'showbiz' about British life as a whole. These successful musicians, actors, and playwrights were not a cultural adornment but rather they constituted what the culture as a whole had become. If nothing else the British had learnt to entertain themselves in the fullest possible way; from now on entertainment was at the very heart of what constituted Britishness.[35]

Albert Finney's sudden stardom and especially his performance in *Tom Jones* (1963) proved that cinema audiences were ready for more full-blooded and less socially refined versions of Britishness and where this son of a Lancashire bookmaker had led others were to follow. Following the international success of *Tom Jones* Finney was only to have an episodic and problematic film career although his own film *Charlie Bubbles* (1968) represented a delightful reflection on the variety of claims that the industrial North could make on those who had moved on to success in London: but meanwhile the British working class had come up with two other actors who were not only to eclipse Finney but who were to remain the most popular and successful British stars throughout the whole era. First there was Sean Connery, a product of working-class Edinburgh: he was born in 1930 the son of a £2-a-week rubber-mill labourer and he had played semi-professional soccer, been invalided out of the Royal Navy, and then had gone through a bewildering range of odd jobs before taking up acting.[36] As a young actor in his early 30s Connery had displayed a number of gifts but they had tended to pull in different directions for as a Shakespearean actor he undoubtedly had power but he rather garbled his words in the style of a Scottish soccer manager, whilst as a contemporary urban heavy he had a physical grace and a charming smile that hinted at other possibilities. His working-class credentials were impeccable but that was not the way his acting career was to develop and it was only in a one-off and untypical film like the 1970 American production of *The Molly Maguires* that he was to be cast in the mould of his ancestors. Rather Connery was to achieve fame by creating for the screen Ian Fleming's secret agent James Bond. The Bond films became hugely popular because they used many of the stylish and sexual idioms of Britain's 'swinging sixties' to take the traditional adventure story into a new era of international technological danger. The success of the whole enterprise very much depended on the playing of Bond for the actor needed to embody the customary virtues of British officer class and yet have sufficient charisma not to be overwhelmed by the epic scope of the dangers he would encounter. Connery was a little beefier than the young Hoagy Carmichael on whom Fleming had modelled his literary hero but in every other respect he was perfect. Here was a Bond who was very much at home in clubland and with the smart international set and yet whose control of irony not only allowed him to parody the conventions of

14 *The Molly Maguires*: Sean Connery, the star with impeccable working-class credentials.

adventure films but to carry the whole audience with him almost as if it were he alone who was allowing them access to a series of private jokes. Much of Connery's poplar success can be explained in terms of the way in which he exuded physical, sexual, and social style as well as good humour but it is interesting to ask whether his unfashionable background allowed him an even wider appeal than that which a more traditional actor could have secured. Alexander Walker has quite rightly stressed that Connery's persona was essentially *classless* although one should not underestimate the extent to which almost any intelligible Scottish accent can be made fashionable and even patrician. Perhaps there was nothing revolutionary about the casting of Connery but nevertheless his selection does offer some indication of how the British cinema of those days was changing. Certainly casting is always a fortuitous process but it is worth noting that several well-known actors had been under consideration and that the eventual decision to entrust the part of Bond to a relatively unknown actor of Celtic and working-class extraction was taken by two American producers, 'Cubby' Broccoli and Harry Saltzman.[37] The whole Bond venture like so much else that was vital in British cinema was now dependent on American finance and inspiration and the somewhat momentous invitation to Connery to bring to life a literary hero who had been spawned out of and initially made popular by one small section of London's social elite was very much an indication that the Americans were in the process of teaching the British studios that in the search for talent one had to do far more than round up the usual suspects and that on the screen there was no substitute for personality and style.

As if to drive home these points Harry Saltzman went on to launch effectively the career of the second great British discovery of those years, Michael Caine. Like Connery, Caine had impeccable working-class credentials: he was born in 1933 in an unfashionable area of London's South Bank, his father was a porter in a fish market, and his mother was a charlady; before taking up acting he had worked as a labourer and in a meat market.[38] In true British style his first film *Zulu* had seen him cast as an upper-class officer but his destiny was to be the pioneer of a new era in the fictional representation of cockneys. The movies had always loved cockneys and used them as the most convenient shorthand way of representing the common people or the masses but the cinema's cockney conventions had been rooted in Dickensian and music-hall stereotypes and had always seemed to limit individual films by pulling them back into well-established stories rather than hinting at contemporary actuality. Caine changed all that by showing that it was possible to talk proper cockney and yet be a full-blooded and contemporary screen personality. After the false start of *Zulu* he very quickly established his identity in two very important and influential films; in *The Ipcress File* (1965) Harry Saltzman cast him as Harry Palmer and used him to show that spies could come from working-class backgrounds and could live very unpretentious life styles, whilst in *Alfie* (1966) his low life of sexual adventures was to be one of the most memorable and significant roles in modern British cinema. Audiences were stunned by the film's very graphic illustration of the fact that there could be a price to pay for sexual encounters but at the same time they were delighted to be introduced to a new friend in the form of Michael Caine. As Alfie, Caine brilliantly created a working-class playboy of a well-known type but he did far more than that for he used the techniques of ironic and cynical humour and of speaking directly to the audience to establish an intimacy with his audience that was something quite new in British cinema. For years to come Caine was to remain the most natural and the most genuinely liked of all British stars.

Connery and Caine were to be the two great British superstars of the next twenty years but their initial breakthrough came at a time when the whole phenomenon of British screen-acting was going through a revolutionary change. Quite simply casting was no longer a problem: the whole range of what was possible in British films had been widened, there was no aspect or nuance of British life which could not be recreated, and at last that stage had been reached at which it could now be said of British films, as it had been said of Hollywood since the coming of sound, that the acting was so natural because the right actor was always in the right part. By the mid- and late 1960s British cinema had become a many-splendoured thing with a wide range of films appealing to many different domestic and American tastes but at every point directors had seemed able to draw on an endless supply of acting talent. There were roles for young actors, attractive actors, and zany actors, as well as musicians and singers, but, of course, as a result of that breakthrough in the early 1960s the ultimate test was still whether actors could realistically and convincingly convey class tensions. The whole phenomenon of the 1960s in Britain was essentially about the opening up of cultural opportunities for regional and working-class talent and the acting profession had been an integral part of that crucial social process. Perhaps inevitably much of the acting talent still came from a theatrical background but of course that great emphasis on realism and autobiographical writing within avant-garde theatre had ensured a new kind of stage actor who was quite capable of transferring an intensity from stage to screen. Lancastrian Robert Shaw developed a malevolent edge by acting in Pinter before becoming the most sought-after screen villain of the era; another Lancastrian Frank Finlay emerged as a screen villain after having developed his talents in Wesker's plays at the Royal Court. Yorkshireman Malcolm MacDowell came from repertory theatre to capture magnificently the arrogance of youth in Lindsay Anderson's 1968 film *If*, and after having made an enormous impact in John Osborne's play *Inadmissible Evidence* the Scot Nicol Williamson went on to star in the film version of that play and then in two Jack Gold films *The Bofors Gun* (1968) and *The Reckoning* (1969), which perhaps more than any other films made at that time confirmed that British cinema was now fully capable of directly confronting the issue of class.

British cinema contrived to feed off the indigenous theatrical tradition in a number of intriguing ways but there were always to be critics who were unhappy about the theatrical base of British acting especially when examined alongside the very different American mode of screen-acting.

According to Gilbert Adair British actors have never learnt 'how not to act'; in every frame they can 'still be seen madly acting away'.[39] This charge of overacting remains generally true but things have improved enormously over the last generation and they have improved because during that time theatre and film have had to exist alongside and come to terms with television. Television has transformed British acting both by ridding it of much of its rhetoric and grand gestures and by confirming that great need for a repertory company of actors who could quietly and effortlessly re-create the whole range of British regional and class types. Early British television was a strange mix of music-hall comedy within a very middle-class Home Counties format and it was by no means certain that it would prove capable of coming to terms with contemporary society. Then very dramatically in the ten years that followed the introduction of commercial television in 1955 the drama and current affairs departments of both BBC and ITV switched their attention to the problems of provincial and class life in modern British history.[40] Suddenly news and documentary programmes were allowing the ordinary people of the country to have their say: for the first time ever people were allowed to describe their own experiences even if they were heavily edited and heavily patronized by interviewers who suspected that this was their own great moment. As real people began to infiltrate the reporting of actuality so television drama came more and more to concern itself with everyday situations. First in single plays and then increasingly in police and crime serials and soap operas the need was for actors who could play natural and regional and low-life types and who could do so without having recourse to overblown histrionics that would just seem ridiculous on the small screen. Billie Whitelaw, Carol White, Tom Bell, and Dennis Waterman ushered in a new era of British acting.

Until the 1970s it was still fashionable to express regret at Britain's failure, unique amongst western industrial cultures, to develop a truly national cinema: only very slowly did a minority come to realize that in effect television had become Britain's national cinema. In that vital decade following the arrival of ITV, television moved into a central position within the national culture primarily because it was never subject to the same pattern of commercial constraints that had cramped British film producers. British cinema had always been run by showmen who could never escape from both the economic and the artistic strangleholds of Hollywood, but British television was run by executives who had a highly developed sense of public service and who were in far more direct contact with the needs and expectations of their mass audience. There were a number of different traditions and different possibilities within the commanding heights of the television services in the 1950s and 1960s but what was vital was the remarkable degree of consensus with regard to the notion of public and cultural responsibility and then the way in which

senior executives were able to recruit a talented generation of programme-makers and programme-writers most of whom were a product of
that social and cultural reawakening that had gone on since the mid-
1950s and nearly all of whom were anxious to come to terms with the
nature of British actuality. The showmen of Wardour Street and the film
studios had never felt under any political or artistic obligation to tackle
British social problems; indeed their political and financial masters had
actively discouraged them from doing so. It was hardly surprising that
creative artists and writers had never felt drawn to the actual process of
film-making: there had been no expectation that films could be made relevant and important. Television had very quickly moved in to fill this
cultural vacuum. In a way it had its own constraints and its own notions
– there were for example strongly developed ideas about the structuring
of programmes and the central role of so-called personalities – but, above
all, there was a strong feeling that the medium of television could be used
both to depict and to analyse the nature of the British experience. Television became a major factor in the British way of life because the
purchasing or hiring of a set became a status symbol during a consumer
boom, but the new national audience was introduced to current affairs
and drama programmes which were produced and written by a very distinctive generation of intellectuals who had been prompted into a new
interest in their own society by academic influences just as they were
being offered new professional opportunities. Historians like E. P. Thompson and social critics like Raymond Williams and Richard Hoggart had
inspired a new interest in the regional and class base of Britishness and
to the extent that social history, the social sciences, and a social analysis
of literature were now becoming fashionable in universities, in academic
journals, and in the influential weekly magazines and Sunday papers so
too did they now become the real inspiration of a whole era of British
television.[41]

Television's cultural revolution was established on a broad front but it
was pioneered by a small number of individual talents who responded to
intellectual and professional promptings and who appreciated, as Alexander Walker has described, the new freedoms allowed by mobile sound-
synchronized cameras, by more flexible procedures than the film technicians had permitted, and by the new low-key acting techniques that
television seemed to invite.[42] The standards and expectations of a new
generation of programme-makers were set by a small group who graduated from current affairs and magazine programmes to televised drama
and films whose creative flair was founded on a mix of political commitment and technical expertise. Furthermore as members of this group
achieved distinction as the makers of televised drama so they moved on
to become feature-film directors and in so doing they helped to establish
the creative link between television and cinema that was to become one

f the features of modern film culture in Britain. Jack Gold, whom we have noted as the director of *The Bofors Gun* (1968) and *The Reckoning* (1969), had come to feature films after a long career in television that had peaked with his 1967 film of Jim Allen's story *The Lump*, which had depicted the angry politics of unionism and non-unionism on a building site. The producer–director team of Tony Garnett and Ken Loach made the nation as a whole aware that a new era had opened with their depiction of working-class London in *Up the Junction* (1965) and especially in their dramatized documentary *Cathy Come Home* (1966), which dealt graphically with the problem of homelessness. They too went on to make feature films: first *Poor Cow* in 1967 and then *Kes* in 1968. More than any other film Ken Loach's adaptation of Barry Hines's *A Kestrel for a Knave* summed up the transformation that television had brought about within British film culture. A young actor, David Bradley, magnificently conveyed the resilience, isolation, and self-sufficiency of a working-class schoolboy and he fully induced audiences to share his view of an adult world that was vindictive, insensitive, petty, and perhaps a little pathetic. *Kes* was made for the big screen but it could only have been made as a result of the new era in television drama. It was television that had sanctioned politically committed scripts, authentic even if unintelligible regional accents, and the use of actors (such as Colin Welland and Brian Glover in *Kes*) who had strong and entirely natural regional identities. *Kes* was a popular success because of the strong yet charming story but it was television that prepared the way for a film that was critical of the methods of schooling at a time when the nation was fiercely debating the way in which secondary education was to be organized and which encouraged Ken Loach to include a brilliantly funny scene in which a fussy and bossy sports master fully reveals his bombastic and frustrated personality during a school soccer game. The new conventions of television had allowed British cinema not only to become relevant, contemporary, and controversial but also to pick up the everyday idioms and jokes of ordinary people.

By the end of the 1960s occasional feature films, television drama, and television reporting were making British audiences far more aware of their own country and were confirming the broad radicalism of many intellectuals and university graduates. In essence the British had become used to the working class describing their own experiences and to having writers and actors taking up those experiences and expanding on them in fictional forms. There had certainly been something of a cultural transformation but it was yet to be proved that these journalistic and artistic breakthroughs had significantly changed the nature of British society. Perhaps neither film nor television was as important as the press in shaping political and social ideas and in any case socially committed drama was still only a small part of the total output of the British film and television studios. There was still only a handful of socially realistic

15 *Kes*: The working-class self-sufficiency of David Bradley.

feature films and the whole structure of film exhibiting and financing in Britain still mediated against independent directors. Television's main problem was its blandness; even a first-class drama would only with difficulty totally hold the attention of its audience and even then its impact would soon be wiped out by a rapidly changing pattern of very different programmes with very different values. Outspoken and powerful plays and films became accepted as episodes in a wider and unceasing pattern of entertainment whilst, as social realism became the basis of soap operas, police series, and situation comedies, so it came to be appreciated as a style rather than as something that implied relevance or urgency. Television had a way of reducing everything to its own level.[43] It soon became obvious that the half-hour comedy series was likely to be the most popular as well as the most original of television's drama forms for within that format outrageous satire and social comment could be combined with comedy in a way that could attract a mass audience. Johnny Speight's *Till Death Us Do Part* was the best thing on British television in the 1960s and 1970s and yet even as Warren Mitchell was using his role as Alf Garnett to expose the ludicrous nature of working-class prejudice he was establishing himself as a greatly loved family favourite. Television had inaugurated a new age of social analysis but it rapidly turned that analysis into mere patterns of conversation. The medium of motion pictures had been given a new versatility but it had also been somewhat diminished.

9 The national experience in Britain and America

In the decades which followed that apparently significant period for British cinema in the 1960s it was very noticeable that debate was dominated by the widely expressed desire that there should be something that could be clearly identified as a 'national cinema'. The general assumption amongst both film-makers and critics was that film remained a weakness, an embarrassment within the culture and that the urgent need was for a new financial dispensation and for new artistic initiatives that would allow a break from the established pattern of film-making and from that overwhelming sense of inferiority in the face of Hollywood.[1] Nearly always it was the successful national cinemas of France, Italy, and other European countries which served as an inspiration and which prompted potential British *auteurs* to believe that they could combine with their technicians to make films which could take their place alongside novels as vehicles of contemporary cultural reflection and analysis. It was all a question of finding the right political and commercial formula, one that ideally would combine American-scale backing with the freedom that European directors had to make artistic statements.[2] At times this waiting for a national cinema was a tedious process and it was not only film fans who tired of the way in which so many false dawns were followed by periods of depression and recrimination. And in any case it was becoming more and more obvious to the public at large that many of those whose main concern was with film were just not keeping up with the rapidly changing pattern of entertainment.

The case for a national cinema was still being argued by the ever-hopeful at a time when the nation as a whole had opted for television and when in any case the High Street cinemas were disappearing at an alarming rate. As we have seen the very reasonable suggestion was soon being made that in effect television had become the British national cinema and perhaps for a while in the 1970s it seemed as if television would entirely kill off the domestic cinema.[3] In the event, however, a slightly more complex situation was to emerge in which new sources of finance, including the television companies themselves, were to guarantee the survival of a British film industry, albeit one that had enormous difficulty in defining any national role, given its declining audience and the almighty power of television. In a very cruel way social and technological change had denied the British their opportunity of having a mass national cinema but the compensation was a whole range of opportunities for recording dramatized fictions and for showing them at the very least to a sectional audience. The distinction between film and television became very blurred, not least in the minds of the audience, but at least scriptwriters and potential directors knew that both television companies and film producers were looking for new material and any one script, the work of an individual writer, an adapter, or a director, could eventually end up as an international blockbuster acclaimed on Oscar night, or as a television film shown to either a large or a small audience, or just as something that would be quietly admired in difficult-to-find London art houses and the Celtic Film Festival. The opportunities for filming fictions were there as never before and certainly the search was on for well-written and original stories but all the while the artistic and commercial pressure of television on film was to be a distinctly confusing influence and the result was a fragmentation of the impact that any particular film could have, a blurring of its meaning within the culture, and a tendency for any filmed fictions to have their impact only within socially separated subcultures. Britain of course has remained a socially divided nation and in a way the development of several strands of entertainment has tended to break up even further any possibility of a mass audience. In the Britain of the 1980s one has a sense of a considerable pool of very able writers and directors confident of being able to produce work for their regular sectional audience but quite unable to imagine how they can capture the attention of the nation as a whole.[4]

Until quite recently the decisive cultural reference point in Britain had been the phenomenon of the early 1960s when the whole question of national identity and values had been opened up by the autobiographical reflections of both writers and academics. Novelists and dramatists had highlighted the tensions that could develop as working-class youths moved away from the terraced houses that had been their homes and began to experience new fashions and values in schools, colleges, offices, and more especially London. Meanwhile Raymond Williams and E. P. Thompson were inspiring a new generation of students to broaden their notion of what constituted British culture by using literary and historical sources to cast light on the conditions that ordinary people had actually experienced. In broad political terms this new emphasis on autobiographical reflection and on the new patterns of social mobility reinforced the commitment of many professional and educated people to the Labour Party and ensured something of a Labour-dominated consensus for much of the 1960s and 1970s, not least in educational circles where the whole approach to the humanities was worked out in terms of a Williams–Thompson prospectus.[5] All the while this new sense of

Britain having at least faced up to its class and regional differences was sustained by those very literary and artistic groups whose work had brought about the new age. First and foremost there was the theatre, which undoubtedly had taken pride of place in that cultural renaissance that Britain had experienced in the latter half of the 1950s. The first voice of the new era had been that of Jimmy Porter, heard in John Osborne's play at the Royal Court, and now as the country became aware of new energies and a new anger it became evident that it was the playwrights who were achieving most with working-class idioms. There were many good writers but above all it was the East End's Harold Pinter and Leicester's Joe Orton who in their very different ways were able to combine their ear for working-class dialogue and appreciation of raw and basic emotions with a sure sense of what constituted a well-written and structured play. Once again the theatre was the most vital form of cultural expression in Britain and it was guaranteed a new lease of life at precisely the moment that television was threatening to carry all before it.[6]

In fact, of course, in the thirty years that have elapsed since Jimmy Porter's début there have been as many crises over the issue of national identity in the British theatre as there have been over the same issue with regard to film. Contemporary British theatre is sustained by a strange amalgam of social pressures, many of them operating as a kind of cultural lag: there is a vague awareness of the need to pay homage to the masterpieces of the past, a continuing sense of theatre-going as the kind of thing that civilized suburbanites should do, and all the time a feeling that tourists should have their expectations fulfilled. But amidst all this the inspiration of the Pinter-Orton era lives on and almost miraculously a considerable stream of native talent is drawn towards a theatre which remains overwhelmingly concentrated in London and the result is that both new plays and revivals have continued to cut through to cultural raw nerves in ways that no other art form can ever quite rival. Of course theatre in Britain can never escape from the charge of being a minority art, an entertainment for a metropolitan elite, and nobody has ever thought seriously about a major revival of provincial theatre especially as public funding is drying up. But to think in these terms is vastly misleading for although theatre indisputably caters for an elite it remains incredibly democratic and genuinely national in the way in which it recruits its talent. The clues to its vitality and relevance are to be found in the quality of writing and directing and even more perhaps in the acting. Until the 1960s the British acting tradition was one in which great stars were surrounded by very competent character actors: today London still needs its virtuoso stars, its successors to Olivier and Gielgud, but what is so noticeable now is the way in which Ian McKellen and Anthony Hopkins are supported by whole troupes of young men and women who can breathe all the passion of contemporary life into plays by Howard Brenton, David Hare, Shakespeare, Webster, or whoever. Since the 1960s the cultural significance of acting in Britain has been transformed and that acting is still seen at its most intense and passionate on the stages of London's sponsored and fringe theatres. Gilbert Adair is quite right to speculate whether this kind of acting is at all suited to film but to argue this is merely to confirm that for a generation now theatre in Britain has been able to generate a degree of passion and emotion that has eluded the cinema.[7] Theatrical writing and acting feed off layers of feeling that have been denied British film: for all its elitism it taps democratic energies and offers genuine catharsis. It was very revealing that Osborne, Pinter, and Orton all went directly from anonymous and lowly backgrounds into careers as actors before they found their voices as writers and between them they gave British theatre an edge which many subsequent careers have helped to sustain.[8]

British film-makers have to live with the superior cultural reputation of the theatre and in particular with the often stunningly high level of performance but that really is as nothing compared with the devastatingly complicated influence of television. From the beginning the country had opted for a national television service and that ensured that standards would be high, that there would be range of clearly identified audience demands, and that programmes would be strongly influenced by the same kind of values that helped to determine the general political consensus. It was this framework that allowed the new cultural patterns of the 1960s to win their greatest victory for during that decade the British found themselves being entertained by a television service that set out in its current affairs programmes, documentaries, and plays to explore all the many different experiences that constituted national life. Television sanctioned autobiographical reflection and sociological investigation and in the process trained a new generation of directors and actors who were quite effortlessly capable of re-creating every social and linguistic nuance of a Britain both past and present. The general impact of television on the Britain of the 1960s and 1970s is a vast and complicated subject but certainly in those years television drama filled out the sense of Britishness in a way that the cinema had never done.[9] It was only the occasional programme like *Cathy Come Home* and *Edna the Inebriate Woman* that would initially bring about a political response and only very occasional plays like those of Colin Welland and Trevor Griffiths which would use labour history as a political reference point but all the while the realities of urban life and especially on housing estates and in high-rise apartments were being spelled out. They were heady days: there were many minor irritants but in general there was great excitement amongst writers, directors, and technicians, a feeling that the nation was being educated into a new political sensitivity and a more sophisticated appreciation of socially realistic drama. It seemed as if a golden era of national cultural debate and analysis was about to be well and truly established.

It never quite worked out that way although the myths of the 1960s were perhaps always to form the context in which so many television people went on working. The problem was that a television service could never afford to become as radical and political as some people wanted and that, as we have suggested, television as a medium tended over a period of time to reduce almost everything it touched, whether it be actuality or fiction, to a kind of background information. The sensation of the previous evening is perhaps keenly debated over the following morning's coffee but this is just swamped by an unbroken stream of very well made and presented diversions in which light comedy and sport always seem well to the fore. One of the main problems was that documentary-type dramas had come more and more to resemble current affairs and news programmes and that audiences were obviously losing interest in constant reminders of the country's problems. British television has never lost its ability to dramatize memorably the difficulties of single-parent families or those living in Northern Ireland but in more recent years it has been interesting to watch as that superb mastery of social reality and class and regional idiom has been siphoned off into situation comedy and its first cousin soap opera. Working-class soap operas are now the most popular programmes on British television and several times a week mass audiences settle down to follow stories which tackle the range of emotional and social problems that ordinary British people would be expected to encounter. Much of the writing and most of the acting that characterizes these serials could never have evolved without the cultural changes of the 1960s and quite occasionally the BBC's *EastEnders* achieves moments of quite disarming realism, but for all that these programmes, like the ubiquitous situation comedies which surround them, owe as much to the Ealing and music-hall tradition as they do to naturalistic acting. Even when the mood of the moment is tragic or tense the mode remains essentially comic: the actors are always slightly sending up their parts and aiming to confirm stereotypes rather than to fill out true individuality. The popularity of such programmes owes much to the nostalgia of viewers who think of this as the world of their childhood and to the way in which, nearly always subconsciously, the format is accepted as a gentle and affectionate satire of old-fashioned preoccupations.[10] Meanwhile lavish praise is also bestowed on an endless stream of television serializations of both nineteenth- and twentieth-century literary classics but these, of course, are just soap operas in costume. Nearly all these dramas are better written, produced, and acted than were the old studio-made British films whose place in the culture they have effectively taken but for all their smoothness and mastery of idiom, especially that of the young, they are not really very different as artifacts from what has gone before. Stock television drama is rarely political, shies away from direct social and cultural confrontations, elevates a limited number of emotional and romantic dilemmas to an absurdly prominent position within the lives of particular families, and often seems locked into an endorsement of community values at the expense of being able to identify with individual heroes or to follow the dilemmas of a character who wants to move out.[11]

The lesson that television tends to be bland and to create its own anaesthetic of familiarity had to be learnt over a number of decades but the respective British channels had trawled deeply in recruiting the best talent of a generation and they are still staffed by men and women who have fought hard to keep television plays and films at the very heart of British culture and to quite a considerable extent they have succeeded. In recent years the most challenging fictions have been provided by television programmes in which first-class writers have been encouraged to provide scripts that have used the full resources of television to move beyond straightforward realism. Perhaps Dennis Potter has always been television's most consistently original writer and it has been fascinating to follow the ways in which he has constantly reworked those 1960s preoccupations of community, class, nostalgia, and social mobility and yet all the while tending to move away from straight realism. *Pennies from Heaven* (1978) and *The Singing Detective* (1986) were both heavily autobiographical and very acute in their observations on class but what made them memorable was the sharpness of the writing and the refraction of Englishness through a perspective provided very significantly by the conventions of popular Hollywood films. Nobody has done more than Potter to guarantee the quality of television writing and to prompt directors into increasingly ambitious acting and editing and he has done this most noticeably by confronting directly that apparently and hitherto paradoxical nostalgia that so many British people over the age of 40 have both for their own working-class childhood and for American popular culture. In the wake of any Potter play or serial the rest of the domestic product suddenly looks very lack-lustre and provincial, but *The Singing Detective* came at a time when it seemed as if the savagely satirical and radically feminist writer Fay Weldon was switching her attention from the novel to television. An adaptation of her *The Life and Loves of a She-devil* was quickly followed by a new serial *The Heart of the Country* and both provided stark reminders of how bland most television writing had become and of how much hypocrisy and smugness still remained to be exposed in Britain. Potter and Weldon seemed to offer every prospect of an inspired post-realist era on British television but of course it remains to be seen to what extent political and social pressures will sustain the capacity for experiment in terms of televised drama.

From the vantage-point of the late 1980s it seems almost certain that the divided nature of British society will continue to inspire documentary-type dramas dealing with the problems of deprivation and race but already one writer has used the medium of television to give quite brilliant fictional expression to the kind of working-class despair that many people took to be characteristic of the period. In *The Boys from the Black Stuff* the writer Alan Bleasdale created a drama which, whilst being rooted very firmly in that very distinctive linguistic and comic Merseyside idiom that had become increasingly familiar since the early days of Alun Owen, also went well beyond the clichés and stereotypes almost to surrealistically expose the social and economic hypocrisies and illogicities of a post-industrial urban world.[12] Ultimately this study of the twilight world of the unemployed and the casually employed came to focus on the personality of Yosser, a part in which the actor Bernard Hill generated the kind of inner and potentially violent anger that should have become one of the hallmarks of social drama in the post-Pinter era but which ever since the early television plays of Pinter himself had been largely confined to the London stage. Bleasdale's collection of plays was notoriously funny, deeply moving, profoundly disturbing, and totally anarchic: it was the kind of material of which any national cinema would have been very proud. But, of course, *The Boys from the Black Stuff* was made for television and so became something of a seasonal wonder discussed in the pubs and by the television critics but then relegated to the edge of the collective memory. The contrast was with *Chariots of Fire*, a film which caricatured elements of the country's ruling class and which concerned the careers of two heroes worked out and defined very much in terms of contemporary American idiom. Not surprisingly Hugh Hudson's film became a cult success in America and so was immediately taken up by first the British film industry as a way to impress the Americans and then by the culture as a whole as an artistic event of great significance. The respective responses to Bleasdale's television plays and to Hudson's film of Colin Welland's story very neatly illustrated the state of filmed drama in the Britain of the 1980s.

In a way the permanent rivalry and occasionally co-operation between film and television provide one of the most fascinating aspects of British life but they do make for some artistic confusion: they complicate the relationship between film-makers and their audience and they certainly make the whole notion of a national cinema somewhat misleading. British films are still largely financed by businessmen and promoted by showmen and so quite naturally they come to us along with a certain amount of razzmatazz, but mostly now these films are the work of writers, directors, and technicians who still believe that theatrically projected films can achieve artistic and emotional statements that cannot be made in any other way.

16 *The Boys From the Black Stuff*: Bernard Hill's Yosser reacts to unemployment with anger and fierce family loyalty.

Almost remarkably in a country in which the point is often made that both television and the theatre have achieved a mastery of form and a confident identity within the culture, the eternal optimism of British film-makers lives on. The problems, however, are enormous.

In those British cinemas that remain open audiences still survive over-whelmingly on a diet of American films and today as in the past the way will have been prepared for those films by publicity in the press and on television and perhaps above all by radio disc jockeys. The American domination of the big screen still constitutes a problem inasmuch as even quite successful British films seem to come along as almost random and fortuitous offerings rather than as part of a continuing cultural experience. Attending the latest '007' film has become something of an anniversary for the declining cinema-going public but perhaps there has been no sense of an enduring British tradition since the demise of that

Carry On series which in the 1960s and 1970s had allowed comedians who quite significantly had owed their fame to radio and television to give one last blast to old music-hall and variety routines. When viewed in the cinema and especially perhaps in provincial theatres British films seem to lack any sense of context: they are arbitrary creations with no point of reference other, of course, than that of television. By the 1980s it was clear that very mercifully the British film industry had left behind that quite dreadful period in which it had become almost solely concerned with making film versions of television situation comedies which had fitted well into their original thirty-minute format but which became very bland and lack-lustre when blown up into full-length big-screen entertainment. It was obvious that in Britain there continued to be an artistic belief in film and yet all the time it seemed difficult to establish a precise line between what should be put on the big screen and what should be left to television and this difficulty was particularly acute for those writers and directors interested in social realism. Over a period of twenty years or so British television had developed its mastery of socially realistic drama but perhaps it also took that length of time for film directors to realize that audiences that went to the cinema expected something that went beyond the conventions of the small screen. In his stark autobiographical trilogy the former miner, Bill Douglas, achieved a very real sense of style but all too often film directors who seek to make social statements in the cinema seem to be just blowing up what is essentially television material.[13] That is true of the uncompromising political films made by Karl Francis and even of the very well-made and relatively successful Northern Ireland story *Cal* made by Pat O'Connor. Critics like Martyn Auty and Chris Peachment have often commented on how so many British directors just go on thinking in television terms and so end up by producing work that is usually dull on the big screen.[14] It may even be, though, that the problem is deeper than that for one senses that British audiences are still a little embarrassed when they are confronted in the cinema with scenes of native domesticity. The set designers have usually done their work well but everything seems just a little too cramped; all the right objects are in their proper places and yet somehow they seem a little unnatural - they take on a life of their own as if they had been highlighted in a still-life painting. One can almost feel individual patrons responding as they recognize familiar objects such as sauce bottles, china dogs, and milk bottles, and the amusement that comes from the recognition of their favourite television programme on that flickering screen in the background is soon eclipsed by the dreadful sound made by those over-crisp newspaper pages. Things are always a little too familiar and then a little too deliberate but perhaps the main visual problem is just that of colour for this nearly always serves to remind audiences that they are watching an artifact. The colour is never quite right in British films and one's impression is in this respect that the maximum alienation occurs during scenes set in and around ordinary homes. And if this was not enough there is still the problem of sound for Britain remains a country of quite distinctive class and regional accents and every director faces the problem of combining authenticity with intelligibility. Enormous advances have been made in this regard but they have not always ensured box-office success and one reason for that may be the fact that many provincial and lower-class accents come out in a curiously flat and somewhat disquieting way. On film at least the subject of British domesticity seems to guarantee bathos.

In the mid-1980s there were real signs that at least some directors were appreciating the need for British cinema to move away from realism and to become more genuinely inventive in cinematic terms. As far as social realism was concerned comedy seems by far the most promising mode and this seemed to cater very much for the tastes of the largely adolescent and student audiences on which many cinemas depend. Bill Forsyth's *Gregory's Girl* and Chris Bernard's *Letter to Brezhnev* seemed to suggest a whole new genre of light comedy based on the need for the urban young to overcome the hostility of the inner city by developing their own fantasies although the tendency still seemed to be towards farce or whimsy rather than really hard-headed comedy. Film comedies in Britain still seem to pull their punches a little and it is almost as if the industry has deliberately refrained from making a totally challenging and anarchic social comment in *The Boys from the Black Stuff* vein. Peter Smith's film of Bleasdale's *No Surrender* was a disappointment in that respect for in a hopelessly cluttered work there just seemed to be too many characters and too many incidents. One senses, though, that the future lies with comedy and that one day very soon a very hard-hitting social comedy will emerge out of one of the North-country's blighted cities. The writer Hanif Kureishi is on record as suggesting that in the Britain of the 1980s 'everything is so horrific' that people are no longer interested in social realism but the whole point about comedy, as he was well aware, is that it can achieve a cutting edge denied straight documentary even as it appeals to mass audiences.[15] The clearest proof of this was Stephen Frears's 1986 film of Kureishi's *My Beautiful Laundrette*, which was surely the most satisfying British film of recent years. Kureishi's script brilliantly captured many facets of the Pakistani experience of England but what was most memorable in the film was the depiction of London's punk culture and in particular the playing of Daniel Day-Lewis as Johnny, who moves on from the National Front to a love-affair with his old school friend Omar. Day-Lewis is a highly skilled actor who in 1986 came before the British public in an amazing variety of different television and film roles but his quite stunning performance as Johnny not only allowed a very telling juxtapositioning of London's punk and Pakistani communities but also came as a dramatic reminder to many film-goers (and television viewers) that for years they had closed their eyes to the significance and meaning of what was going on amongst young whites in Britain's inner cities. In setting out to comment on race in London and to explore his own identity Hanif Kureishi had come up with the lesson that the punks were really far more alien that the Pakistanis.

So many British middle-class intellectuals and graduates look back with nostalgia to the 1950s and 1960s that they often seem to forget that the cultural achievements which moulded and sustained their values and social identity were very mild affairs as compared with the fact that the general sanctioning of a youth culture was creating new social and cultural divisions that were to be very bit as real as those which had been thrown up by industry in earlier times. For several generations education had been the central reference point in determining the values of the young and in particular grammar-school students had played a decisive role within the culture by forging a link between the classes and by virtually robbing their secondary-modern contemporaries of any cultural identity at all. In the 1960s the social hold of education was irreversibly diluted and henceforth the values of both the home and the school had to exist alongside those worked out by young people themselves. The young went into a ghetto that was defined most markedly by age itself, by dress, by language, and above all by music that was made familiar at first by records and then more noticeably by discos and in particular the transistor radio. So-called 'pop' or 'rock' music became the most creative, dynamic, and original aspect of British cultural life but by its very nature it was a subculture that tended not to have meaningful links with the broader patterns of entertainment that together constitute a form of national consensus. As people aged and certainly as they took up careers they tended to move out of the subcultural ghetto into an adult world that was even further removed from the experience of the young than had been that 'mandarin' culture of the 1950s which had prompted Jimmy Porter into rebellion. Even so it is perhaps surprising that pop music has had so little impact in terms of broader cultural patterns. There have been a number of promising films such as Derek Jarman's *Jubilee*, which in 1978 used the occasion of Queen Elizabeth II's Silver Jubilee to show that a very new London was coming into being, and Franc Roddam's use of the Who's album *Quadrophenia* was to evoke the initial days of rebellion in the 1960s. But one is left with an enormous sense of lost opportunities. In 1976 Nicholas Roeg quite brilliantly combined the conventions of pop and of science fiction in *The Man Who Fell to Earth* and that film should have inspired a whole new era in British cinema and should have launched the singer and actor David Bowie into a film career that would have inspired other musicians such as Sting to take up the challenge. What has denied the British a glorious era of musically inspired cinema has been the very firmness of lines between the subcultures as well as that very old realization that films made so entirely in the national idiom would not do well in America. The cultural and commercial restraints are as real as ever but just as real is the continuing failure of the artistic imagination. In 1986 a hugely expensive and ambitious attempt was made to make a statement about the young in Britain of that generation but the text that was chosen was a brilliant novel that had been written by Colin MacInnes as long ago as 1959. Perhaps not surprisingly the film of *Absolute Beginners* was a hopeless mishmash of musical, cinematic, and cultural styles that ended up as neither social history nor cultural comment. What is revealing is the contrast between the mediocrity and uncertainty of that film on the one hand and the often quite startling excellence of so many British advertisements and pop videos on the other. It is difficult not to conclude that it is with these forms that British pop-culture has really come into its own, and to accept that is only to confirm one's sadness and one's disbelief that so much musical and technical talent have not been able to sustain a truly great pop or rock cinema. Of course investors are very conservative and always have two eyes firmly fixed on the American market but the truth remains that the British produce very few contemporary artists who think primarily in terms of cinematic innovation or who are capable of transcending class and subcultural barriers. Orthodox middle-class and middlebrow culture serves to disguise the continuing heterogeneity of British society and it is very much that formidable heterogeneity which now, as in the past, blocks any progress towards a national cinema.

Things are different in the United States quite simply because film has held its place within the national culture. Of course there have been immense changes: that great studio system of Hollywood which had held such a monopoly and which had guaranteed the uniformity of American cinema has virtually gone and not surprisingly audience figures have declined. But Americans and especially young Americans still go to the movies in their millions and the film industry and film-makers still receive the full support of the critics and commentators in sustaining the view that many of the best and most successful movies are hugely relevant to an understanding of what is happening within American society as a whole.[16] Quite simply film remains an integral and essential part of the continuing debate on the very nature of America and the meaning of the American experience. To comprehend the place of film in contemporary America one first has to appreciate the very different role played by television as compared with the British example for leaving aside the genuinely national role played by televised sport in America it is generally true that the overall level of programmes has been determined by the tastes of working-class audiences. Consequently television plays a far smaller part in the lives of the young and especially in the lives of the socially mobile high-school and college students. The new American film industry that has emerged is now just one strand within the structure of corporate America; it has achieved for itself a distinctive niche within the culture as the provider of high-quality entertainment to a very loyal audience of young people. In any one year only a very small number of really successful films are needed to guarantee the profitability of the industry and in this respect the sure-fire pattern has been for films in which very charming if perfectly ordinary American citizens are exposed to precisely the fantastic and horrible adventures that television could never create, let alone show. So these blockbusters provide the commercial base of the industry but meanwhile the theatres have to be kept going for the rest of the year and the interest of that potentially loyal audience has to be maintained.[17] It is within this context that what, on the face of things, appears to be a new American cinema has developed. In fact regular film-goers have increasingly found themselves in a position of not knowing what to expect for between the blockbusters there are always lots of surprises. Above all the new American cinema has been characterized by diversity and audiences, especially those in major cities and college towns, have been given a wider range of choice than was ever the case in the past. Now between the fantastic adventure stories there is every likelihood of the film-goer discovering movies which examine the dilemmas of Vietnam veterans, condemn American involvement in Central America, or portray very precisely the nature of life within a particular ethnic community. Certainly America's post-Hollywood cinema has been characterized by a tremendous degree of enterprise and by sheer inventiveness and for those who had grown up in earlier decades there were two very great surprises. First there has been the emergence of a genuine director's cinema. With the passing of the studio there was a marked decrease in the power of producers and editors and soon there were directors like Woody Allen and Brian De Palma who could only be described as *auteurs* and who built up their own regular audience. In this process one could trace the greatly increased influence of European cinema and it was significant that several British and European directors now responded to the new freedom by actually choosing to work in America. The second great surprise was the way in which the United States itself now began to 'star' in movies for increasingly films were made on location and not necessarily in New York or in California. For years Hollywood had closed its eyes to the drama of the big cities such as Chicago and Pittsburgh and to the scenic beauties of so many areas of America such as the South but now there was every chance that even routine crime stories or melodramas would be given an added dimension by being set in a very particular and lovingly photographed location. Suddenly the film camera was celebrating the beauty and diversity of

America and individual states rushed to give tax concessions to potential film projects. Suddenly there was a steady flow of entertaining, intriguing, and often controversial American movies and it did not take the annual Oscar ceremony or *Time*'s review of the year to convince most socially and culturally aware Americans that they needed to keep up with what film-makers were saying about their country. Hollywood had gone but America was still hugely entertained by the movies and entertained furthermore in ways that were distinctly and quite possibly significantly American.

When one considers the extent to which the Vietnam War and the rebellion of youth had politicized the country in the 1960s it was not surprising that American directors should react to the end of the studio era by making films that were socially and politically significant. Indeed for a period in the late 1970s it even seemed that the American cinema was setting out to celebrate the independence and militancy of American labour. Certainly audiences in New York and other centres of sophisticated viewing would have been aware of a new clutch of labour-history documentaries: *Union Maids* and *Rosie the Riveter* recalled past struggles while *Harlan County* depicted the continuing struggle in the nation's most militant coalfield. In a sense these documentaries were precisely the kind of film that would have been shown routinely on British television but there was a feeling that the film world was making up for lost time and assuaging its guilt by turning to this forgotten aspect of the American experience. This seemed to be confirmed by the feature film *Norma Rae*, which told the tale of a dispute in a Southern mill-town in which the largely female work-force became unionized. Even the casual movie-goers would have been struck by the unusual features of this film with its strong anti-management position, its quite uncompromising depiction of the very ordinary and stark conditions in which American operatives lived, and Sally Field's totally unaffected performance in the title role. More discerning members of the audience would also have appreciated that this was not just a random movie dealing with a labour dispute but rather one that had been consciously planned both as a tribute to an era that had passed and as a celebration of the new freedoms that American film-makers had recently acquired. The movie was the work of Martin Ritt, one-time Communist and veteran of the Group Theatres, the black list and the Actors-Studio, a director whose central reference point had always been the New York of the 1930s and who had survived through the bad years to make films like *Hud* (1963), *The Molly Maguires* (1970), and *The Front* (1976) which to some degree had reflected the values that he had learnt at that time.[18] Clearly *Norma Rae* was made as a straightforward statement of class principles but the action of the movie rests on the way in which the rebellions and radical instincts of Norma Rae, the local leader, are prompted by the outside organizer, who happens to be a

17 *Norma Rae*: Sally Field introduces audiences to the reality of radical working women.

Jewish intellectual from New York City. Here then was a tribute from Ritt to that great interaction between the worker and the New Yorker which had formed one of the corner-stones of American radicalism and one of the touchstones of American cultural values generally for at least a couple of generations. The new mood of the 1970s had allowed Martin Ritt to reflect on his own experiences and on how the movies as a whole had moved so decisively away from what they had promised in the 1930s. His film was an exercise in nostalgia but nevertheless was one which seemed to confirm the way in which movies were now going.[19] It was no wonder that there were now scholarly journals such as *Jump Cut* and the *Journal of Popular Film and Television* which concerned themselves in part with the social message of the movies.[20]

In point of fact, of course, as the contributors to the journals were to argue the social message of the movies had not greatly changed and neither was it going to. Rosie the Riveter and Norma Rae became well-known names but there was never to be any wave of films dealing with American labour history or indeed with the contemporary labour struggle. Rather the situation was one in which American film-makers became more prepared to set their stories in working-class communities, partly because that in itself seemed to be a guarantee of critical and sectional popularity at a time when what were thought of as serious issues were fashionable and partly because such settings fitted in with the new practice of location shooting. In the vast majority of cases the new working-class films were to concern themselves with the talents, successes, and accompanying dilemmas of individual heroes and heroines – to that extent they were to conform to well-established Hollywood norms – but nevertheless the appealing freshness and vitality of the stories was in no small part due to the convincing depiction of working-class living conditions. It seemed as if a new dimension had been almost effortlessly added to the American movie for the new settings and the total command of idiom promised a new seriousness even as they guaranteed entertainment though that sheer novelty. In *Jump Cut* Mary Bufwack very convincingly argued that three country-and-western films, which had obviously been made with that kind of music's vast following in mind, ultimately came to rely on very much the standard Hollywood biopic conventions with the emphasis on emotional dilemmas rather than a faithful depiction of the working-class communities that had produced the musicians. What struck Bufwack about *Coalminer's Daughter*, *Honeysuckle Rose*, and *The Night the Lights Went Out in Georgia* was that there had been little attempt to deal with any political issues or with the way in which country music tended to operate as a collective defence mechanism within working-class communities but when she nevertheless conceded that the films did represent a notable advance on how white working-class supporters of country music in Appalachian and other rural areas had normally been depicted she was perhaps appreciating the more positive way in which most film-goers would have reacted to these films.[21] Audiences were beginning to appreciate new pleasures now afforded by the movies and in particular they sensed that what was going on was a filling out of America as they were introduced to its rich diversity through the agencies of stunning photography and fine naturalistic acting such as that of Sissy Spacek in *Coalminer's Daughter*.

During the course of the 1980s it became increasingly clear that the movies were in fact celebrating the physical diversity of America and although one soon tired of car chases through San Francisco there was the regular pleasure of discovering the ingenious ways in which directors and cameramen would respond to new locations and especially to new cities. It is very much within this framework that one has to examine those increasingly frequent but nevertheless random films which had reason to look at the working class. In the best films there was always a convincing integration of plot and location but there were also occasions when one was well aware that directors were consciously 'slumming it' and had tried to exploit a working-class theme or location rather than using it quite naturally. With *Blue Collar* (1978) one had been genuinely excited by the notion of a movie about auto workers and one was thrilled to be confronted with that very rare thing, a big-screen depiction of working-class America, but then we were cheated for although what Michael Omi describes as 'the heist-caper format' entertained us it nevertheless kept us at arm's length from all the important questions about labour relations, trade unions, and race relations that we really wanted answered.[22] Paul Schrader's *Blue Collar* was perhaps the most spectacular but not the last

18 *Blue Collar*: The realities of Detroit but only in the interests of routine entertainment.

example of a film that could have achieved greatness but which settled for routine entertainment. One was left wondering when Detroit would graduate to the cinema that its history would suggest. In *The California Dolls* Peter Falk worked hard to bring alive the character of the immigrant's son who ended up managing a couple of female wrestlers but one longed for a film to look more closely at the steelworks of Akron, Toledo, and Youngstown which were being used just as a backdrop. In more recent years one has felt similarly cheated by that hopelessly muddled and badly edited disco film *Flashdance*, which annoyingly only hinted at a working-class industrial background in Pittsburgh, that most filmically neglected of all American cities, but without doubt the worst offender was the Eddie Murphy vehicle *Beverly Hills Cop*, which opened with a stunning title sequence which suggested that we were about to see the best film ever about the decline of industrial Detroit, only to switch to the familiar territory of Los Angeles once the action commenced. There have been other films which have offered tantalizing glimpses of working-class reality as their plots called for such scenes and perhaps the best indication of how blue-collar America tends to be both exploited and marginalized came in *An Officer and a Gentleman* when the uniformed hero whose successful career we had seen take shape dramatically strides into the factory to claim his working-class girlfriend and presumably to take her on to better things. This marvellous moment of sheer bravado occasioned both tears and cheers within the film and amongst audiences but one was left with the afterthought that what had occurred here as a piece of not entirely justified melodrama was really one of those moments that not only called for a better film but which could have served as the starting-point for any director wanting to make a serious film about American society.

There have been moments of embarrassment and frustration but more often one has been aware of how directors have been able successfully to incorporate ordinary America into the films without any sense of affectation and in so doing they have weaned the film away from that Hollywood dependence on the ritzy hotel and the manicured suburb. In 1981 Francis Ford Coppola embarked on a second career as an experimental director and he deliberately filmed his *One from the Heart* in a studio set but nevertheless the movie realistically depicted the relationship between a girl who worked in a store and a man who worked in a scrap-yard. The bright glamour of the doubly artificial Las Vegas contrasted beautifully with Frederic Forest's memorably and deliberately flat portrayal of a lack-lustre and anonymous worker. More recently Gene Hackman achieved very much the same effect while playing a steelworker in Bud Yorkin's *Twice in a Lifetime*, a fairly routine domestic drama which deserves to be remembered as one of the most fully sustained depictions of working-class family life and one which was given a degree of novelty and freshness by its use of Oregon locations. One of the great British myths about the United States is that the Americans do not have 'pubs' and Yorkin's film is one of a number that have in recent years used a bar-room location to bring together groups of ordinary Americans. Again the contrast is with the old Hollywood films, in which the only bars depicted were either those in fashionable hotels or the speak-easies of the Prohibition era: it was very noticeable that the suburbanites never went to bars. Now at last the world's film audiences could see now normal American blue-collar and white-collar workers spent their leisure hours and perhaps Edward Zwick's *About Last Night* provided the best example of a movie which used a bar, in this case an Irish bar in Chicago, to bring its characters together. Zwick's film was an adaptation of a David Mamet play and one of the exciting prospects of the late 1980s was that there would be further films of his dramatizations of everyday life in Chicago. Nearly all the time now one has this sense of discovering the real America in movies and this is every bit as true of the farming states as it is of the big cities. One of the most remarkable features of 1983 and 1984 was a spate of so-called 'back to the land' films which rooted melodramas of everyday rural life very much in stunning and authentic locations. The plots were fairly conventional but the sheer power and caprice of nature as it could so often be manifested in the vastness of America was well conveyed and audiences were left in no doubt as to the mythic fascination that the land could hold. And once more it was the acting that authenticated the cultural experience, with Mel Gibson and Sissy Spacek in *The River*, Sally Field in *Places in the Heart*, and Jessica Lange and Sam Shepard in *Country* all looking and behaving as if to the farm born. Sam Shepard's performance was particularly appropriate for almost single-handedly he was in the process of giving the American West a new mythology and a new set of cultural credentials. With Shepard everything was of a piece, his interest in his own family's migration, the symbolic naturalness of his dialogue which had contributed to his enormous success as a dramatist, and his own distinguished appearance and beautifully underplayed acting technique which made him ideal for playing modern, thoughtful, and thoroughly independent cowboys. He was indeed, Leonard Melfi noted, the Gary Cooper of the post-hippy era.[23]

Increasingly one sensed that American cinema was both free and confident enough to deal with almost any aspect of the national experience and certainly with any setting that its tales of melodrama or entertainment might require. In the vast majority of films, though, there was no great sense of the structure of society constituting a political problem as such: the emphasis was always on the momentum of the story rather than on a sustained examination of the social whys and wherefores. It was only in films dealing with Vietnam veterans that one in any way suspected that the problems were the heart of the matter. Nevertheless there were some kinds of American films that seemed more concerned than others to say something about the nature of society and in particular deal with differences in life style and in values. There can be no doubt, for example, that one is always far more aware of class in those films which depict distinctive ethnic communities or neighbourhoods, for the obvious reason that the director will be at pains to establish both the essential 'otherness' and the undeniable solidarity of families and groups within his chosen section of society. Paradoxically, then, we are never so aware of confronting the realities of everyday life in America than when we are being shown the customs and values that have been developed by an immigrant group. In a way the attraction of such films is again partly explained by their very novelty but audiences are also quite obviously benefiting from that very precise and highly developed sense of being American that has often shaped the personalities and philosophies of the writer, the director, and quite possibly many of the cast. These films have an added edge and power and they allow us all to have a heightened sense of the American experience. Undoubtedly the Italians have made the biggest impact: of *Mean Streets*, which he made in 1973, Martin Scorsese said that he had done it to exorcize the demons of his childhood and certainly to sit through it was to feel as if one had spent the whole day drinking and fighting with Harvey Keitel and Robert De Niro in Tony's Bar in Little Italy.[24] We are taken back to a very similar world in John Travolta's great 1978 hit *Saturday Night Fever*, a film which was to be attacked by many people for its sheer unpleasantness and for its exploitation of what Peter Steven felt to be a somewhat depoliticized Brooklyn working-class background.[25] Of course the contrast between the sheer mediocrity of life in Brooklyn and the glamour of Manhattan's discos was deliberately exaggerated but audiences were left in no doubt that Travolta was depicting just the kind of violence and animal magnetism that Italian neighbourhoods were capable of producing. The film reminded many people of Paddy Chayevsky's story *Marty*, which had been filmed in 1955, but in this respect it is interesting to compare the critic Leslie Halliwell's comment that the earlier film, in which Ernest Borgnine had played an unattractive Brooklyn butcher who went dancing on Saturday night, was characterized by 'new naturalistic dialogue' which falls 'happily on the ear' with his view that in the Travolta film 'all the characters seemed to have crawled from under stones'.[26] Conventions had changed and so, of course, had Brooklyn.

The product of the ethnic ghetto is just a special kind of American but undoubtedly that kind of background can add levels of nostalgia and sentiment to any review of the socializing process but it can also encourage a much clearer understanding. It certainly seems to encourage directors to keep asking questions about the American experience. It is fascinating that, having tackled some of the big issues, Francis Ford

Coppola should begin making smaller films, such as *The Outsider* in which he explores the nature of adolescence, and in so doing encouraged the emergence of a new generation of young American actors who would guarantee that film would not lose its ability to keep up with the passage of the years. Meanwhile Woody Allen after a period of analysing his own Manhattan set retreated into history and into his own working-class background and quite suddenly in both *The Purple Rose of Cairo* and *Radio Days* we were given moments of very affectionate and perceptive insight into a past world in which, of course, the movies had flourished. All the time it is the films made by the children of immigrants that seem to be the most penetrating and the most socially adventurous and inquisitive and it is certainly these qualities which made Michael Cimino's *The Deer Hunter* seem to be one of the boldest, most intriguing,

19 *The Deer Hunter*: At last the American cinema gets to a steel town.

and most controversial films made for many years. In their immediate reactions the majority of critics went off in search of interpretations of the Vietnam War, with the least perceptive of them concentrating on whether the experience of soldiers had been realistically depicted. The best discussion of the film was provided by Dennis Wood, who emphasized the basic comparison that Cimino was making between the meaninglessness of the war and the meaninglessness of everyday work in the steel-mill at Clairton and then the inability of the community to cope with the suicide of one of its most loved products.[27] It was a difficult and not entirely unflawed film but one that could be cherished for the way in which it deliberately lingered on the working-class Ukrainian community that lived around the steelworks. One was fully aware that the wedding ceremony in the church (and especially the music) and then the subsequent reception and dance were all lulling one into a sentimental and nostalgic acceptance of class and community but the combined effect of the industrial setting, the great family set pieces and the acting was to leave you in no doubt that men who came from such a background would love each other and relate to each other in a way that no crazy economic or military logic could ever question. A film had been made that had earned the love that it wanted to test and it had rooted that love in a very specific working-class community. In part one was just charmed by Robert De Niro but in this as in all his films one was aware of how that charm had developed and how it was always related to other people. In *The Deer Hunter* a director was using workers to make a profound statement but he used them not as a stage army or as an excuse for melodrama but rather as complex and passionate individuals within a strange world in which the familiar and reliable were always likely to be challenged by the horrific and the illogical.

De Niro is the bravest, most versatile, and most accomplished actor of his generation but he has a cult or sectional rather than a mass following. Even in the post-Hollywood era of today there are still stars of the traditional sort whose very name will guarantee the success of a particular film whatever its inherent merits, and what is especially fascinating is that the two greatest stars of the mid-1980s were both fully conscious of the capacity of the popular feature film to impart some kind of social message. Essentially they were both populists who rooted their films in what they took to be the values and prejudices of working-class Americans and then shaped their own roles to express precisely the kind of individual freedom and success that were thought to be the birthright of every American. This was the basic formula that was worked out with varying degrees of sensibility and sophistication in the many films that starred Sylvester Stallone and Clint Eastwood. Stallone will always be remembered as Rambo, the 'vet' who went back to 'Nam' to win the war that the intellectuals and journalists had not let American fighting men win the first time around, but it is interesting to trace the antecedents of that character. This New York Sicilian actor began his career as the rather pathetic and inarticulate keeper of pigeons in *The Lords of Flatbush* but within two years he had graduated from satirizing Brando in Brooklyn to becoming something more than a mere boxing contender in Philadelphia. America was ripe for the *Rocky* myth and at the end of that film as the emerging champion jogged up the steps of Philadelphia's Museum of Art triumphantly to salute both his own success and the whole city Stallone was both celebrating his own relationship with the city in which he had spent his youth and pointing to the kind of individual breakthrough that most ordinary Americans always worked to believe in. Rocky's salute was indeed a reclaiming of the nation on behalf of the people. Stallone was already far more than an actor: he had written *Rocky* and he was now to co-author *F.I.S.T.*, a film in which he played Johnny Kovacs, a product of Cleveland's Hungarian community who drifts into trade unionism in the depression era and who by the 1950s had become a union boss and a national figure. It was an enormously ambitious film and it had consider-able value as an almost drama-documentary of the way in which immi-grants ('good simple people who like beer and lots of laughs') were unionized and then of the way in which a union having fought off scabs and blacklegs could become caught up with racketeers. The film is hopelessly long and by the end Stallone has to settle for schmaltz as he struggles to ensure that in spite of his flaws Kovacs remains a hero. Certainly we retain some sympathy for Kovacs although the ending is far too contrived to sustain any meaningful mythology, but long before that Stallone has already registered his main point that what was thought of as ethnic loyalty was far more important than politics or the organized solidarity of the working class. Trade unionism had been a useful instru-ment at one point before it became just another routine feature of corporate America but all the time there remained deeper loyalties. Having unsuccessfully tackled the great details and myths of history in Coppola fashion it was not surprising that Stallone rushed back to the uncluttered and instantly appreciated message of *Rocky* and Rambo. As Robert Mazzocco has suggested he was very much the 'comic-book' hero come alive.[28] In Peter Goldman's description Stallone was now 'film-maker to a damn-mad blue-collar America that does not want to take it anymore' but whilst that seemed to guarantee him a mass following, not only in America but throughout the world, it also ensured the increasing hostility of both intellectuals and non-film-goers.[29] Increasingly he seemed to be destroying that bond between film heroes and liberal intellectuals which had survived since the New Deal and to be heralding in a new era of concern about the impact of popular-front film on the masses.[30]

The workers and the young have cheered Stallone but perhaps they are more intrigued by the more enigmatic and demanding personality of Clint Eastwood and it is entirely appropriate that we should end with the man who has been described as Hollywood's last great star. What is interesting about Eastwood is that he is so difficult to place: obviously he was the cowboy with no name who rode into town from out of nowhere and we could take it for granted that he was something of a loner, a silent type who did things his own way. But after that what could be said? For Norman Mailer his face was that of 'a murderer or a saint', for Mazzocco 'the plebeian allure' came along with 'a patrician grace', whilst for Jack Nachbar Eastwood was 'the last American puritan'.[31] Certainly he was, in the words of *Newsweek*, 'a thoroughly American icon' and in a sense he had taken over from Henry Fonda as the classic American Everyman, but an Everyman who now had the entrepreneurial talents and artistic freedom to create his own cinema. Intellectuals have always had a weakness for genre cinema and encouraged by his massive success as the no-name cowboy Eastwood has produced a whole series of westerns and detective movies in which he has really teased the liberal establishment. He has just played out variations on the theme of puritan individualism and left the thinking classes to argue about whether he was a sexist, a Fascist, a Reaganite conservative, or just an old-fashioned Progressive. Through all of this, though, Eastwood has maintained his loyalty to America's working class and its history, the explanation of this being, as *Newsweek* and other authorities have argued, the way in which the Great Depression of the 1930s has always remained the touchstone of his values and his individualism. Eastwood's father had wandered around California looking for jobs and undoubtedly the films that treat depression themes form by far his most personal statements.[32] *Honkytonk Man* is the story of the Okie who gets to sing at the Grand Old Opry before he dies and we can see it as a tribute to Eastwood senior, as an allegory of Clint's own life, and as a moving depiction of how basic American values expressed in traditional idioms can carry the nation as a whole through hardship: whilst looking at it Norman Mailer 'felt a tenderness for America'.[33] Of course Eastwood could predict that the liberal intelligentsia would soon make this into a cult movie for a nostalgia for the 1930s was a basic aspect of their faith but his affection for the common man is not restricted to the historic past. As an entrepreneur he is fully aware of the nature of his mass following but in the movies that he makes for that audience Eastwood is well able to identify with them. *Every Which Way But Loose* and *Any Which Way You Can* are marvellously funny invitations to blue-collar and redneck audiences to laugh away their prejudices and to take comfort from the fact that one of the nation's best-known men has exactly the same tastes and pleasures as they do and that he can walk into a bar and drink beer from a bottle in a way that suggests that all is well in America. Eastwood's unique and pre-eminent position as a star can be

20 *Honkytonk Man*: Clint Eastwood and son Kyle line up to pay homage to values learnt in the Depression.

explained by the way in which he combines this appeal to the masses with a special hold on the attention and affection of many educated film-goers. He has given his liberal followers some nasty moments but few really doubted that here was the latest reincarnation of the thoroughly independent, professional, and yet highly principled hero that so many of them had supported in countless films since the depression. It was obvious that there were many Americans who were quite prepared to face up to the fact that the nation had its problems but they could do that only because they were aware that there were still heroes who knew how to solve those problems in ways that were time-honoured and formed the very basis of the culture.

10   Workers and the film

Film was born in the age of the masses and from the beginning the commercial film industry was largely concerned with producing fictional films that would appeal specifically to those masses. In the early decades that great crowd of working people who were drawn into picture-houses were not surprised to see the kinds of communities in which they lived, the kinds of homes in which they reared their families, and even occasionally the kind of workplace where they spent their days depicted in the movies. Most early feature films had been inspired by late nineteenth-century melodrama and popular fiction and so the film companies were quite happy to play it safe by ensuring that their moving pictures were centred above all on the dramas that arose out of everyday life. The great innovators in the film world were the comedians but, inspired by the one-time labourer and steelworker Mack Sennett, they also took great care to let their humour and their pranks, however absurd, grow quite naturally out of a very familiar social setting. At the very time when so many of Europe's creative artists and intellectuals were turning their backs on realism and even on accessibility, America's showmen had come up with an entertainment that fascinated and intrigued the masses because it was based on a scientific miracle and yet could be so easily accepted because of the social milieu in which its fictions were based.

The early feature film provided ample proof that it could realistically depict almost any aspect of contemporary social life and certainly that it could cover all the ground necessary to bring to life the works of nineteenth-century writers whether great or obscure. But as the American industry became more and more concentrated in Hollywood it became clear that social realism was not going to be the dominant theme as far as feature films were concerned. In fact Hollywood was to create its own fictional world: it certainly retained an interest in the broad themes of popular literature - romance, adventure, comedy, and the twists of fate - but more and more it was able to take these ingredients away from urban tenements and industrial or peasant settings and to set them either in slightly idealized versions of the past or in a very busy and upbeat version of contemporary city life. It is always dangerous to generalize about the content of Hollywood's output because the industry could always afford to experiment, to cater for sectional interests, and to indulge eccentric or visiting European directors; there were always to be films rooted in Victorian melodrama or set very realistically on the Manhattan waterfront but increasingly when the masses went to the cinema they no longer expected to see that real world with which they were so familiar. They had, of course, so thoroughly accepted all the conventions of film that they were quite happy to be led into the new world that the movies were creating. That 'world of entertainment' which was thereafter always accepted as Hollywood's distinctive creation had emerged out of an interplay of political, social, and cultural forces. As the highly concentrated film industry became very much the concern of a few entrepreneurs it was readily appreciated that feature films were being sent out to a highly politicized America. On the one hand there were the urban reformers waiting to clean up cities and control every potentially dangerous form of entertainment and on the other hand there was the fact that those very working people who were likely to be depicted in social melodramas were in real life sustaining their own political challenge. Politically it was a complicated and angry society and this, coupled with the way in which Hollywood's audience continued to grow both at home and abroad, gave producers every incentive to be less specific as far as the social content of films was concerned and to concentrate on creating fictional worlds that would be generally accepted. Certainly the very development of the American film industry on that distant West Coast should be seen as an indication that films were not going to be shaped by the political pluralism of the urban East or Midwest. Nevertheless the producers were well aware of what paying customers throughout America and the rest of the world actually wanted to see and there were two messages in particular that shaped the content of movies. The first point was that whilst increasingly working-class audiences could more or less be taken for granted it had become obvious that better films would bring in a more respectable down-town audience that would boost profits as well as provide valuable political support. On the whole that new audience was less interested in the drama of everyday life. The second point was that all audiences seemed to react to individual actors and actresses and seemed in particular to be attracted to films in which their favourites were billed to appear. Soon the star system was confirming that Hollywood's stock-in-trade would be films of adventure and romance in which the focus would always be on the varying fortunes but ultimate success of attractive men and women. Quite rightly the historian Lary May has identified the former mining engineer Douglas Fairbanks as the star who more than any other took the movies away from the world of industry and tenement and into a fantasy world that would specifically appeal to audiences that wanted films to confirm the excitement of urban life.[1]

By the second and third decades of the twentieth century it was apparent that Hollywood's showmen had created a new empire but equally apparent that their empire was one with which no educated or respectable person would want to be associated. Of course the reformers and the authorities were always on the look-out for lewdness, radicalism, sacrilege, or disrespect but as long as films were purged of these evils then it was quite enough to sustain the notion that all cinema had to offer was meaningless and trivial entertainment for people who were not capable of taking life seriously.[2] An inescapable fact of the Hollywood-dominated silent cinema of the period between the First World War and the early years of sound is that it was largely ignored not only by all intellectuals and vast sections of the middle class but also by all those sections of the working class who associated social stature and social improvement either with the religious denominations or with an active role in trade unions, political parties, or adult education classes. For the schoolteacher, the minister of religion, the conductor of the choir, and the trade union secretary the movies were an irrelevance except inasmuch as they actually weakened minds and stunted personalities by deflecting them from worthwhile considerations: what they offered was a diversion for the young, for women, for those exhausted after physical labour, and for those incapable of spiritual or mental endeavour. A clear distinction was made by social and civic leaders (and accepted by many respectable working-class patriarchs and matriarchs) between the worthwhile agencies that moulded working-class culture and another set of essentially passive and useless activities. Film-going was better than going to bars but not quite as worthwhile as attendance at sport, where at least there was an incentive for the participants to stay fit and the possibility that the audience would develop some communal identity.[3] This formidable body of contemporary opinion would need to be respected and even to be accepted were it not for the fact that so many subsequent groups were to discover for themselves the joys of precisely that silent cinema which the anxious and respectable citizens of an earlier era had been so prepared to reject. It is the grossest form of cultural arrogance for later elites and scholars not to accept that the qualities they are able to detect in a form of entertainment were not perceived by the masses for whom it had originally been devised.[4] In going to the movies of course those people whom St John Ervine described as 'celluloid nit-wits' were momentarily turning their backs on reality as defined by employers, ministers, and Socialists but in general they were paying to enter comfortable and possibly luxurious halls where as patrons they were treated with respect and offered extremely well-made and well-acted films that they knew were being enjoyed by similar audiences all over the world. Not for one moment did those audiences take the world of the movies to be the real world but the whole point of film was that it allowed a temporary but total suspension of disbelief. It was always appreciated that the movies had created a fantasy world but it was a world peopled by a very attractive and increasingly familiar repertory company of stars. We may surmise that the vast majority of film-goers were quite content with the transient pleasures of each particular show but there must have been many individual fans for whom the moving fictions added a level of complexity to their imagined world. They would often have been told that the world of the movies was a false world but nevertheless they would find themselves responding to glimpses of urban sophistication, style, and wit, to the nuances of a whole variety of international and historical subcultures, to situations in which beautiful women played a far more important and liberated role than in real life, to a very precise code of romantic love, and to narrative patterns which constantly emphasized the extent to which individual men and women were the heroes and heroines of their own lives and honour-bound to develop notions of personal integrity. Film fits into the general pattern of all fictions: once their conventions are accepted and disbelief is suspended then those who respond are complicating their lives through their awareness of new possibilities as well as of alternative social codes and values. For most working-class people the range of social possibilities had been defined by employers, politicians, educationalists, and religious leaders but now in the movies there was confirmation that romance and adventure could be self-generated either in the mind or by a more open commitment to the range of urban possibilities. We need to remember that it was amongst the urban masses that the first 'film buffs' were to be found.

It was only in the 1930s that educated and respectable people began to take the movies seriously and allowed themselves for the first time to enthuse about films other than the comedies of Chaplin. Of course the American film in particular had greatly changed: the coming of sound and the attempts of the studios to breathe new life into a medium that had become a little stale had apparently taken the movies one or two steps out of the world of make-believe and rooted them just a little more in a recognizably contemporary America. It so happened that the direction now taken by the movies was precisely that which had been adopted by so many educated people and in particular by those who belonged to the opinion-forming groups. The depression, the New Deal, and the devastating political changes in Europe had now sanctioned a new interest in the full ramifications of democracy and especially in the role of the common man and woman in that newly appreciated dispensation. It had always been assumed that the movies belonged to the common man, were an integral part of some kind of popular culture, but now as the new talking films gave increasing evidence of their capacity to pick up the idiom of the vernacular and to reflect patterns of urban life so there developed a new appreciation that the previously despised medium of the American and indeed British cinema could be used to say something worth while and to buttress democracy. Those who had so consistently denigrated the product of the American and British studios had always conceded (albeit on the evidence of a small number of films) that the Russian and German national cinemas had graduated to the level of art because they had been shaped by directors who took their standards from contemporary painting and photography and from the novel but now it could be seen that the English-language film could develop a more humble but certainly quite valid and worthwhile role as a vehicle for depicting and glorifying the real-life drama of ordinary people. A key to the politics of the 1930s in both America and Britain was the way in which a new cohort of middle-class radicals used the concept of a proletariat as the foundation both of their values and of their strategies and the cultural corollary of that was the demand that the novel, the photograph, art, drama, and above all the vastly more popular and influential film should play a vital role in explaining to the middle and working classes alike precisely those qualities that were now taken as being fundamental to a decent society and as the main defence against Fascism. That was the central truth as it appeared to groups at the centre of things intellectual and artistic in New York and London and as it was disseminated through pamphlets and journals, through university and high-school staffrooms, and through branches of all the radical political parties.

And so to their surprise working people began to see communities resembling their own in the movies and increasingly found themselves reading critics who hailed the new realism and spoke of how film was developing that capacity to reflect all the drama of actuality both in America and to a lesser extent in Britain. As it transpired the rise of the social-problem film which so excited the critics did not arouse such enthusiasm amongst the masses and with hindsight we are able to appreciate that so many of the controversial and pioneering films of that highly politicized decade represented a compromise between the political opportunism of one or two of the studios and the cultural and social affectations of journalistic and cultural elites. Perhaps patrons in Pennsylvania and South Wales who found themselves watching films about working-class communities much like their own, but in which there were no trade unions and in which all the good ideas came from either middle-class reformers or very talented working men played by well-known stars, might just have realized that they were living through difficult days in which both showmen and intellectual elders were stumbling about trying to find new social and artistic mythologies. It would indeed be surprising if there were ordinary film-goers who did not sense in their bones what we can now see to have been the aesthetic and intellectual confusion of the 1930s. It was a confusion that operated at several levels but which had at its core the general notion that all the arts were to be judged by the standard of whether they made obvious the social and moral qualities of ordinary people. Everything seemed possible as a new cultural fervour developed; quite conveniently all the modern developments in the novel were forgotten and it was assumed that it was just a matter of time before a towering genius from the Midwest or the North of England would write the great proletarian novel and in so doing restore that great literary form back to its true nineteenth-century centrality; meanwhile drama and photography, which had the potential to be more accessible and democratic, were pointing the way forward. At every point the political imperative sustained optimism even as it closed the door on all the artistic, philosophical, and essentially subjective concerns that had dominated the worlds of art and of ideas for at least a generation. And surely it could only have been unrealistically optimistic to believe that a commercial cinema that had almost totally eschewed politics, and certainly radical politics, would now suddenly and seriously commit itself to dramatizing the actuality of working-class life. That new expectation of cinema that developed amongst radical intellectuals and their large army of fellow-travellers in the 1930s had its roots in a suspension of so many aesthetic and cultural standards and in a totally hopeless misunderstanding of the conventions of a popular cinema which had been established by that relationship between showmen and their mass audiences.

The whole basis of popular cinema was that audiences had developed an expectation of tales which were full of humour, romance, or adventure and which were set in a world that was recognizably related to real life without in any way being a mirror-image of it. Nobody expected or even desired to see any analysis of political and socio-economic realities and yet within the narrow but widely accepted conventions of film drama the *sine qua non* of acceptability was that characters and the situations which they confronted had to be within the limits of possibility. The pact that had developed between the studios and their audiences was something very rarely discussed in any public way but it was nevertheless a very definite and demanding reality. It was a pact that for all the relative cheapness of cinema entertainment guaranteed audiences movies that were made to a very high technical standard and brought into being by carefully selected and very photogenic actors and actresses. Films only had any meaning if they worked and that meant that good stories had to be well told and had to concern interesting people. In the new decade there were the additional challenges of dialogue and music and once again the showmen had to measure up to the highest standards in a very high percentage of their total output. Of course the whole basis of cinematic fiction was provided by stock situations, stereotypes, and clichés but within the overall formula there was always that expectation of a new moment of suspense, a new flash of humour, a new display of style, or a new manifestation of sex and when these pleasures came they were created by men and women who were so acceptable in their screen form that it hardly seemed relevant to ask whether they actually existed in real life.

And so it was in an era characterized by vast differences and by quite considerable social tension that the producers who controlled American and British films had devised a fictional world that fairly closely corresponded to what was though of as reality and yet one that could essentially bypass the major political and economic questions of the day. Out of life they could extract melodramas that created their own logic and suspense and from the street they recruited actors who could cut themselves off from many aspects of everyday life and yet still be accepted as real people. The more one examines that pact between showmen and audiences, the more one realizes the extent to which the whole edifice of the movies rested on the way in which the stars and supporting players sustained the apparent reality of the fictions they were enacting. Film was obviously a technical miracle but just as miraculous was the way in which it had totally eliminated any awareness that the people on show were merely actors. The very essence of the cinematic experience was that during the running time of a particular film few if any members of the audience would ever think of the fictional characters as anything other than real people and certainly would not think of the actors as having entirely separate private lives. This seemed to be the case whether the individual actor was a newcomer or a veteran and in some ways familiarity was important in the case of supporting players as it made them all the more acceptable in their type-cast roles as servants, waiters, or policemen. Casting had always been vital and had become even more so with the coming of sound: great care had to be taken now to master the detail of real-life society in which the nuances of class were so obvious and important. Writing during the Second World War George Orwell suggested that the old pre-1918 British society had been one in which any particular person's social class could immediately be 'placed' by 'his clothes, manners and accent' and in truth very much the same could have been said of both Britain and America right down to 1939.[5] The great triumph of film and especially the American film was that it had successfully negotiated the mine-field of class. It had done this in part by building up a repertory company of actors which could cover the whole range of social types and in that company there were specialists, character actors, and vaudeville veterans who could breathe life into whatever stereotypes they were offered. But of course the supporting players were never as important as the leads and both the American and the British studios always knew that all their most expensive and sophisticated fictions would only be profitable if given life by attractive or intriguing stars. Those stars, chosen as they were on the basis of their ability to look glamorous or to generate tension in front of the camera, tended to come from a variety of different backgrounds but, of course, the film industry had successfully defined conventions which allowed their rising stars to be comfortably and effortlessly incorporated into the world of fiction film.

In the 1930s, as we have seen, many critics and writers on film were excited into believing that the American film was beginning to hint at the possibility of a wider range and of a new maturity as an artistic medium. They were impressed in part by the new social-problem films and also by the new generation of naturalistic actors who could so dramatically act out contemporary urban dramas or scenes from America's past. Hollywood, though, remained fully in control of its product and was well able to resist any drift towards a more fully realistic examination of urban, rural, political, or industrial realities in contemporary society. Instead that new urban idiom that Hollywood had mastered and much of that naturalistic acting was deliberately channelled into genre films which treated crime, Prohibition, and policing methods as well as the history of the West in carefully defined and highly stylized ways. Then a few years later the war film became another very convenient format for expressing and yet containing themes and energies suggested by the real America. Certainly, as Priestley has so perceptively argued, Hollywood was feeding off many aspects of American life but it always did so very much on its own terms and in particular those terms constituted a refusal to look very closely at the realities of working-class life.[6] In the 1930s Hollywood had appeared to waver but then in the 1940s and 1950s as America enjoyed a spectacular boom the studios were more than happy to reflect their times by rooting their drama in the largely middle-class world of downtown apartments and prosperous suburbs. Crime films would continue to hint at problems in the tenements but Hollywood's real world now was provided by the anxieties which accompanied social improvement. Middle-class drama, of course, was precisely what the studios were best able to provide for ever since the arrival of sound the West Coat had drawn heavily on the models provided by Broadway and from New York had come the notion of the American gentleman with his deep reassuring East-Coast or even mid-Atlantic accent, his relaxed urban charm, his range of formal city and informal weekend clothes, and his variety of very elegant and highly articulate female friends. What Hollywood had done in the 1930s was to create a fictional America in which Broadway models of middle-class charm and style existed alongside new conventions of naturalistic action developed within the studios themselves.[7] The smart metropolitan conventions had been mastered exactly and in truth they were always to provide a kind of base in what remained an overwhelmingly middle-class fictional world but perhaps the real secret of Hollywood's success was precisely the way in which tension developed as more naturalistic actors were introduced into that middle-class ethos. The society depicted in the movies was very definitely a step or two removed from the experience of the bulk of Hollywood's audience but on the screen Americans saw a confirmation of the prosperity that was now on offer and they could see also the emergence of a new suburban society in which very ordinary Americans could begin to behave more like the ladies and gentlemen of a previous era. Like America itself Hollywood had shaken off the Great Depression and could return to the themes with which it had always been happiest: the movies would go on reflecting the charm, energy, and vitality of individual Americans but only within a framework which saw their having to come to terms with very definite and specific historical processes and social trends.

In the decades following the Second World War it became a familiar notion that the American film offered 'models for the middle-class life style' but in 1962, as we have seen, the sociologist Herbert Gans was to argue that it would be more accurate to talk in terms of how Hollywood portrayed 'people with working-class traits' who were seeking that middle-class life style.[8] What Gans thought of as having been crucial was the way in which the vastly popular action film had dictated the need for heroes with qualities and characteristics which were far more likely to occur in individuals from a relatively underprivileged background. The emphasis was on physical danger and so a largely working-class audience was far happier with heroes who succeeded because of charm, courage, and strength rather than wealth, education, and privilege. But success, of course, was the vital thing and the whole point about the bulk of American films was that all the outstanding qualities of individual Americans were ultimately rewarded and fulfilled within a wider culture. Chuck Kleinhans has written about the way in which traditionally Hollywood could only deal with working-class heroes within the framework of the 'success myth' but the point about that myth is that there were so many aspects of the culture that made it seem very real.[9] The startling success of the economy seemed to confirm the political and educational rhetoric whilst in terms of the cinema the fictional success of heroes and heroines was realistically depicted by attractive and yet ordinary Americans who had obviously themselves started out on farms, in small towns, or in anonymous neighbourhoods. Hollywood succeeded because it celebrated the beauty, vitality, and diversity of individual Americans at precisely the same time as it celebrated and propagated the notion that society as a whole allowed a resolution of so many tensions. The movies never showed that real world in which most Americans lived but they had successfully developed conventions and above all an acting style which allowed audiences to accept that what they were seeing was an authentic version of America. Everything up there on the screen was a fiction and of course much of the action was highly melodramatic and far-fetched but most of it worked and it worked because it was all happening to real Americans, Americans who had all come from somewhere and who were now well on their way to success in a way that was thoroughly American. In this respect it is interesting to note that for all the protests and academic analyses that have attended the question of how both blacks and women have been depicted in the movies the only real adjustment that film-makers have made is to come up with one or two particularly attractive or charismatic stars. Perhaps more than ever American films owe both their popularity and their charm to a quite small range of male, and with one exception, white actors.[10]

If Hollywood's fictional world was several steps removed from the social reality in which most Americans lived their lives it was of course even further removed from the reality experienced by British audiences. And yet, as we have seen, all those commercial considerations which ensured that the British were to see more American films than they were to see of their native product were reinforced by cultural considerations which meant that sections of the British audience and especially critics came to prefer imported Hollywood films. If one examines the history of British and American cultural relations in the modern era there is nothing in the least surprising about this preference for from the advent of jazz and dance-band music through the era of the musical and popular song and right down to the age of television people from all backgrounds and from all ages in Britain have been prepared to be swept off their feet by the American idiom.[11] In part the popularity of the American film was explained by its quality and by its relative strangeness: it was simply fascinating to see such well-told stories being enacted in such exotic settings. But in Britain also the nature of American film acting was crucially important in determining the effortless acceptance of all of Hollywood's conventions. It was important that the English that was spoken could generally be understood and that so many of the male and female stars were attractive but even in Britain what was absolutely crucial was that the casting had been so perfect and the acting so natural. However far-fetched the tale and fanciful the twists it was always assumed that these were precisely the kinds of tensions and adventures that could possibly crop up in the lives of the very real people who were being shown on the screen. And this of course was precisely the point of contrast with British films. Hollywood had built on Broadway models and then merged them with new naturalistic acting but the British studios had never successfully escaped from the West End conventions. The notion of middle-class ladies and gentlemen was roughly the same in both New York and London and yet, whilst Hollywood could use the Broadway stereotype as one base in a far wider and more open society, the British studios found it difficult to escape from that Home Counties middle-class world in any terms other than that of caricature. In 1941 Orwell believed that there was now a new type of British person who could not be readily placed in any of the old class divisions but such types were still in a minority and in any case they had not yet been identified and celebrated within the culture. In America the middle-class world that was portrayed in film seemed to be one that was just about achieved in real life and most people were familiar with actual success stories, whereas in Britain the middle-class world of the home-produced film was quite obviously rooted in the Home Counties and was one in which there were well-defined notions of who did and who did not belong. Within the narrow range that British cinema had created for itself it could achieve many good things but the real problem was that unlike Hollywood the British studios could not create stories or acting styles that could effectively deal with the tension between the middle-class world and individuals or groups from other sections of society. The whole nature of social and historical myth in America continued with the new prosperity to prompt films into reconciling differences of social class whereas in Britain there were no cultural incentives to tempt writers, producers, and actors into more ambitious social dramas. If one needed to move out of the comfortable middle-class world it was far easier to resort to comedy and to caricature. It was only in the late 1950s and early 1960s that British culture began to sustain new myths about social mobility and at last a group of novelists and playwrights began to provide stories that rested on very real social tensions and which suggested that new acting styles would be needed in any dramatic presentation of these stories. Now for the first time British films began to feed off the same kind of social tensions that had long been basic to Hollywood's fiction. For any number of political and commercial reasons neither American nor British producers had ever wanted social or political realism in their films but at least Hollywood had concerned itself with tensions and energies that grew out of a real society and a truly national mythology. The coming of sound had ensured that actors would play a full part in rooting American films within the culture but it was only in the 1960s that British studios began to take up stories and employ new actors in such a way as to suggest that something like a national cinema was possible.

It was Dwight MacDonald who commented that for the movies the subject of work was rather like 'the dark side of the moon'.[12] Of course over the years film audiences came to know a great deal about the work of cowboys and detectives but they were to learn almost nothing about routine labouring, manufacturing, selling, and clerking and they were shown even less of the trade union politics that were associated with those activities. Early on the showmen had been faced with the challenge of making films that would not prejudice their own long-term commercial interests, would not anger middle-class politicians and interest groups, and yet would offer the masses something of an escape from the economic and political realities of everyday life. The need for political compromise, the findings of audience research, and sheer entrepreneurial instinct and bravado all combined to establish the conventions of the English-speaking world's feature film. The masses seemed happy and so indeed did the serious-minded guardians of middle-class values for the conventions of the feature film seemed to ensure that it would remain essentially a meaningless and trivial entertainment based on a liaison between uncouth trades-people and the quiescent working class. There were times when the showmen themselves seemed to acquiesce in this view as they cynically admitted that their only concern was the manufacture of tinsel for the masses, but there were other occasions when they would more readily congratulate themselves on having devised an entertainment that fitted very nicely into the contemporary English-speaking culture.

At one point Scott Fitzgerald's Monroe Stahr describes his job as a movie mogul as one in which he took people's 'own favourite folklore, dressed it up and gave it back to them': anything beyond that was 'sugar'.[13] The movies were essentially a retelling of the old stories, a reworking of old fables and adages, a rejuggling of clichés and stereotypes. Nobody went to the cinema expecting startling revelations or profound insights or even to be surprised: rather they went to see stories told well in a way that was totally believable, they went to be amused, and they went to see fascinating people. Fundamental to the movies was a pact between producers and audiences and that pact ensured success and contentment within well-defined expectations. In this respect the feature film played very much the same role as that popular fiction whose place in the culture it had come to augment: both quite clearly operated within conventions that ensured that they would be accepted by the masses as their own and the stories would concern believable people who would encounter real-life dilemmas before achieving a successful resolution. What was different and more potent about films was that from the very beginning they began to show a glory in new kinds of glamour and urban style and they came to rely very heavily on the charm of attractive people. In common with mass-circulation fiction, vaudeville, and the popular song the movies now helped to confirm a sense of shared experience and to offer a sense of tenderness and comfort. They were rooted in the same sense of humanity as those older forms of popular culture, but now together with new kinds of music the movies began to create their own values and to hint that many of the older qualities that had formed the basis of the popular mentality would be given a new twist in the modern urban world. Above all feature films seemed to concentrate on individual men and women and the way in which they were able to cope with all the challenges and dilemmas that they experienced. In time this fascination with the story of an individual's experience became the hallmark of the English-speaking world's cinema.

The showmen had been greatly relieved by their success in developing a popular cinema that was under no obligation to depict the problems of work and the details of politics for quite apart from the difficulty of having to take sides and confront philosophies there was the obvious fact that those subjects would have been inherently dull. They soon realized that the subsequent decades were to confirm that the story of one strike was very much like that of another and that there could often be considerable repetition in the presentation of the Socialist case. If it was dangerous to tackle such subjects it would also be difficult to effectively dramatize other collective responses or collectivist arguments. And so the movies opted for the hero, for the man or woman who was never to be shown as being too closely tied to work, who certainly had to accept all kinds of constraints within a community, and who would undoubtedly experience vast mountains of emotional anguish but who would overcome all these things without having recourse to unions or politicians. The films were to be about personal experience and the charm, resourcefulness, and ingenuity that individuals could use to ensure at least survival. In developing this convention the film studios were given a new twist to an age-old need for individual heroics but what was new was partly the sheer power of the projected image, which as good as brought the heroes alive, and also the fact that this new breakthrough in popular culture had come at a time when the whole question of the place of masses within the culture was being given a new urgency.

There was much about the movies that was trivial and routine but the power of the medium and the fascination with the stories that were told ensured that they would play an important role in the way in which modern democratic society evolved in both the United States and the United Kingdom. Undoubtedly the greatest contribution of the movies was to offer sheer pleasure and diversion to audiences of hard-working people and adolescents with time on their hands but all the time and in a largely undetected manner they were also giving dramatic expression to the notion that ultimately an individual was responsible for his own well-being within a society. Going to the movies was very much a communal activity and indeed much of the pleasure came from the shared experience but unlike the political or religious meeting and even the theatre and music-hall the film tended to communicate directly with individual members of the audience. If there was an unwritten pact between the movies and the masses there were also an even more meaningful relationship between individual films and their stars on the one hand and the lone viewer on the other. Regular cinema-going was something that could be done in groups or it could be part of a courting ritual but it was also an invitation to encounter a new emphasis on individual style and mobility that ran counter to many of the influences within working-class experience. Films meant different things to different people and within the local situation they offered a message that could be taken privately. But films of course were not local products, they came from a wider world, the world primarily of the future, and in that sense whatever their degree of social otherness they could be taken as being in tune with history.

In the present century both the United Kingdom and the United States have developed into mature political democracies and have avoided major domestic strife in spite of the facts that their respective citizens have experienced considerable differences in levels of prosperity and that influential groups have argued the need for a purely class approach to social action. In both countries the reality of class and the possibility of sustained class struggle have been negated primarily by the general levels of income, by the degree of social mobility, and by the extent to which the cultures as a whole were seen to sanction individual freedom and fulfilment. For much of the century the feature film played a part in condoning the logic that was basic to both cultures and both economies, and that was that individual responsibility was the sole test of maturity within a pluralistic, democratic society. In the United States the movies both depicted and celebrated an individualism that many thought had been fundamental to the national experience and was now the only hope for the future. America had been a created society that had always rested on a clear notion of citizenship and on a few political tenets that could be readily understood: now, in an age of mass migration, of urbanization, and of threatened dislocation, the movies were at hand to hint at all the problems even as they suggested that whatever the impulses to political action all the old adages about self-sufficiency and relying on one's own resources remained true.[14] All the time the American film was to portray people that were being socialized rather than politicized but it also never ceased to imply that it was to those who succeeded within what the culture allowed that the prizes went.

The movies were not openly political, they did not shout out their case. Carl Laemmle used to talk about the bell that the showmen consistently rang and stressed that it was a bell that always rang out for entertainment.[15] Nevertheless the opportunity was always there for women, for adolescents, for romantics, for the sensitive, and for all of those who had not entirely fallen for the message of the Socialist, the preacher, and even the teacher to consider how intriguing some of the emotional and psychological problems of life could be and how awfully simple the economic realities were. In fact one suspects that this is how films operated throughout the English-speaking world. In Great Britain that very simple message of self-help which had been the hallmark of Victorian culture had been gradually lost sight of and there was an increasing tendency to look down at the rather crude assumptions that seemed to govern the whole of American life. In particular it was the considerable success of the British labour movement which seemed to point to the great difference between the cultures: the issue of class had been elevated into one of considerable importance in the industrial and party politics of Britain and there seemed to be significant support for the notion that there were specific class grievances which could only be alleviated by constraints on business. Beneath the rhetoric of political life and the logic of class organization, though, the Hollywood movie worked in Britain very much as it did in its own country for in truth the realities of everyday existence were the same in both countries. Even in the relatively less fluid society of Britain it was generally appreciated that economic independence within the well-established and readily comprehended conventions of the day could lead on to new degrees of freedom and entertainment. American films became popular because their style and their energy were always hinting at what the twentieth century was now putting on offer whereas the home-based cinema had been forced by a considerable array of political and artistic obstacles into caricaturing existing class styles and mentalities rather than pointing to the way in which they would become irrelevant. More than anything what Britain had needed was somebody who took film seriously and who understood the direction in which society was moving. Meanwhile the most popular home-grown heroes in the classic years of the cinema were those charming and nicely spoken gentlemen who seemed to their fans to be the very quintessence of Englishness but who pointed backwards rather than forwards and who could never have been truly national heroes.[16] In time as acting conventions changed, as new writers emerged, and as television and the theatre began to explore new themes the British were to be given authentic heroes from every section of their culture, but so resistant was society as a whole to change that very few indeed of these new heroes could ever become truly national in their appeal. Perhaps indeed British society is too complex and too rigid to be reduced to any simple cinematic formula but rather one suspects it is a case of cultural and artistic as well as political moulds that need to be broken.

In the modern era both Britain and America have had a large but diminishing working class and they have both experienced considerable social mobility. The feature film was classically designed to entertain the working class but circumstances ensured that it should unequivocally come out on the side of progress and mobility. The workers of course had never wanted to see their problems analysed in the movies and many of them would have been delighted that film-going may have played a small part in encouraging their children and their successors to move away from some of the awful jobs and awful conditions that an older economy had once required. In general society has become far more like the movies once were and meantime many of the best and most successful new movies will continue to confirm both the values that ordinary people esteem most highly and their expectations that their kind of hero will

21 *Breaking Away*: Paul Dooley as the ex-cutter and Dennis Christopher as his son who will never be a cutter.

succeed on their behalf. Very simply those movies offer the advice 'Go thou and do likewise'.

In the 1980s the American film industry continued to produce scores of movies for its predominantly young audience and it was fascinating to observe the way in which so many of those movies seemed preoccupied with notions of class and with standards of social behaviour. More than ever before American films were prepared to admit that there were class differences and in many films the action seemed to focus on the anxiety of a young hero as he moved from his humble and unfashionable background into the big-city world in which he would succeed. Perhaps the most obvious signs of this new interest in social awareness were the constant references within the dialogue to the colleges and universities at which the main characters had been educated. At times it almost seemed as if American film directors had been inspired by Paul Fussell's observation that an American who felt 'class-secure' was a rare specimen indeed.[17] Undoubtedly this new era of class anxiety in the cinema was inspired by the 1979 film *Breaking Away*, which very significantly was directed by an Englishman Peter Yates. In this quite unprecedented study of class Yates has his young hero develop an interest in things Italian as he attempts to establish an identity that would mark him off from both the snooty students at the university in Bloomington and his own very ordinary family headed by his father, who sells cars. The only other source of pride at hand is the fact that his father had once worked in the local quarries - had been 'a cutter'. Incensed by the attitudes of students the young protagonist describes himself to his father as 'a cutter': the father's response is to remind his son sharply that it was only he who had actually been a cutter. More than ever before American films are concerned with what young people make of themselves but in concentrating on how the sons of cutters first learn how to respect the values of their fathers before moving on to face challenges of their own movies are only really doing what they have always done.

References

1 Showmen and the nature of the movies

1 The best discussion of the city as a cultural experience is provided by Jonathan Raban, *Soft City*, London, 1974.
2 For 'popular culture' see Stuart Hall and Paddy Whannel, *The Popular Arts*, London, 1964; Raymond Williams, *Keywords*, London, 1976; and Dwight Macdonald, 'Masscult and midcult', *Partisan Review*, spring 1960, reprinted in Dwight Macdonald, *Against the American Grain*, London, 1963.
3 Raymond Williams, *Culture and Society, 1780–1950*, London, 1958, pp. 295 ff., and 'British film history: new perspectives', in James Curran and Vincent Porter (eds) *British Cinema History*, London, 1983, p. 14.
4 For music-hall see D. F. Cheshire, *Music Hall in Britain*, Newton Abbott, 1974, and for vaudeville, Douglas Gilbert, *American Vaudeville*, New York, 1940.
5 George Moore, *Something of Myself*, London, 1937, quoted by Cheshire, op. cit., p. 88.
6 Michael Chanan, *The Dream that Kicks: the Prehistory and Early Years of Cinema in Britain*, London, 1980, p. 218.
7 Vachel Lindsay, 'Thirty differences between the photoplays and the stage', in his book *The Art of the Moving Picture*, New York, 1915, reprinted in David Denby (ed.), *Awake in the Dark*, New York, 1977, p. 15.
8 Max Beerbohm, 'At the Tivoli', *Saturday Review*, 1898, 'In a music hall', *Saturday Review*, 1901, quoted by Cheshire, op. cit., p. 90. Also S. N. Behrman, *Conversation with Max*, London, 1960, p. 219.
9 George Gissing, *The Private Papers of Henry Ryecroft*, London, 1903, 'Winter', no. 5.
10 Arnold Bennett, *Your United States*, London, 1912, p. 118. The whole world of pre-1914 London is best evoked in Arthur Ransome, *Bohemia in London*, London, 1907, and D. H. Rolph, *London Particulars*, London, 1980.
11 Raymond Williams, *The Long Revolution*, London, 1961, p. 265.
12 Chanan, op. cit., p. 21. Chanan was much influenced by E. P. Thompson, *The Making of the English Working Class*, London, 1963.
13 Hall and Whannel, op. cit., p. 56.
14 Colin MacInnes, *Sweet Saturday Night*, London, 1967, p. 179.
15 Chanan, op. cit., chapter 23 *passim*.
16 MacInnes, op. cit., pp. 177 ff.
17 Robert Sklar, *Movie-made America*, New York, 1975, p. 14.
18 Robert Roberts, *The Classic Slum*, Manchester, 1971, chapter 8, 'Culture'; and Gareth Stedman Jones, *Languages of Class*, Cambridge, 1983, pp. 204 ff.
19 *Exhibitors Film Exchange*, Chicago, 22 July 1915.
20 *Bioscope*, London, 2 October 1908, p. 14 and 24 June 1908, p. 3.
21 *Bioscope*, 2 October 1908, p. 8.
22 ibid.

23 *Moving Picture World*, New York, 4 January 1908, p. 4.
24 Gilbert Seldes, *An Hour with the Movies and the Talkies*, London, 1929, p. 33.
25 ibid., p. 34.
26 *Bioscope*, 24 June 1909.
27 'The nickelodeon', *Moving Picture World*, 4 May 1907, p. 140.
28 *Moving Picture World*, 23 March 1907, p. 40.
29 W. Stephen Bush, 'The triumph of the gallery', *Moving Picture World*, 13 December 1913, reprinted in Stanley Kauffmann and Bruce Henstell, *American Film Criticism*, New York, 1972, p. 67.
30 Pare Lorentz in the *Forum*, September 1928, reprinted in Pare Lorentz, *Lorentz on Film*, New York, 1975, p. 18.
31 *Mirror*, Manchester, New Hampshire, quoted in *Moving Picture World*, 26 October 1907.
32 *Moving Picture World*, 4 January 1908.
33 *Bioscope*, 2 October 1908, p. 8.
34 James Agee, 'Comedy's greatest era', *Life Magazine*, 3 September 1949, reprinted in James Agee, *Agee on Film*, London, 1963, p. 7.
35 Kenneth Macpherson in *Close Up*, July 1927, no. 1.
36 *Moving Picture World*, 4 May 1907.
37 Phrase used in the short film *Sunshine* (1983) which appealed for audiences to support the film industry's efforts to provide Sunshine Coaches for the disabled.
38 Terry Ramsaye, *A Million and One Nights - the History of the Motion Picture*, New York, 1926, and 'The rise and place of the motion picture', in Gordon S. Watkins (ed.), *The Motion Picture Industry, Annals of the American Academy of Political and Social Science*, November 1947, vol. 254, p. 1; Russell Merritt, 'Nickelodeon theatres 1905-1914: building an audience for the movies', in Tino Balio (ed.) *The American Film Industry*, Madison, 1976, p. 59. See also Garson Kanin's novel *Moviola*, New York, 1979, part 1, 'Gold in the streets'.
39 *Exhibitors Film Exchange*, Chicago, 29 July 1915, p. 18.
40 *Bioscope*, 4 December 1908.
41 *Exhibitors Film Exchange*, 1 July 1915, p. 8.
42 *Exhibitors Film Exchange*, 18 September 1915.
43 Bosley Crowther, *The Lion's Share*, New York, 1957, p. 19.
44 Quoted and discussed in *Moving Picture World*, 18 May 1907, p. 168.
45 *Bioscope*, 6 November 1908.
46 Garth Jowett, *Film: the Democratic Art*, Boston 1976.
47 In the *Kinematograph Year Book* of London there was a regular 'Busybodies and meddlers' section.
48 *Moving Picture World*, 29 June 1907. Boosting paid off for Chicago for the latest developments there were always more widely reported than in other cities.
49 *Exhibitors Film Exchange*, 24 June 1915.
50 'There is no crowd so fickle as the crowd that has gathered together to be amused', *Bioscope*, 25 February 1909.
51 Seldes, op. cit., p. 37.
52 Harry Weiss, 'The future of feature films', *Exhibitors Film Exchange*, 11 September 1915.
53 Leading comment, *Exhibitors Film Exchange*, 22 July 1915, p. 18.
54 *Bioscope*, 25 February 1909, p. 3.
55 Lary May, *Screening out the Past*, Chicago, 1980, chapter 7, 'The new frontier: "Hollywood"'.

2 Towards significance in the silent era

1 Lewis Jacobs, *The Rise of the American Film*, New York, 1939 (p. 137 of 1968 edition).

2 These films were reviewed in the *Bioscope*: *The Quarry Man*, 6 November 1980; *A Workingman's Dream*, 13 November 1908; *Unemployed and Unemployable*, 31 December 1908; *The Miner's Daughter*, 21 January 1909; and *Hard Times*, 4 February 1909.

3 *New York Dramatic Mirror*, 25 December 1909, p. 15, reprinted in Anthony Slide, *Selected Film Criticism, 1868-1911*, Metuchen, NJ, and London, 1982, p. 25.

4 *Motion Picture World*, 9 April 1910, p. 553, reprinted in Slide, op. cit., p. 43.

5 For Griffith see Richard Schickel, *D. W. Griffith*, London, 1984; Kevin Brownlow, *The Parade's Gone By*, New York, 1968; the essay by Arthur Lenning in Joseph McBride (ed.), *Persistence of Vision*, Madison, 1968; and D. W. Griffith, 'My early life', *Photoplay*, July 1916, reprinted in Harry M. Geduld, *Focus on D. W. Griffith*, Englewood Cliffs, NJ, 1971. There is a revealing recollection in Rodney Ackland and Elspeth Grant, *The Celluloid Mistress*, London, 1954, pp. 57 ff.

6 Heywood Broun in the *New York Tribune*, 7 September 1916, reprinted in Stanley Kauffmann and Bruce Henstell, *American Film Criticism*, New York, 1972, p. 97.

7 W. Stephen Bush in the *Moving Picture World*, 18 July 1914, reprinted in Slide, op. cit., p. 144.

8 *Moving Picture World*, 20 June 1914, reprinted in Slide, op. cit., p. 150.

9 Both *Business is Business* and *Out of Darkness* were reviewed in the *Exhibitors Film Exchange*, 11 September 1915, pp. 8 and 11.

10 *Exhibitors Film Exchange*, 23 October 1915, p. 18.

11 *Exhibitors Film Exchange*, 6 November 1915, p. 18.

12 *Exhibitors Film Exchange*, 2 October 1915, p. 7.

13 Lary May, *Screening Out the Past*, Chicago, 1980, pp. 122 ff. for a brilliant discussion. Also Brownlow, op. cit., and Robert Windeler, *Mary Pickford: Sweetheart of the World*, London, 1973.

14 James Agee, 'Comedy's greatest era', *Life Magazine*, 3 September 1949, reprinted in James Agee, *Agee on Film*, London, 1963, p. 7.

15 For Sennett see Eric Rhode, *A History of the Cinema*, London, 1976, and Jacobs op. cit. (1968 edn), pp. 209 ff.

16 *Kinematograph Year Book*, 1917, p. 145.

17 Bennett praised Chaplin in *Close Up*, December 1927, no. 6. Gilbert Seldes dedicated his *An Hour with the Movies and the Talkies*, London, 1929, to Chaplin.

18 Gilbert Seldes, 'The keystone the builders rejected' in his book *The Seven Lively Arts*, New York, 1923, reprinted in David Denby, *Awake in the Dark*, New York, 1977, p. 22. To read back through American film criticism is to become aware of the enormous pioneering significance of Seldes in shaping responses to the movies. He worked in radio and television production and became Dean of Annenberg school at the University of Pennsylvania.

19 William Hunter, *Scrutiny of Cinema*, London, 1932, p. 44.

20 Edmund Wilson's review of *The Gold Rush* appeared in *New Republic*, 2 September 1925, reprinted in Edmund Wilson, *The American Earthquake*, London, 1958, p. 69.

21 James Agate, 'Hey but he's doleful', *Saturday Review*, 1 October 1921,

reprinted in James Agate, *Around Cinemas*, London, 1946, p. 13. Hunter, op. cit.

22 J. B. Priestley, *Midnight on the Desert*, London, 1937, p. 195.

23 *Robert Wagner's Script*, 15 February 1936, vol. 15, no. 353, reprinted in Anthony Slide, *Selected Film Criticism, 1931-1940*, Metuchen, NJ, and London, 1982, p. 161.

24 Raoul Sobel and David Francis, *Chaplin: Genesis of a Clown*, London, 1977, p. 160.

25 Walter Kerr, *The Silent Clowns*, New York, 1975, quoted by David Robinson in his excellent *Chaplin*, London, 1983, p. 177.

26 A translation of Boris Shumiatski's *Pravda* review was printed in *New Masses*, 24 September 1935, vol. 16, no. 13, p. 29.

27 Charmion Von Wiegard, 'Little Charlie, What now?', *New Theatre*, March 1936, vol. 3, no. 3.

28 Charles Chaplin, 'Does the public know what it wants?', *Adelphi*, January 1924, vol. 1, no. 8, p. 702, reprinted in Peter Haining, *The Legend of Charlie Chaplin*, London, 1982.

29 Welford Beaton in the *Film Spectator*, 26 May 1928. Beaton was a Canadian critic who went to work in Hollywood and who edited this outspoken journal, which always urged its readers to think seriously about the nature of the movies.

30 Seldes, 1929, op. cit., p. 8.

31 HD,'The cinema and the classics', *Close Up*, July 1927, no. 1.

32 Kenneth Macpherson, 'As is', *Close Up*, July 1927, no. 1, p. 5. Macpherson was the editor of *Close Up*, a journal published in Switzerland and which was concerned not just with film as art but rather with the whole quality of English life. It ran from July 1927 to September 1933. See Paul Rotha and Richard Griffith, *The Film Till Now*, London, 1951 edition, p. 416.

33 Seldes, 1929, op. cit., pp. 115 ff.

34 Clifford Howard, 'Cinemaphobia', *Close Up*, July 1929, vol. 5, no. 1, p. 60.

35 HD in *Close Up*, September 1928, vol. 3, no. 3, p. 20; Kenneth Macpherson in *Close Up*, October 1927, vol. 1, no. 4, p. 14; and Walter Kron in *Close Up*, November 1930, vol. 7, no. 5, p. 39.

36 Hugh Castle, 'The future of the British cinema', *Close Up*, April 1929, vol. 4, no. 4, p. 35.

37 Clifford Howard, 'The waning of the stars', *Close UP*, May 1928, vol. 2, no. 5.

38 Seldes, 1929, op. cit., p. 115.

39 Welford Beaton in the *Film Spectator*, 14 April 1928, p. 6.

40 Bryher in *Close Up*, June 1932, vol. 9, no. 2, p. 132.

41 Ernest Betts, 'On being bored with films', *Close Up*, July 1928, vol. 3, no. 1, p. 45.

42 Pare Lorentz, 'The stillborn art', *Forum*, September 1928, reprinted in Pare Lorentz, *Lorentz on Film*, New York, 1975, p. 18.

43 Welford Beaton in *Film Spectator*, 26 May 1928.

44 *Exhibitors Herald*, Chicago, 14 January 1922, p. 34.

45 Ben M. Hall, *The Remaining Best Seats*, New York, 1961, pp. 17 and 43.

46 James Agate, 'Some films and a moving picture', *Saturday Review*, 30 September 1922, reprinted in Agate, 1946, op. cit., p. 21.

47 James Agate, 'Babylon at Brixton', *Tatler*, 25 September 1929, reprinted in Agate, 1946, op. cit., p. 52.

48 *Variety*, 30 March 1927, p. 15.

49 *Cinematograph Times*, 19 January 1929, vol. 1, no. 7, p. 27.

50 Pare Lorentz, 'Moral racketeering in the movies', *Scribner's*, September 1930, reprinted in Lorentz, 1975, op. cit., pp. 53 ff.

51 Kenneth Macpherson in *Close Up*, February 1929, vol. 4, no. 2.

52 *Life*, 1 January 1925, reprinted in Anthony Slide, *Selected Film Criticism, 1921-1930*, Metuchen, NJ, and London, 1982, p. 127.

53 *Exceptional Photoplays*, December-January 1924-5, vol. 5, nos 3 and 4, reprinted in Slide, *1921-1930*, op. cit., p. 124.

54 John Russell Taylor, *Strangers in Paradise: the Hollywood Emigrés 1933-50*, London, 1983.

55 Written just before his death in 1940, 'Mightier than the sword' appeared first in *Esquire* and then in Scott Fitzgerald, *The Pat Hobby Stories*, New York, 1962.

56 For Vidor's autobiographical reflections see Charles Higham and Joel Greenberg, *The Celluloid Muse: Hollywood Directors Speak*, London, 1969, pp. 223 ff., and Richard Schickel, *The Men Who Made the Movies*, New York, 1975, pp. 131 ff.

57 Robert Sherwood in *Life*, 10 December 1925, reprinted in Kauffmann and Henstell, op. cit., p. 167.

58 Bryher, 'The war from three angles', *Close Up*, July 1927, no. 1, p. 16. For a discussion of *The Big Parade* see Michael T. Isenberg, 'The Great War viewed from the twenties', in John E. O'Connor and Martin A. Jackson (eds), *American History/American Film*, New York, 1979.

59 *Kinematograph Weekly*, 16 February 1928.

60 Pare Lorentz in *Judge*, 10 March 1928, reprinted in Lorentz, 1975, op. cit., p. 14. *Photoplay*, December 1927, vol. 33, no. 1, reprinted in Slide, *1921-1930*, op. cit., p. 76.

61 Welford Beaton, 'Crowd subjected to too much supervision', *Film Spectator*, 24 December 1927.

62 *Close Up*, October 1928, vol. 3, no. 4, p. 347. For Vidor's career and work see Clive Denton, 'King Vidor' in Stuart Rosenthal and Judith M. Kass (eds) *The Hollywood Professionals*, vol. 5, London and New York, 1976, and John Baxter, *King Vidor*, New York, 1976.

63 *Exhibitors Herald*, 28 January 1922, pp. 67 ff.

64 *Variety*, 13 April 1927.

65 Agate, 1946, op. cit., p. 22. I saw *Broken Blossoms* at the London Film Festival in 1983 and Lillian Gish was present on that occasion to introduce the film.

66 James Agate, *The Common Touch*, London, 1926, p. 151.

67 Welford Beaton in the *Film Spectator*, 24 December 1927, p. 4.

68 Kenneth Macpherson in *Close Up*, July 1927, no. 1.

69 Kenneth Macpherson in *Close Up*, August 1927, no. 2, p. 9 and April 1928, vol. 2, no. 4, pp. 57 ff.

70 Clifford Howard in *Close Up*, July 1929, vol. 5, no. 1, p. 65.

71 Dorothy Richardson in *Close Up*, April 1928, vol. 2, no. 4, p. 49, and 'The cinema in Arcady', *Close Up*, July 1928, vol. 3, no. 1, p. 55.

3 The 'sociological punch' of the talkies

1 There is an excellent analysis of Hollywood at the start of the 1930s in Robert Sklar, *Movie-made America*, New York, 1975, pp. 161 ff.

2 Welford Beaton, 'Get out of the rut', *Film Spectator*, 8 November 1930, p. 5.

3 Ed Kuykendahl in the *Film Daily Year Book*, 1932, p. 534.

4 Ralph A. Bauer, 'When the lights went out: Hollywood, the depression and the thirties', *Journal of Popular Film and Television*, winter 1981, vol. 8, no. 4, p. 24.

5 Frank T. Daugherty's reviews appeared in the *Film Spectator*, 18 May, 21 September, and 14 December 1929 and 1 March 1930.

6 John Clellan Holmes, '15 cents before 6.00 pm: the wonderful movies of the thirties', *Harpers*, December 1965, vol. 231/1387, p. 52; Welford Beaton, *Film Spectator*, 11 October 1930, p. 5.

7 Frank T. Daugherty in the *Film Spectator*, 21 September 1929, p. 14.

8 Welford Beaton in the *Film Spectator*, 25 April 1931, p. 7.

9 See especially Robert Warshow, *The Immediate Experience*, New York, 1962, part 2, 'The gangster as tragic hero', and Andrew Bergman, *We're in the Money: Depression America and its Films*, New York, 1971.

10 Dalton Trumbo in the *Film Spectator*, 4 July and 15 August 1931. Dalton Trumbo had now joined the staff of this journal.

11 Welford Beaton in the *Film Spectator*, 8 November 1930, p. 5.

12 Welford Beaton in the *Film Spectator*, 2 November 1929, reprinted in Anthony Slide, *Selected Film Criticism, 1921-1930*, Metuchen, NJ, and London, 1982, p. 127.

13 Welford Beaton in the *Film Spectator*, 12 September 1931, p. 6.

14 George Blaisdell in the *International Photographer*, October 1931, vol. 3, no. 9; *Photoplay*, October 1931, vol. 40, no. 5; both reprinted in Anthony Slide, *Selected Film Criticism, 1931-40*, Metuchen, NJ, and London, 1982, pp. 250 ff.

15 For *The Public Enemy* see Garth Jowett, 'Bullets, beer and the Hays Office', in John E. O'Connor and Martin A. Jackson (eds) *American History/American Film*, New York, 1979, p. 57, and Henry Cohen (ed.), *The Public Enemy*, Wisconsin/Warner Bros Screenplay Series, Madison, 1981.

16 James Shelley Hamilton in the *National Board of Review Magazine*, May 1931, reprinted in Stanley Kauffmann and Bruce Henstell, *American Film Criticism*, New York, 1972, p. 251.

17 Seton Margrave in the *Daily Mail*, 4 January 1932.

18 Lincoln Kirstein, 'James Cagney and the American hero', *The Hound and Horn*, April/June 1932, reprinted in Kauffmann and Henstell, op. cit., p. 262.

19 Patrick McGilligan, *Cagney: the Actor as Auteur*, New York, 1975.

20 Michael Freedland, *James Cagney*, London, 1974.

21 Warshow, op. cit., p. 87.

22 Kauffmann and Henstell, op. cit., p. 252.

23 ibid., p. 264.

24 Wallace Beery had once worked in a circus and it was said that every time a circus came to Hollywood one or more of the elephants would recognize him 'and trumpet joyfully'! See Alva Johnston, 'Jumbo' *New Yorker*, 9 November 1935, reprinted in *Profiles* (Penguin Books), London, 1944.

25 Otis Ferguson in the *New Republic*, 6 June 1934, reprinted in Robert Wilson (ed.), *The Film Criticism of Otis Ferguson*, Philadelphia, 1971, p. 37.

26 Frank Daugherty, 'Gang stuff by Cagney', *Film Spectator*, 6 June 1931, p. 10.

27 Gore Vidal greatly enjoyed this story as he recalled his days at MGM in 'Who makes the movies?', *New York Review of Books*, 25 November 1976, reprinted in Gore Vidal, *Pink Triangle and Yellow Star*, London, 1982.

28 'Warner Brothers', *Fortune*, December 1937, vol. 16, no. 6, p. 212, and Douglas Gomery, *The Hollywood Studio System*, London, 1986, p. 110.

29 John E. O'Connor (ed.), *I am a Fugitive from a Chain Gang*, Wisconsin/Warner Bros Screenplay Series, Madison, 1981.

30 *Robert Wagner's Script*, 12 November 1932, vol. 8, no. 196, reprinted in Slide, op. cit., p. 122.

31 William A. Barrett in the *National Board of Review Magazine*, November 1932, reprinted in Kauffmann and Henstell, op. cit., p. 274.

32 Pare Lorentz in *Vanity Fair*, December 1932, reprinted in Kauffmann and Henstell, op. cit., p. 276.

33 Pare Lorentz in *Vanity Fair*, May 1933, reprinted in Kauffmann and Henstell, op. cit., p. 286.

34 *Robert Wagner's Script*, 21 November 1931, vol. 6, no. 145, reprinted in Slide, op. cit., p. 9. Like the *Hollywood Spectator* this highly respected critical journal was published in Los Angeles itself. Both publications were avidly read by the trade.

35 Pare Lorentz in *Vanity Fair*, May 1933, reprinted in Kauffmann and Henstell, op. cit., p. 286.

36 Jerome Lawrence, *Actor: the Life and Times of Paul Muni*, New York, 1974.

37 The findings of the Payne Fund's eleven projects and eight volumes were summarized in Henry James Forman, *Our Movie Made Children*, New York, 1933. There is a full analysis in Sklar, op. cit.

38 Wendell S. Dysinger and Charles A. Ruckwick, *The Emotional Responses of Children to the Motion Picture Situation*, New York, 1933, p. 119.

39 Herbert Blumer, *Movies and Conduct*, New York, 1933, pp. 195 ff.

40 Forman, op. cit., p. 12.

41 Herbert Blumer and Philip M. Hauser, *Movies, Delinquency and Crime*, New York, 1933, p. 202.

42 Forman, op. cit., p. 262. At this point Forman was citing the work of Paul G. Cressey and F. M. Thrasher but according to Sklar (op. cit., p. 325) their projected volume, *Boys, Movies and City Streets*, never appeared. Surely one of the great unpublished titles?

43 Forman, op. cit., pp. 43 ff.

44 Charles C. Peters, *Motion Pictures and Standards of Morality*, New York, 1933, pp. 129 ff.

45 Forman, op. cit., p. 179; W. W. Charters, *Motion Pictures and Youth*, New York, 1933, p. 60.

46 Blumer, op. cit., p. 199.

47 Bauer, op. cit., p. 24; Peter Roffman and Jim Purdy, *The Hollywood Social Problem Film*, Bloomington, 1981, p. 65.

48 Paul Rotha and Richard Griffith, *The Film Till Now*, London, 1951 edition, p. 436.

49 Otis Ferguson in the *New Republic*, 29 August 1934, reprinted in Wilson, op. cit., p. 44.

50 Richard Schickel, *The Men Who Made the Movies*, New York, 1975, p. 149.

51 Roffman and Purdy, op. cit., p. 124.

52 John Baxter, *King Vidor*, New York, 1976, p. 52.

53 Otis Ferguson in the *New Republic*, 9 May and 29 August 1934, reprinted in Wilson, op. cit., pp. 34 and 44.

54 William Troy in the *Nation*, 10 April 1935, reprinted in Kauffmann and Henstell, op. cit., p. 300.

55 Jeffrey Richards, *Visions of Yesterday*, London, 1973, pp. 232 ff.

56 Otis Ferguson in the *New Republic*, 19 December 1934, reprinted in Wilson, op. cit., p. 59.

57 Letters in Box 14603 of the Warner Bros Archive at Princeton indicate the close personal contact between the Warner brothers and first Governor and then President Roosevelt.

58 Lawrence, op. cit., pp. 184 ff.
59 The various drafts are to be found in the Scripts File of *Black Fury* at the Warner Film Library, Wisconsin Center for Film and Theater Research, the State Historical Society of Wisconsin, Madison.
60 Dialogue File, Madison.
61 James R. Silke, *Here's Looking at You Kid: Fifty Years of Fighting, Working, and Dreaming at Warner Bros*, Boston, 1976, p. 66. Joseph Breen was director of the Production Code Office.
62 Press-book, Madison.
63 Lawrence, op. cit., pp. 204 ff.
64 James Shelley Hamilton, 'Paul Muni and the labor problem', *National Board of Review Magazine*, May 1935, vol. 10, no. 5, p. 13. The National Board of Review of Motion Pictures had been formed in New York in 1909: it was a voluntary body which was 'opposed to legal censorship', but which co-ordinated a number of local Better Films Committees as well as using its journal to review new releases. Throughout the 1930s the dramatist James Shelley Hamilton was Secretary of its Review Committee.
65 Otis Ferguson in the *New Republic*, 24 May 1935, reprinted in Wilson, op. cit., p. 73.
66 Monroe Greenthal Papers, Box 2, Madison.
67 For contemporary reactions to *Red Salute* and *Riff Raff* see *New Theatre*, October 1935, vol. 2, no. 10, and *New Masses*, October 1935, vol. 17, no. 1.
68 Raymond Moley, *The Hays Office*, New York, 1945, p. 124.
69 Material relating to the background of *Black Legion*, Box 12677 H, Warner Bros Archive, Princeton.
70 Press-book and poster, Madison.
71 Box 12677 H, Warner Bros Archive, Princeton.
72 Script File, Madison.
73 Archie Mayo, Interview with Radie Harris, 22 January 1937, Box 12677 H, Warner Bros Archive, Princeton.
74 Janet Graves, 'Hollywood trademarks', *Cinema Arts*, September 1937, vol. 1, no. 3, p. 39.
75 James Shelley Hamilton in the *National Board of Review Magazine*, February 1937, vol. 12, no. 2, p. 8.
76 Otis Ferguson, 'Hollywood's half a loaf', *New Republic*, 10 June 1936, reprinted in Wilson, op. cit., p. 135.

4 'The propaganda mills of the 1930s'

1 Robert Warshow, *The Immediate Experience*, New York, 1962, p. 5.
2 There is a collection of clippings covering the 1931 Harlan County Strike in the Samuel B. Ornitz Papers at Madison (US Mss 48 AN). See in particular the *New York Times*, 17 November 1931. See also Tony Bubka, 'The Harlan County coal strike of 1931', *Labor History*, winter 1970, vol. 11, p. 181.
3 Daniel Aaron, *Writers on the Left*, New York, 1961.
4 Jerre Mangione, *The Dream and the Deal: the Federal Writers' Project, 1935–1943*, New York 1972, p. 30.
5 Alice Evans, 'Theatre and trade unions', *New Theatre*, August 1935, vol. 2, no. 8, p. 23.
6 Henry Hart (ed.), *American Writers Congress*, New York, 1936, p. 136. For a discussion of the four congresses that were held see Aaron, op. cit.

7 William Alexander, *Films on the Left*, Princeton, 1981.

8 For a useful anthology, see Harvey Swados (ed.), *The American Writers and the Great Depression*, New York, 1966, and for a critical assessment William Stott, *Documentary Expression and Thirties America*, New York, 1973.

9 Henry Hart, op. cit., p. 86.

10 Harry Alan Potamkin, 'The mind of the movie', *New Freeman*, 20 August 1930, reprinted in Lewis Jacobs (ed.), *The Compound Cinema: the Film Writings of Harry Alan Potamkin*, New York, 1977, p. 158.

11 *New Theatre*, November 1935, vol. 2, no. 11, p. 23.

12 Louis Norden, 'Luck comes to the proletariat', May 1935, vol. 2, no. 5, p. 17.

13 *Film Front* (National Film and Photo League, New York), 15 February 1935, vol. 1, no. 4, p. 12.

14 *New Masses*, 11 December 1934, vol. 13, no. 11, p. 30.

15 Jacobs, op. cit., p. 151.

16 Harry Alan Potamkin, 'Gabriel over Roosevelt', *New Masses*, May 1933, reprinted in Jacobs, op. cit., p. 515.

17 Harry Alan Potamkin, *The Eyes of the Movie*, Film and Photo League, International Pamphlets, no. 38, 1934, reprinted in Jacobs, op. cit., p. 264. Potamkin died in 1933 at the age of 33 and this pamphlet was put together from notes by Irving Lerner.

18 *Film Front*, 24 December 1934, vol. 1, no. 1, p. 2.

19 In a piece called 'Hollywood's riff-raff' in *New Theatre*, October 1935, vol. 2, no. 10, Joel Faith and Louis Norden spoke of 'Willie Hearst and his girlfriend Marion Davies's being 'cosily ensconced at Warner Bros'. See also 'Warner Brothers' in *Fortune*, December 1937, vol. 16, no. 6, in which the Burbank studio was described as 'a moated feudal city'.

20 William Randolph, 'Heil Hearst', *New Masses*, 9 April 1935, vol. 15, no. 2, p. 9, and *Film Front*, 15 February 1935, vol. 1, no. 4, p. 13.

21 'Peter Ellis' (Irving Lerner) in *New Masses*, 3 September 1935, vol. 16, no. 10, p. 29.

22 Quoted in Larry Ceplair and Steven Englund, *The Inquisition in Hollywood: Politics in the Film Community, 1930–1960*, Berkeley, 1983, p. 97.

23 Jay Rand in *New Masses*, July 1935, vol. 16, no. 4, p. 29.

24 *Film Front*, 24 December 1934, vol. 1, no. 1, p. 5.

25 'Peter Ellis' (Irving Lerner) discussed 'the crude patriotic propaganda of *Ruggles of Red Gap*' in *New Masses*, 26 March 1935, vol. 14, no. 12, p. 29.

26 *New Masses*, 22 October 1935, vol. 17, no. 4, p. 30, and *New Theatre*, October 1935, vol. 2, no. 10, p. 23.

27 Jay Rand in *New Masses*, July 1935, vol. 16, no. 4, p. 30.

28 ibid.

29 *Film Front*, 24 December 1934, vol. 1, no. 1, p. 7.

30 Harry Alan Potamkin, 'The mind of the movie', *New Freeman*, 20 August 1930, reprinted in Jacobs, op. cit., p. 154.

31 Herbert Kline in *New Theatre*, February 1936, vol. 3, no. 2, p. 26.

32 Arthur Draper in *New Theatre*, January 1936, vol. 3, no. 1, p. 30.

33 John R. Chaplin in *Film Front*, 15 March 1935, vol. 1, no. 5, p. 4.

34 'Peter Ellis' (Irving Lerner) in *New Masses*, 16 October 1934, vol. 13, no. 3, p. 30.

35 'Peter Ellis' (Irving Lerner) in *New Masses*, 5 February 1935, vol. 14, no. 6, p. 30.

36 Phillip Russell in *Film Front*, 15 February 1935, vol. 1, no. 4, p. 10.

37 Albert Maltz in *New Theatre*, May 1935, vol. 2, no. 5, p. 8.

38 *Film Front*, ibid., p. 16.

39 Robert Stebbins in *New Theatre*, January 1936, vol. 3, no. 1, p. 41.

40 Edmund Wilson, *The Boys in the Back Room*, San Francisco, 1941. These 'Notes on Californian novelists' had first appeared in *New Republic*.

41 Fred Lawrence Guiles, *Hanging on in Paradise*, New York, 1975, p. 7.

42 ibid., p. 15.

43 Harold Cantor, *Clifford Odets: Playwright-Poet*, Metuchen, NJ, 1978, p. 50.

44 James Shelley Hamilton in *National Board of Review Magazine*, September-October 1936, vol. 11, no. 7, p. 8.

45 John R. Chaplin in *Film Front*, 15 March 1935, vol. 1, no. 5, p. 5.

46 Hart, op. cit., p. 174.

47 John R. Chaplin in *Film Front*, 15 March 1935, vol. 1, no. 5, p. 5.

48 Ceplair and Englund, op. cit., pp. 47 ff.

49 Joris Ivens in *New Theatre*, October 1936, vol. 3, no. 10, quoted in Alexander, op. cit., p. 124.

50 Pare Lorentz in *McCall's*, July 1938, reprinted in Pare Lorentz, *Lorentz on Film*, New York, 1975, p. 154.

51 Wilson, op. cit., p. 70. Nathanael West's *The Day of the Locust* was published in 1939, the year before his death.

52 F. Scott Fitzgerald, *The Last Tycoon*, Notes printed in 1965, Penguin edition, London, p. 191. This novel was first published in 1941, the year after the author's death.

53 The reference to 'people's own favourite folklore' comes in ibid., p. 128 of the Penguin edition.

54 For West and Fitzgerald in Hollywood see Tom Dardis, *Some Time in the Sun*, London, 1976.

55 Horace McCoy, *They Shoot Horses, Don't They?*, New York, 1935. The quotation is from the Black Box omnibus edition, London, 1983, p. 69.

56 Horace McCoy, *I Should Have Stayed at Home*, New York, 1938; Black Box edition, London, 1983, p. 447. (This edition also includes *Kiss Tomorrow Goodbye* and *No Pockets in a Shroud* and an interesting introduction by Paul Buck.)

57 This has been done splendidly by Gordon de Marco in his Riley Kovachs thrillers, *October Heat*, San Francisco, 1979, *The Canvas Prison*, San Francisco, 1982, and *Frisco Blues*, London, 1985.

58 Fitzgerald, op. cit., p. 14 of Penguin edition.

59 Ceplair and Englund, op. cit., p. 116; they were thinking of *Blockade* (United Artists, 1938).

60 Robert Forsythe in *New Masses*, vol. 18, no. 8, 18 February 1936, p. 29.

61 Chaplin's telegram to Monroe Greenthal, Director of Publicity at United Artists, was sent on 24 January 1936 and is in the Monroe Greenthal File at Madison, Box 2.

62 As previously noted a translation of Shumiatski's *Pravda* review was printed in *New Masses*, 24 September 1935, vol. 16, no. 13, p. 29.

63 Charmion Von Wiegard, 'Little Charlie, What Now?' *New Theatre*, March 1936, vol. 3, no. 3.

64 Otis Ferguson in the *New Republic*, 19 February 1936, reprinted in Robert Wilson (ed.), *The Film Criticism of Otis Ferguson*, Philadelphia, 1971, p. 117, and in Stanley Kauffmann and Bruce Henstell, (eds), *American Film Criticism*, New York, 1972, p. 331.

65 'Peter Ellis' (Irving Lerner) in *New Masses*, 19 March 1935, vol. 14, no. 11, p. 29.

66 *New Theatre*, September 1935, vol. 2, no. 9, p. 33.

67 'Peter Ellis' (Irving Lerner) in *New Masses*, 25 February 1936, vol. 18, no. 9, p. 30.

68 Robert Stebbins in *New Theatre*, February 1936, vol. 3, no. 2, p. 22.

69 James Shelley Hamilton in *National Board of Review Magazine*, May 1936, vol. 16, no. 5, p. 11.

70 Robert Stebbins in *New Theatre*, May 1936, vol. 3, no. 5, p. 17.

71 Patterson Murphy in *Esquire*, January 1940, reprinted in Kauffmann and Henstell, op. cit., p. 377.

72 Richard Griffith in the *National Board of Review Magazine*, November 1939, vol. 14, no. 8, p. 13. This judgement was incorporated into Paul Rotha and Richard Griffith, *The Film Till Now*, London, 1949, p. 452.

73 Otis Ferguson in the *New Republic*, 22 April 1936, reprinted in Robert Wilson, op. cit., p. 128.

74 Otis Ferguson in the *New Republic*, 1 November 1939, reprinted in Robert Wilson, op. cit., p. 273.

75 Ceplair and Englund, op. cit., p. 309.

76 'MacLeish on Spain', *Cinema Arts*, September 1937, vol. 1, no. 3, p. 104.

77 *Variety*, 3 February 1937.

78 *National Board of Review Magazine*, January 1937, vol. 12, no. 1, p. 5. Almost certainly this is James Shelley Hamilton writing.

79 Otis Ferguson in *New Republic*, 13 October 1937, reprinted in Robert Wilson, op. cit., p. 199.

80 *National Board of Review Magazine*, October 1937, vol. 12, no. 7, p. 12.

81 James Dugan, 'Changing the reel', 1 September 1940, vol. 34, no. 3, p. 28.

82 Charles Glenn in *New Masses*, vol. XXXIV, 11 June 1940, p. 31.

83 James Dugan in *New Masses*, vol. XXXIV, 26 March 1940, p. 29.

84 James Dugan in *New Masses*, vol. XXXIV, 9 January 1940, p. 28.

85 Edmund Wilson, op. cit., p. 61.

86 Mel Gussow, *Don't Say Yes Until I Finish Talking: a Biography of Darryl F. Zanuck*, New York, 1971, section 2, chapter 3. My feeling that Zanuck was perhaps the most powerful and creative of Hollywood studio heads is confirmed in Douglas Gomery's *The Hollywood Studio System*, London, 1986.

87 Edmund Wilson, op. cit.; James Shelley Hamilton in the *National Board of Review Magazine*, February 1940, vol. 15, no. 2, p. 16. (This magazine later voted *The Grapes of Wrath* as the best film of 1940 with *The Great Dictator* as runner-up; see *National Board of Review Magazine*, January 1941, vol. 16, no. 1, p. 14.

88 Otis Ferguson in the *New Republic*, 12 February 1940, reprinted in Robert Wilson, op. cit., p. 282.

89 Edwin Locke in *Films*, spring 1940, reprinted in Kauffmann and Henstell, op. cit., p. 385.

90 James Shelley Hamilton in the *National Board of Review Magazine*, February 1940, vol. 15, no. 2, p. 19. (Later *Of Mice and Men* was chosen as the third best film of the year; see *National Board of Review Magazine*, January 1941, vol. 16, no. 1, p. 14).

91 Gussow, op. cit.

92 Cecilia Ager in *Photoplay Magazine*, 29 October 1941, p. 23, reprinted in Anthony Slide, *Selected Film Criticism 1941-1950*, Metuchen, NJ, 1982, p. 82.

93 Otis Ferguson in the *New Republic*, 1 December 1941, reprinted in Robert Wilson op. cit., p. 396.

94 Alfred Kazin, *Starting Out in the Thirties*, New York, 1965, p. 30 of Vintage Book edition. This memoir remains the best evocation of the New York City discussed in this chapter.

95 See chapter 3, p. 54.

96 Warshow, op. cit. p. 3.

97 Otis Ferguson in the *New Republic*, 13 October 1937, reprinted in Robert Wilson, op. cit., p. 198.

98 Walter Wanger in *Foreign Affairs*, October 1938, reprinted in John Eugene Harley, *The World-wide Influence of the Cinema*, Los Angeles, 1940, p. 4. Wanger was at the time President of the Academy of Motion Picture Arts and Science and very much the industry's leading spokesman.

5 'The faintest dribble of real English life'

1 G. A. Atkinson in the *Sunday Express*, 20 March 1927 (Sydney Carroll Collection, BFI Library).

2 For this period see Jeffrey Richards, *The Age of the Dream Palace: Cinema and Society in Britain 1930-1939*, London, 1984.

3 St John Ervine, 'Why I denounce the pictures', *Observer*, 5 November and 12 November 1933.

4 Review of *Pier 13*, *The Times*, 23 January 1933.

5 Seton Margrave in the *Daily Mail*, 14 March 1932.

6 L'Estrange Fawcett, *Films, Facts and Forecasts*, London, 1927.

7 Arthur Dent in the *Daily Film Renter*, 1 January 1934.

8 J. B. Priestley, 'English films and English people', *World Film News*, November 1936, vol. 1, no. 8, p. 3.

9 J. B. Priestley, *Midnight on the Desert*, London, 1937, pp. 166 ff.

10 Elizabeth Bowen, 'Why I go to the cinema', in Charles Davy (ed.), *Footnotes to the Film*, London, 1938, p. 205.

11 Seton Margrave in the *Daily Mail*, 4 January 1932; Richard Carr, 'Cagney - king of the corner boys', *World Film News*, October 1937, vol. 2, no. 7, p. 17.

12 *Daily Worker*, 24 January, 7 August, and 9 September 1936.

13 Trevor Blewitt, 'Films cash in on reality', *Daily Worker*, 26 October 1936.

14 Eric Knight, 'The passing of Hollywood', *Cinema Quarterly*, summer 1933, vol. 1, no. 4, p. 216.

15 Ernest Betts, 'British films discover England', *Daily Mail*, 21 August 1930.

16 Charles B. Cochran, letter to the *Observer*, 20 July 1933.

17 Jane Morgan in the *Daily Worker*, 2 May 1938.

18 'Names still sell pictures', *Daily Film Renter*, 21 February 1934. See also Herbert Wilcox, 'Find me a real British film hero', the *Daily Mail*, 14 September 1932.

19 Ian Dalrymple in the *Spectator*, 28 January 1938; Victor Saville in *Film Weekly*, 19 March 1938 (Balcon Scrapbooks, BFI Library).

20 *Daily Worker*, 13 April 1936.

21 This article from the *Newcastle Evening Chronicle*, July 1936, is retained in the Ernest Dyer Scrapbooks, no. 3, p. 48, BFI Library. See also his comments on the 1936 Hays Report in which he argued that the burden of the report was 'that films of real life pay', *Newcastle Evening Chronicle*, 2 June 1936, in Scrapbook no. 3, p. 8. At the end of the year 'Evans' (Dyer) selected *Fury* as his best film (Scrapbook no. 3, p. 40).

22 David E. Thomas in the *Daily Worker*, 9 May 1938.

23 Jane Morgan in the *Daily Worker*, 16 May 1938.

24 *The Times*, 9 August 1938, quoted by John Eugene Harley, *The World-wide Influence of the Cinema*, Los Angeles, 1940, p. 61.

25 Priestley, 1936, op. cit., p. 3.

26 One's sense of this British film culture emerges from a reading of contemporary reports, especially *The Film in National Life*, London, 1932, the Annual Reports of the BFI (published from 1934 onwards), articles in *Sight and Sound* and *Cinema Quarterly*, and the writings of Paul Rotha, some of which were collected in his book *Rotha on the Film*, London, 1958. The story of Socialist efforts has been usefully summarised by Bert Hogenkamp in *Deadly Parallels: Film and the Left in Britain 1929-39*, London, 1986.

27 *Minutes of Evidence Taken Before the Committee on Cinematograph Films*, Board of Trade Paper, 1936.

28 D. F. Taylor in *Sight and Sound*, 1933-4, vol. 2, no. 8, p. 128.

29 John Grierson, 'The course of realism' in Davy, op. cit.; Paul Rotha's review, 'The movies and reality', *Sight and Sound*, summer 1937, vol. 6, no. 22, p. 90.

30 Graham Greene, 'Is it criticism?', *Sight and Sound*, autumn 1936, vol. 5, no. 19, p. 64.

31 See Arthur Vesselo's review of *Steel*, *Sight and Sound*, summer 1936, vol. 5, no. 18., p. 32.

32 J. B. Priestley, *Rain upon Godshill*, London, 1939, pp. 78 ff.

33 Richards, op. cit., pp. 169 ff.

34 Graham Greene's review of *Shipyard Sally*, *Spectator*, 18 August 1939, reprinted in Graham Greene, *The Pleasure Dome*, London, 1972, (ed. John Russell Taylor).

35 Richards, op. cit., pp. 191 ff.

36 Terry Ramsaye (ed.) *Fame: Annual Audit of Screen and Radio Personalities*, New York, 1937, p. 50.

37 Aubrey Flanagan in ibid., p. 290.

38 Sidney Bernstein, *The Bernstein Questionnaire*, 1937, BFI Library, p. 29.

39 P. L. Mannock, 'British comedians cash in', *Daily Herald*, 20 May 1938.

40 John Grierson, 'The course of realism', in Davy, op. cit., p. 158.

41 ibid. The essay is also printed in Forsyth Hardy (ed.), *Grierson on Documentary*, London, 1946, pp. 132 ff.

42 Priestley, 1939, op. cit.

43 Aubrey Flanagan in *Ramsaye*, op. cit., p. 290.

44 Jane Morgan in the *Daily Worker*, 10 January 1938.

45 P. L. Mannock in the *Daily Herald*, 30 December 1938.

46 P. L. Mannock in the *Daily Herald*, 23 December 1928.

47 King Vidor, *On Film Making*, London, 1973, pp. 54 and 222. The extent to which the film was made in the American style was emphasized in the *Exhibitors Service Sheet* distributed in the USA. The information given here was that Cronin had written the novel with Donat in mind as the star of any film that would be made.

48 *The Times*, 5 January 1939.

49 *Film Comment*, July-August 1973, p. 40.

50 Alan Page in *Sight and Sound*, 1938-9, vol. 7, no. 28, p. 160.

51 *Catholic Herald*, 26 January 1940. See the Scrapbook (item 25) in the Carol Reed Collection, BFI Library.

52 Cited by Tony Aldgate, 'Ideological consensus in British feature films, 1935-1947', in K. R. M. Short (ed.), *Feature Films as History*, London 1981, p. 105.

53 See clippings in the Carol Reed Scrapbook, *BFI Library*, and especially in the *Birkenhead News*, 16 August 1939, and the *Daily Film Renter*, 18 August 1939.

54 *Newcastle Evening Chronicle*, 4 August 1939 (Carol Reed Collection - item 27, BFI Library.

55 Graham Greene in the *Spectator*, 26 January 1940, reprinted in Greene, 1972, op. cit., p. 265.
56 *Daily Express*, 19 January 1940.
57 *Manchester Guardian*, 20 January 1940.
58 Elizabeth Young in the *Tribune*, 26 January 1940.
59 *Liberty Magazine*, 16 August 1941. The American clippings form item 35 of the Carol Reed Collection at the BFI.
60 Graham Greene in the *Spectator*, 15 March 1940, reprinted in Greene, 1972, op. cit., p. 275.
61 *News Review*, 1 June 1939. See the Scrapbooks in the Balcon Collection, BFI Library.
62 The changed editing was mentioned by Dilys Powell in her review in the *Sunday Times*, 10 March 1940 (Carol Reed Collection).
63 *Listener*, 11 March 1982, a report on the radio programme *Desert Island Discs*, in which Osborne chose a Paul Robeson recording as one of his eight records.
64 *Picturegoer and Film Weekly*, 23 March 1940 (Balcon Collection).
65 W. H. Auden, 'As it seemed to us', *New Yorker*, 3 April 1954, reprinted in W. H. Auden, *Forewords and Afterwords*, New York, 1973, p. 514.
66 Evelyn Waugh, *Put Out More Flags*, London, 1942, p. 47 of Penguin edition. The hero in question was Basil Seal.
67 George Orwell, *The Road to Wigan Pier*, London, 1937, and J. B. Priestley, *English Journey*, London, 1933.
68 See Peter Stead, 'Wales in the movies', in Tony Curtis (ed.), *Wales: the Imagined Nation*, Bridgend, 1986.

6 'The wartime drama of the common people'

1 George Perry, *The Great British Picture Show*, London, 1974.
2 Richard Meran Barsam, *Nonfiction Film: a Critical History*, New York, 1973.
3 'The man on the screen', *Documentary News Letter*, May 1940, vol. 1, no. 5, p. 3.
4 Dilys Powell, *Films Since 1939*, London, 1947, pp. 14 ff.
5 Barsam, op. cit., p. 180 of British edition.
6 Powell, op. cit., p. 39.
7 Ernest Betts, 'The shelterers' verdict', *Sunday Express*, 20 April 1941, Ernest Betts Collection, BFI Library.
8 Roger Manvell 'They laugh at realism', *Documentary News Letter*, March 1943, vol. 4, no. 3, p. 188.
9 Guy Morgan, 'A filmgoer's war diary', in Guy Morgan (ed.), *Red Roses Every Night*, London, 1948, p. 70.
10 'Feature film propaganda', *Documentary News Letter*, 1942, vol. 3, no. 5; *The Bernstein Questionnaire*, 1946-7, p. 6, BFI Library.
11 Clive Coultass, *The British Realist Film: a Historical Perspective*, 1978, unpublished MS, Imperial War Museum.
12 *Documentary News Letter*, 1943, vol. 14, no. 4, p. 200.
13 ibid.
14 Mary Lou Jennings, *Humphrey Jennings: film-maker, Painter, Poet*, London, 1982.
15 Humphrey Jennings Collection, BFI Library, Files 8 and 16.
16 Barsam, op. cit., p. 178; Roy Armes, *A Critical History of the British Cinema*, London, 1978, p. 151.
17 These comments are taken from the detailed half-page advertisement in the

Documentary News Letter, May 1943, vol. 4, no. 5, p. 218.

18 The film was shown at a World Food Conference held at Hot Springs Virginia and received 'prolonged applause'; *Documentary News Letter*, May 1943, vol. 4, no. 5. The background to the film is told in Paul Rotha (ed.) *Rotha on the Film*, London, 1958, pp. 98 ff.

19 Doreen Willis, 'Why no labour films?', *Documentary News Letter*, January–February 1947, vol. 6, no. 55, p. 68.

20 Paul Rotha, *Documentary Diary*, London, 1973, p. 286.

21 Powell, op. cit., p. 19.

22 Jeffrey Richards, *The Age of the Dream Palace: Cinema and Society in Britain 1930–1939*, London, 1984, p. 119.

23 Edgar Anstey in the *Spectator*, 6 June 1941 and 2 January 1942, Edgar Anstey Collection, BFI Library. The Rank Cards consisting of Viewers' Reports are in the BFI Library, Special Collections: this report was dated 2 April 1941.

24 *Kine Weekly*, 10 April 1941, BFI File.

25 William Whitebait in the *New Statesman*, 7 June 1941.

26 Ernest Betts in the *Sunday Express*, 1 June 1941.

27 Edgar Anstey in the *Spectator*, 6 June 1941.

28 *Kine Weekly*, 10 April 1941.

29 Ernest Betts in the *Sunday Express*, 1 June 1941. For Betts *Love on the Dole* was an 'earthy, bitter, soul-disturbing affair, lit with the torches of despair, the fires of desperation'.

30 Ernest Betts, 'The shelterers' verdict', *Sunday Express*, 20 April 1941, Ernest Betts Collection, BFI Library.

31 ibid.

32 Ernest Betts in the *Sunday Express*, 16 March 1941, Ernest Betts Collection.

33 Edgar Anstey in the *Spectator*, 1 May 1942.

34 Edgar Anstey in the *Spectator*, 17 March 1944.

35 Nicholas Pronay, 'The first reality: film censorship in liberal England', in K. R. M. Short (ed.), *Feature Films as History*, London, 1981.

36 Nicholas Pronay and Jeremy Croft, 'British film censorship and propaganda during the Second World War', in James Curran and Vincent Porter (eds.), *British Cinema History*, London, 1983.

37 Edgar Anstey in the *Spectator*, 2 January 1942.

38 Charles Barr, *Ealing Studios*, London, 1977, p. 37.

39 Sue Aspinall, 'Women, realism and reality in British films, 1943–1953', in Curran and Porter, op. cit.

40 Rank Card, 14 April 1942.

41 Rank Card, 22 September 1943.

42 *The Way Ahead*, Press-book, BFI Library.

43 C. A. Lejeune, *Chestnuts in her Lap*, London, 1947, p. 136. This review was written in 1944 when the film went on general release.

44 ibid., p. 153. The film under review was *Blood on the Sun*.

45 ibid., p. 128. These comments were made at the time of the film's opening in London in 1944: in 1947 Lejeune added the note 'I am still hoping'.

46 Powell, op. cit., p. 20.

47 *Documentary News Letter*, 1944, vol. 5, no. 1, p. 1.

48 Leonard England, 'The cinema in the first three months of the war', Topic Collection no. 17, Film, Box no. 2, File H, the Tom Harrison Mass-Observation Archive, Sussex University. Dorothy Sheridan's guide *The Mass-Observation Records 1937–1949*, Sussex University Library, 1983, not only explains the archive but also the ways in which it has been used by historians.

49 'Worktown', Film Survey, 1938, Box W.29, Mass-Observation Archive.
50 Interview, 16 November 1939, Box no. 4, File 4 (A).
51 Film Report, 14 February 1942, Box no. 4, File 4 (F).
52 'Report on *Picturegoer* letters', Box no. 5.
53 *The Cinema Audience*, Wartime Social Survey, New Series, no. 376, June/July 1943.
54 *The Bernstein Questionnaire*, 1946-7, p. 9, BFI Library.
55 Frederic Mullally, *Films: an Alternative to Rank*, London, 1946, p. 2.
56 Larry Ceplair and Steven Englund, *The Inquisition in Hollywood: Politics in the Film Community, 1930-1960*, Berkeley, 1983, pp. 180 ff. The best introduction to this whole subject is provided by Garth Jowett, *Film: the Democratic Art*, Boston, 1976, chapter 12, 'Hollywood goes to war'.
57 Ceplair and Englund, op. cit., p. 181.
58 Joe Morella, Edward Z. Epstein, and John Griggs, *The Films of World War II*, Syracuse, NJ, 1973.
59 Edgar Anstey in the *Spectator*, 19 February 1943.
60 James Agee in the *Nation*, 20 February 1943, reprinted in James Agee, *Agee On Film*, London, 1963, p. 28.
61 Bosley Crowther in the *New York Times*, 21 July 1944.
62 James Agee in the *Nation*, 29 July 1944, reprinted in Agee, 1963, op. cit., p. 107.
63 *Documentary Film Classics*, National Audio Visual Center, Washington, DC. This excellent catalogue of films 'produced by the US Government' was written by William J. Blakefield.
64 Dorothy B. Jones, 'The Hollywood war film 1942-1944', *Hollywood Quarterly* (Berkeley), October 1945, vol. 1, no. 1. Cf. Arthur F. McClure, 'Hollywood at war: the American motion picture and World War II', *Journal of Popular Film*, spring 1972, vol. 1, no. 2.
65 Colin Shindler, *Hollywood Goes to War*, London, 1979, p. 40.
66 The dust-jacket of Shindler's book is graced by a still from *Guadalcanal Diary*: William Bendix shaves and at the same time keeps an eye on a pin-up photo of Betty Grable.
67 John T. McManus in *Photoplay Magazine*, 7 October 1945, reprinted in *New York Motion Picture Critics Reviews*, 8 October 1945, vol. 2, no. 34, p. 82.
68 Philip Dunne in *Hollywood Quarterly*, January 1946, vol. 1, no. 2.
69 Shindler, op. cit., p. 79.
70 Richard Griffith, *Samuel Goldwyn - the Producer and His Films*, New York, 1956, pp. 37 ff.
71 James Agee in the *Nation*, 14 April 1946, reprinted in Agee, 1963, op. cit., p. 229.
72 Abraham Polonsky in *Hollywood Quarterly*, April 1947, vol. 2, no. 3, p. 257.
73 Jones, op. cit.

7 The post-war age of anxiety

1 Dilys Powell in the *Listener*, 31 July 1947.
2 James Agee in the *Nation*, 10 January 1948, reprinted in James Agee, *Agee on Film*, London, 1963, p. 289.
3 James Agee in the *Nation*, 13 April 1946, reprinted in Agee, 1963, op. cit., p. 194.
4 Pauline Kael, *Kiss Kiss Bang Bang*, New York, 1968 (p. 406 Bantam edition).

5 James Agee in the *Nation*, 11 October 1947, reprinted in Agee, 1963, op. cit., p. 279.

6 D. A Yerrill, 'The technique of realism', *Sight and Sound*, spring 1948, vol. 17, no. 65, p. 23.

7 Richard Winnington in the *News Chronicle*, 24 April 1948, reprinted in Richard Winnington, *Film Criticism and Caricatures 1943-53*, London, 1975, pp. 79 and 94.

8 Edgar Anstey on BBC Third Programme, 12 October 1947, transcript in Edgar Anstey Collection, BFI Library.

9 Garfield had started out in New York's Group Theatre. See F. L. Guiles, *Hanging on in Paradise*, New York, 1975, p. 15.

10 Stephen Belcher in *New Movies* (National Board of Review), November 1947, vol. 22, no. 6, reprinted in Anthony Slide, *Selected Film Criticism 1941-1950*, Metuchen, NJ, 1982.

11 For Chandler see Frank MacShane, *The Life of Raymond Chandler*, London, 1976, and for earlier comment on how Cain's novels were written with film in mind and constituted 'a kind of Devil's parody of the movies' see Edmund Wilson, *The Boys in the Back Room*, San Francisco, 1941, p. 14.

12 Manny Farber, *Negative Space*, London, 1971, p. 290. This marvellous essay had first appeared in *Commentary* in 1957.

13 Rank Card, 12 November 1947.

14 Peter Roffman and Jim Purdy, *The Hollywood Social Problem Film*, Bloomington, 1981, p. 262, and John Baxter, *King Vidor*, New York, 1976, p. 66.

15 *Variety*, 19 October 1949, Cinema Audience File, Performing Arts Library, Lincoln Center, NYC.

16 James R. Silke, *Here's Looking at You Kid: Fifty Years of Fighting, Working, and Dreaming at Warner Bros*, Boston, 1976, p. 299.

17 Larry Ceplair and Steven Englund, *The Inquisition in Hollywood: Politics in the Film Community, 1930-1960*, Berkeley, 1983, pp. 239 ff.

18 The psychological and dramatic dimensions of the hearings are reflected in the way in which Eric Bentley published the actual dialogue in play form with the titles *Are You Now or Have You Ever Been?*, New York, 1972, and In David Zane Mairowitz's analysis of the American left, *The Radical Soap Opera*, New York, 1974.

19 'Movies: end of an era?', *Fortune*, April 1949, vol. 39, no. 4, p. 144.

20 *Box-Office*, 22 May 1948, p. 25.

21 *Fortune*, April 1949, vol. 39, no. 4, pp. 99 ff., and Eric Johnson, 'Our critics', *Variety*, 5 January 1949.

22 *New York Times*, 27 February 1949.

23 'The progress of the British film', in John Lehmann (ed.), *The Penguin New Writing*, London, 1944.

24 *Chestnuts in her Lap*, London, 1947, p. 163; the model she had in mind in 1945 was *Brief Encounter*.

25 *Tendencies to Monopoly in the Cinematograph Film Industry*, Board of Trade, 1944 (normally known after its chairman's name as the Palache Report).

26 Alan Wood, *Mr Rank: a Study of J. Arthur Rank and British Films*, London, 1952, and James L. Limbacher, *The Influence of J. Arthur Rank on the History of the British Film*, Dearborn, Mich., BFI Library.

27 This whole story is succinctly told in Peter Forster, 'J. Arthur Rank and the shrinking screen', in Michael Sissons and Philip French (eds), *Age of Austerity 1945-1951*, London, 1963.

28 Paul Rotha in 'By guess and by God', *Tribune*, 19 September 1952, reprinted

in Paul Rotha (ed.) *Rotha on the Film*, London, 1958, p. 299. Here Rotha reviews Alan Wood's *Mr Rank* and gives his own views on the crisis years.

29 Penelope Houston, 'Hollywood warning', *Sequence*, winter 1947, no. 2, p. 15.

30 See especially J. P. Meyer, *British Cinemas and their Audiences*, London, 1948, and Mark Abrams, 'The British cinema audience', *Hollywood Quarterly*, winter 1947-8, vol. 3, no. 2, p. 55.

31 James Monahan, 'The year's work in the feature film', in Roger Manvell (ed.), *The Year's Work in the Film*, London, 1950.

32 The reviews by Milton Shulman and Fred Majdelany are in Edgar Anstey (ed.), *Shots in the Dark*, London, 1951, p. 62. Also Rank Card, 20 April 1949.

33 Rank Card, 23 September 1947. The film is analysed in Jeffrey Richards and Anthony Aldgate, *The Best of British*, Oxford, 1983.

34 Lindsay Anderson in *Sequence*, summer 1950, no. 11. p. 39.

35 Rank Card, March 1950.

36 *Kine Weekly*, 4 January 1945, p. 163.

37 *Daily Herald*, 19 September 1951, Balcon Collection.

38 Kenneth Tynan in the *Evening Standard*, 9 September 1951, Balcon Collection.

39 Michael Balcon, 'The road to survival', *Kine Weekly*, 14 December 1950.

40 *Manchester Guardian*, 11 August 1951, Balcon Collection.

41 James Monahan, 'The year's work in the feature film', in Manvell, op. cit., p. 21.

42 Thomas Spencer in the *Daily Worker*, 24 January 1951.

43 Honor Arundel in the *Daily Worker*, 21 January 1950.

44 Rank Card, 8 August 1952.

45 Rank Card, 12 March 1952.

46 Thomas Spencer in the *Daily Worker*, 17 February 1951.

47 Lindsay Anderson, 'Angles of approach', *Sequence*, winter 1947, no. 2, p. 5.

48 Gavin Lambert, 'British films', *Sequence*, winter 1947, no. 2, p. 9.

49 William Whitebait in the *New Statesman*, 13 May 1950.

50 Paul Rotha and Richard Griffith, *The Film Till Now*, London, 1949.

51 Alan Ross, *The Forties*, London, 1950.

52 The mood of the time is best reflected in the literary magazine *Horizon*, whose editor Cyril Connolly had written that 'those who really care for books can never settle down to the impermanent world of the cinema' (*Horizon*, October 1947, no. 93/94).

53 Oliver Martin in the *Daily Worker*, 6 January 1951; Thomas Spencer in the *Daily Worker*, 10 February 1951.

54 William Whitebait in the *New Statesman*, 13 May 1950.

55 John Howard Lawson, *Film in the Battle of Ideas*, New York, 1953.

56 *California Quarterly*, summer 1953, vol. 11, no. 4, Herbert Biberman and Gale Sondergaard Papers, Madison.

57 Typescript, 26 October 1954, Box 2/4, Madison.

58 *Hollywood Review*, March-April 1953.

59 *Los Angeles Times*, 5 November 1954.

60 *Frontier*, May 1953, vol. 4, no. 7, p. 5; *Los Angeles Times*, 20 Mây 1954.

61 *New York Times*, 13 March 1954.

62 Peter Biskind, *Seeing is Believing: How Hollywood Taught us to Stop Worrying and Love the Fifties*, New York, 1983 (p. 173 of the 1984 London edition).

63 ibid., pp. 25 ff.

64 Parker Tyler, *The Hollywood Hallucination*, New York, 1944, and quoted in the preface to his *Magic and Myth of the Movies*, New York, 1947.

65 Manny Farber, 'The group', first published in *Commentary* in 1952; reprinted in Farber, 1971, op. cit.

66 James T. Farrell, *The League of Frightened Philistines*, New York, 1945.

67 Gilbert Seldes, *The Great Audience*, New York, 1950. Dwight Macdonald, *Against the American Grain*, New York, 1962. For a summary of the debate Harold Leonard, 'Recent American film writing', *Sight and Sound*, summer 1947, vol. 16, no. 62, p. 73.

68 Robert Warshow, 'The Legacy of the 1930s', *The Immediate Experience*, New York, 1962, pp. 7 ff. (The article appeared originally in *Commentary*, vol. 8, no. 12, December 1947.)

69 Seldes, op. cit., p. 263.

70 Warshow, op. cit., p. xxvii. For a study of Warshow, Macdonald, and other critics, see Edward Murray, *Nine American Film Critics*, New York, 1975.

71 Hortense Powdermaker, *Hollywood: the Dream Factory*, New York, p. 14.

72 Farber, 1971, op. cit., p. 82.

73 Peter Biskind, 'The politics of power in *On the Waterfront*', *Film Quarterly*, fall 1975, vol. 29, no. 1, p. 26, BFI Library File. (See also Biskind, 1983, op. cit., pp. 169 ff.)

74 Columbia Pictures, Production Notes (BFI).

75 Biskind, 1983, op. cit., p. 27.

76 Elia Kazan in *Movie*, winter 1971-2, no. 19, p. 8 (BFI).

77 For the story of the film, see Kenneth R. Hey, 'Ambivalence as a theme in *On the Waterfront*', in Peter C. Rollins (ed.) *Hollywood as Historian*, Lexington, Ky, 1983.

78 Biskind, 1983, op. cit., p. 33.

79 Kael, op. cit., p. 72; Hal Hinson, 'Some notes on method acting', *Sight and Sound*, summer 1984, vol. 53, no. 3, p. 200.

80 Farber, 1971, op. cit., p. 76.

81 Norman Mailer, *Advertisements for Myself*, New York, 1959. The section called 'Hipsters' includes Mailer's essay 'The white negro' (first published in *Dissent*, 1957) together with subsequent discussion and notes.

82 Norman Mailer, 'Tango, last tango', in Bernardo Bertolucci, *Last Tango in Paris*, London, 1976; reprinted in Normal Mailer, *Pieces and Pontifications*, New York, 1982.

83 Gerald Nicosia, *Memory Babe: a Critical Biography of Jack Kerouac*, New York, 1983 (p. 170 of Penguin edition).

84 The phrase 'street-socialism of the 1930s' is used by Hilary Miller in her *Mailer: a Biography*, New York, 1982 (p. 72 of NEL edition).

85 Pauline Kael, 'Marlon Brando: an American hero', in Kael, op. cit., p. 231.

86 Joan Mellen, *Big Bad Wolves: Masculinity in the American Film*, New York, 1977, p. 189.

87 Mailer, 1976, op. cit.

88 Mellen, op. cit., p. 214.

89 See especially *The Public Appraises Movies*, Princeton, 1957, in which Opinion Research Corp. demonstrated that 52 per cent of the motion-picture audience was under 20 whilst only 6 per cent was over 50.

8 British working class heroes

1 Gavin Lambert, 'Notes on the British cinema', *Hollywood Quarterly*, fall 1956, vol. 11, no. 1.

2 Pauline Kael, 'Commitment and the straight-jacket', *Film Quarterly*, fall 1961,

vol. 15, no. 1. Gilbert Adair examines the history of British film criticism in *Sight and Sound*, autumn 1982, vol. 51, no. 4, p. 248.

3 Penelope Houston in *Sight and Sound*, October/December 1954, vol. 24, no. 2, p. 85.

4 Lindsay Anderson, 'The last scene of *On the Waterfront*', *Sight and Sound*, January/March 1955, vol. 24, no. 3, p. 127.

5 Richard Winnington, *Film Criticism and Caricatures 1943-53*, London, 1975, pp. 140 ff.

6 William Whitebait in the *New Statesman*, 22 August 1959, BFI File. ·

7 *News Chronicle*, 11 December 1959.

8 *Daily Worker*, 28 February 1959.

9 Kael, op. cit.

10 Raymond Durgnat, *A Mirror for England*, London, 1970, p. 139.

11 C. A. Lejeune in the *Observer*, 13 March 1960, BFI File.

12 Normal Cecil in *Films in Review*, January 1960, vol. 12, no. 1.

13 The best introduction to the debate on British culture in these years is provided by Robert Hewison in *In Anger: Culture in the Cold War*, London, 1981, and *Too Much: Art and Society in the Sixties*, London, 1986.

14 Kenneth Tynan's review, which appeared first in the *Observer* in May 1956, is reprinted in John Russell Taylor, *John Osborne: Look Back in Anger: a Casebook*, London, 1968, p. 49.

15 Taylor, op. cit., p. 44.

16 Kael, op. cit.

17 According to the early pages of his autobiography, *A Better Class of Person*, London, 1981, John Osborne himself was once referred to as 'Welsh Fulham upstart'.

18 Gavin Lambert in *Hollywood Quarterly*, summer 1959, vol. 12, no. 4, p. 39.

19 Ann Lloyd and Graham Fuller (eds), *The Illustrated Who's Who of the Cinema*, London, 1983, p. 195.

20 David Thomson, *A Biographical Dictionary of the Cinema*, London, 1975, p. 231.

21 James Leahy, *The Cinema of Joseph Losey*, London, 1967, p. 57.

22 Michael Ciment, *Conversations with Losey*, London and New York, 1985, p. 293.

23 ibid., p. 272.

24 Alexander Walker, *Hollywood England*, London, 1974, p. 84.

25 ibid., p. 142.

26 Nina Hibbin in the *Daily Worker*, 28 January 1961, BFI File.

27 *Kine Weekly*, 27 October 1960.

28 For Sillitoe as a writer see Stuart Laing, *Representations of Working-class life, 1957-1964*, London, 1986, pp. 65 ff. The film is analysed by Anthony Aldgate in Jeffrey Richards and Anthony Aldgate *The Best of British*, Oxford, 1983.

29 For an interesting view see Arthur Marwick, 'Images of the working class since 1930', in Jay Winter (ed.), *The Working Class in Modern British History*, London, 1983, and also John Hill, *Sex, Class and Realism: British Cinema 1956-1963*, London, 1986.

30 Herbert J. Gans, 'Hollywood films on British screens: an analysis of the functions of American popular culture abroad', *Social Problems*, spring 1962, vol. 9, no. 4, p. 324.

31 Vernon Young, 'Kinds of loving in the international film', *Hudson Review*, 1962; reprinted in Vernon Young, *On Film*, Chicago, 1972, p. 167.

32 Elizabeth Sunderland in *Film Quarterly*, summer 1961, vol. 14, no. 4, p. 58.

33 Dwight Macdonald, 'Masscult and midcult', *Partisan Review*, spring 1960, reprinted in Dwight Macdonald, *Against the American Grain*, New York, 1962, p. 64.
34 Kael, op. cit.
35 Christopher Booker fully appreciated the follies of 'English life in the Fifties and Sixties' but his study *The Neophiliacs*, London, 1969, nicely traced the new patterns of social mobility.
36 Curtis Hutchinson on Sean Connery, *Film Review*, September 1986, p. 14.
37 Walker, op. cit., pp. 181 ff.
38 Iain McAsh, interview with Michael Caine, *Film Review*, May 1987, p. 8.
39 Gilbert Adair, *Myths and Memories*, London, 1986, p. 23.
40 The chronology is best understood by a reading of John Russell Taylor, *Anger and After*, London, 1962. See also Peter Lewis, *The Fifties*, London, 1978.
41 Raymond Williams was certainly the most influential cultural critic of this era: *Culture and Society 1780–1950*, London, 1958, and *The Long Revolution*, London, 1961, were his central texts but he looked more closely at television in *Communications*, London, 1962.
42 Walker, op. cit., pp. 370 ff.
43 There is a useful discussion in John Ellis, *Visible Functions*, London, 1982, pp. 109 ff.

9 The national experience in Britain and America

1 The mood is described in John Walker, *The Once and Future Film: British Cinema in the Seventies and Eighties*, London, 1985.
2 The significance of the commercial formula is best appreciated by the contrast between Alexander Walker's volume on the 1960s, *Hollywood England*, London, 1974, and his later work, *National Heroes: British Cinema in the Seventies and Eighties*, London, 1985. As Walker explains, in the first book the emphasis is on film-making, in the second, on business.
3 'British Cinema: life before death on television', *Sight and Sound*, spring 1984, vol. 53, no. 2, p. 114, especially the contribution of Simon Perry. Also David Docherty *et al.*, *The Entertainment Film in British Life*, London, 1984.
4 See James Park, *Learning to Dream: the new British Cinema*, London, 1984, and Marty Auty and Nick Roddick, *British Cinema Now*, London, 1985.
5 For the context in which the Williams-Thompson influence operated it is necessary to read Perry Anderson's 'Components of the national culture', *New Left Review*, July/August 1968, no. 50. Their influence is assessed from the right in George Watson, 'Was the new left a success?', *Encounter*, October 1975, vol. 45, no. 4, p. 13.
6 John Russell Taylor, *Anger and After*, London, 1962.
7 Gilbert Adair, *Myths and Memories*, London, 1986.
8 The emergence of this 'edge' is most fully conveyed in John Osborne, *A Better Class of Person*, London, 1981, and John Lehr, *Prick Up Your Ears: the Biography of Joe Orton*, London, 1978. For the theatre in national life see John Pick, *The West End: Mismanagement and Snobbery*, London, 1984.
9 See Christopher Booker, *The Neophiliacs*, London, 1969, and Robert Hewison, *Too Much: Art and Society in the Sixties*, London, 1986.
10 For a detailed study of the pioneering working-class 'soap', Richard Dyer *et al.*, *Coronation Street*, London, 1981.

11 For a detailed analysis of one series, *Days of Hope* (director Ken Loach, writer Jim Allen), see Tony Bennett *et al.*, *Popular Television and Film*, London, 1981, (BFI and the Open University). Perhaps the most ambitious television series, *Brideshead Revisited*, is discussed by Nick Roddick in *Sight and Sound*, winter 1981-2, vol. 51, no. 1, p. 58.

12 Alan Bleasdale's Play *The Black Stuff* was shown by the BBC in 1980 to be followed in 1982 by the five-part *The Boys from the Black Stuff*, directed by Jim Goddard.

13 Bill Douglas's trilogy consisted of *My Childhood* (1971), *My Ain Folk* (1972), and *My Way Home* (1979). In 1987 he completed *Comrades*, a more ambitious film telling the story of the Tolpuddle Martyrs.

14 See their comments in Martyn Auty and Chris Peachment, 'Brit pix bite back', *Time Out*, 10 May 1984, no. 716.

15 Quoted by David Robinson, *Sight and Sound*, winter 1985-6, vol. 55, no. 1, p. 56.

16 James Monaco, *American Film Now*, New York, 1979.

17 The strange story of profits and losses in the American film industry was told by David Pirie in 'Hollywood's last hurrah?', *The Times*, 21, 22, and 23 February 1983. See also Alan Trustman, 'Who killed Hollywood?', *Atlantic*, January 1978, p. 65. Trustman attributes the idea of one winner paying for fifty 'stinkers' to paramount's Frank Yablans and so he thinks of the film industry as having been 'Yablansized'.

18 Ann Lloyd and Graham Fuller (eds), *The Illustrated Who's Who of the Cinema*, London, 1983, p. 373; *National Film Theatre Programme*, September/November 1972, p. 38.

19 Henry A. Grant gave a detailed analysis of *Norma Rae* in 'Character, culture and class', *Jump Cut*, no. 22.

20 For the background to *Jump Cut* see Peter Seven (ed.), *Jump Cut: Hollywood, Politics and Counter Cinema*, Toronto, 1985.

21 Mary Bufwack, 'Taking the class out of country', *Jump Cut*, no. 28.

22 Michael Omi, 'Race relations in *Blue Collar*, *Jump Cut*, no. 26.

23 Quoted in Ellen Oumano, *Sam Shepard*, New York, 1986.

24 Monaco, op. cit., p. 154.

25 Peter Steven in *Jump Cut*, no. 25.

26 Leslie Halliwell, *Halliwell's Film Guide*, London, 1982 edition.

27 Dennis Wood, 'All the words we cannot say: a critical commentary on *The Deer Hunter*', *Journal of Popular Film and Television*, 1980, vol. 67, no. 4, p. 366.

28 Robert Mazzocco, 'The supply-side star' (Clint Eastwood), *New York Review of Books*, April 1982, vol. 29, no. 5, p. 38.

29 Peter Goldman, 'Rocky and Rambo', *Newsweek*, 23 December 1985. For Stallone's international appeal see the article by Richard Grenier in the *International Herald Tribune*, 23 September 1985.

30 For growing intellectual fears, see Jeffrey Richards, 'Yobbery with violence: on the new cult of barbarism', *Encounter*, January 1986, vol. 7, no. 2, p. 5, and Anthony Lejeune, 'When all the World loved Hollywood', *The Times*, 28 June 1986.

31 Normal Mailer, 'Norman Mailer meets Clint Eastwood', *Observer*, Colour Supplement, 29 January 1984; Mazzocco, op. cit.; Jack Nachbar, 'Clint, an American icon', *Newsweek*, 23 September 1985.

32 Michael Freedland, 'When Eastwood held a fistful of sorrows', *TV Times*, 9-16 August 1986.

33 Mailer, op. cit.

10 Workers and the film

1 Larry May, *Screening Out the Past*, Chicago, 1980, pp. 109 ff.
2 For a fascinating discussion see Kathleen D. McCarthy, 'Nickel, vice and virtue: movie censorship in Chicago 1907-1915', *Journal of Popular Film*, 1976, vol. 5, no. 1, p. 38.
3 For a self-improving worker's dismissal of film see B. L. Coombes, *Miner's Day*, London, 1945.
4 Hence my enthusiasm for the magnificent analysis of the pleasures of film provided by Elizabeth Bowen, 'Why I go to the cinema', in Charles Davy (ed.), *Footnotes to the Film*, London, 1938, p. 205. Novelists and writers have frequently acted as the spokespeople for film fans; see Peter Stead, 'The people and the pictures', in Nicholas Pronay and D. W. Spring (eds), *Propaganda, Politics and Film, 1918-1945*, London, 1982.
5 George Orwell, *The Lion and the Unicorn: Socialism and the English Genius*, London, 1941, and *The Collected Essays*, vol. 2, London 1968, p. 77.
6 J. B. Priestley, 'English films and English people', *World Film News*, November 1936, vol. 1, no. 8, p. 3. This 1936 essay by Priestley remains one of the best discussions of the difference between Hollywood and British films.
7 Alistair Cooke, 'The English in America', *Listener*, 16 May 1946, and see also the discussion of Ronald Colman and Herbert Marshall in Sheridan Morley, *Tales from the Hollywood Raj*, London, 1983.
8 Herbert J. Gans, 'Hollywood films on British screens: an analysis of the functions of American popular culture abroad', *Social Problems*, spring 1962, vol. 9, no. 4, p. 325.
9 Chuck Kleinhans, 'Contemporary working class film heroes', *Jump Cut*, no. 2; Peter Steven (ed.) *Jump Cut: Hollywood, Politics and Counter Cinema*, Toronto, 1985, p. 64.
10 See especially Molly Haskell, *From Reverence to Rape: the Treatment of Women in the Movies*, New York, 1974, and Thomas Cripps, *Slow Fade to Black: the Negro in American Films*, New York, 1977.
11 Tony Palmer, *All You Need is Love: the Story of Popular Music*, London, 1976.
12 Quoted in Edward Murray, *Nine American Film Critics*, New York, 1975.
13 F. Scott Fitzgerald, *The Last Tycoon*. Notes printed in 1965, Penguin edition, London, p. 128. First published in 1941.
14 Cf. Raymond Durgnat, *A Mirror for England*, London, 1970, p. 176.
15 Carl Laemmle in the *Film Daily Year Book*, 1932, p. 35.
16 There is an excellent analysis in Jeffrey Richards, *Visions of Yesterday*, London, 1973, pp. 64 ff., and for a prediction that 'kitchen-sink drama is on the wane' and that 'the great British Gentleman' was poised to return see David Quinlan, 'Revival of the League of Gentlemen', *TV Times*, 23-27 August 1985.
17 Paul Fussell, *Class, Style and Status in the USA*, Arrow edition, London, 1984, p. 50.

Index of films

Note: Illustrations are indicated by **bold** figures.

Index of names

Note: Illustrations are indicated by **bold** numbers.

PACE UNIVERSITY LIBRARIES

3 5061 00565529 6